Forbidden
Dance

ALSO AVAILABLE FROM TOKYOPOP®

REALITY CHECK
REBIRTH
REBOUND
REMOTE June 2004
RISING STARS OF MANGA December 2003
SABER MARIONETTE J
SAILOR MOON
SAINT TAIL
SAIYUKI
SAMURAI DEEPER KYO
SAMURAI GIRL REAL BOUT HIGH SCHOOL
SCRYED
SGT. FROG March 2004
SHAOLIN SISTERS
SHIRAHIME-SYO: SNOW GODDESS TALES December 2004
SHUTTERBOX
SNOW DROP January 2004
SOKORA REFUGEES May 2004
SORCEROR HUNTERS
SUIKODEN May 2004
SUKI February 2004
THE CANDIDATE FOR GODDESS April 2004
THE DEMON ORORON April 2004
THE LEGEND OF CHUN HYANG
THE SKULL MAN
THE VISION OF ESCAFLOWNE
TOKYO MEW MEW
TREASURE CHESS March 2004
UNDER THE GLASS MOON
VAMPIRE GAME
WILD ACT
WISH
WORLD OF HARTZ
X-DAY
ZODIAC P.I.

NOVELS

KARMA CLUB APRIL 2004
SAILOR MOON

ART BOOKS

CARDCAPTOR SAKURA
MAGIC KNIGHT RAYEARTH
PEACH GIRL ART BOOK April 2004

ANIME GUIDES

COWBOY BEBOP ANIME GUIDES
GUNDAM TECHNICAL MANUALS
SAILOR MOON SCOUT GUIDES

CINE-MANGA™

CARDCAPTORS
FAIRLY ODD PARENTS MARCH 2004
FINDING NEMO
G.I. JOE SPY TROOPS
JACKIE CHAN ADVENTURES
KIM POSSIBLE
LIZZIE MCGUIRE
POWER RANGERS: NINJA STORM
SPONGEBOB SQUAREPANTS
SPY KIDS
SPY KIDS 3-D March 2004
THE ADVENTURES OF JIMMY NEUTRON: BOY GENIUS
TRANSFORMERS: ARMADA
TRANSFORMERS: ENERGON May 2004

TOKYOPOP KIDS

STRAY SHEEP

For more information visit www.TOKYOPOP.com

10103

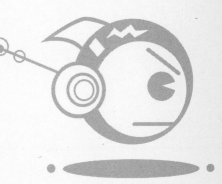

ALSO AVAILABLE FROM TOKYOPOP®

MANGA

.HACK//LEGEND OF THE TWILIGHT
@LARGE
A.I. LOVE YOU February 2004
AI YORI AOSHI January 2004
ANGELIC LAYER
BABY BIRTH
BATTLE ROYALE
BATTLE VIXENS April 2004
BIRTH May 2004
BRAIN POWERED
BRIGADOON
B'TX January 2004
CARDCAPTOR SAKURA
CARDCAPTOR SAKURA: MASTER OF THE CLOW
CARDCAPTOR SAKURA: BOXED SET COLLECTION 1
CARDCAPTOR SAKURA: BOXED SET COLLECTION 2
   March 2004
CHOBITS
CHRONICLES OF THE CURSED SWORD
CLAMP SCHOOL DETECTIVES
CLOVER
COMIC PARTY June 2004
CONFIDENTIAL CONFESSIONS
CORRECTOR YUI
COWBOY BEBOP: BOXED SET THE COMPLETE
   COLLECTION
CRESCENT MOON May 2004
CREST OF THE STARS June 2004
CYBORG 009
DEMON DIARY
DIGIMON
DIGIMON SERIES 3 April 2004
DIGIMON ZERO TWO February 2004
DNANGEL April 2004
DOLL May 2004
DRAGON HUNTER
DRAGON KNIGHTS
DUKLYON: CLAMP SCHOOL DEFENDERS
DV June 2004
ERICA SAKURAZAWA
FAERIES' LANDING January 2004
FAKE
FLCL
FORBIDDEN DANCE
FRUITS BASKET February 2004
G GUNDAM
GATEKEEPERS
GETBACKERS February 2004
GHOST! March 2004
GIRL GOT GAME January 2004
GRAVITATION
GTO

GUNDAM WING
GUNDAM WING: BATTLEFIELD OF PACIFISTS
GUNDAM WING: ENDLESS WALTZ
GUNDAM WING: THE LAST OUTPOST
HAPPY MANIA
HARLEM BEAT
I.N.V.U.
INITIAL D
ISLAND
JING: KING OF BANDITS
JULINE
JUROR 13 March 2004
KARE KANO
KILL ME, KISS ME February 2004
KINDAICHI CASE FILES, THE
KING OF HELL
KODOCHA: SANA'S STAGE
LAMENT OF THE LAMB May 2004
LES BIJOUX February 2004
LIZZIE MCGUIRE
LOVE HINA
LUPIN III
LUPIN III SERIES 2
MAGIC KNIGHT RAYEARTH I
MAGIC KNIGHT RAYEARTH II February 2004
MAHOROMATIC: AUTOMATIC MAIDEN May 2004
MAN OF MANY FACES
MARMALADE BOY
MARS
METEOR METHUSELA June 2004
METROID June 2004
MINK April 2004
MIRACLE GIRLS
MIYUKI-CHAN IN WONDERLAND
MODEL May 2004
NELLY MUSIC MANGA April 2004
ONE April 2004
PARADISE KISS
PARASYTE
PEACH GIRL
PEACH GIRL CHANGE OF HEART
PEACH GIRL RELAUNCH BOX SET
PET SHOP OF HORRORS
PITA-TEN January 2004
PLANET LADDER February 2004
PLANETES
PRIEST
PRINCESS AI April 2004
PSYCHIC ACADEMY March 2004
RAGNAROK
RAGNAROK: BOXED SET COLLECTION 1
RAVE MASTER
RAVE MASTER: BOXED SET March 2004

Forbidden Dance 3

created by ***Hinako Ashihara***

TENSHI NO KISS

Translator - Takae Brewer
English Adaptation - Tisha Ford
Editor - Jodi Bryson
Retouch and Lettering - Rubina Chabra
Cover Layout - Matt Alford

Sr. Editor - Julie Taylor
VP of Production - Ron Klamert
President & C.O.O. - John Parker
Publisher & C.E.O. - Stuart Levy

A TOKYOPOP® Manga

TOKYOPOP Inc.
5900 Wilshire Blvd. Suite 2000
Los Angeles, CA 90036

Email: editor@TOKYOPOP.com
Come visit us online at www.TOKYOPOP.com

"TENSHI NO KISS" 3

ISBN: 1-59182-347-1

First TOKYOPOP printing: January 2004

10 9 8 7 6 5 4 3 2 1

Printed in the USA

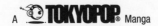

Forbidden Dance

Volume 3

Written and Illustrated by
Hinako Ashihara

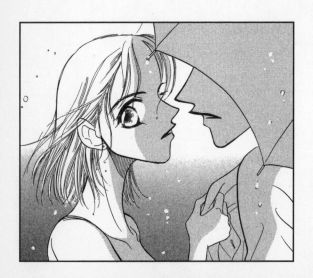

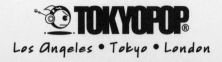

Los Angeles • Tokyo • London

FORBIDDEN DANCE 3

CONTENTS

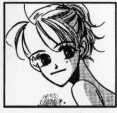

AYA FUJI
HIGH SCHOOL STUDENT.
SHE HAS BEEN TRAINING IN
CLASSICAL BALLET SINCE
SHE WAS VERY YOUNG.

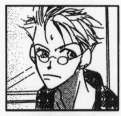

AKIRA HIBIYA
LEADER OF THE
ALL-MALE DANCE
TROUPE "COOL."

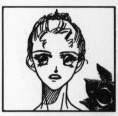

DIANA ROBERTS
A WORLD FAMOUS
BALLERINA.

STORY

AYA IS A HIGH SCHOOL STUDENT WHO LOVES BALLET. DURING A
PERFORMANCE AT A BALLET COMPETITION, SHE INJURED HER FOOT
AND DEVELOPED A MORBID FEAR OF DANCING ON STAGE. SHE QUIT
DANCING BECAUSE OF THE PSYCHOLOGICAL EFFECTS OF HER ACUTE
STAGE FRIGHT. ONE DAY, AYA GOES TO A BALLET PERFORMANCE OF
"COOL" AND IS DEEPLY MOVED BY AKIRA'S STYLE OF DANCING.
THIS MOTIVATES AYA TO BEGIN DANCING AGAIN. AYA WISHES TO
DANCE WITH AKIRA AND ASKS AKIRA TO LET HER JOIN "COOL."
DESPITE THE STRICT REQUIREMENT SET FORTH BY AKIRA, AYA
SUCCESSFULLY BECOMES A MEMBER OF "COOL." DIANA ROBERTS,
A WIDELY-RECOGNIZED BRITISH DANCER, COMES TO SEE AKIRA.
SHE CAME FOR AN IMPORTANT PERFORMANCE IN JAPAN, HIDING
THE FACT SHE HAS A SEVERE ANKLE INJURY. IN ORDER TO HELP
DIANA THROUGH HER PREDICAMENT, AYA SECRETLY TAKES OVER
THE SECOND ACT. THANKS TO AYA, DIANA SUCCESSFULLY FINISHES
THE FINAL ACT, BUT SHE COLLAPSES AS SOON AS THE CURTAIN
GOES DOWN...

* BETSU COMI FLOWER COMICS*

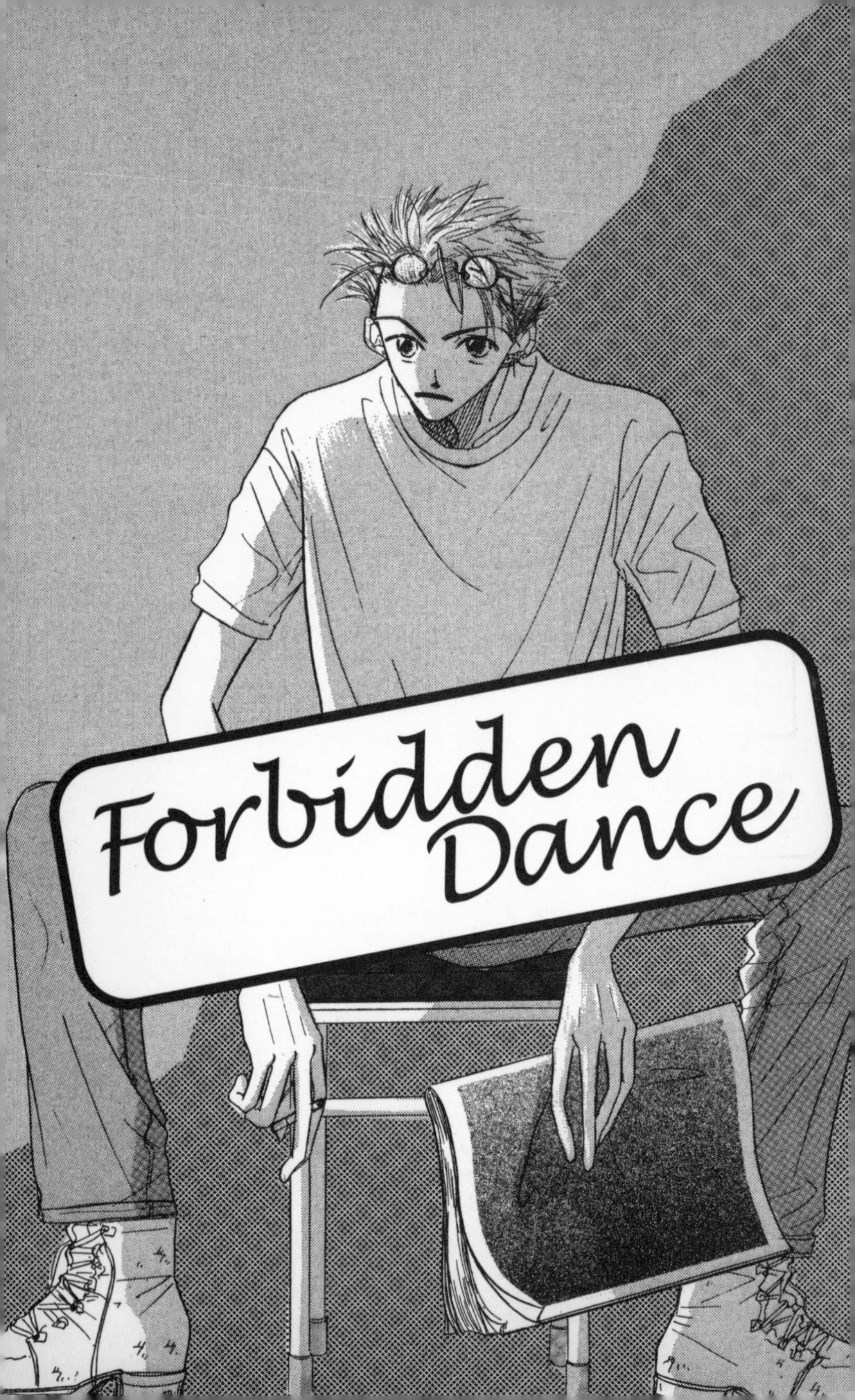
Forbidden Dance

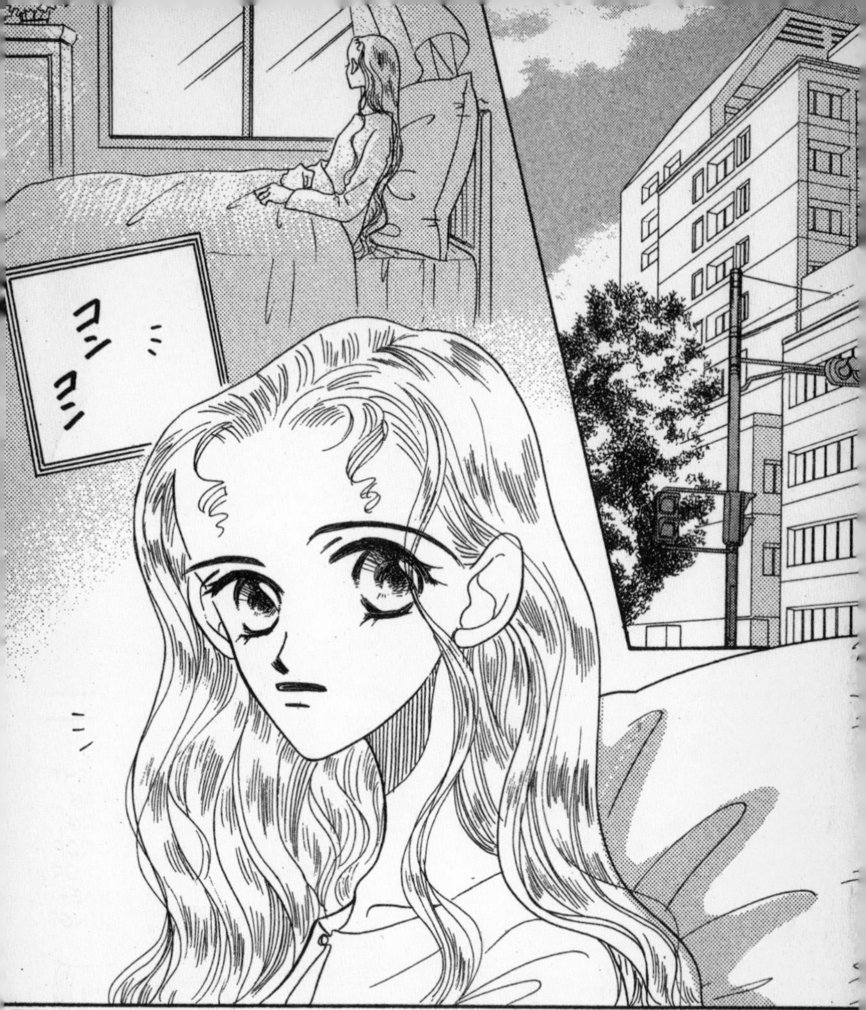
コンコン

Ashihara's Diary

-◆- Mr. Suehiro -◆- Age 85

He is pretty old, but looks like he has another 50 years to live. I have never had an old character like him. The good news is his face is pretty easy to draw. Elderly people are often hard to draw, you know?

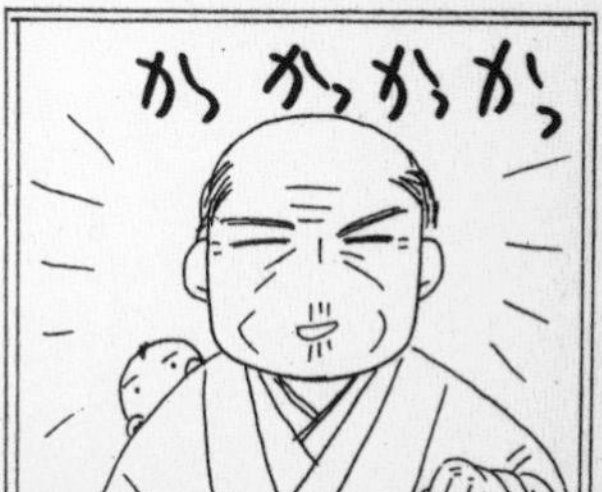
かっ かっかっかっ

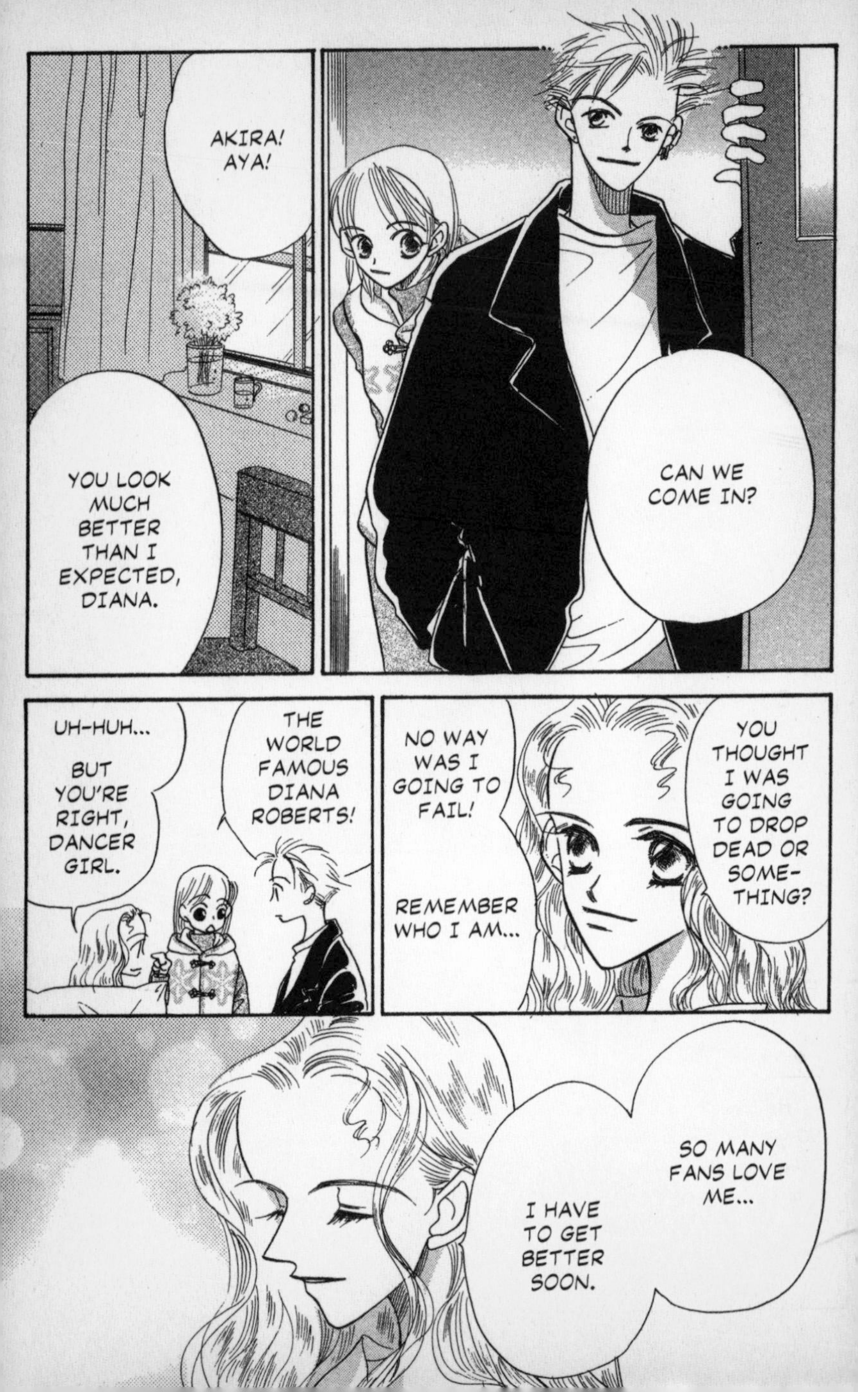
CAN WE COME IN?
AKIRA! AYA!
YOU LOOK MUCH BETTER THAN I EXPECTED, DIANA.
YOU THOUGHT I WAS GOING TO DROP DEAD OR SOME-THING?
NO WAY WAS I GOING TO FAIL!
REMEMBER WHO I AM...
THE WORLD FAMOUS DIANA ROBERTS!
UH-HUH...
BUT YOU'RE RIGHT, DANCER GIRL.
SO MANY FANS LOVE ME...
I HAVE TO GET BETTER SOON.

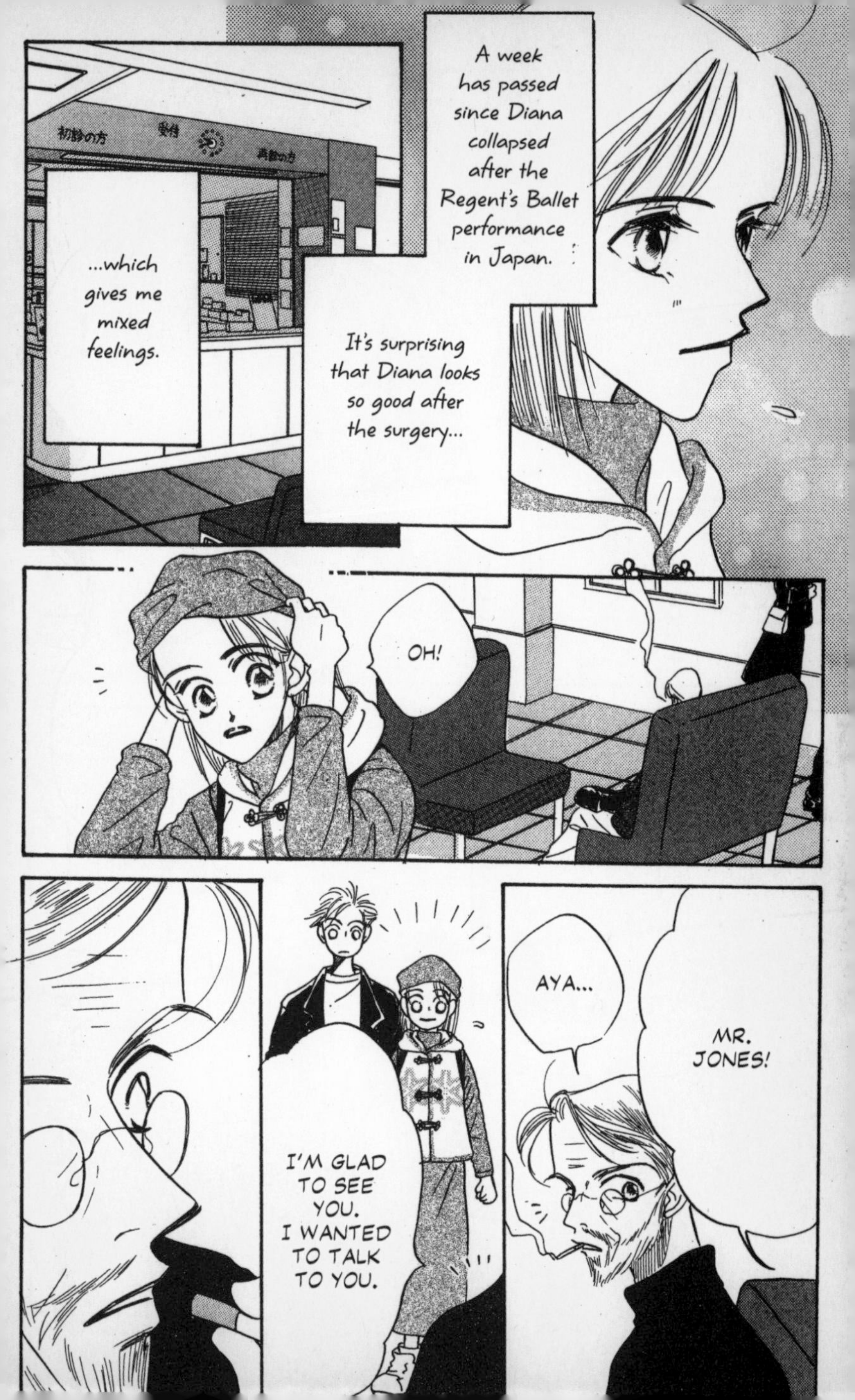

A week has passed since Diana collapsed after the Regent's Ballet performance in Japan.
It's surprising that Diana looks so good after the surgery...
...which gives me mixed feelings.
初診の方
受付
再診の方
OH!
MR. JONES!
AYA...
I'M GLAD TO SEE YOU. I WANTED TO TALK TO YOU.

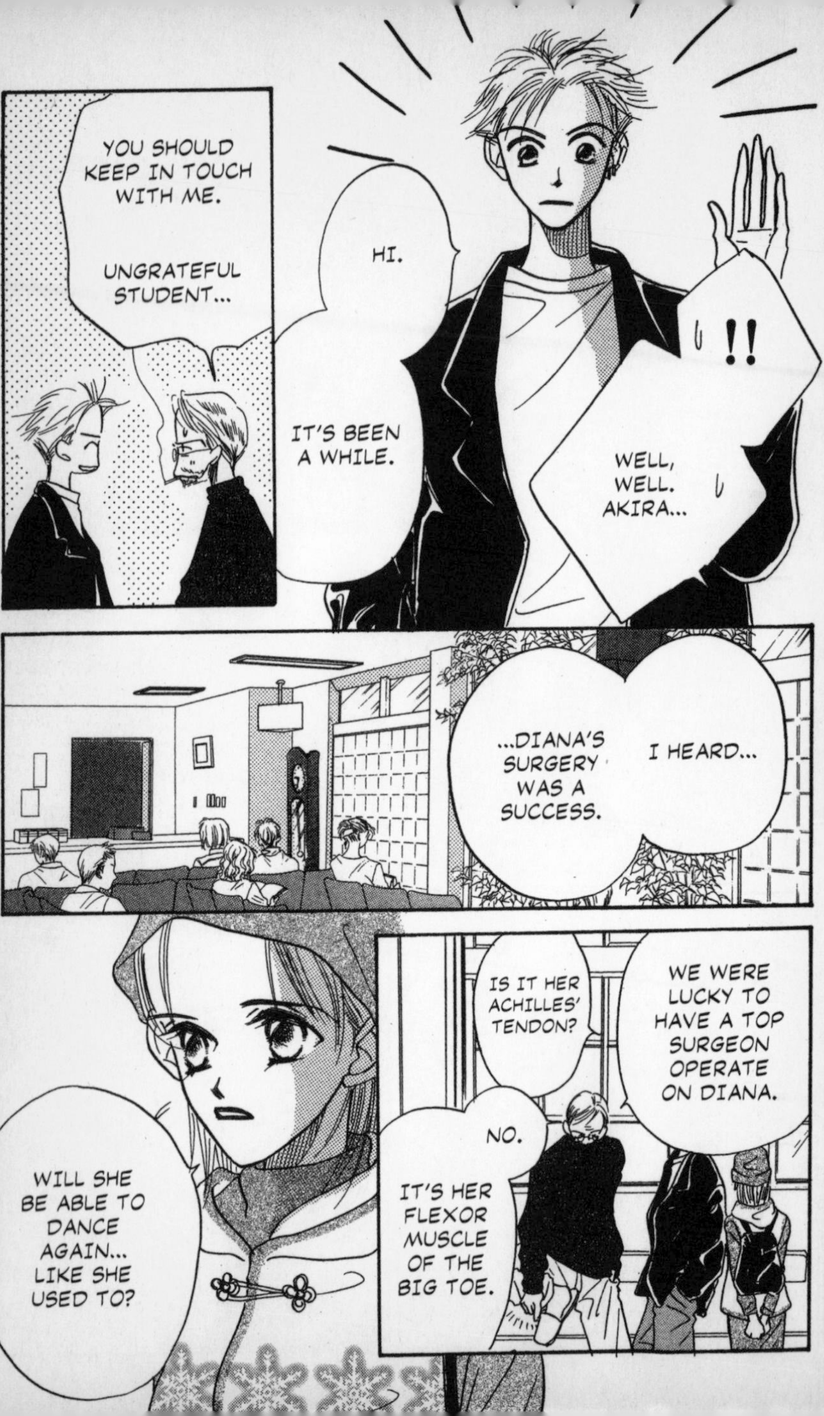
!!
WELL, WELL. AKIRA...
HI.
IT'S BEEN A WHILE.
YOU SHOULD KEEP IN TOUCH WITH ME.
UNGRATEFUL STUDENT...
I HEARD...
...DIANA'S SURGERY WAS A SUCCESS.
WE WERE LUCKY TO HAVE A TOP SURGEON OPERATE ON DIANA.
IS IT HER ACHILLES' TENDON?
NO.
IT'S HER FLEXOR MUSCLE OF THE BIG TOE.
WILL SHE BE ABLE TO DANCE AGAIN... LIKE SHE USED TO?

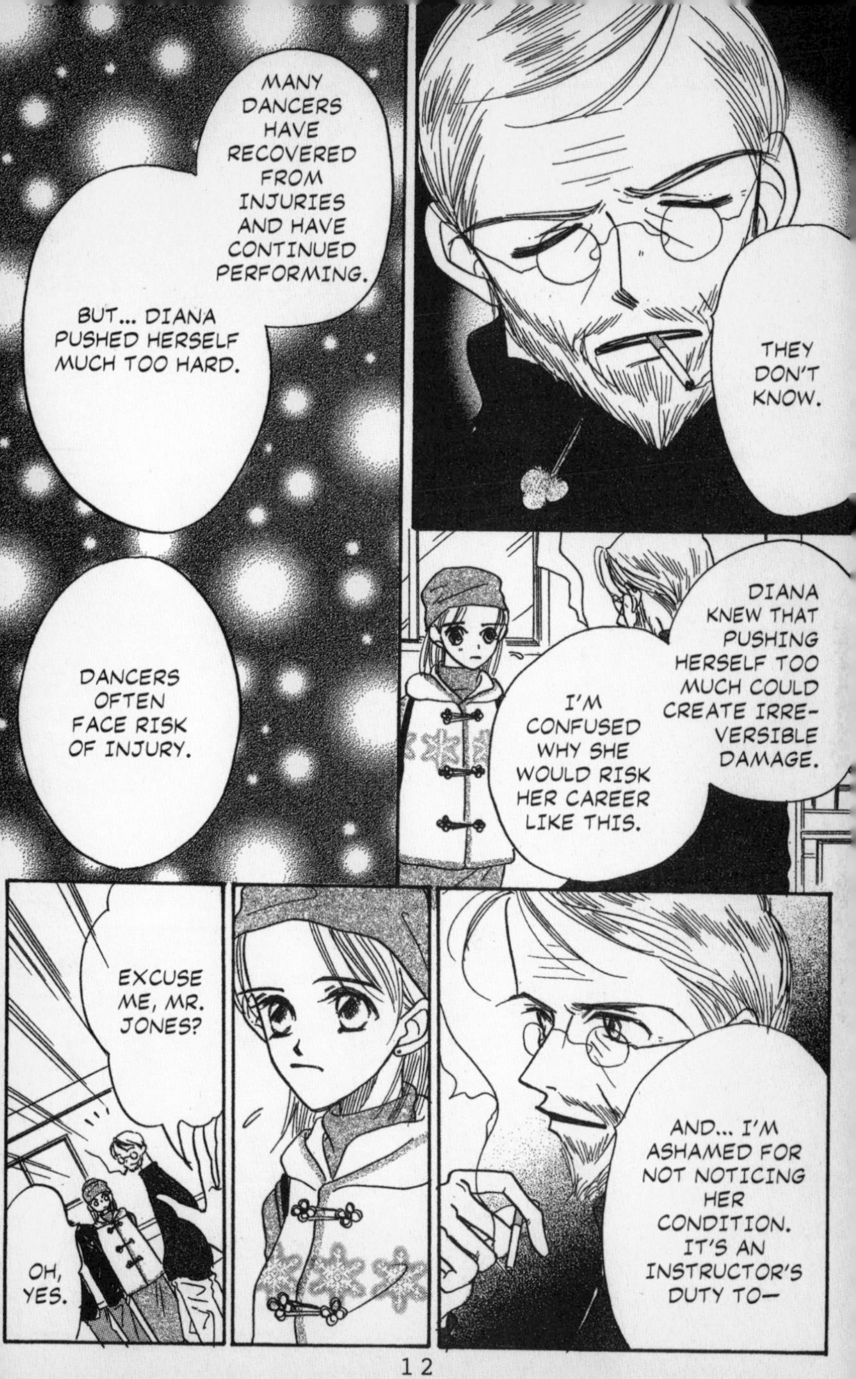
THEY DON'T KNOW.
DIANA KNEW THAT PUSHING HERSELF TOO MUCH COULD CREATE IRRE-VERSIBLE DAMAGE.
I'M CONFUSED WHY SHE WOULD RISK HER CAREER LIKE THIS.
MANY DANCERS HAVE RECOVERED FROM INJURIES AND HAVE CONTINUED PERFORMING.
BUT... DIANA PUSHED HERSELF MUCH TOO HARD.
DANCERS OFTEN FACE RISK OF INJURY.
AND... I'M ASHAMED FOR NOT NOTICING HER CONDITION. IT'S AN INSTRUCTOR'S DUTY TO—
EXCUSE ME, MR. JONES?
OH, YES.

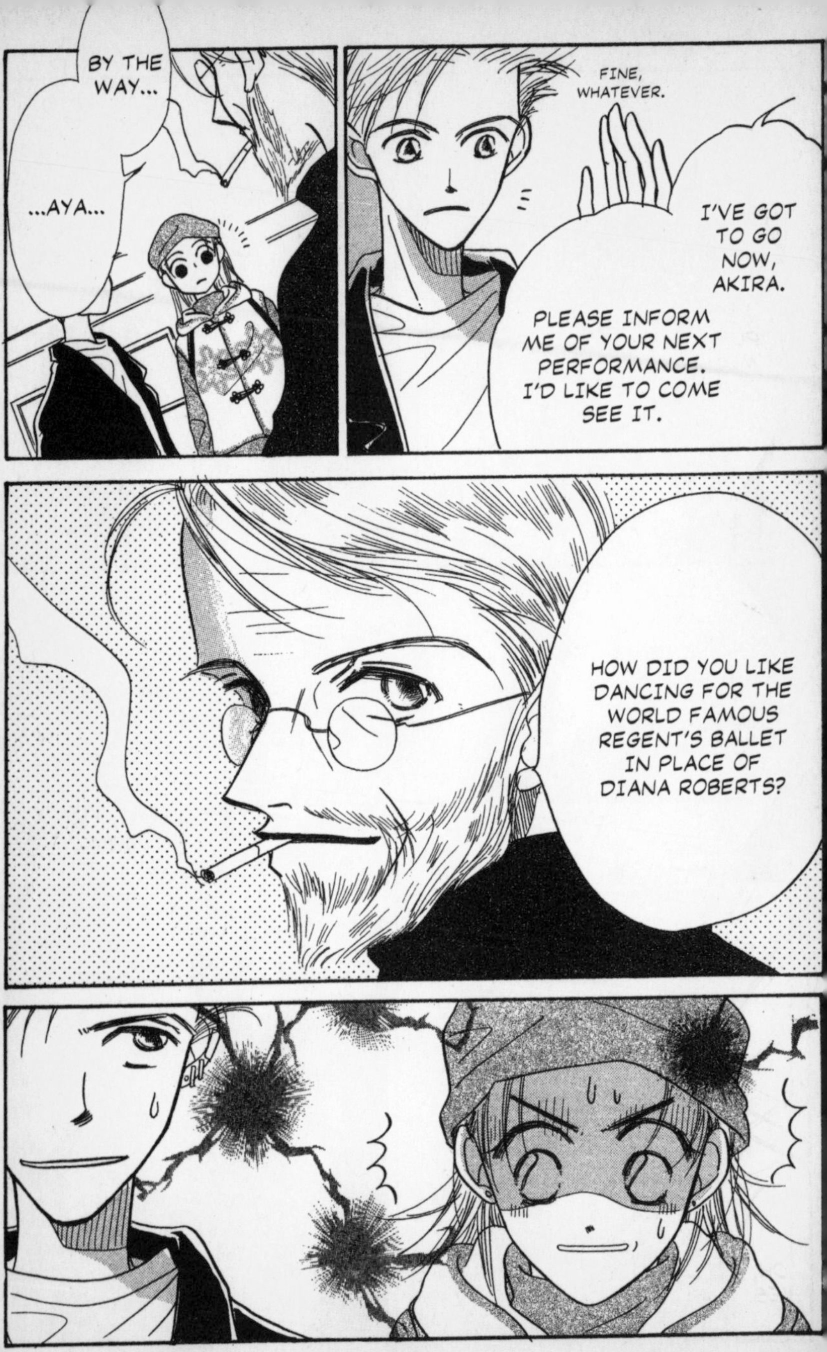
I'VE GOT TO GO NOW, AKIRA.
PLEASE INFORM ME OF YOUR NEXT PERFORMANCE. I'D LIKE TO COME SEE IT.
FINE, WHATEVER.
BY THE WAY...
...AYA...
HOW DID YOU LIKE DANCING FOR THE WORLD FAMOUS REGENT'S BALLET IN PLACE OF DIANA ROBERTS?

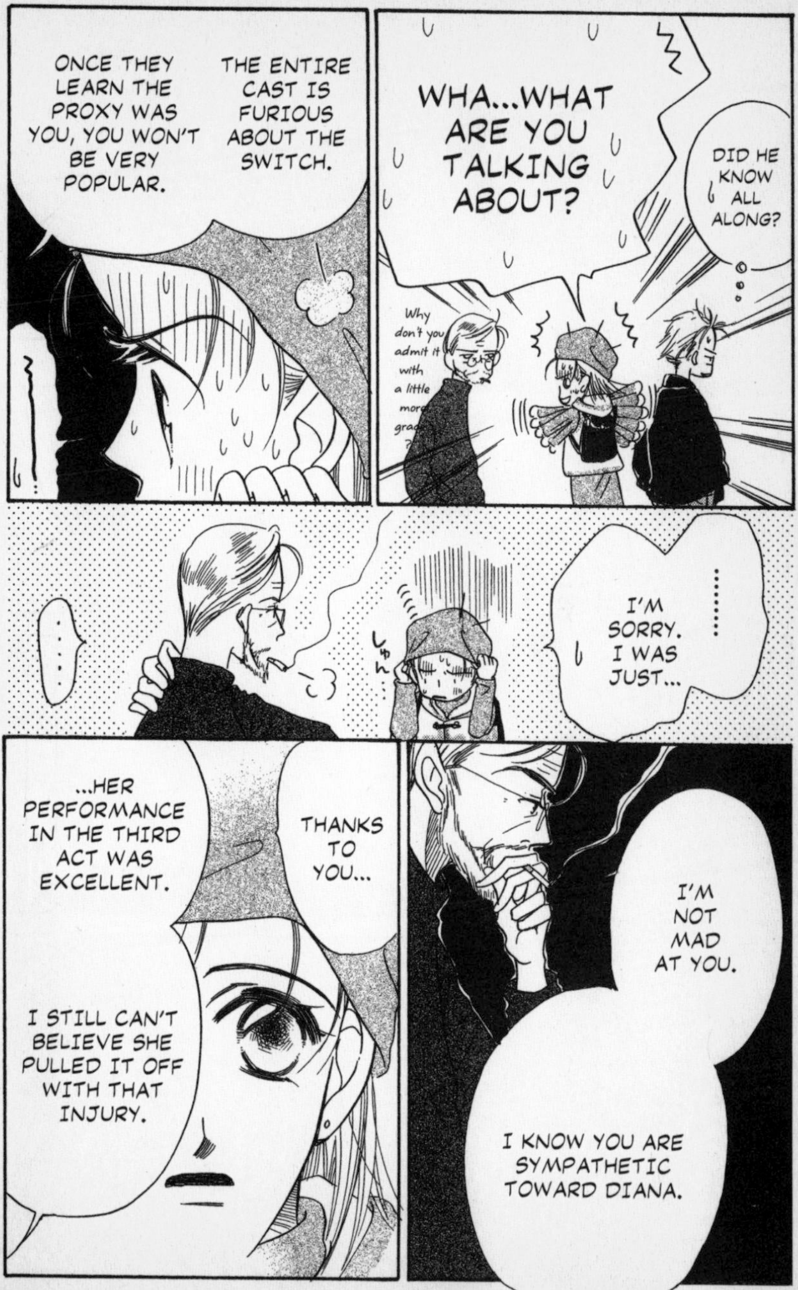
WHA...WHAT ARE YOU TALKING ABOUT?
DID HE KNOW ALL ALONG?
Why don't you admit it with a little more grac
THE ENTIRE CAST IS FURIOUS ABOUT THE SWITCH.
ONCE THEY LEARN THE PROXY WAS YOU, YOU WON'T BE VERY POPULAR.
......
I'M SORRY. I WAS JUST...
しゅん…
.....
I'M NOT MAD AT YOU.
I KNOW YOU ARE SYMPATHETIC TOWARD DIANA.
THANKS TO YOU...
...HER PERFORMANCE IN THE THIRD ACT WAS EXCELLENT.
I STILL CAN'T BELIEVE SHE PULLED IT OFF WITH THAT INJURY.

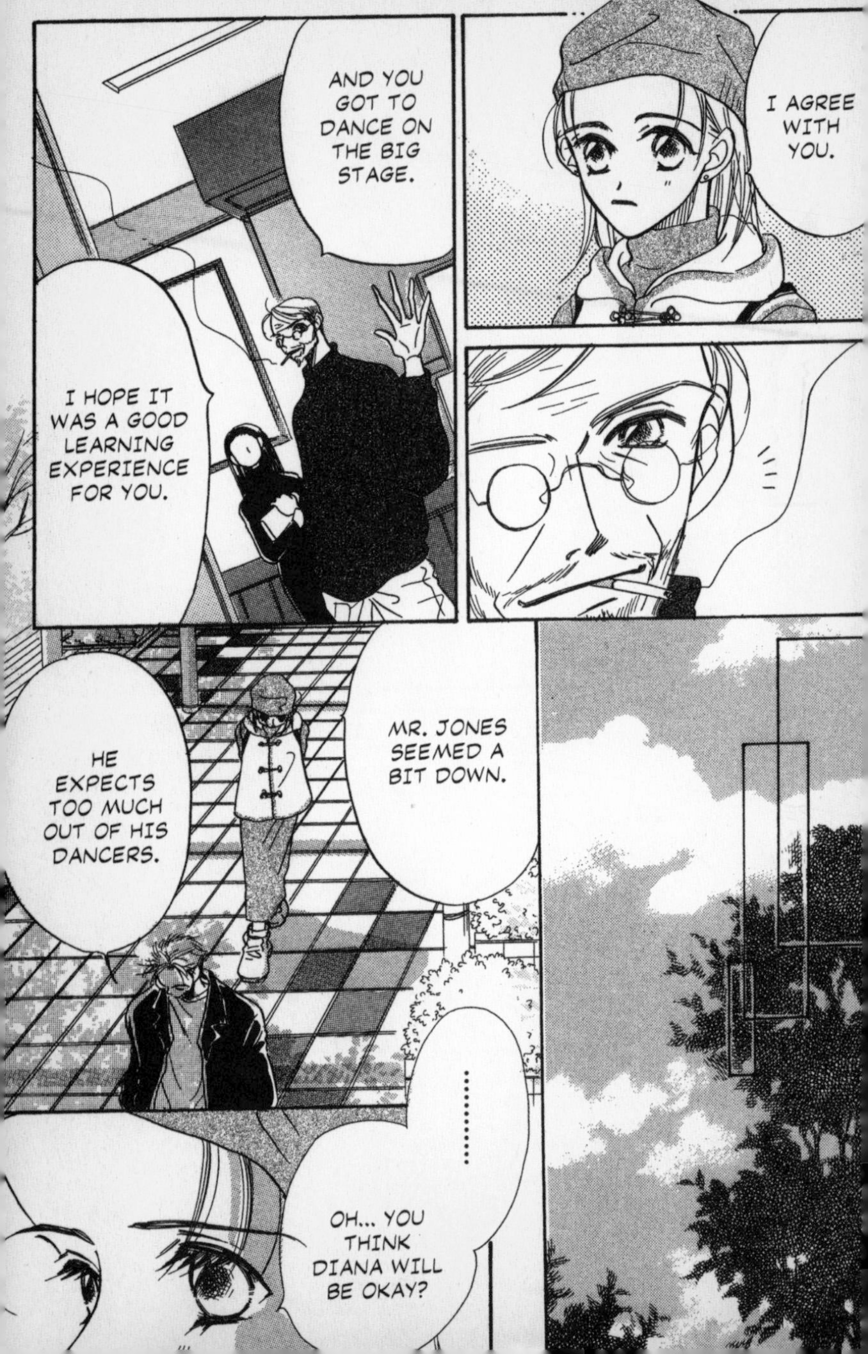
I AGREE WITH YOU.
AND YOU GOT TO DANCE ON THE BIG STAGE.
I HOPE IT WAS A GOOD LEARNING EXPERIENCE FOR YOU.
MR. JONES SEEMED A BIT DOWN.
HE EXPECTS TOO MUCH OUT OF HIS DANCERS.
....
OH... YOU THINK DIANA WILL BE OKAY?

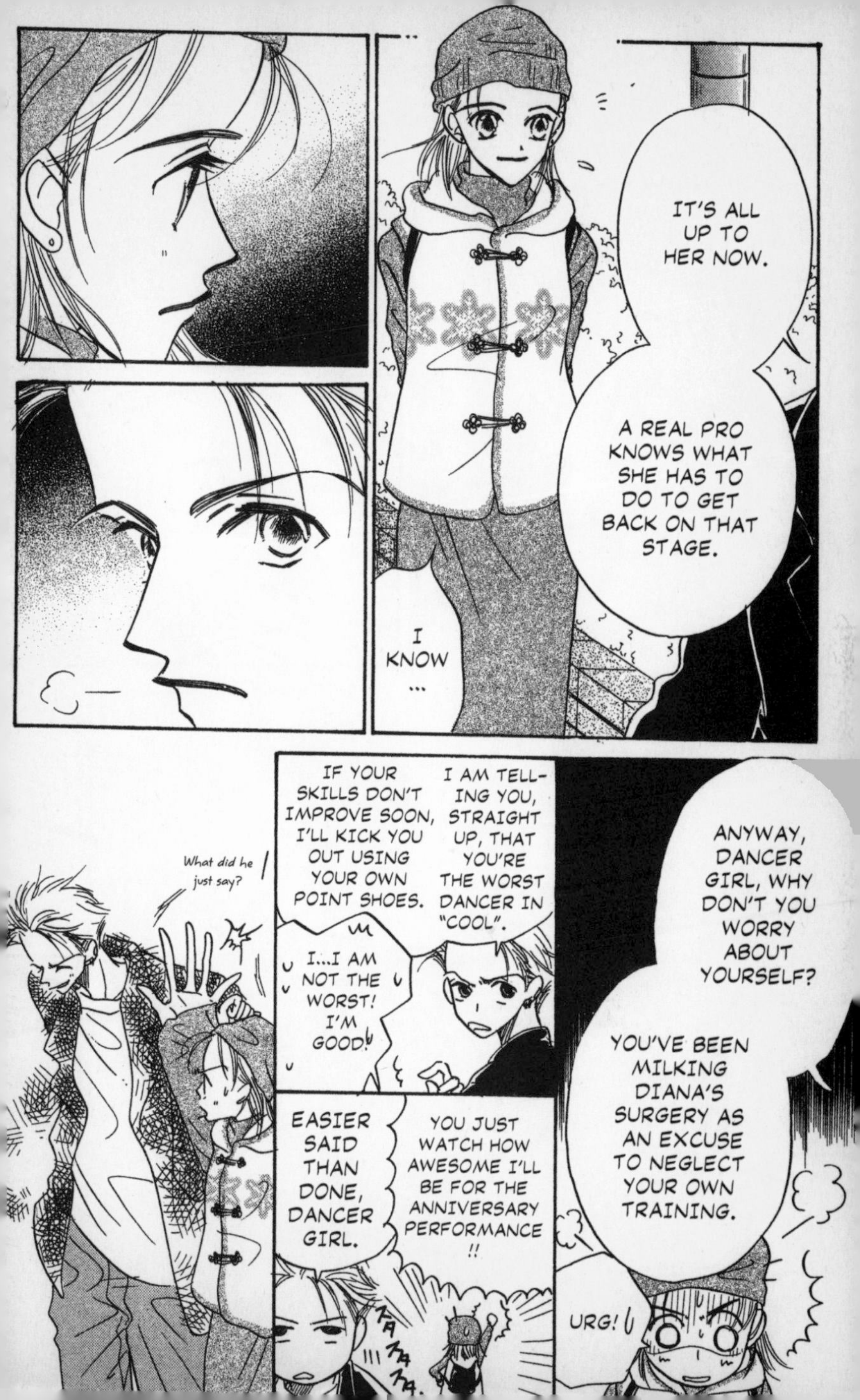
IT'S ALL UP TO HER NOW.
A REAL PRO KNOWS WHAT SHE HAS TO DO TO GET BACK ON THAT STAGE.
I KNOW ...
ANYWAY, DANCER GIRL, WHY DON'T YOU WORRY ABOUT YOURSELF?
YOU'VE BEEN MILKING DIANA'S SURGERY AS AN EXCUSE TO NEGLECT YOUR OWN TRAINING.
URG!
I AM TELLING YOU, STRAIGHT UP, THAT YOU'RE THE WORST DANCER IN "COOL".
IF YOUR SKILLS DON'T IMPROVE SOON, I'LL KICK YOU OUT USING YOUR OWN POINT SHOES.
I...I AM NOT THE WORST! I'M GOOD!
YOU JUST WATCH HOW AWESOME I'LL BE FOR THE ANNIVERSARY PERFORMANCE !!
EASIER SAID THAN DONE, DANCER GIRL.
What did he just say?

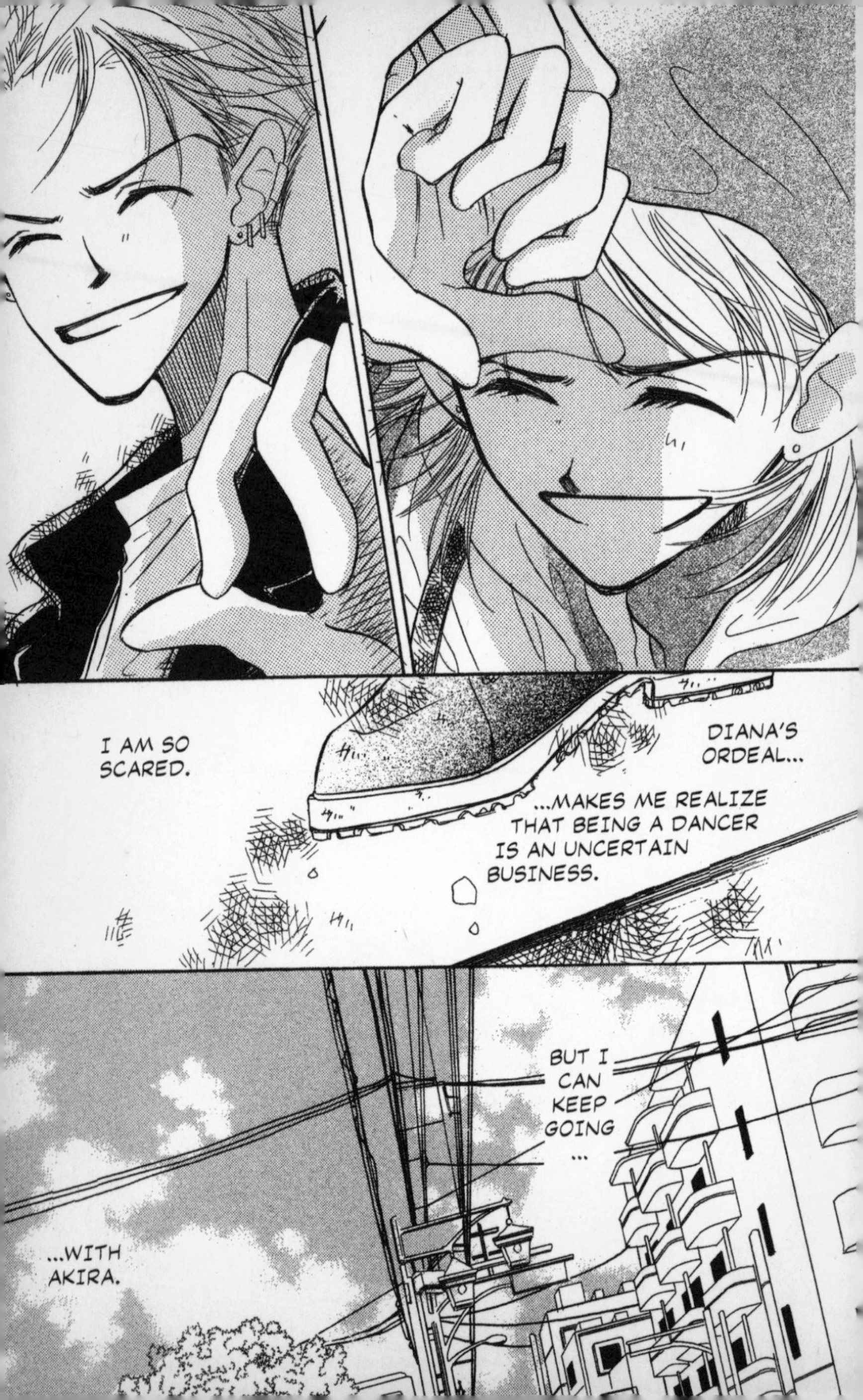
DIANA'S ORDEAL...
...MAKES ME REALIZE THAT BEING A DANCER IS AN UNCERTAIN BUSINESS.
I AM SO SCARED.
BUT I CAN KEEP GOING ...
...WITH AKIRA.

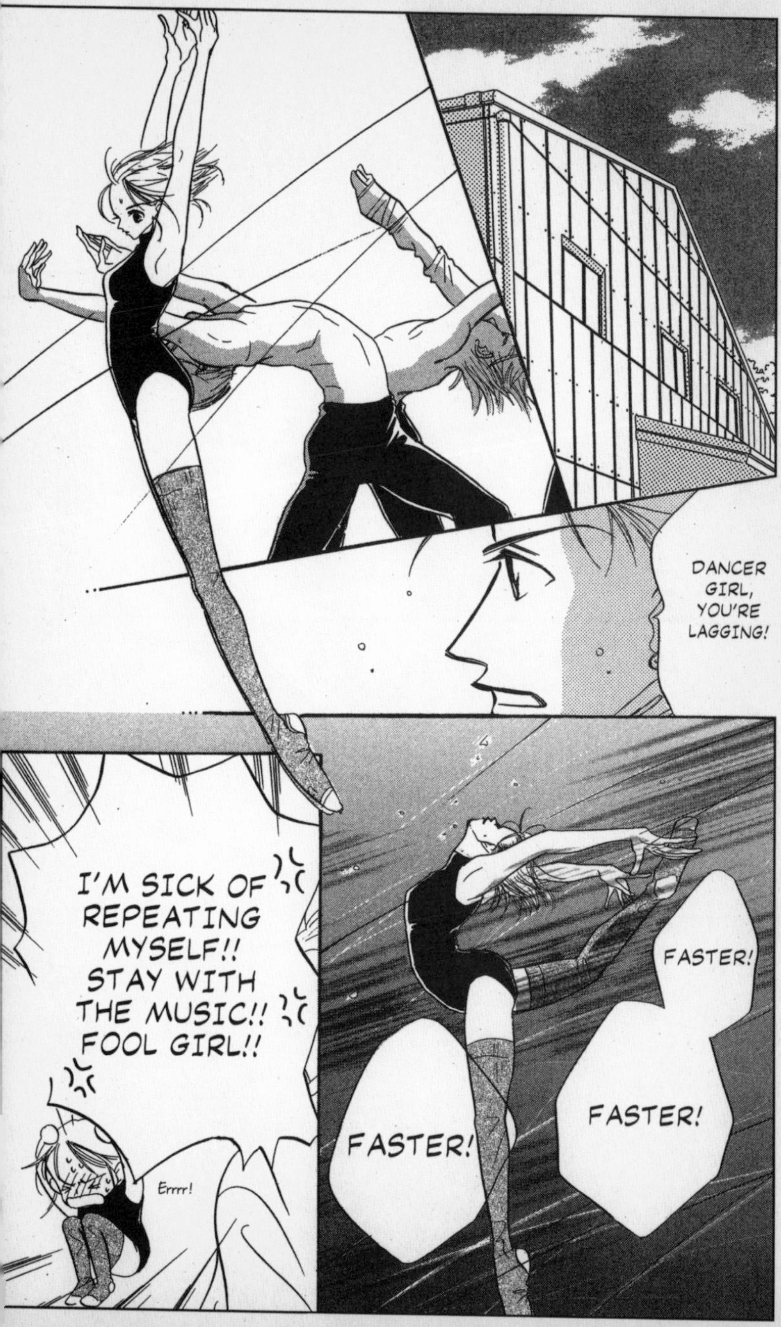
DANCER GIRL, YOU'RE LAGGING!
FASTER!
FASTER!
FASTER!
I'M SICK OF REPEATING MYSELF!! STAY WITH THE MUSIC!! FOOL GIRL!!
Errrr!

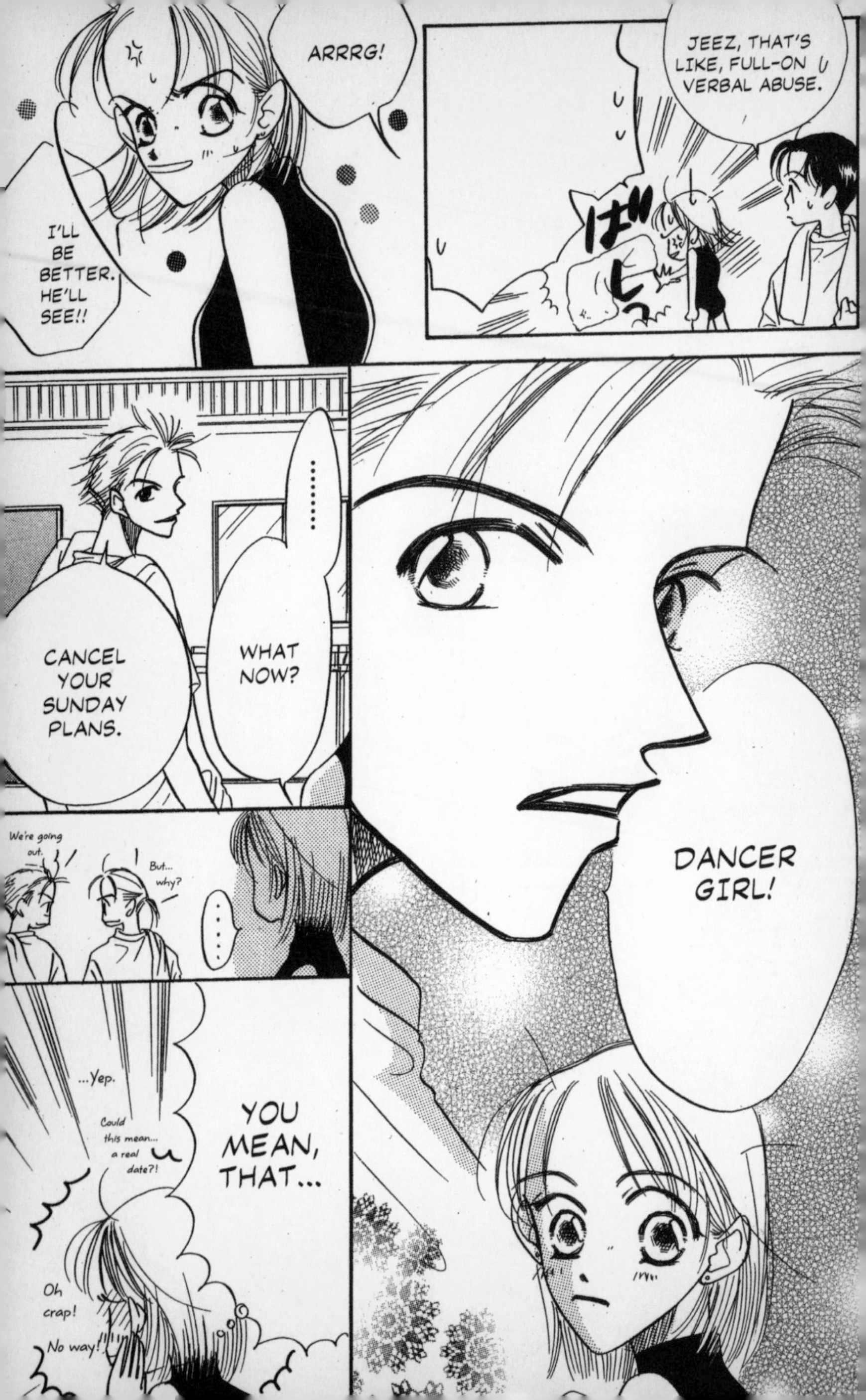
JEEZ, THAT'S LIKE, FULL-ON VERBAL ABUSE.
ばしっ
ARRRG!
I'LL BE BETTER. HE'LL SEE!!
DANCER GIRL!
....
WHAT NOW?
CANCEL YOUR SUNDAY PLANS.
.....
We're going out.
But... why?
YOU MEAN, THAT...
...Yep.
Could this mean... a real date?!
Oh crap!
No way!!

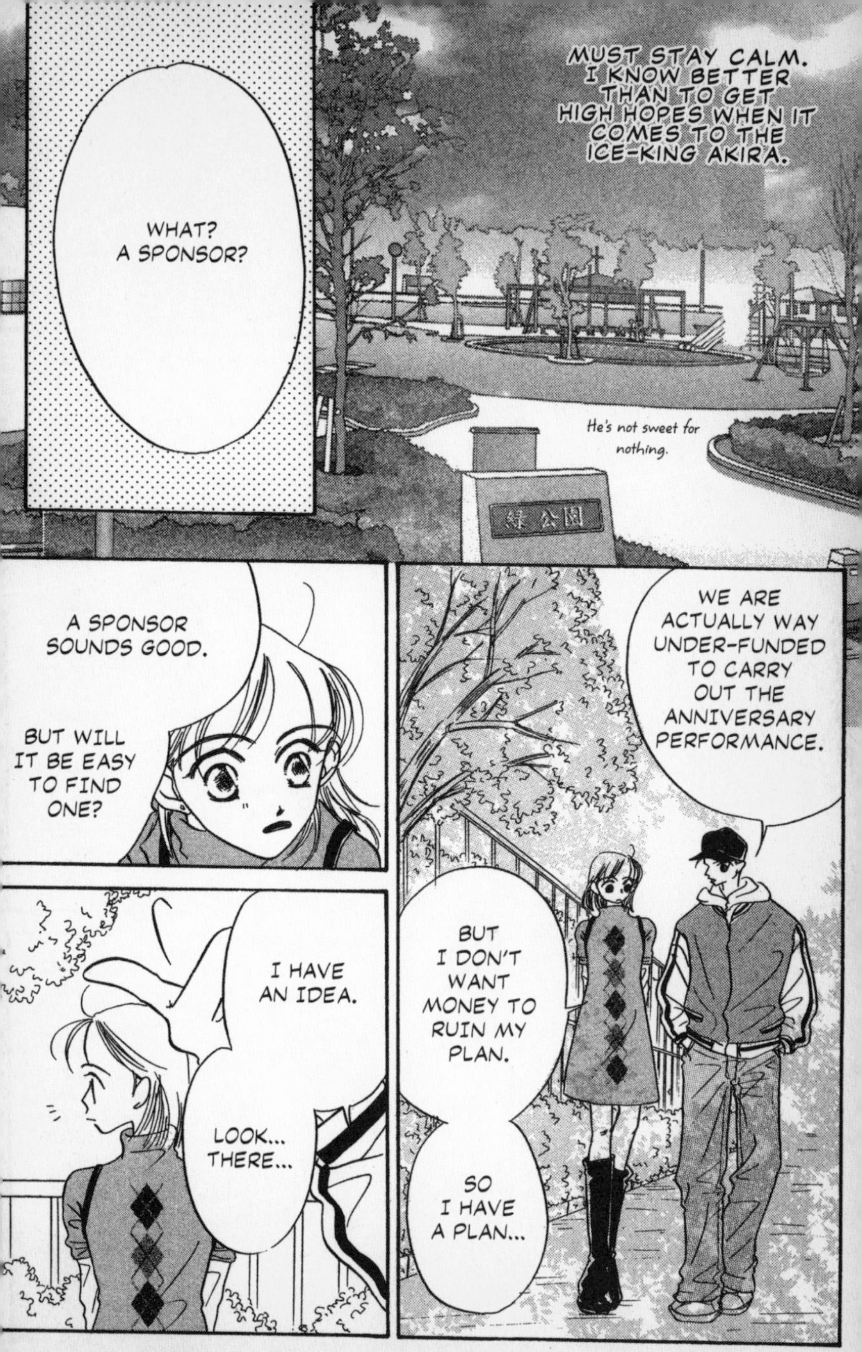
MUST STAY CALM. I KNOW BETTER THAN TO GET HIGH HOPES WHEN IT COMES TO THE ICE-KING AKIRA.
He's not sweet for nothing.
緑公園
WHAT? A SPONSOR?
WE ARE ACTUALLY WAY UNDER-FUNDED TO CARRY OUT THE ANNIVERSARY PERFORMANCE.
BUT I DON'T WANT MONEY TO RUIN MY PLAN.
SO I HAVE A PLAN...
A SPONSOR SOUNDS GOOD.
BUT WILL IT BE EASY TO FIND ONE?
I HAVE AN IDEA.
LOOK... THERE...

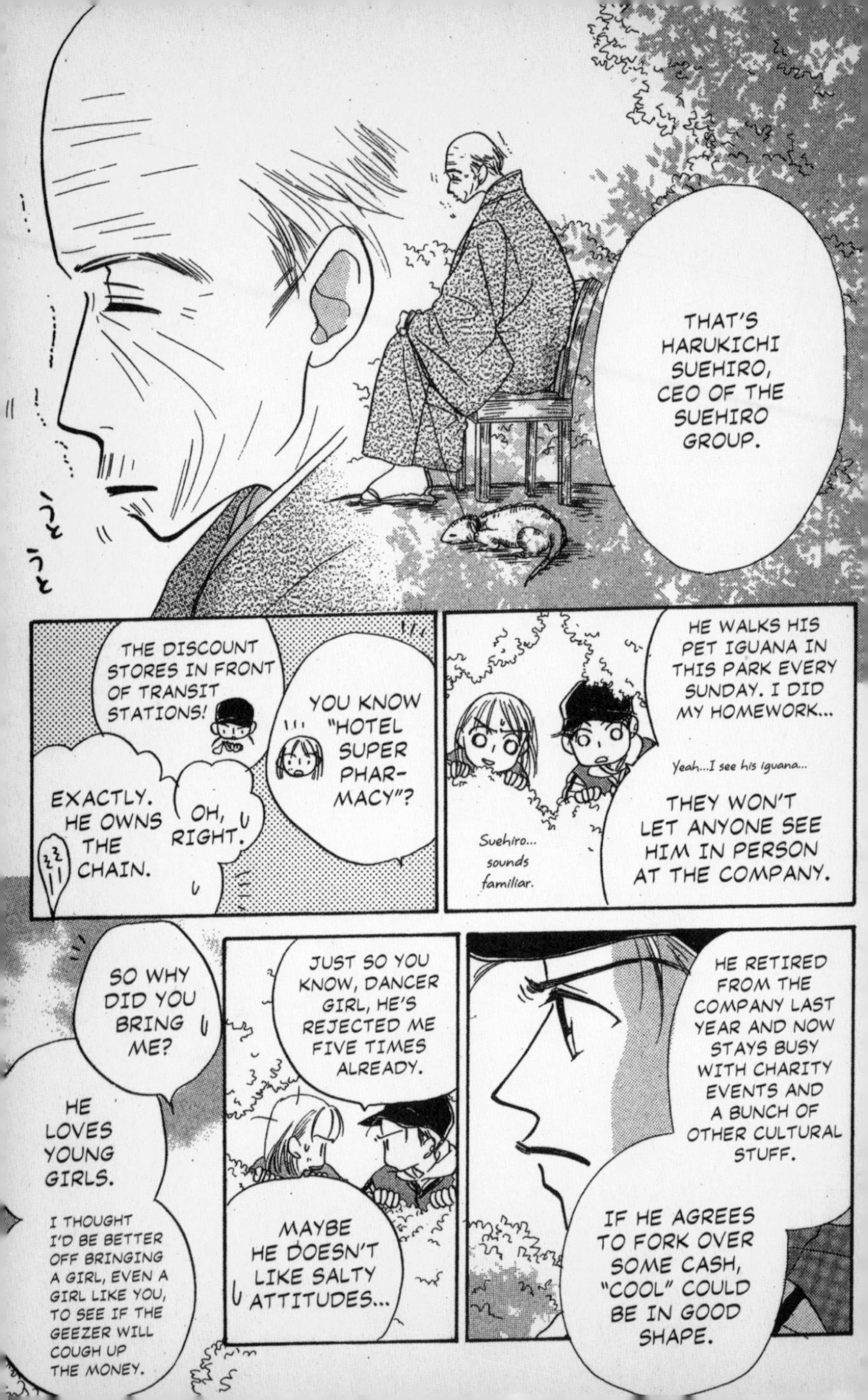
THAT'S HARUKICHI SUEHIRO, CEO OF THE SUEHIRO GROUP.
うと うと
HE WALKS HIS PET IGUANA IN THIS PARK EVERY SUNDAY. I DID MY HOMEWORK...
Yeah...I see his iguana...
THEY WON'T LET ANYONE SEE HIM IN PERSON AT THE COMPANY.
Suehiro... sounds familiar.
YOU KNOW "HOTEL SUPER PHARMACY"?
THE DISCOUNT STORES IN FRONT OF TRANSIT STATIONS!
OH, RIGHT.
EXACTLY. HE OWNS THE CHAIN.
HE RETIRED FROM THE COMPANY LAST YEAR AND NOW STAYS BUSY WITH CHARITY EVENTS AND A BUNCH OF OTHER CULTURAL STUFF.
IF HE AGREES TO FORK OVER SOME CASH, "COOL" COULD BE IN GOOD SHAPE.
JUST SO YOU KNOW, DANCER GIRL, HE'S REJECTED ME FIVE TIMES ALREADY.
MAYBE HE DOESN'T LIKE SALTY ATTITUDES...
SO WHY DID YOU BRING ME?
HE LOVES YOUNG GIRLS.
I THOUGHT I'D BE BETTER OFF BRINGING A GIRL, EVEN A GIRL LIKE YOU, TO SEE IF THE GEEZER WILL COUGH UP THE MONEY.

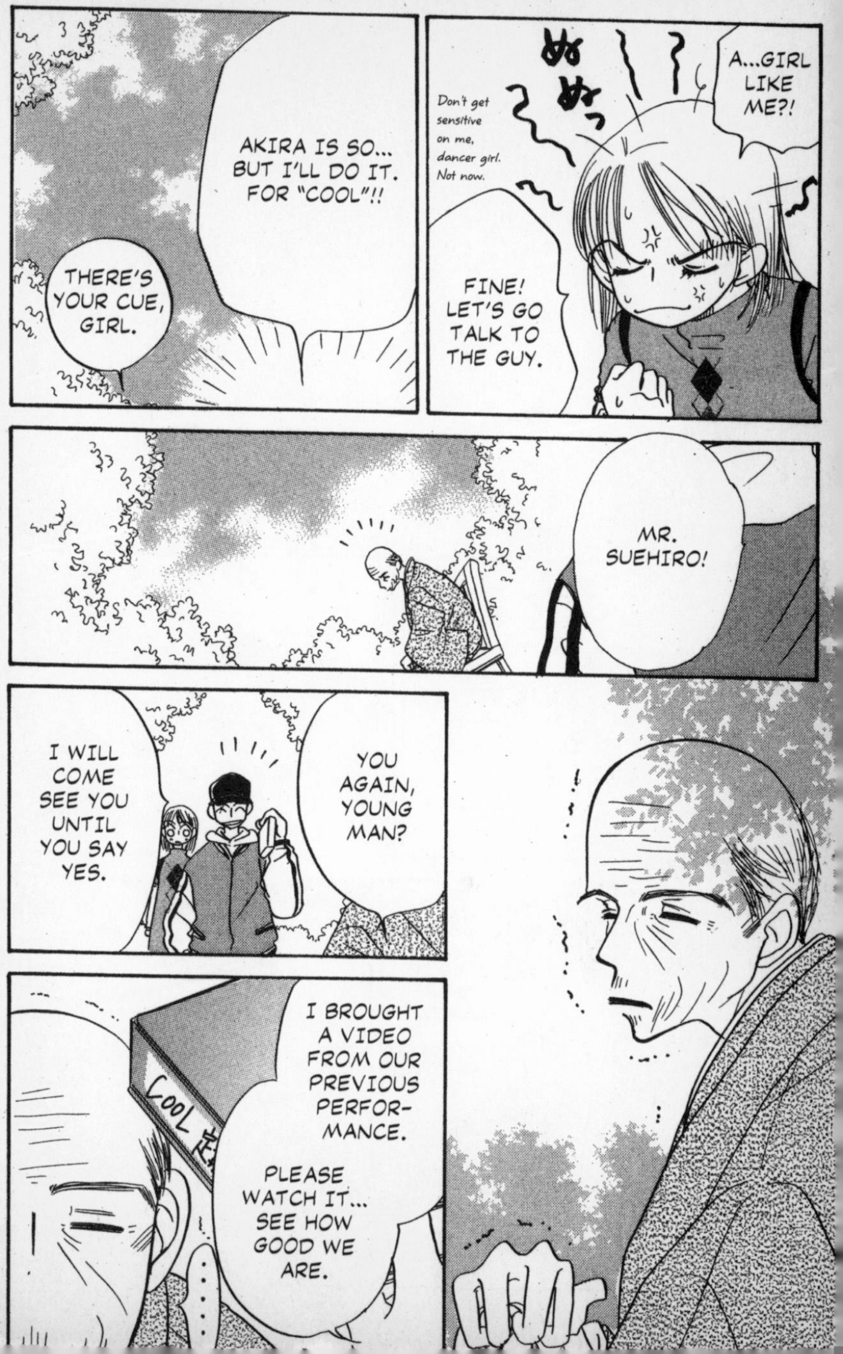

A...GIRL LIKE ME?!
ぬぬっ
Don't get sensitive on me, dancer girl. Not now.
FINE! LET'S GO TALK TO THE GUY.
AKIRA IS SO... BUT I'LL DO IT. FOR "COOL"!!
THERE'S YOUR CUE, GIRL.
MR. SUEHIRO!
YOU AGAIN, YOUNG MAN?
I WILL COME SEE YOU UNTIL YOU SAY YES.
I BROUGHT A VIDEO FROM OUR PREVIOUS PERFOR-MANCE.
PLEASE WATCH IT... SEE HOW GOOD WE ARE.
COOL

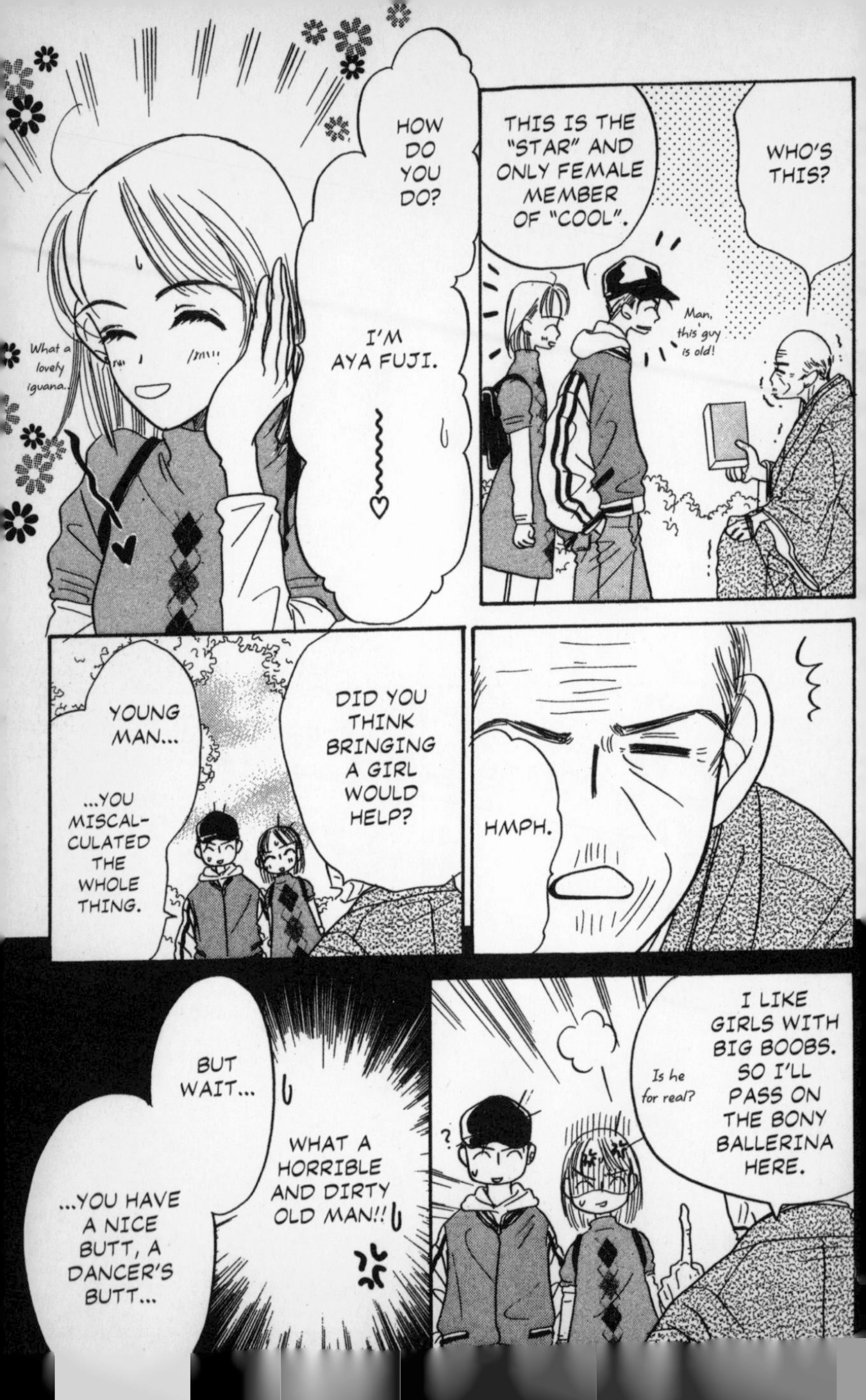
WHO'S THIS?
THIS IS THE "STAR" AND ONLY FEMALE MEMBER OF "COOL".
Man, this guy is old!
HOW DO YOU DO?
I'M AYA FUJI.
What a lovely iguana...
HMPH.
DID YOU THINK BRINGING A GIRL WOULD HELP?
YOUNG MAN...
...YOU MISCALCULATED THE WHOLE THING.
I LIKE GIRLS WITH BIG BOOBS. SO I'LL PASS ON THE BONY BALLERINA HERE.
Is he for real?
BUT WAIT...
...YOU HAVE A NICE BUTT, A DANCER'S BUTT...
WHAT A HORRIBLE AND DIRTY OLD MAN!!

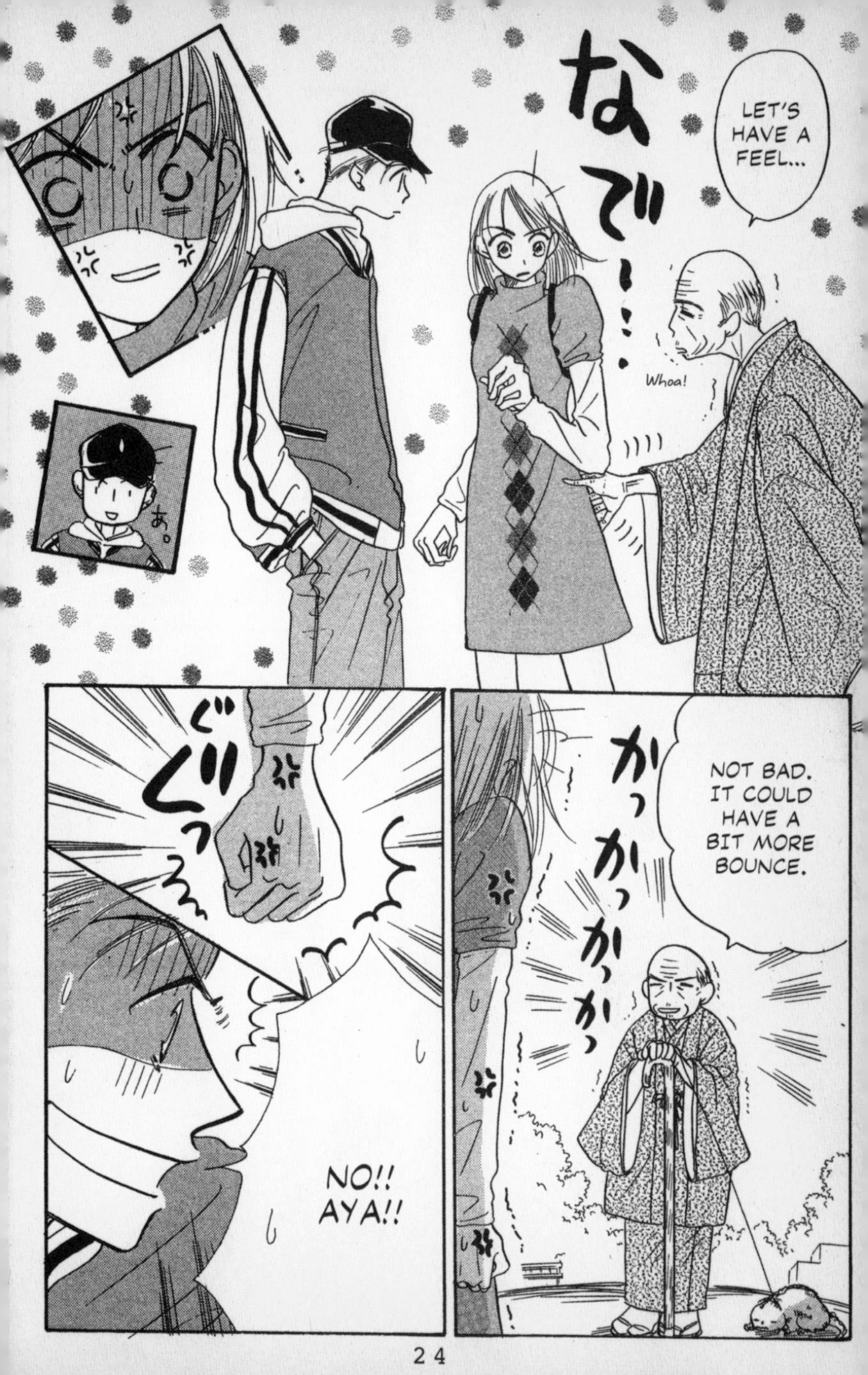
LET'S HAVE A FEEL...
なでー…
Whoa!
あ。
かっかっかっかっ
NOT BAD. IT COULD HAVE A BIT MORE BOUNCE.
ぐりぐっ
NO!! AYA!!

Ashihara's Diary

No. 1

Hello there.
This is Ashihara. Thanks for reading Forbidden Dance Volume 3. Hope you enjoy the book.

*

I finished up the last episode of Forbidden Dance the other day. The series continued for one year and four months (if my memory is correct). It felt like a long time when I was writing it, but now that the series is over, it was really a brief amount of time. It was still hard work, though. Still I really enjoyed working on the series. A lot of people who practice ballet sent me letters, which made me happy. Thanks again for all the support!

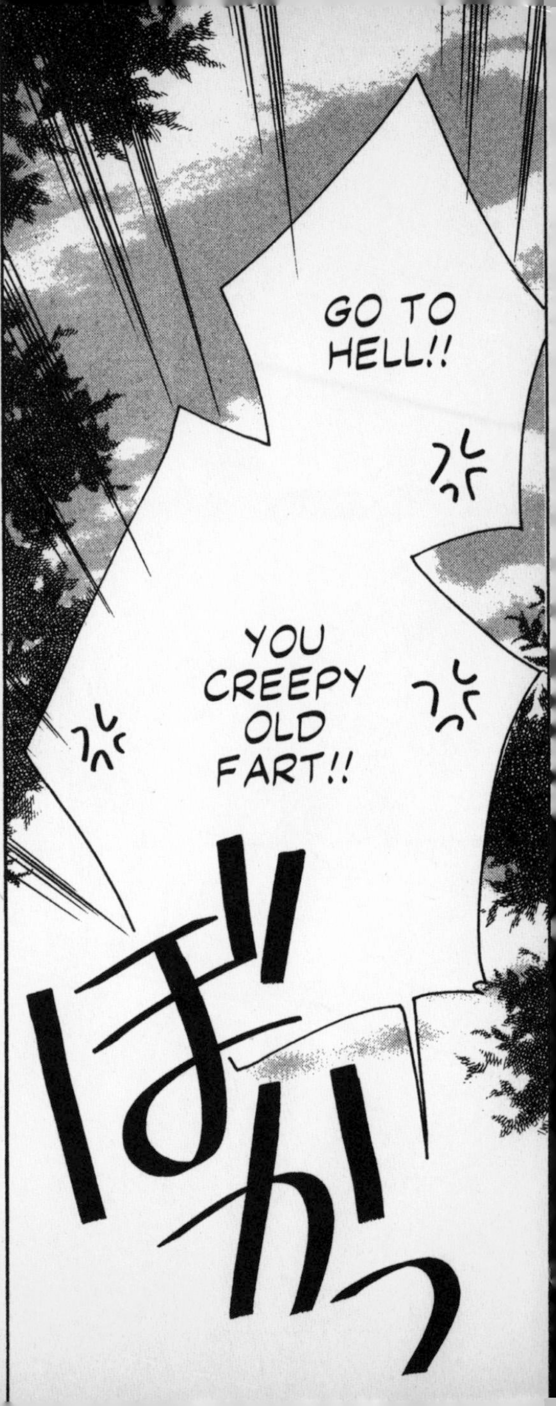
GO TO HELL!!
YOU CREEPY OLD FART!!
ばかっ

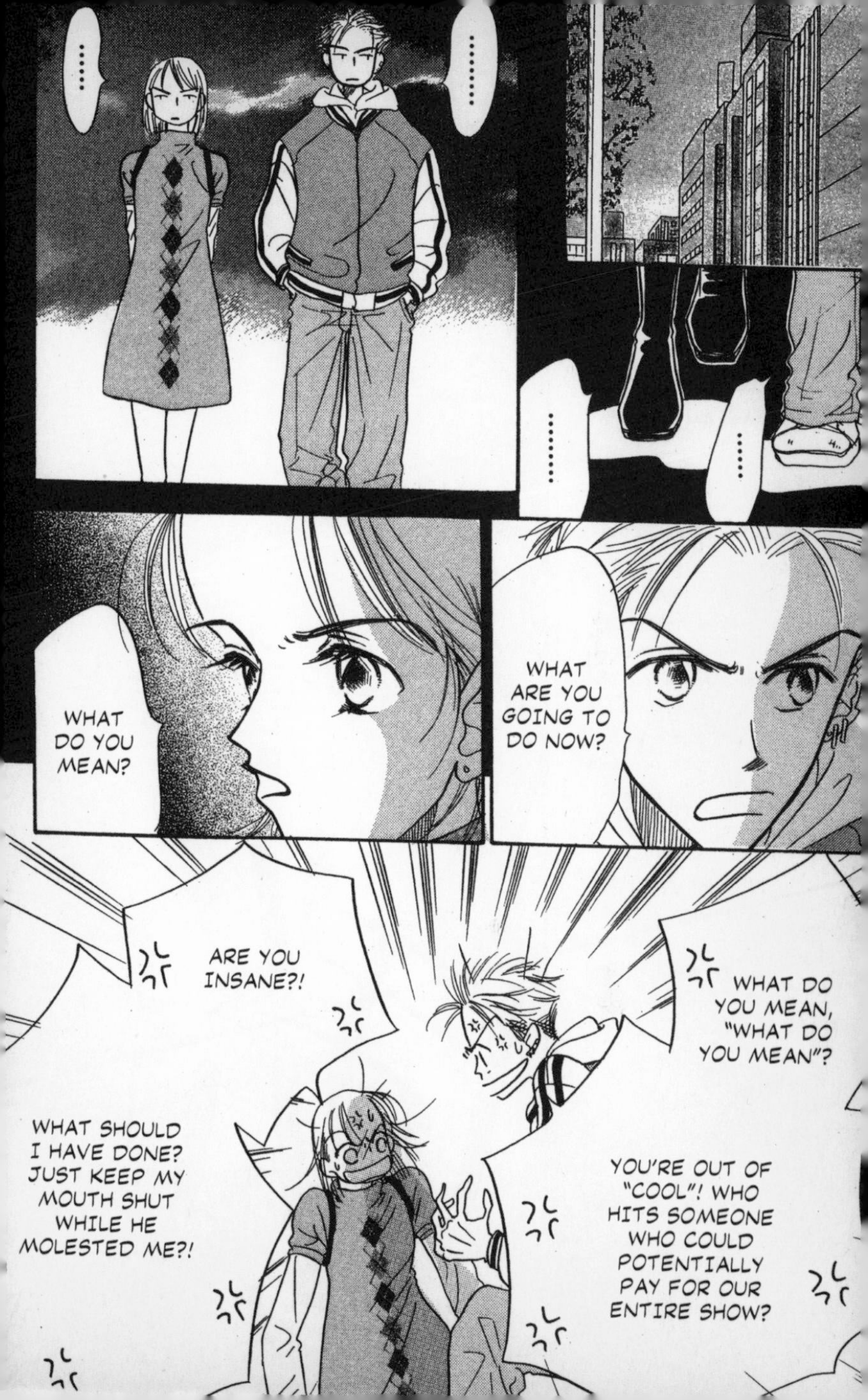
......
....
....
......
WHAT ARE YOU GOING TO DO NOW?
WHAT DO YOU MEAN?
WHAT DO YOU MEAN, "WHAT DO YOU MEAN"?
ARE YOU INSANE?!
YOU'RE OUT OF "COOL"! WHO HITS SOMEONE WHO COULD POTENTIALLY PAY FOR OUR ENTIRE SHOW?
WHAT SHOULD I HAVE DONE? JUST KEEP MY MOUTH SHUT WHILE HE MOLESTED ME?!

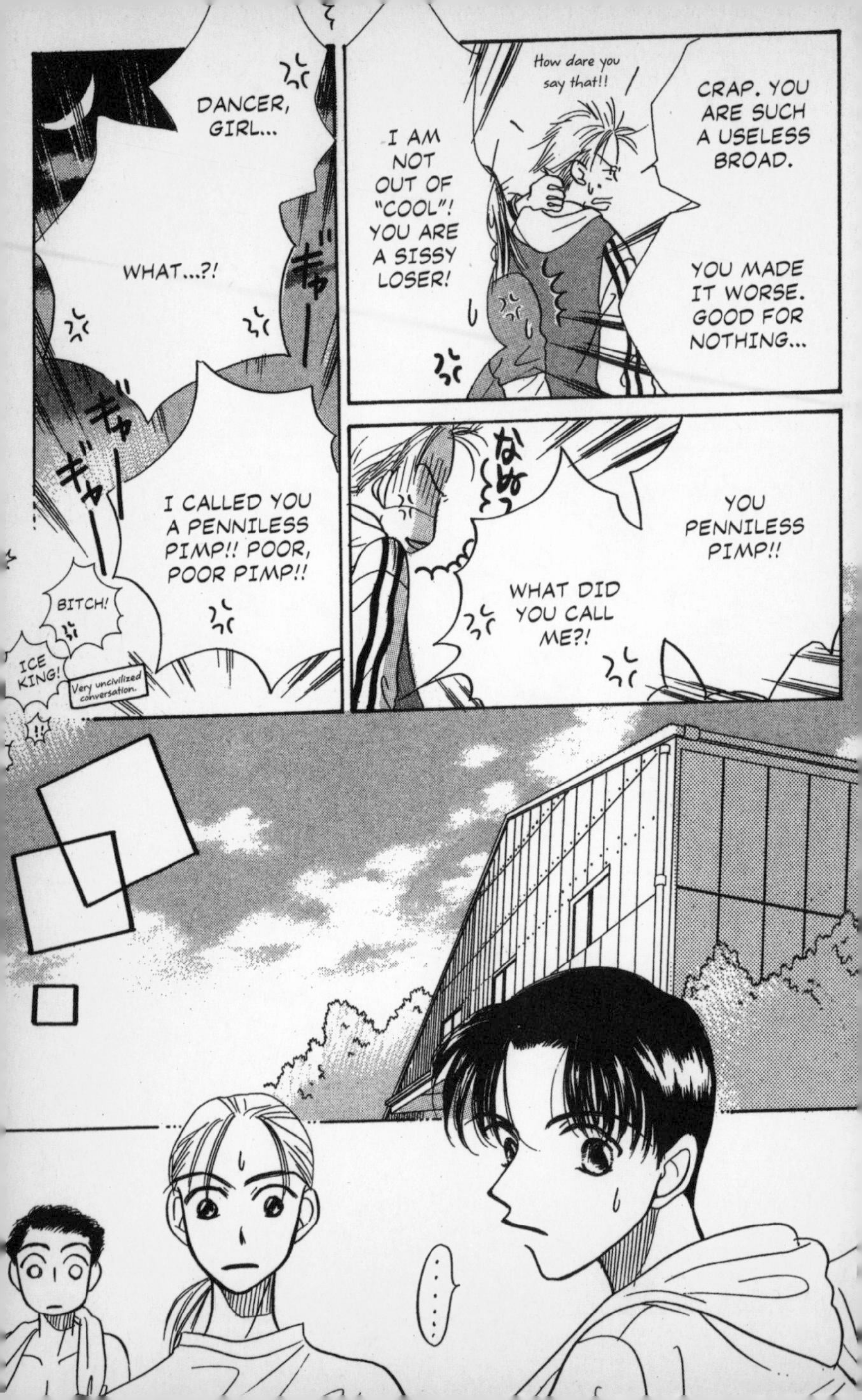
CRAP. YOU ARE SUCH A USELESS BROAD.
How dare you say that!!
I AM NOT OUT OF "COOL"! YOU ARE A SISSY LOSER!
YOU MADE IT WORSE. GOOD FOR NOTHING...
なぬっ
YOU PENNILESS PIMP!!
WHAT DID YOU CALL ME?!
ギャー
DANCER, GIRL...
WHAT...?!
ギャ
ギャ
I CALLED YOU A PENNILESS PIMP!! POOR, POOR PIMP!!
BITCH!
ICE KING!
Very uncivilized conversation.
!!
......

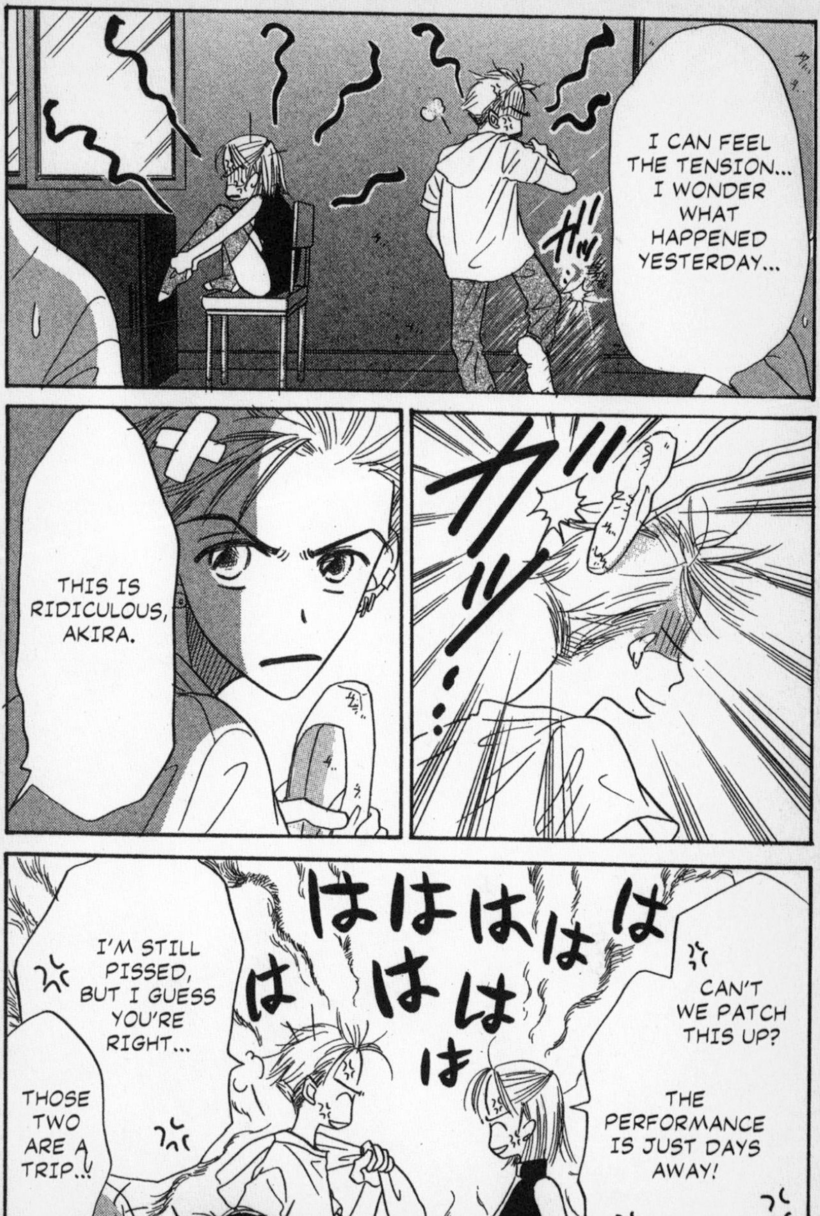
I CAN FEEL THE TENSION... I WONDER WHAT HAPPENED YESTERDAY...
ガッ
ガツ...
THIS IS RIDICULOUS, AKIRA.
CAN'T WE PATCH THIS UP?
THE PERFORMANCE IS JUST DAYS AWAY!
ははははははは
I'M STILL PISSED, BUT I GUESS YOU'RE RIGHT...
THOSE TWO ARE A TRIP..!

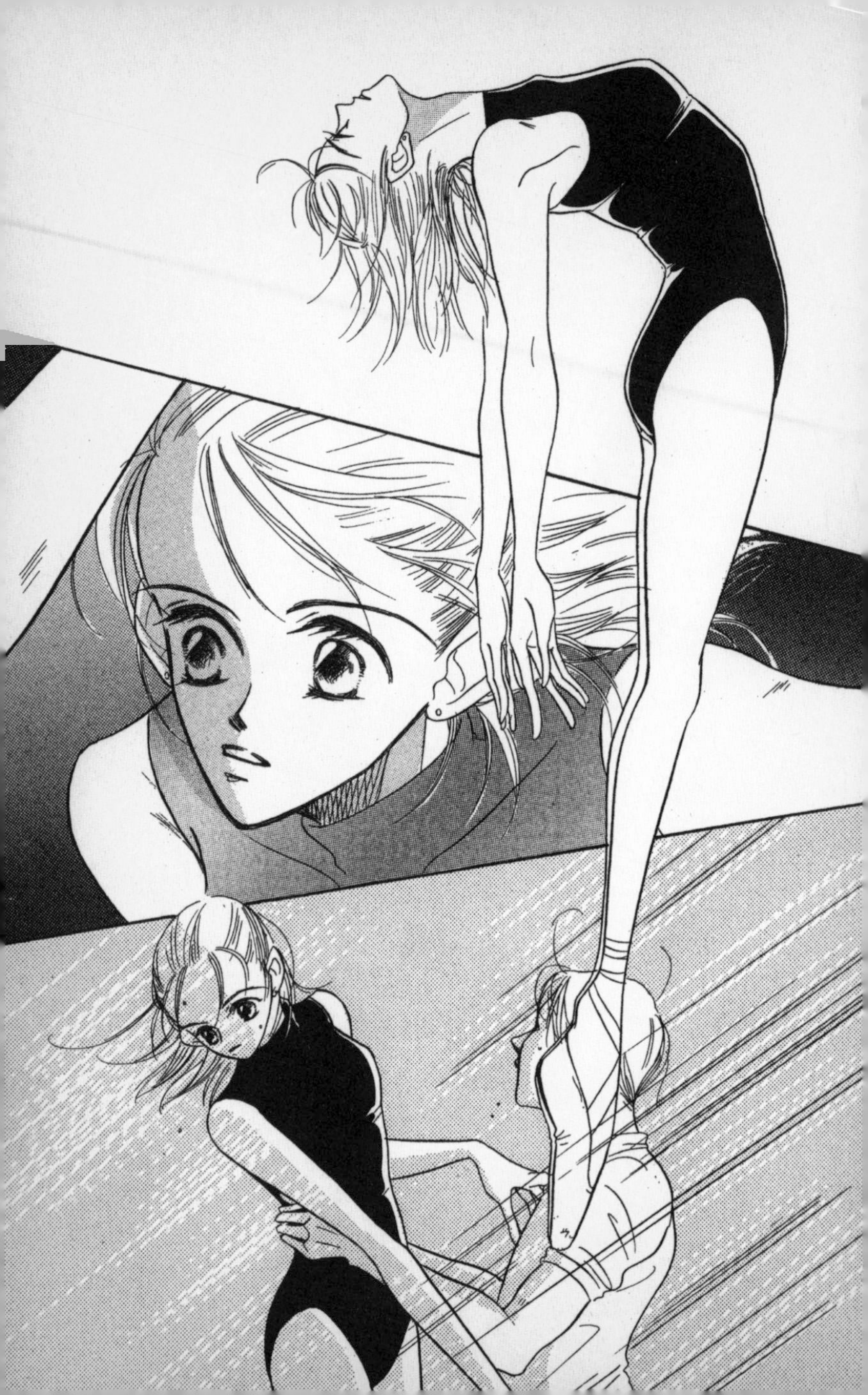

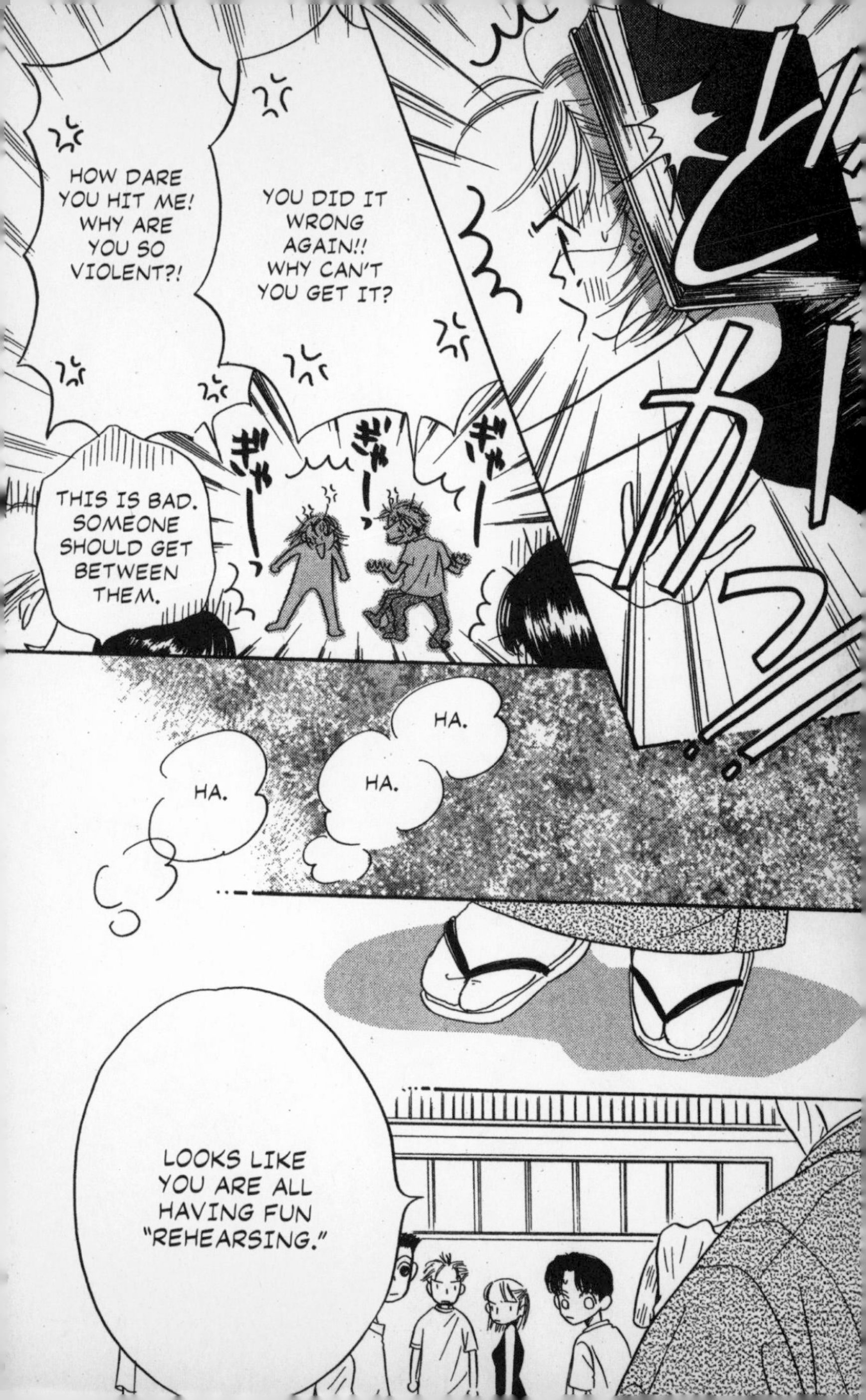
YOU DID IT WRONG AGAIN!! WHY CAN'T YOU GET IT?
HOW DARE YOU HIT ME! WHY ARE YOU SO VIOLENT?!
ぎゃー
ぎゃーっ
ぎゃーっ
THIS IS BAD. SOMEONE SHOULD GET BETWEEN THEM.
HA.
HA.
HA.
LOOKS LIKE YOU ARE ALL HAVING FUN "REHEARSING."

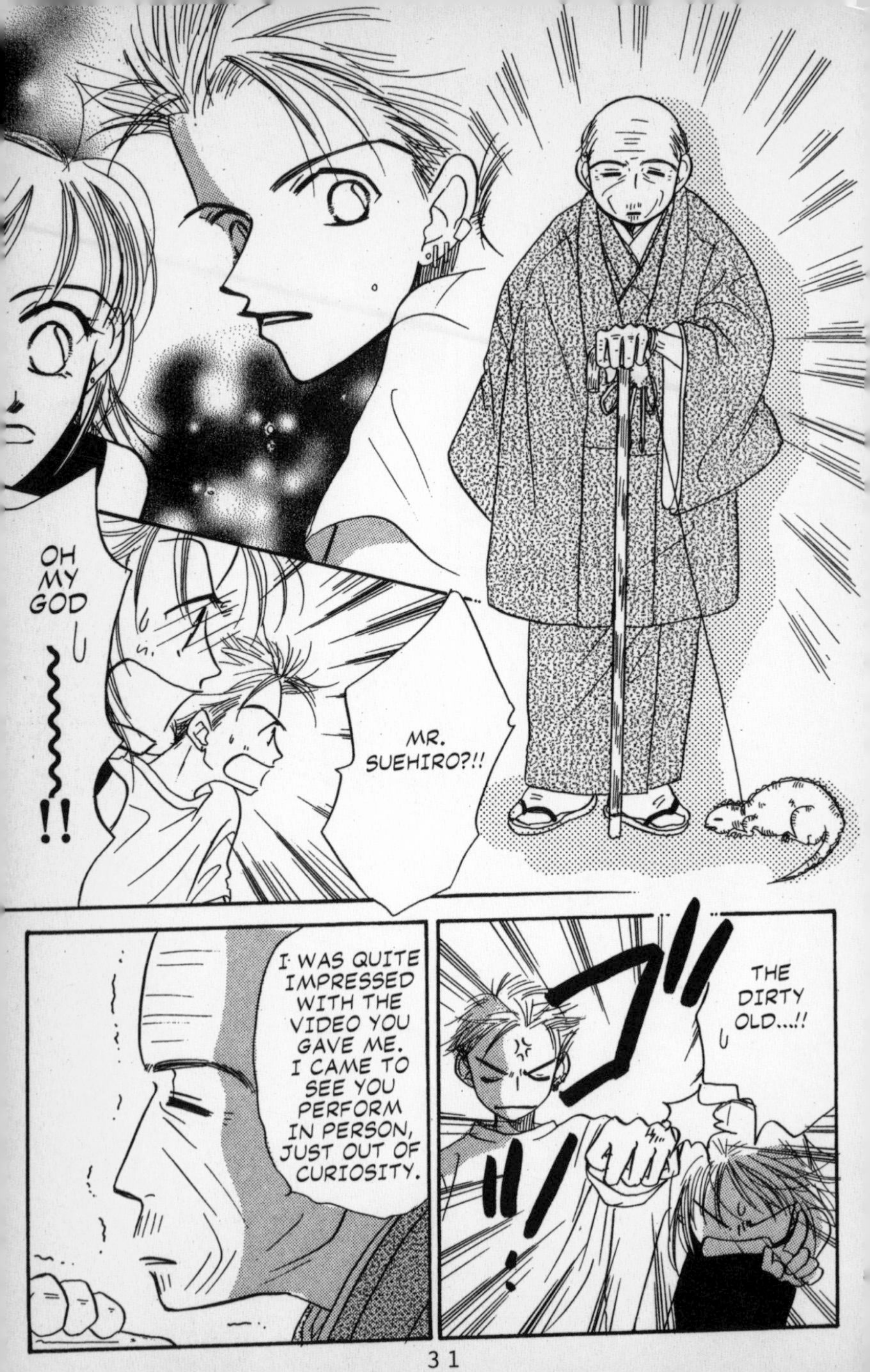
MR. SUEHIRO?!!
OH MY GOD ~~~ !!
THE DIRTY OLD...!!
I WAS QUITE IMPRESSED WITH THE VIDEO YOU GAVE ME. I CAME TO SEE YOU PERFORM IN PERSON, JUST OUT OF CURIOSITY.

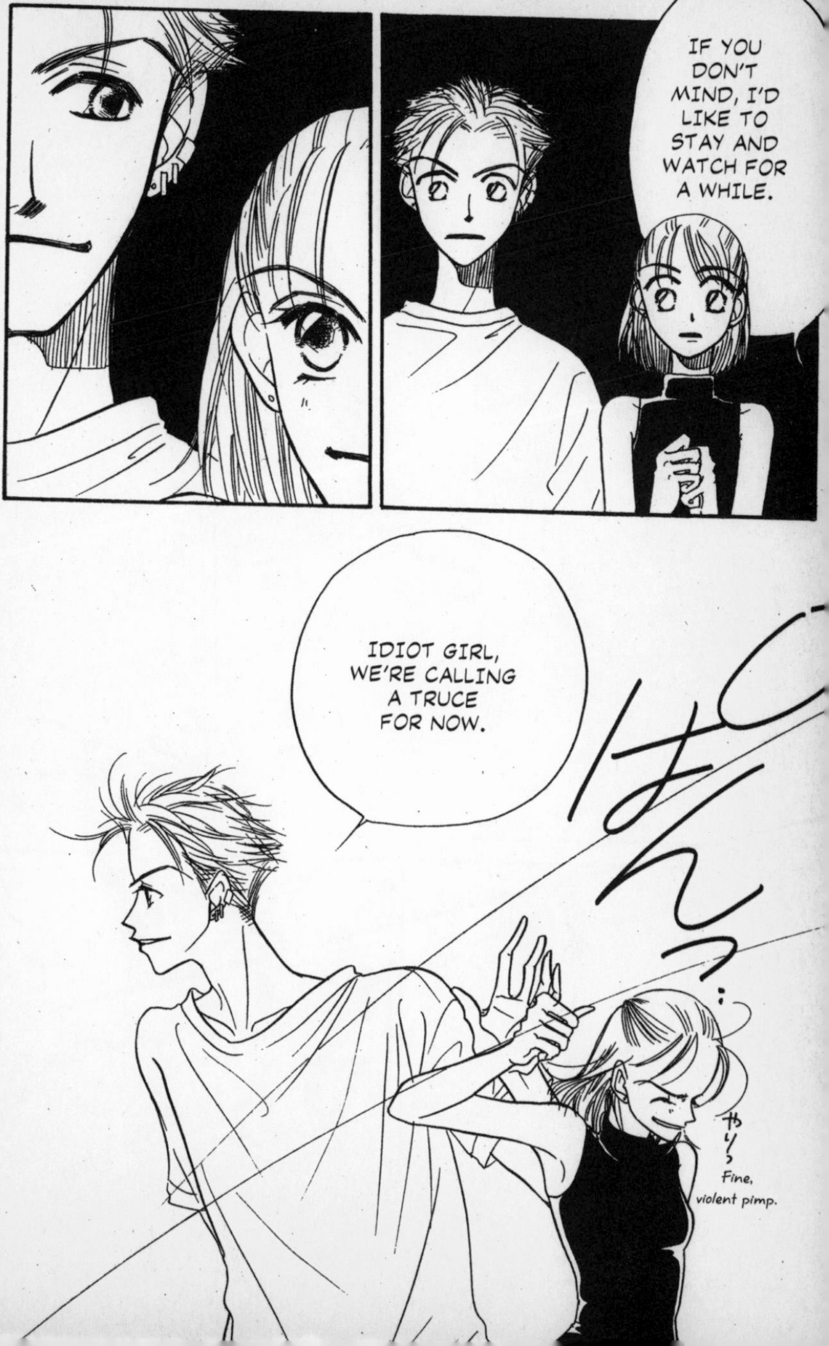
IF YOU DON'T MIND, I'D LIKE TO STAY AND WATCH FOR A WHILE.
IDIOT GIRL, WE'RE CALLING A TRUCE FOR NOW.
はんっ
やりっ
Fine, violent pimp.

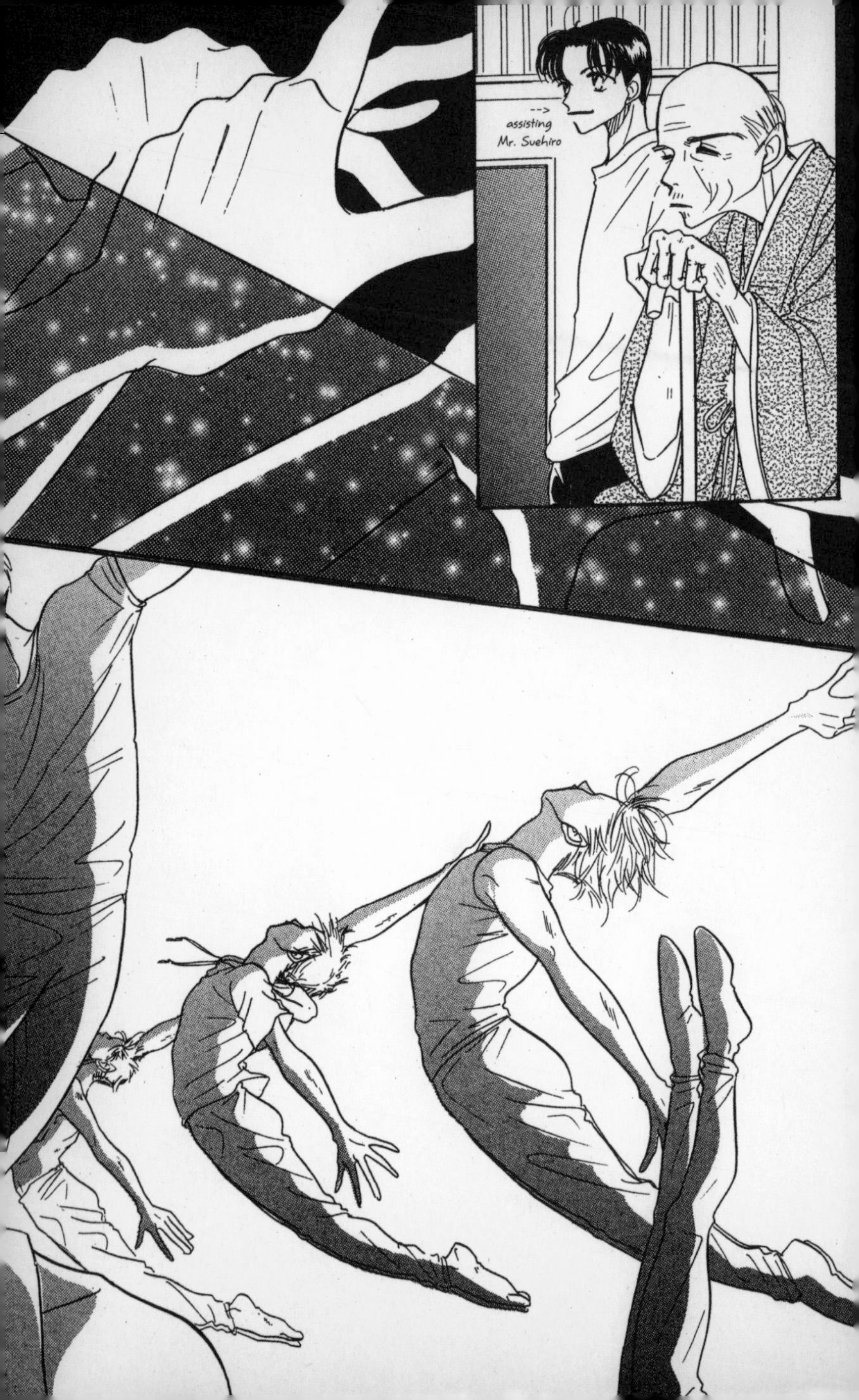
-->
assisting
Mr. Suehiro

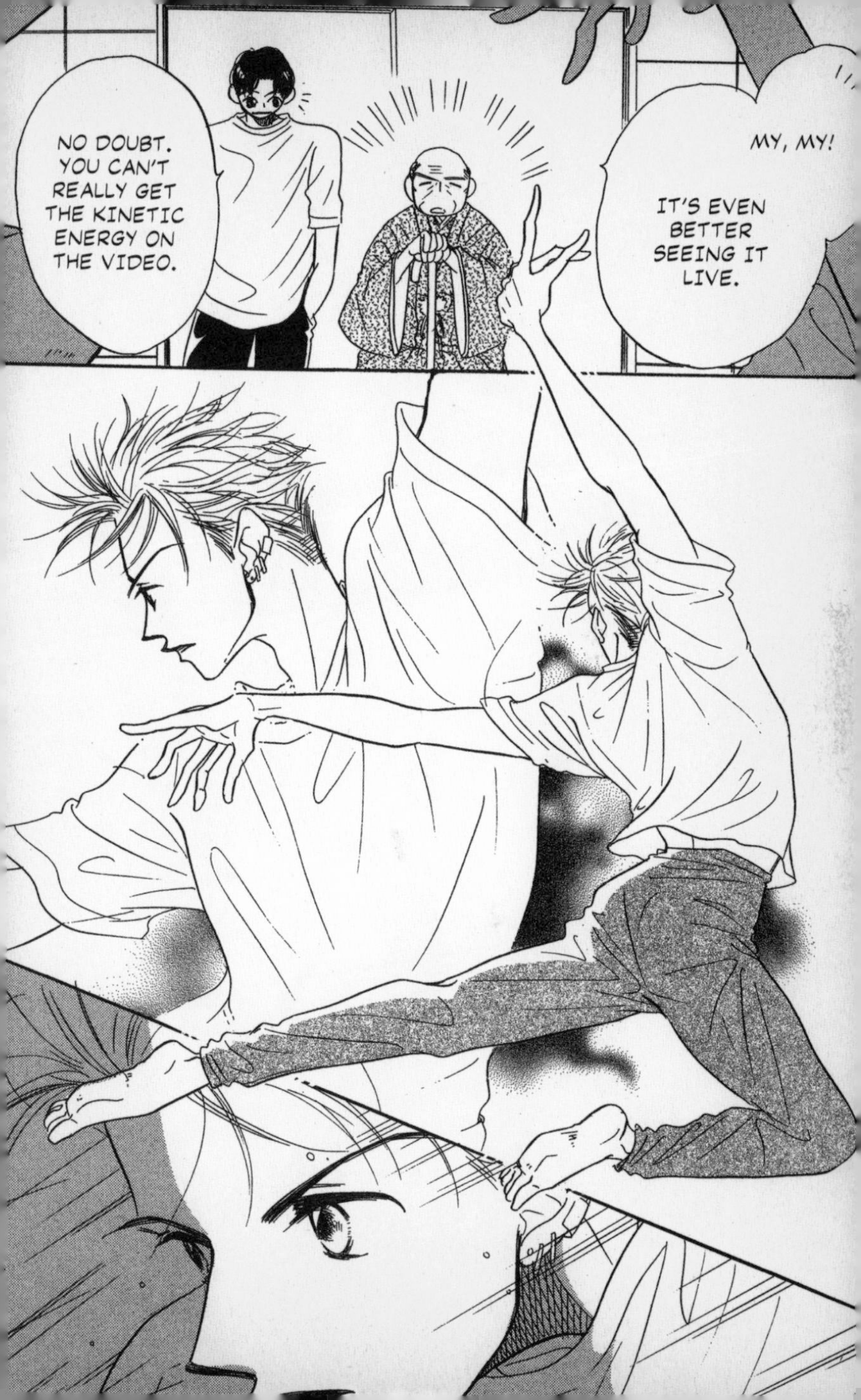
MY, MY!
IT'S EVEN BETTER SEEING IT LIVE.
NO DOUBT. YOU CAN'T REALLY GET THE KINETIC ENERGY ON THE VIDEO.

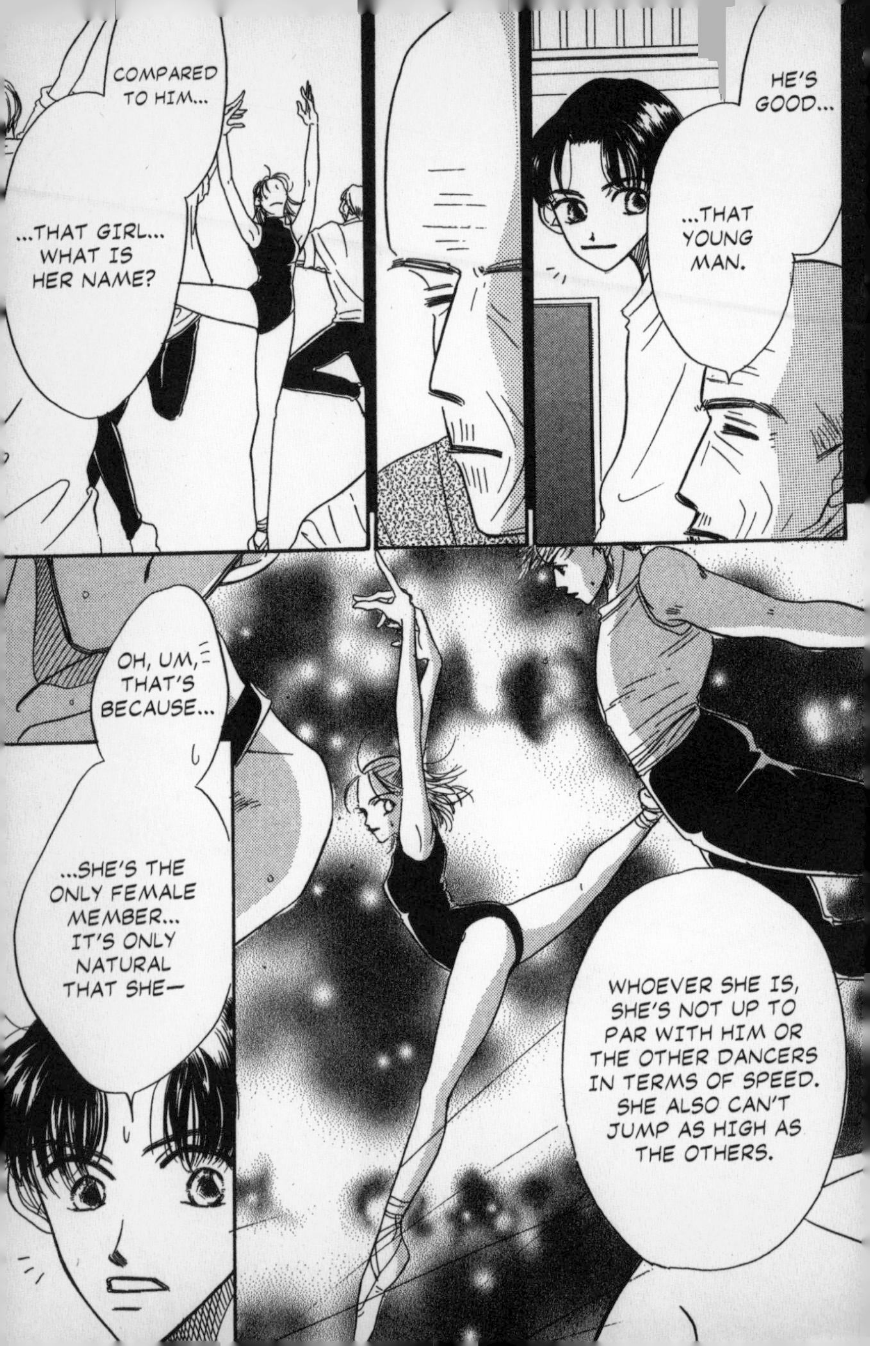
HE'S GOOD...
...THAT YOUNG MAN.
COMPARED TO HIM...
...THAT GIRL... WHAT IS HER NAME?
WHOEVER SHE IS, SHE'S NOT UP TO PAR WITH HIM OR THE OTHER DANCERS IN TERMS OF SPEED. SHE ALSO CAN'T JUMP AS HIGH AS THE OTHERS.
OH, UM, THAT'S BECAUSE...
...SHE'S THE ONLY FEMALE MEMBER... IT'S ONLY NATURAL THAT SHE—

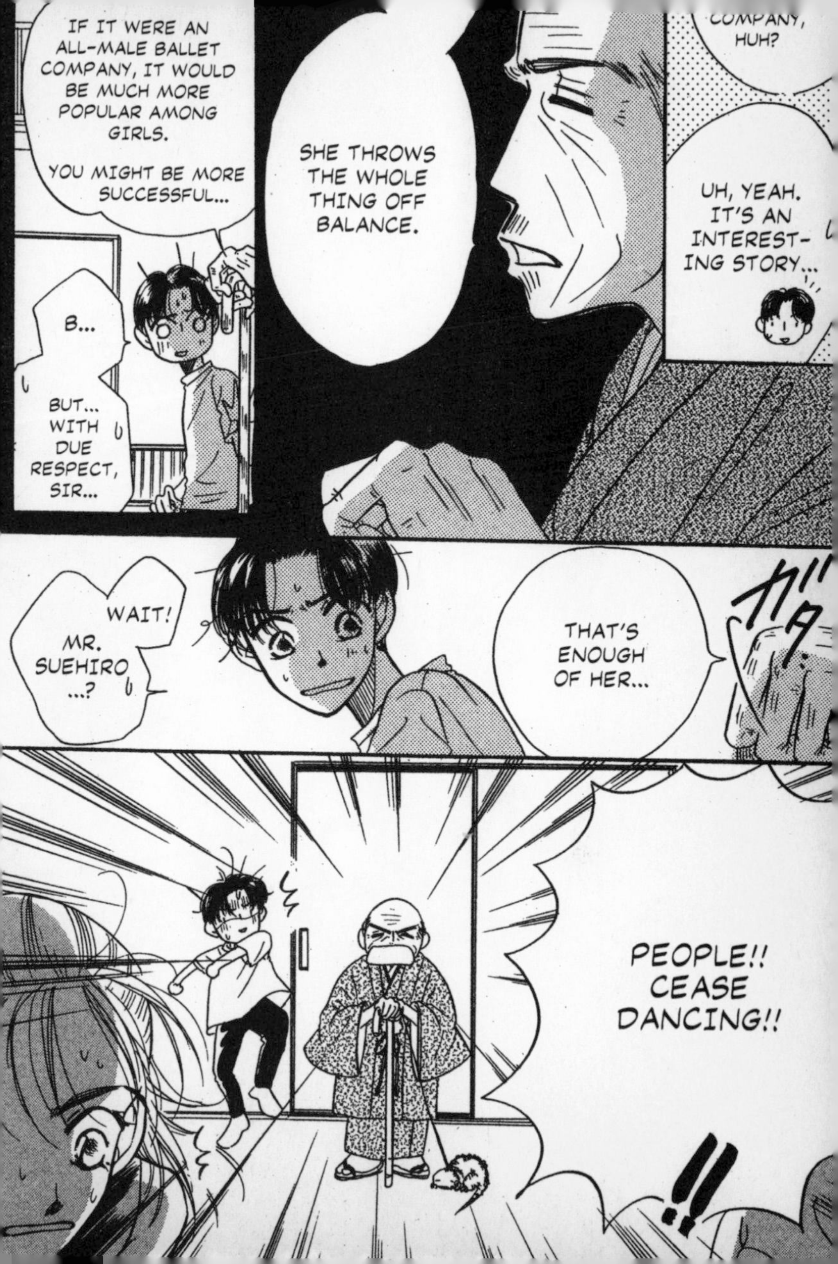
COMPANY, HUH?
UH, YEAH. IT'S AN INTEREST-ING STORY...
SHE THROWS THE WHOLE THING OFF BALANCE.
IF IT WERE AN ALL-MALE BALLET COMPANY, IT WOULD BE MUCH MORE POPULAR AMONG GIRLS.
YOU MIGHT BE MORE SUCCESSFUL...
B...
BUT... WITH DUE RESPECT, SIR...
THAT'S ENOUGH OF HER...
WAIT! MR. SUEHIRO ...?
PEOPLE!! CEASE DANCING!!
!!

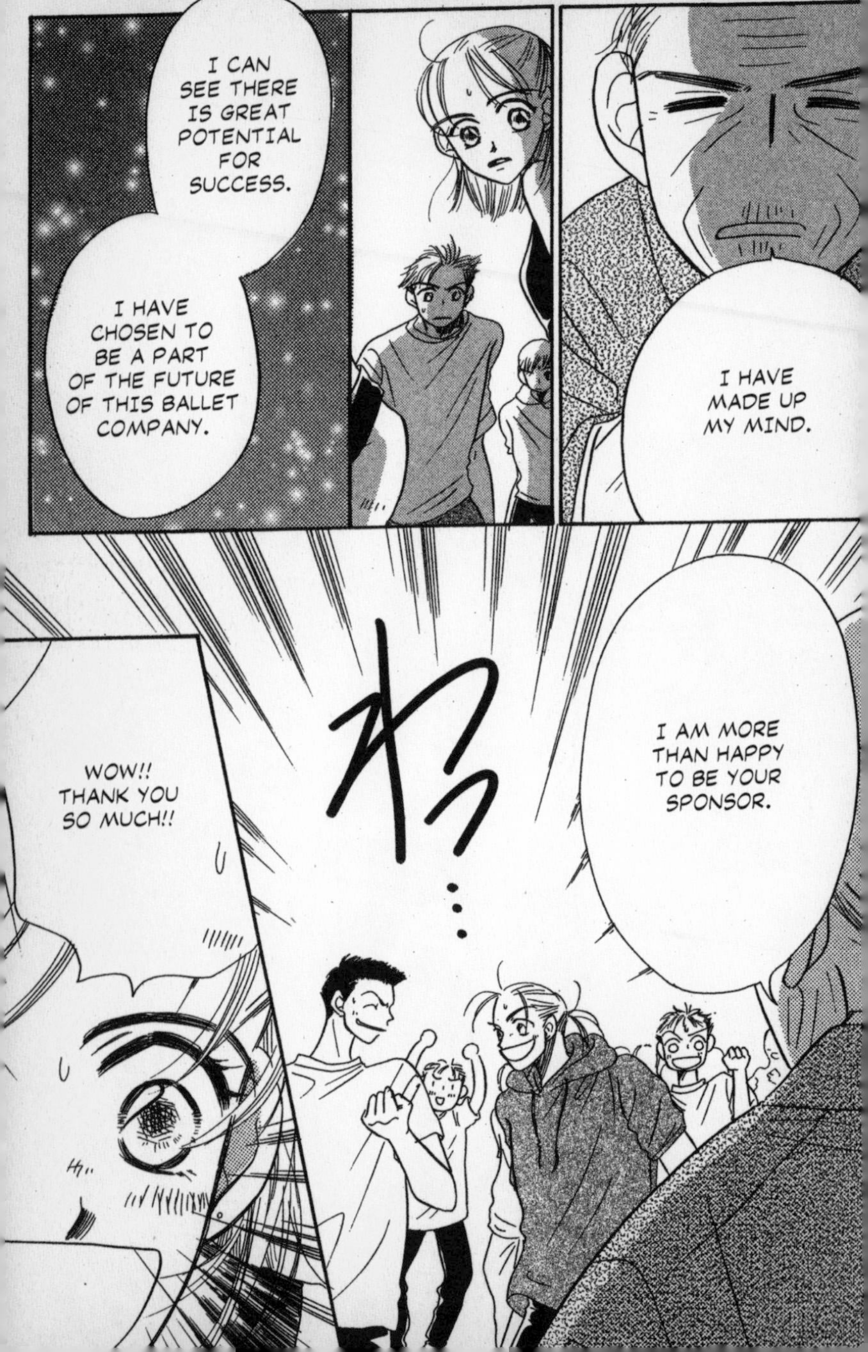

I HAVE MADE UP MY MIND.
I CAN SEE THERE IS GREAT POTENTIAL FOR SUCCESS.
I HAVE CHOSEN TO BE A PART OF THE FUTURE OF THIS BALLET COMPANY.
I AM MORE THAN HAPPY TO BE YOUR SPONSOR.
WOW!! THANK YOU SO MUCH!!

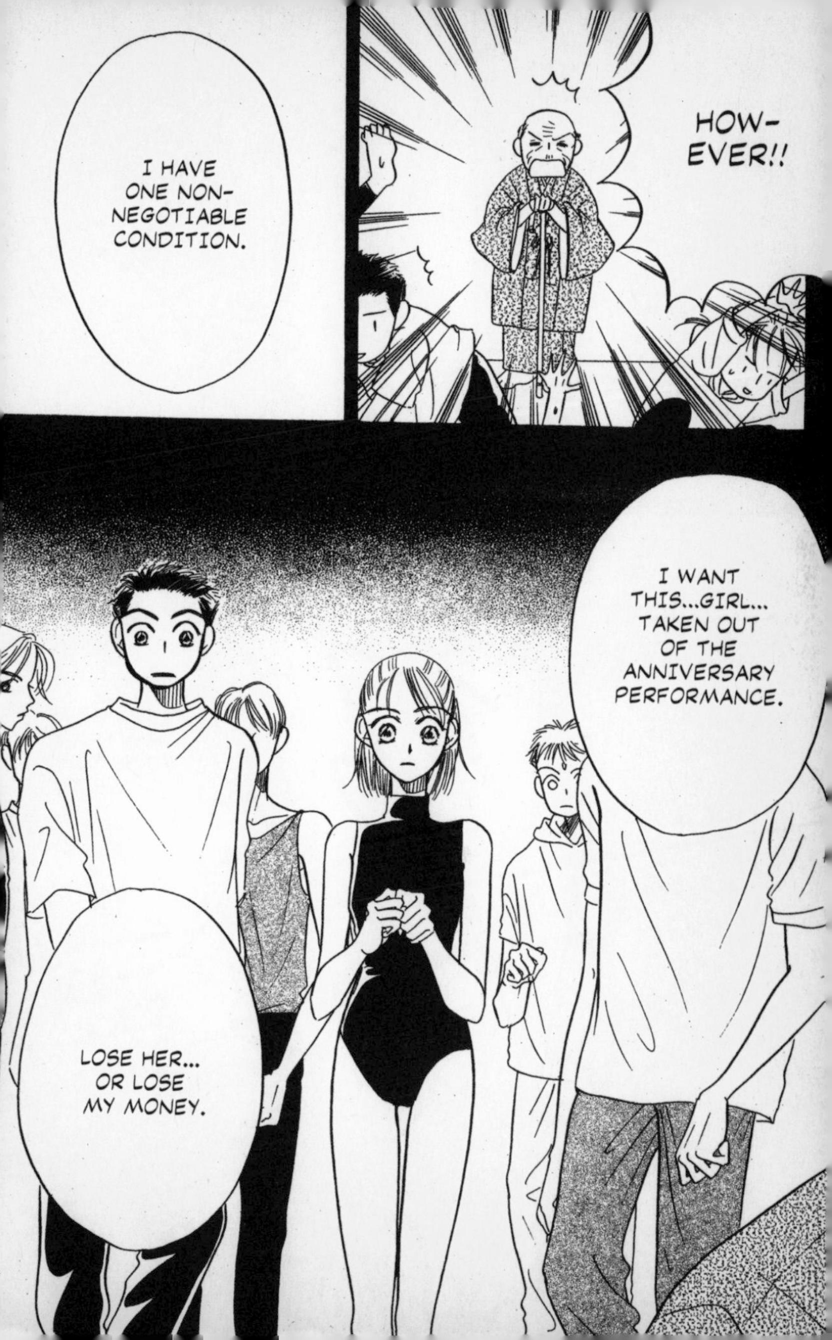
HOW-EVER!!
I HAVE ONE NON-NEGOTIABLE CONDITION.
I WANT THIS...GIRL... TAKEN OUT OF THE ANNIVERSARY PERFORMANCE.
LOSE HER... OR LOSE MY MONEY.

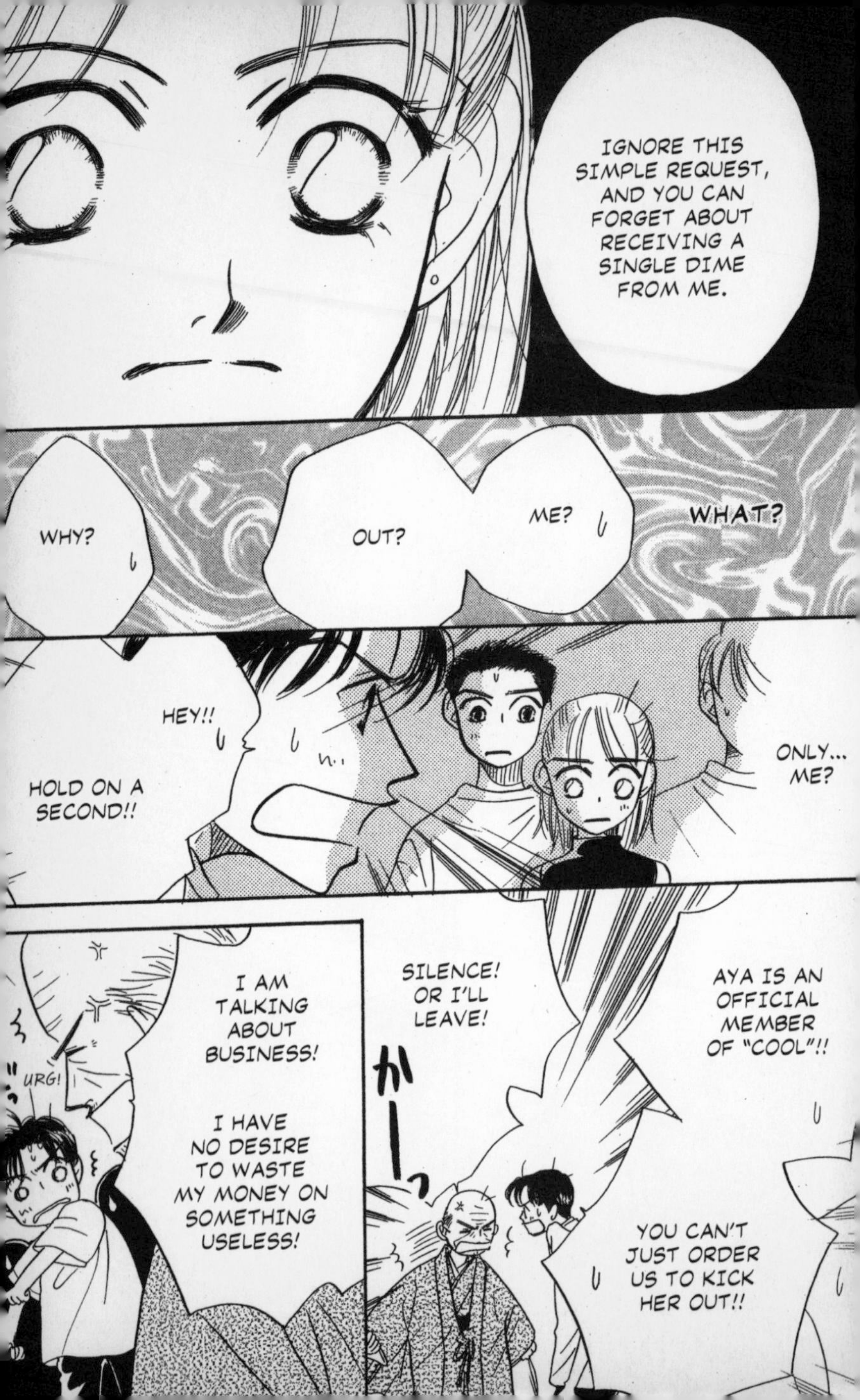
IGNORE THIS SIMPLE REQUEST, AND YOU CAN FORGET ABOUT RECEIVING A SINGLE DIME FROM ME.
WHAT?
ME?
OUT?
WHY?
ONLY... ME?
HEY!!
HOLD ON A SECOND!!
AYA IS AN OFFICIAL MEMBER OF "COOL"!!
YOU CAN'T JUST ORDER US TO KICK HER OUT!!
SILENCE! OR I'LL LEAVE!
かーっ
I AM TALKING ABOUT BUSINESS!
I HAVE NO DESIRE TO WASTE MY MONEY ON SOMETHING USELESS!
URG!

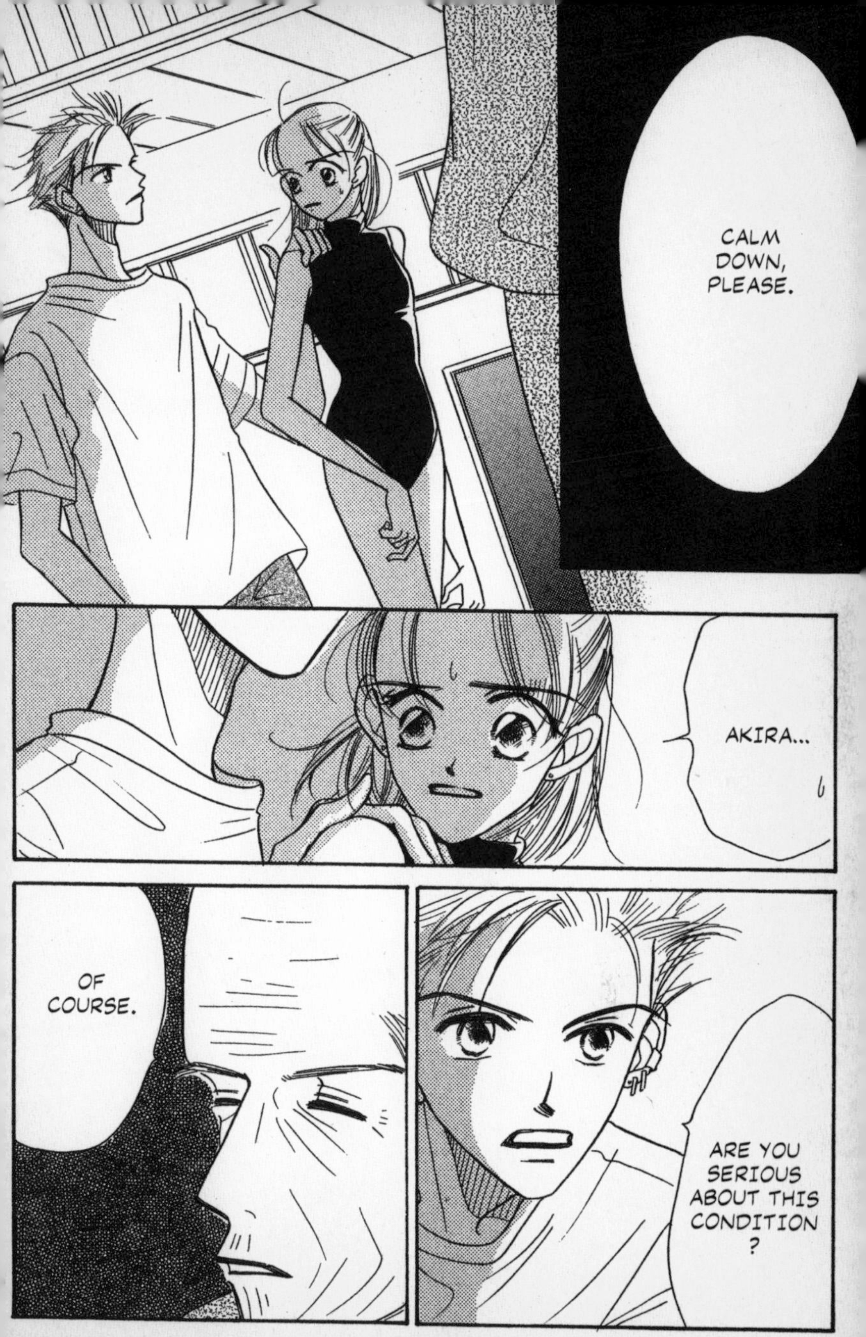
CALM DOWN, PLEASE.
AKIRA...
ARE YOU SERIOUS ABOUT THIS CONDITION?
OF COURSE.

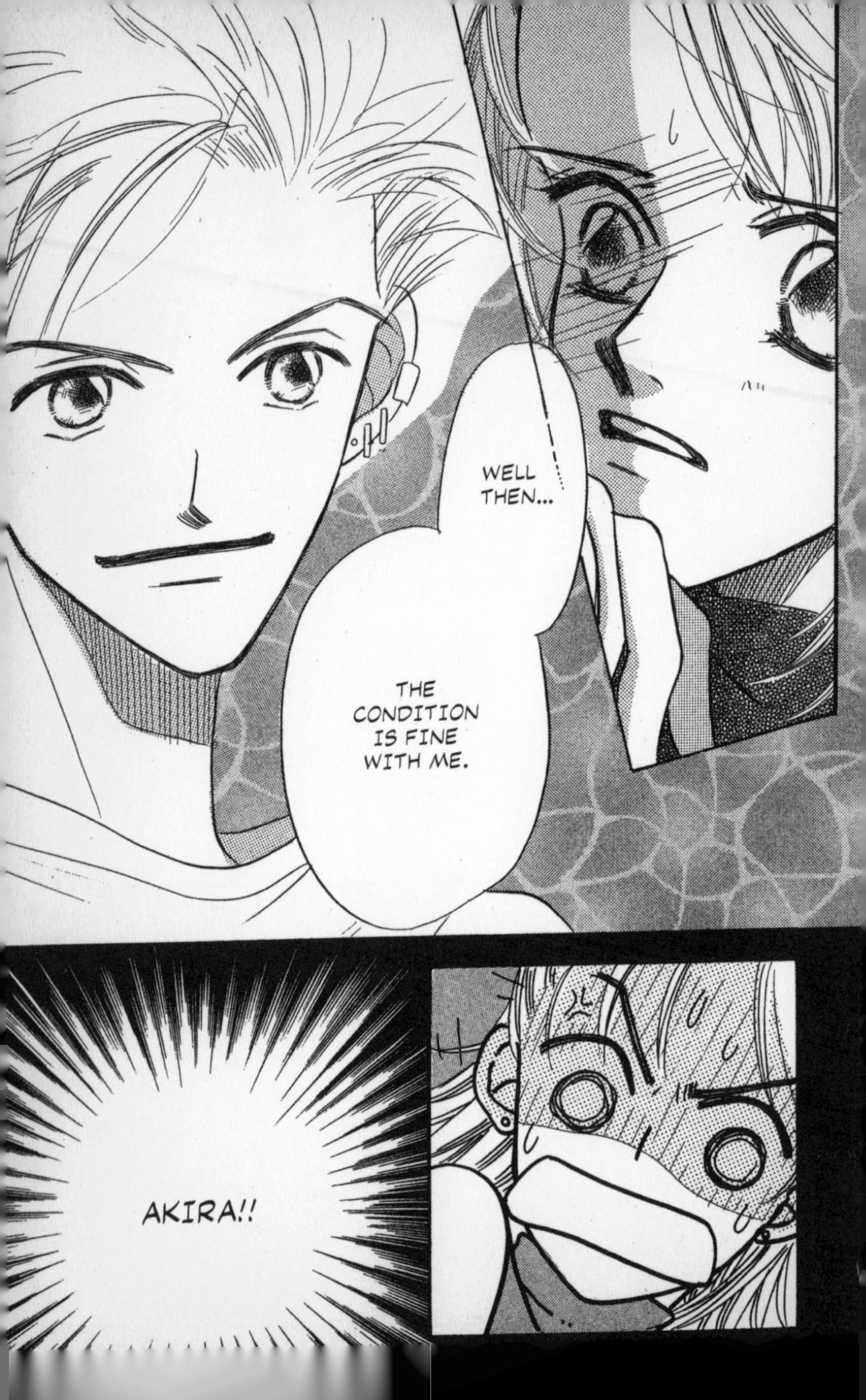
WELL THEN...
THE CONDITION IS FINE WITH ME.
AKIRA!!

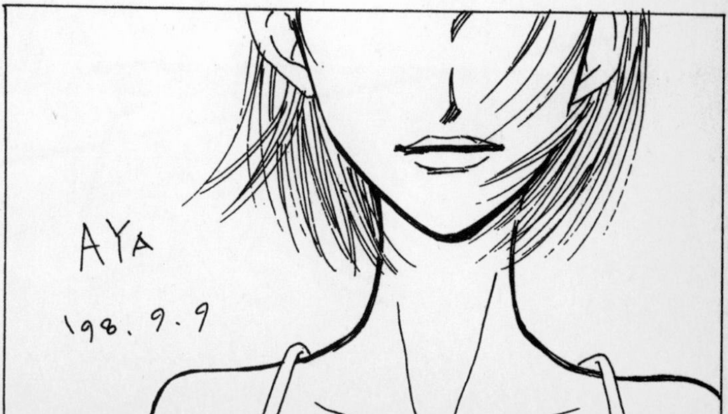
AYA
'98. 9. 9

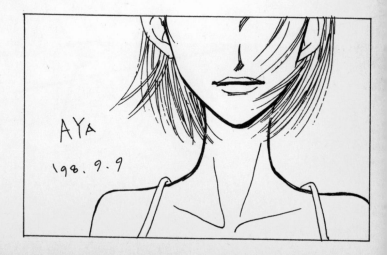

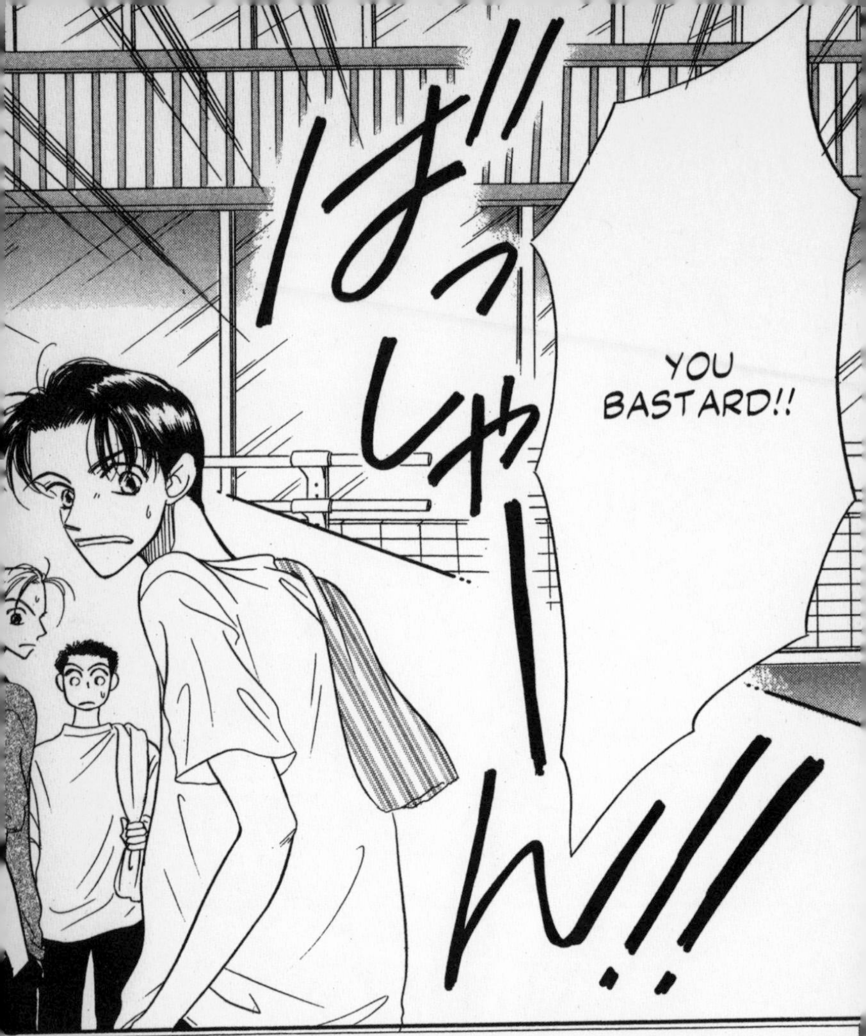
YOU BASTARD!!
ばっしゃーん!!

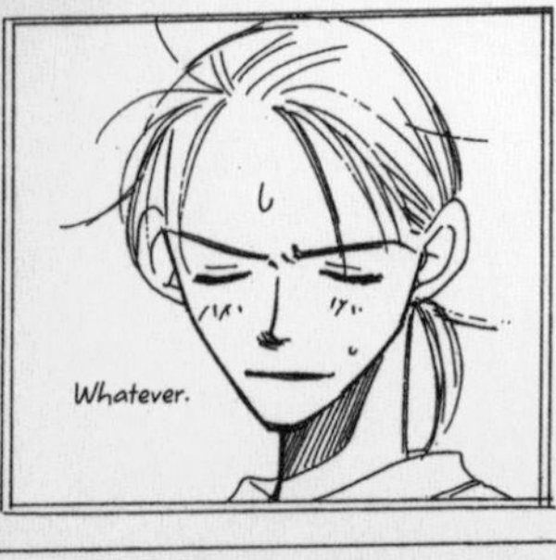
Whatever.

Ashihara's Diary

Yamane — Age 24

He makes a frequent appearance in the latter half of the series. He tends to get the short end of the stick. He was supposed to be a character that is not so dependable in a pinch, but a good mediator when things are going well.

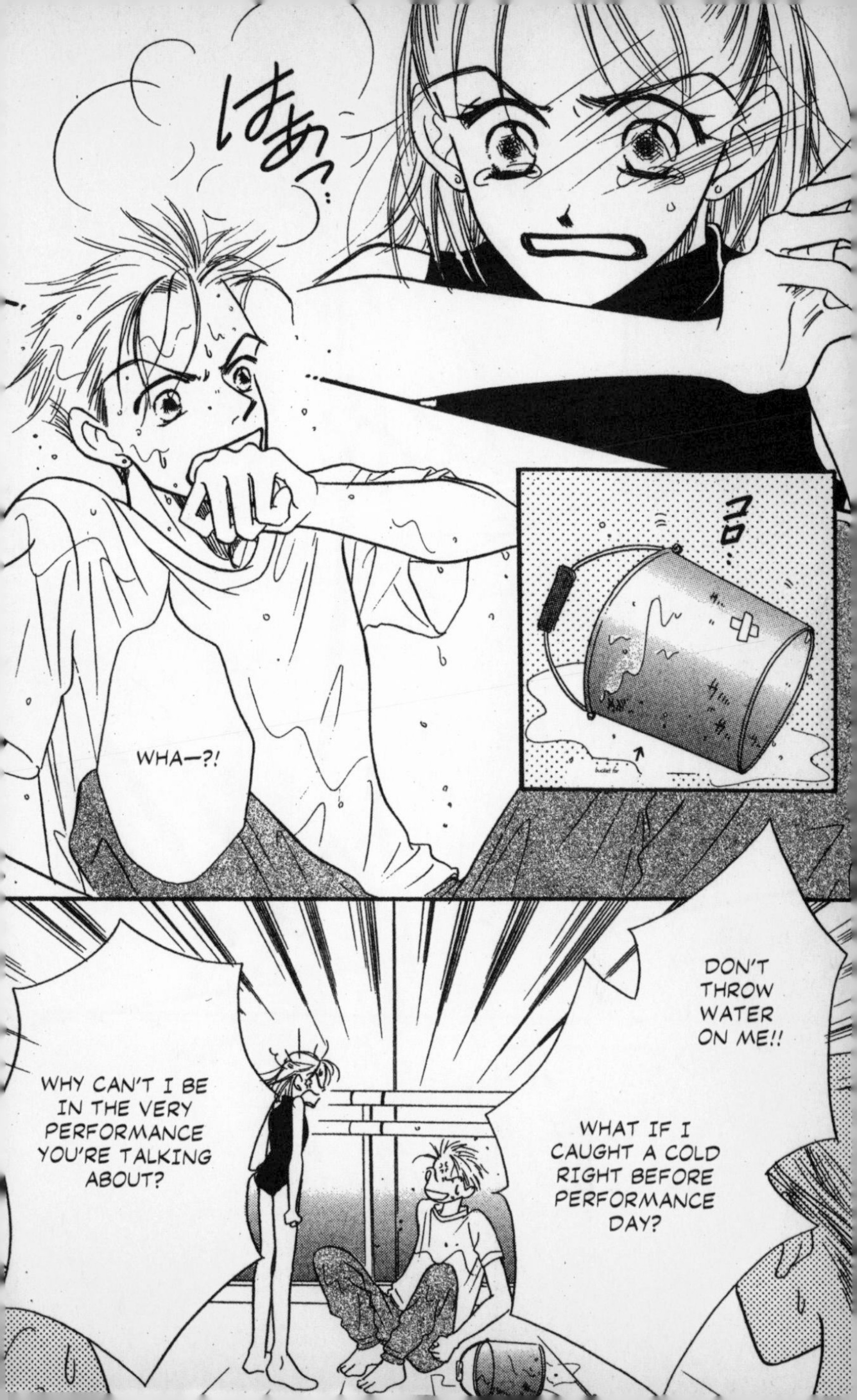
はあっ
ゴロ
WHA—?!
DON'T THROW WATER ON ME!!
WHAT IF I CAUGHT A COLD RIGHT BEFORE PERFORMANCE DAY?
WHY CAN'T I BE IN THE VERY PERFORMANCE YOU'RE TALKING ABOUT?

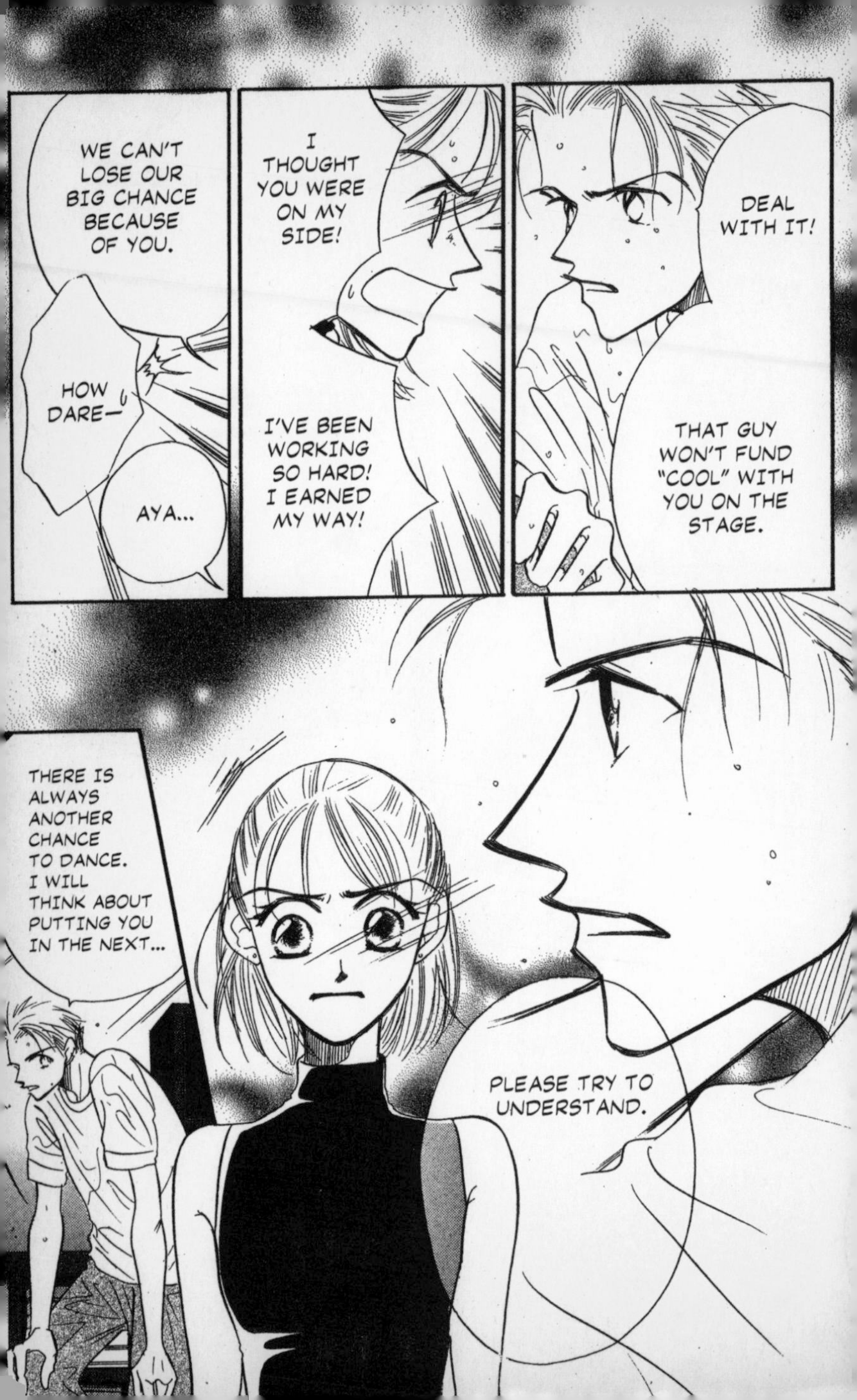
DEAL WITH IT!
THAT GUY WON'T FUND "COOL" WITH YOU ON THE STAGE.
I THOUGHT YOU WERE ON MY SIDE!
I'VE BEEN WORKING SO HARD! I EARNED MY WAY!
WE CAN'T LOSE OUR BIG CHANCE BECAUSE OF YOU.
HOW DARE—
AYA...
THERE IS ALWAYS ANOTHER CHANCE TO DANCE. I WILL THINK ABOUT PUTTING YOU IN THE NEXT...
PLEASE TRY TO UNDERSTAND.

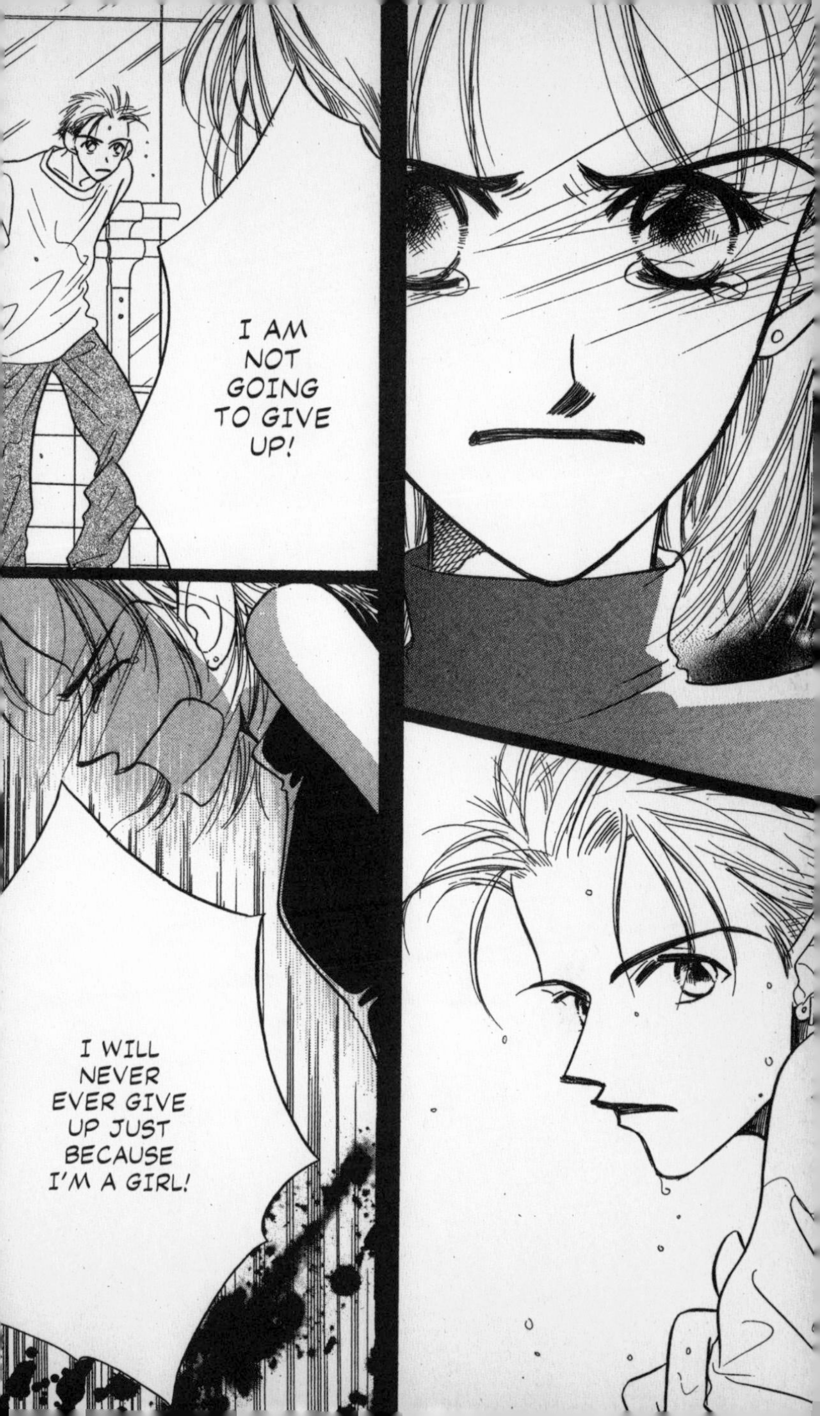
I AM NOT GOING TO GIVE UP!
I WILL NEVER EVER GIVE UP JUST BECAUSE I'M A GIRL!

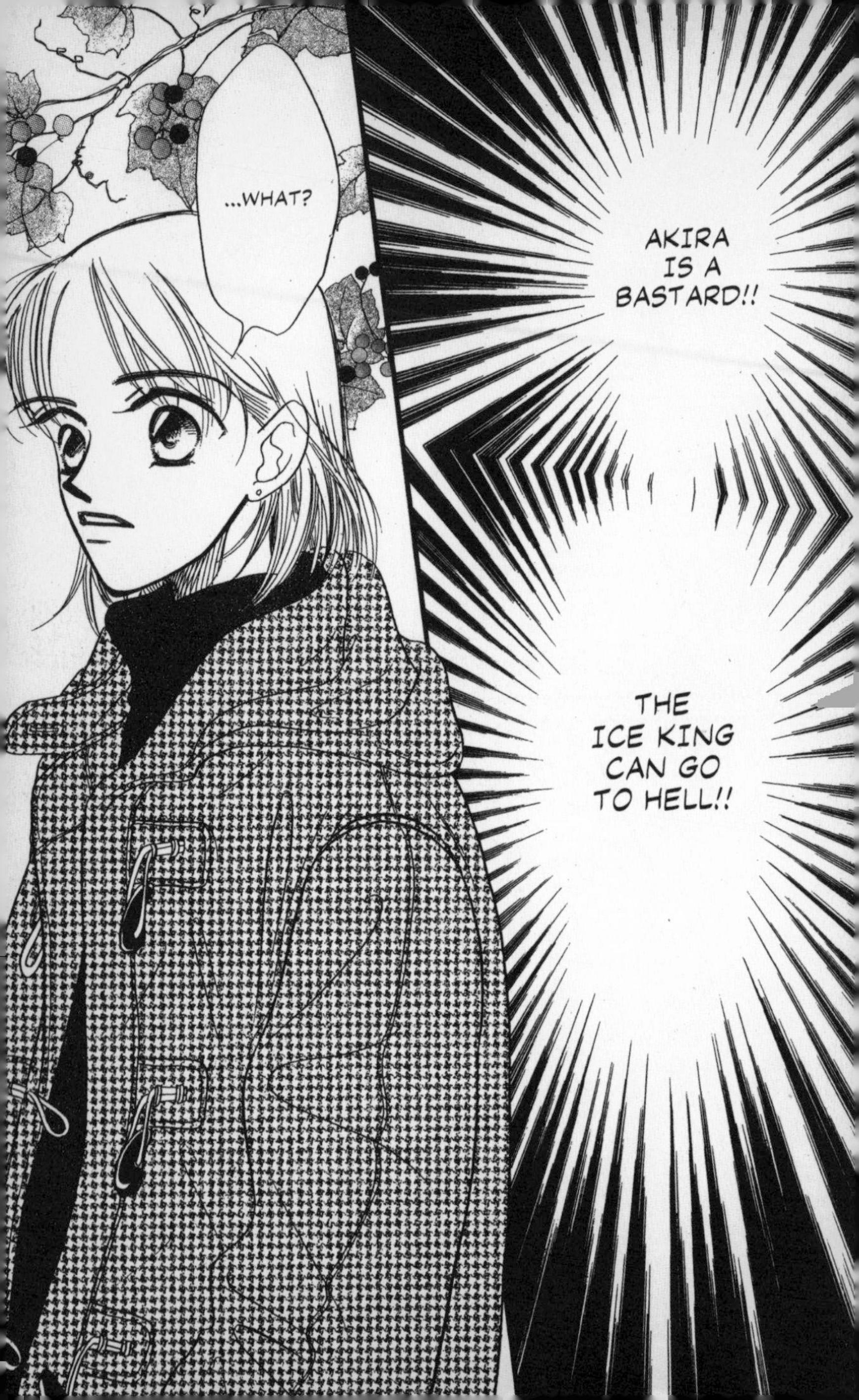
AKIRA IS A BASTARD!!
THE ICE KING CAN GO TO HELL!!
...WHAT?

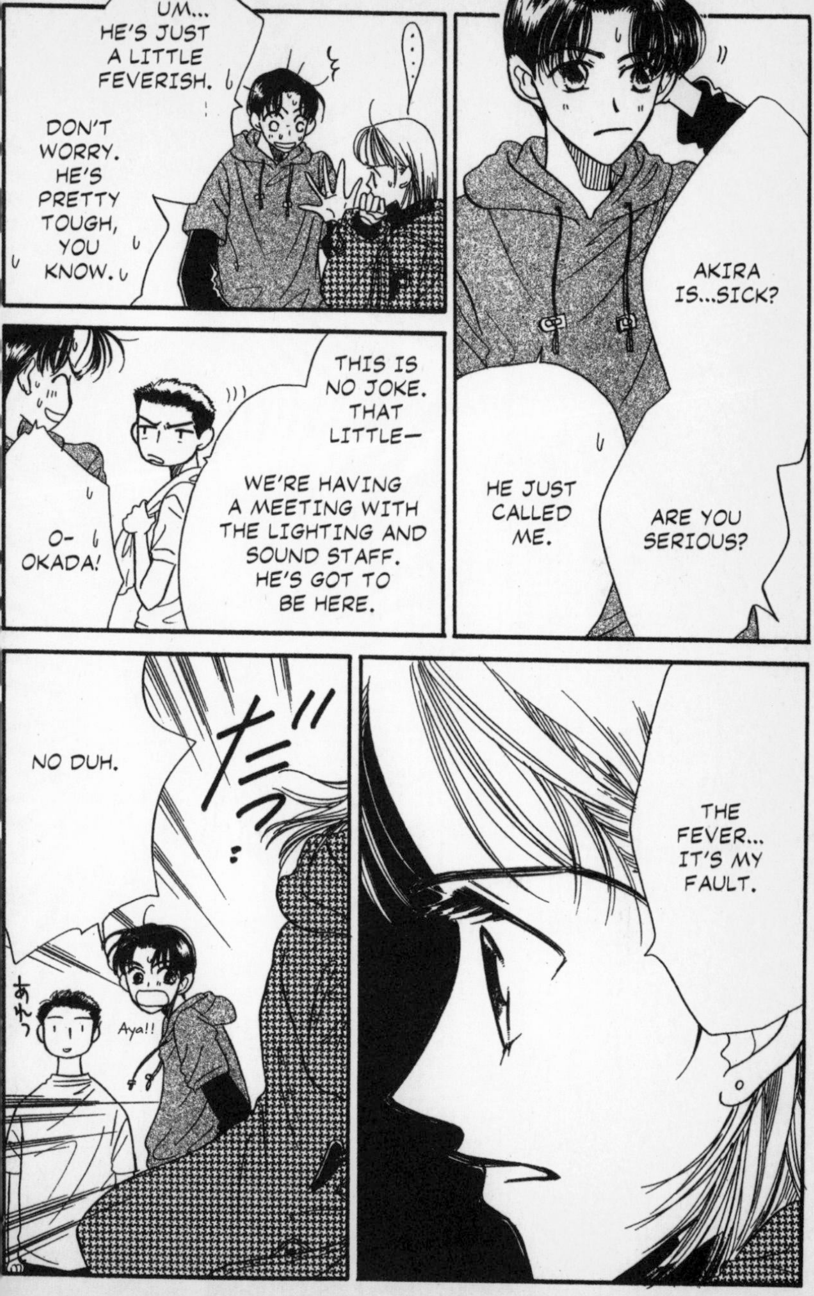
AKIRA IS...SICK?
ARE YOU SERIOUS?
HE JUST CALLED ME.
UM... HE'S JUST A LITTLE FEVERISH.
DON'T WORRY. HE'S PRETTY TOUGH, YOU KNOW.
THIS IS NO JOKE. THAT LITTLE—
WE'RE HAVING A MEETING WITH THE LIGHTING AND SOUND STAFF. HE'S GOT TO BE HERE.
O-OKADA!
THE FEVER... IT'S MY FAULT.
ダッ
NO DUH.
Aya!!
あれっ

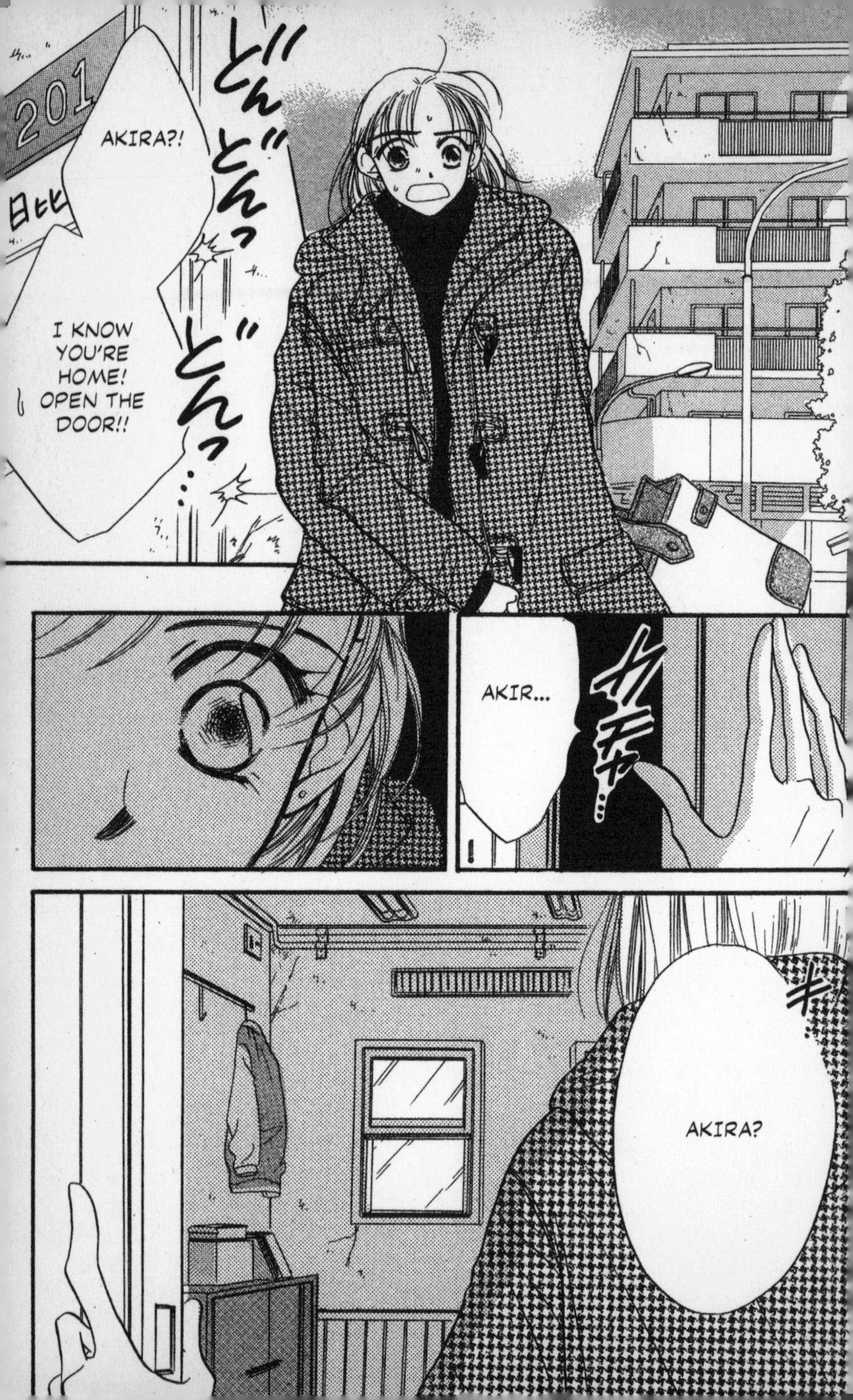
201
日比
どんどんっ
AKIRA?!
どんっ…
I KNOW YOU'RE HOME! OPEN THE DOOR!!
ガチャ
AKIR...
AKIRA?

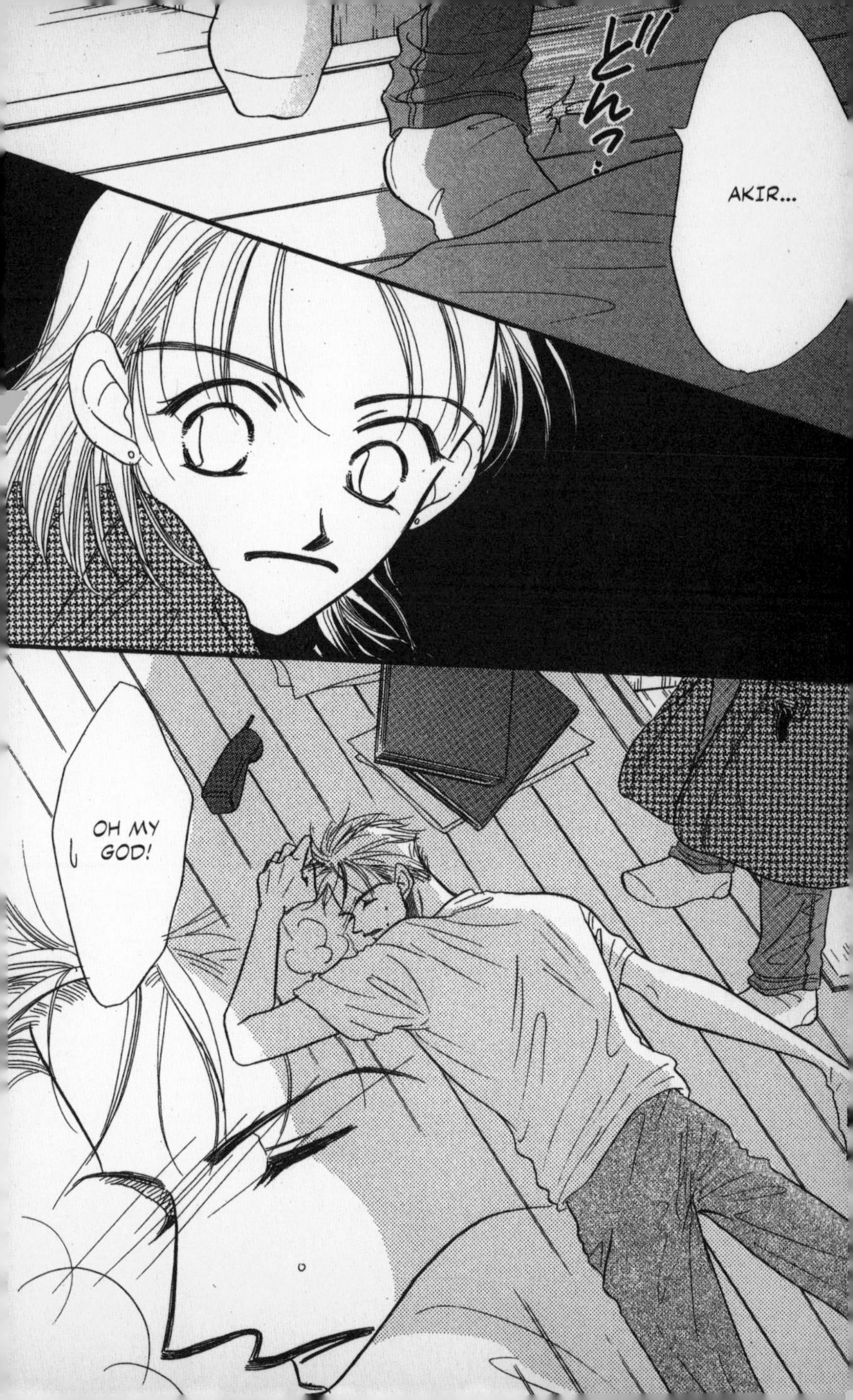
AKIR...
どんっ..
OH MY GOD!

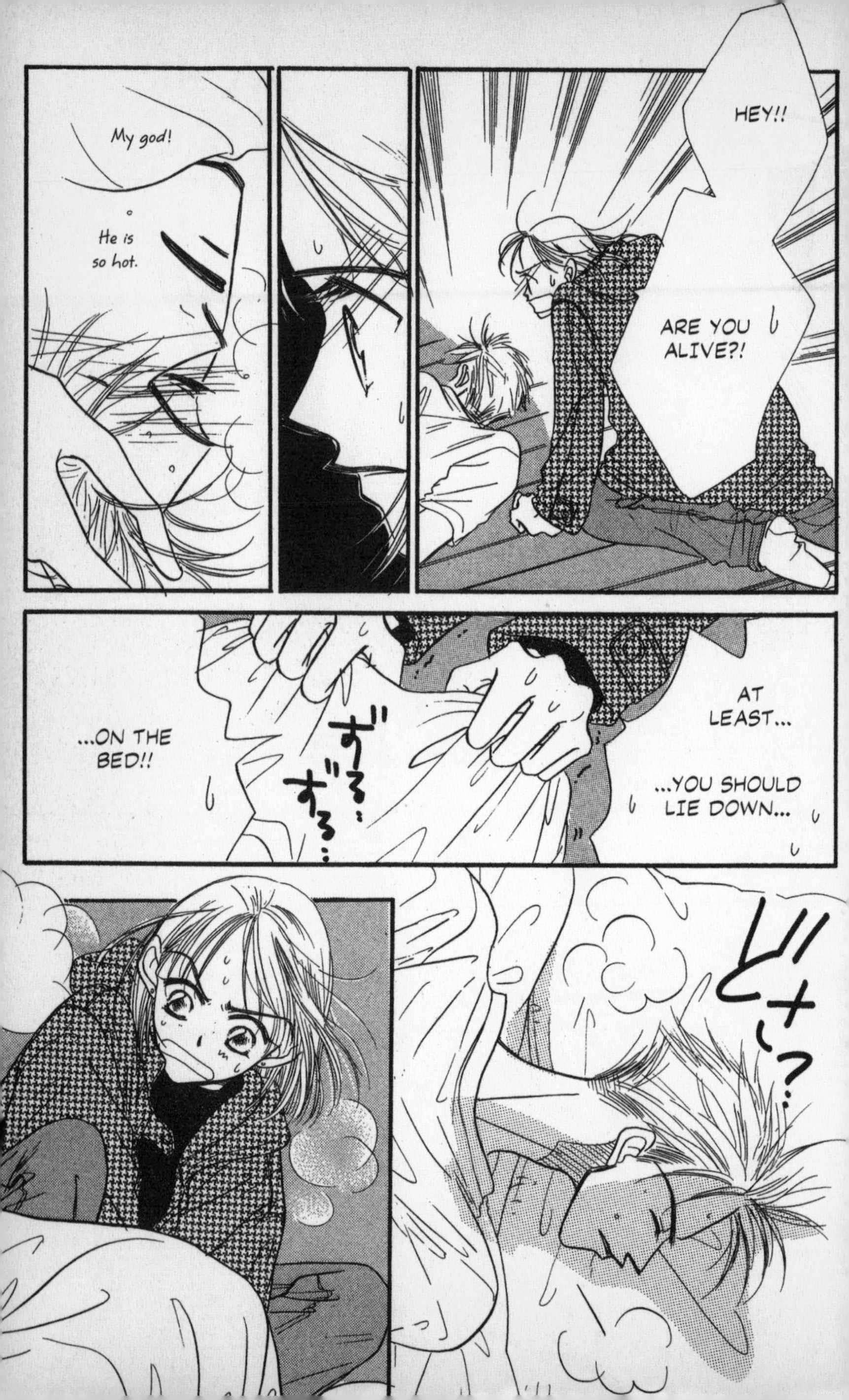
HEY!!
ARE YOU ALIVE?!
My god!
He is so hot.
AT LEAST...
...YOU SHOULD LIE DOWN...
ずる…ずる…
...ON THE BED!!
どさっ

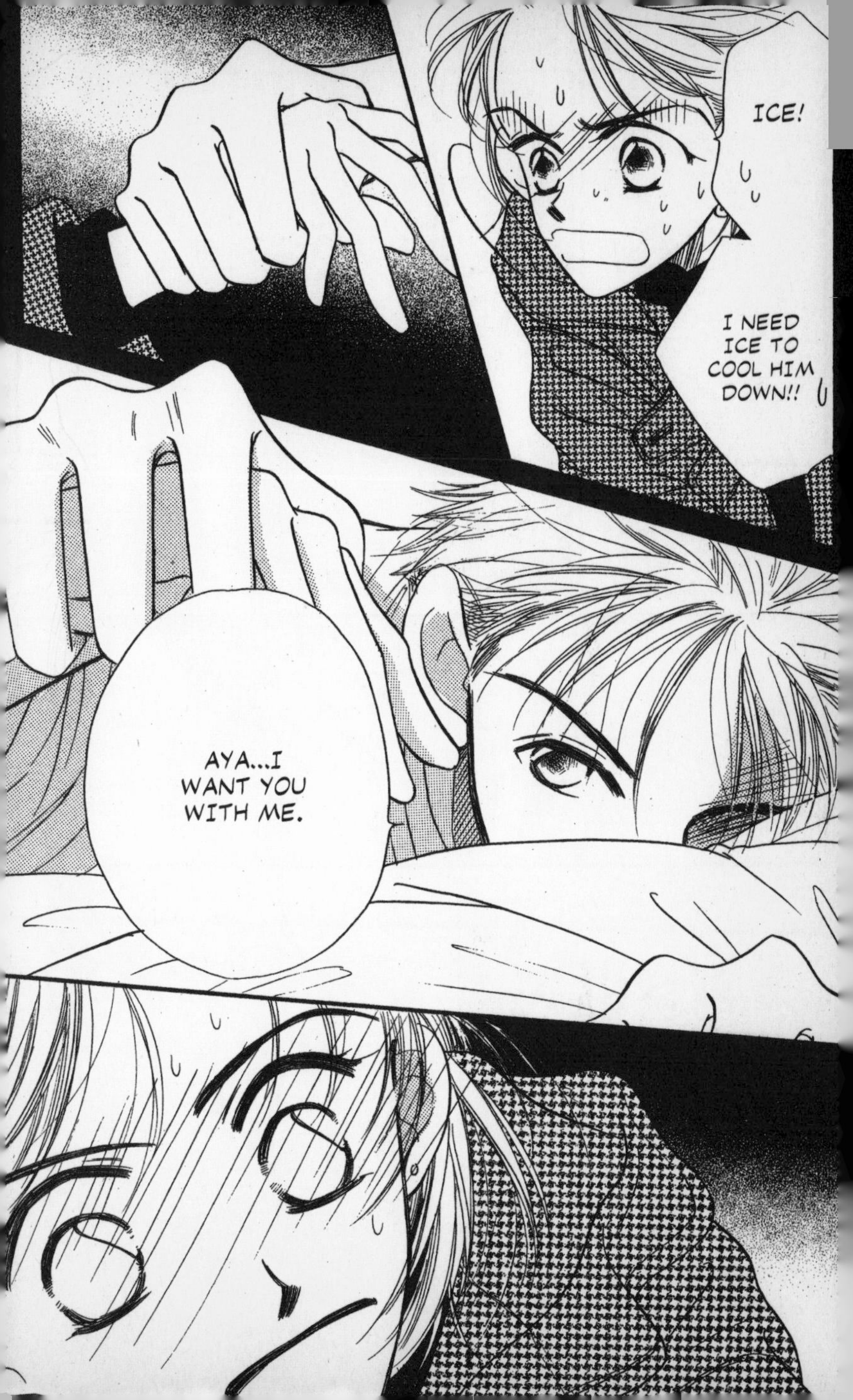
ICE!
I NEED ICE TO COOL HIM DOWN!!
AYA...I WANT YOU WITH ME.

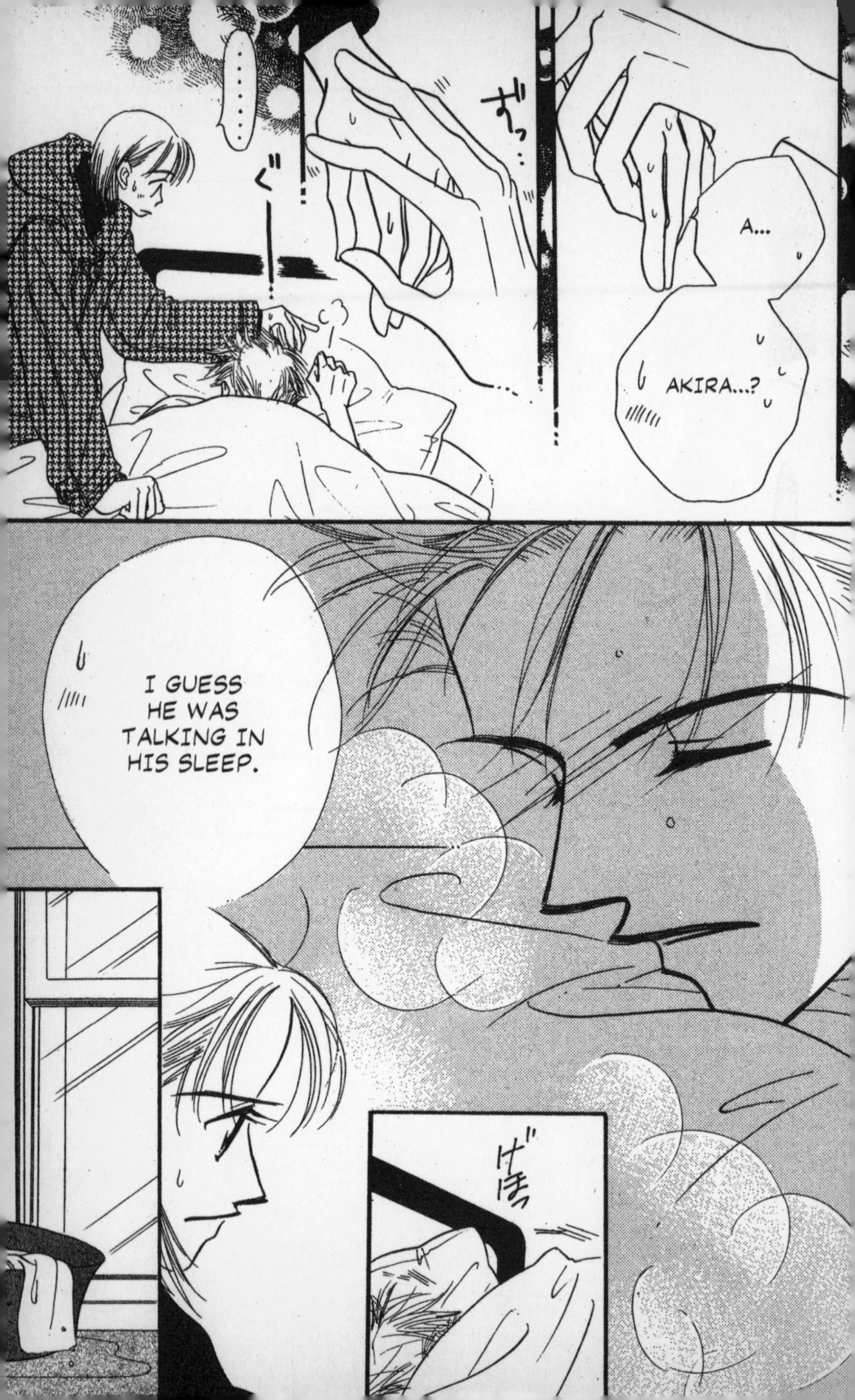
A...
AKIRA...?
ずっ…
……
ぐー
I GUESS HE WAS TALKING IN HIS SLEEP.
げほっ

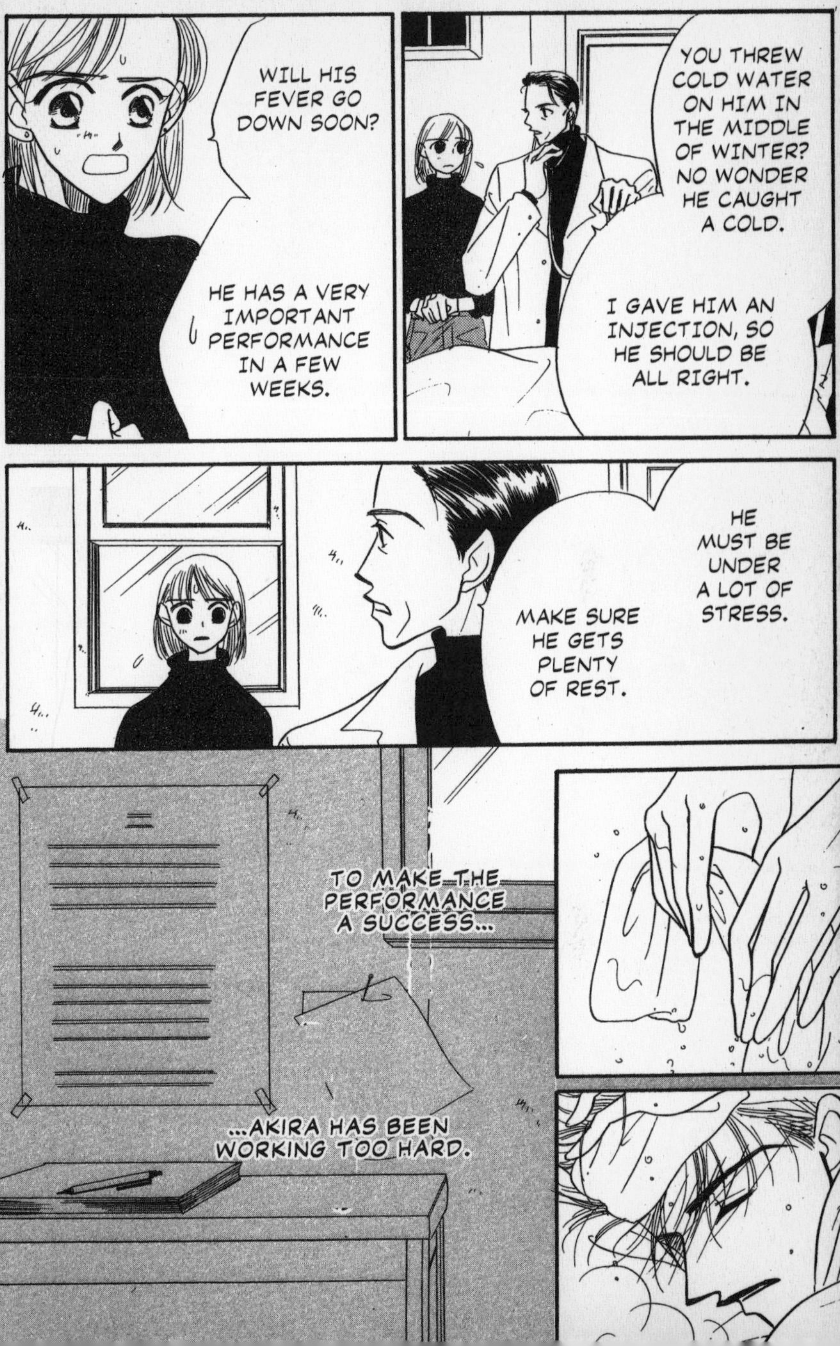
YOU THREW COLD WATER ON HIM IN THE MIDDLE OF WINTER? NO WONDER HE CAUGHT A COLD.
I GAVE HIM AN INJECTION, SO HE SHOULD BE ALL RIGHT.
WILL HIS FEVER GO DOWN SOON?
HE HAS A VERY IMPORTANT PERFORMANCE IN A FEW WEEKS.
HE MUST BE UNDER A LOT OF STRESS.
MAKE SURE HE GETS PLENTY OF REST.
TO MAKE THE PERFORMANCE A SUCCESS...
...AKIRA HAS BEEN WORKING TOO HARD.

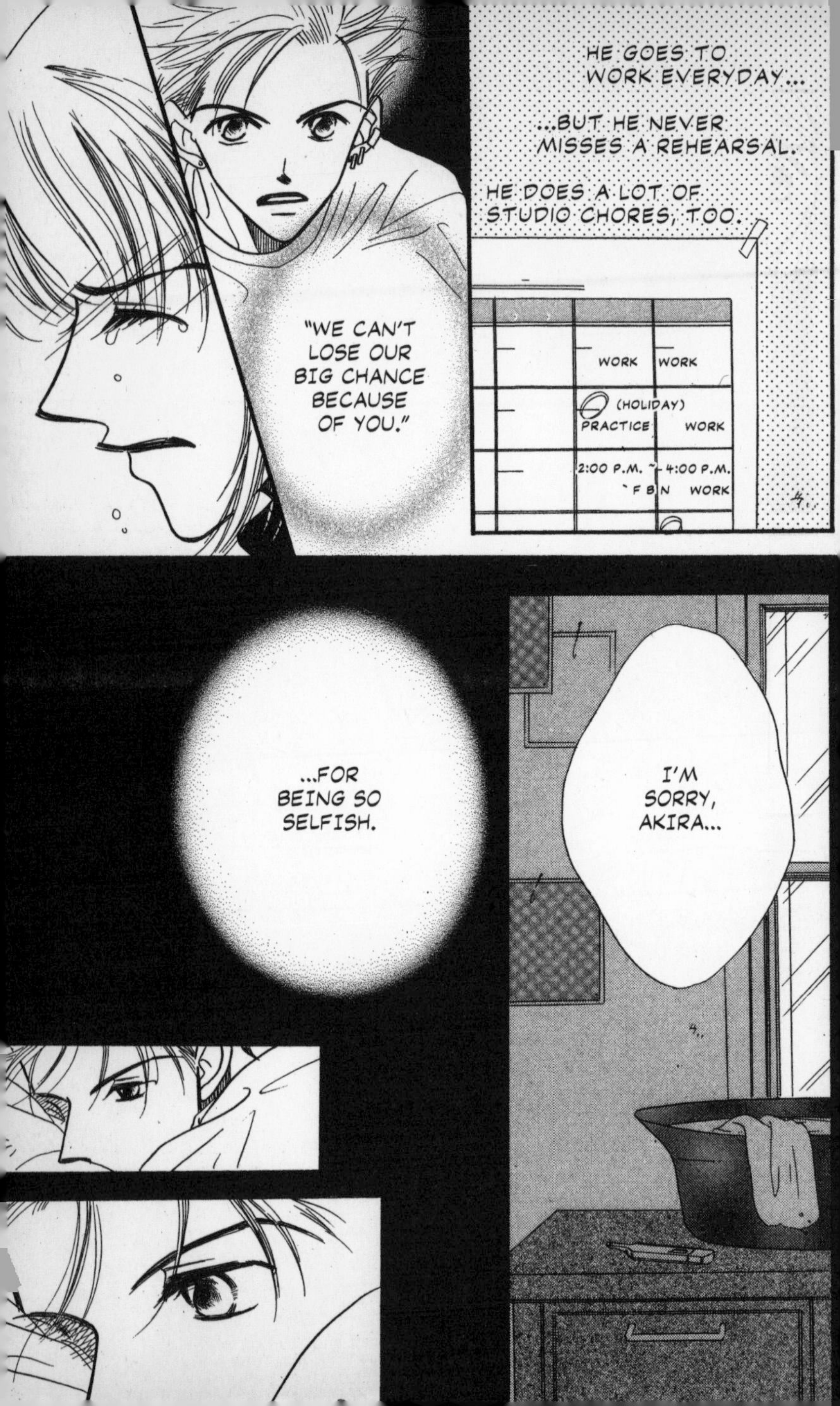
HE GOES TO WORK EVERYDAY...
...BUT HE NEVER MISSES A REHEARSAL.
HE DOES A LOT OF STUDIO CHORES, TOO.
WORK WORK
(HOLIDAY)
PRACTICE WORK
2:00 P.M. ~ 4:00 P.M.
F B N WORK
"WE CAN'T LOSE OUR BIG CHANCE BECAUSE OF YOU."
I'M SORRY, AKIRA...
...FOR BEING SO SELFISH.

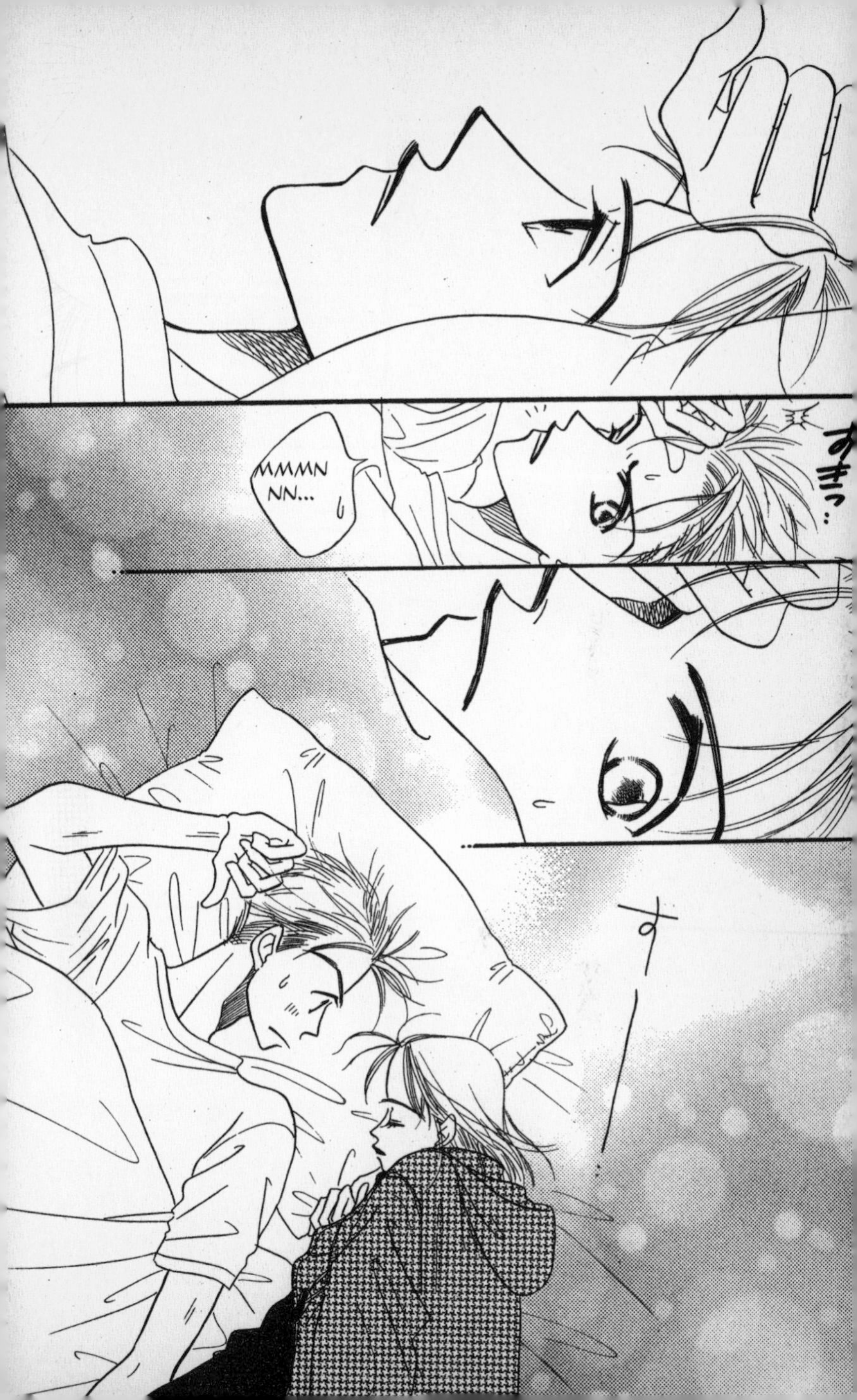
すきっ…
MMMN NN...
す

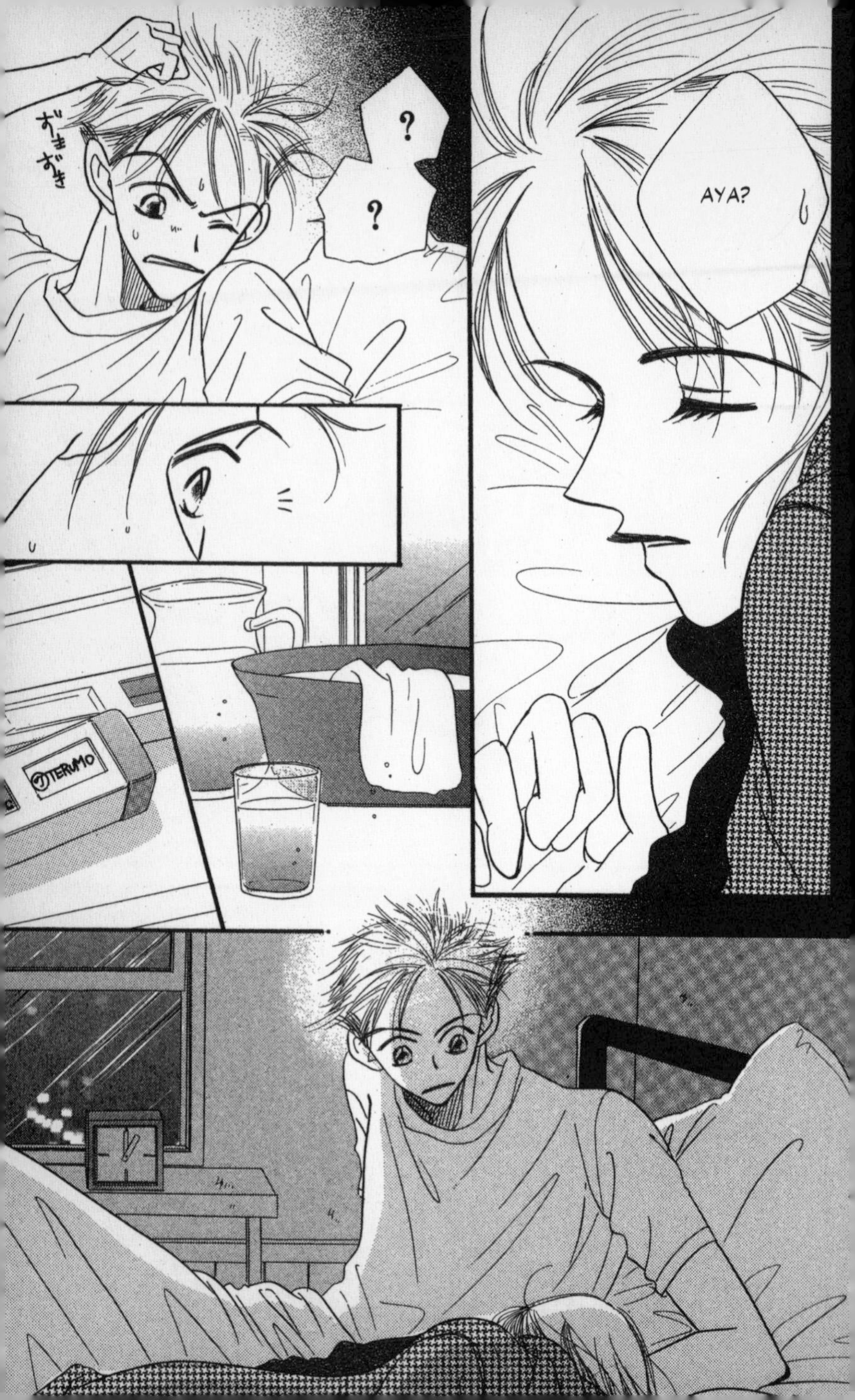
AYA?
?
?
ずきずき
TERUMO

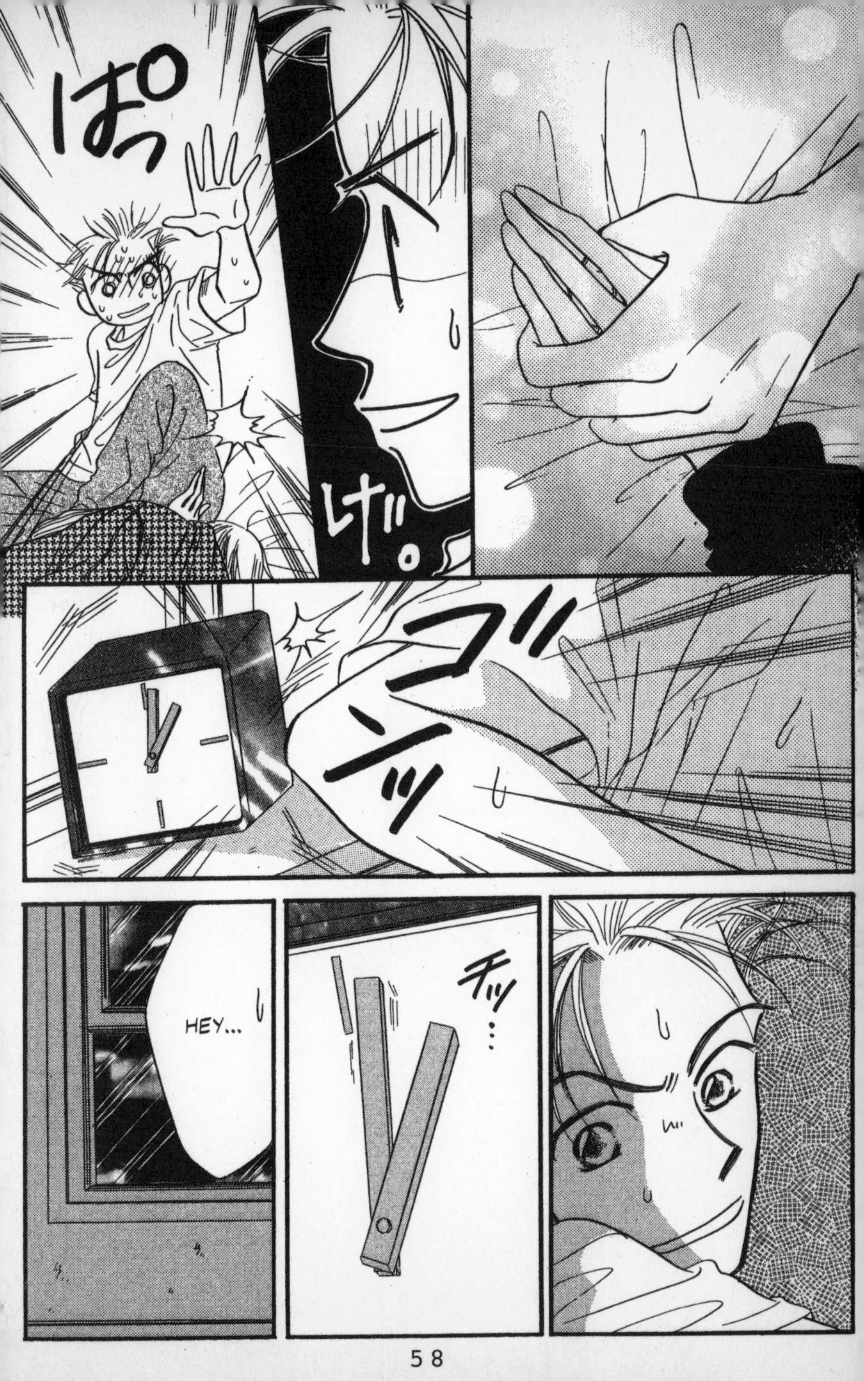
げ。
ぱっ
ゴンッ
チッ…
HEY...

Ashihara's Diary

No. 2

The most difficult scenes to draw were the dancing scenes. I am not very good at sketching. Once I started the series, I realized my lack of experience even more and regretted that I hadn't practiced sketching enough. I'm determined to practice more.

*

As you have already noticed, there are some scenes in England in this volume. I've been to England myself — not really on business but for pleasure. I was hoping to go to England because I knew I would write some scenes related to that country. Then I happened to go on a trip to England, all of a sudden.

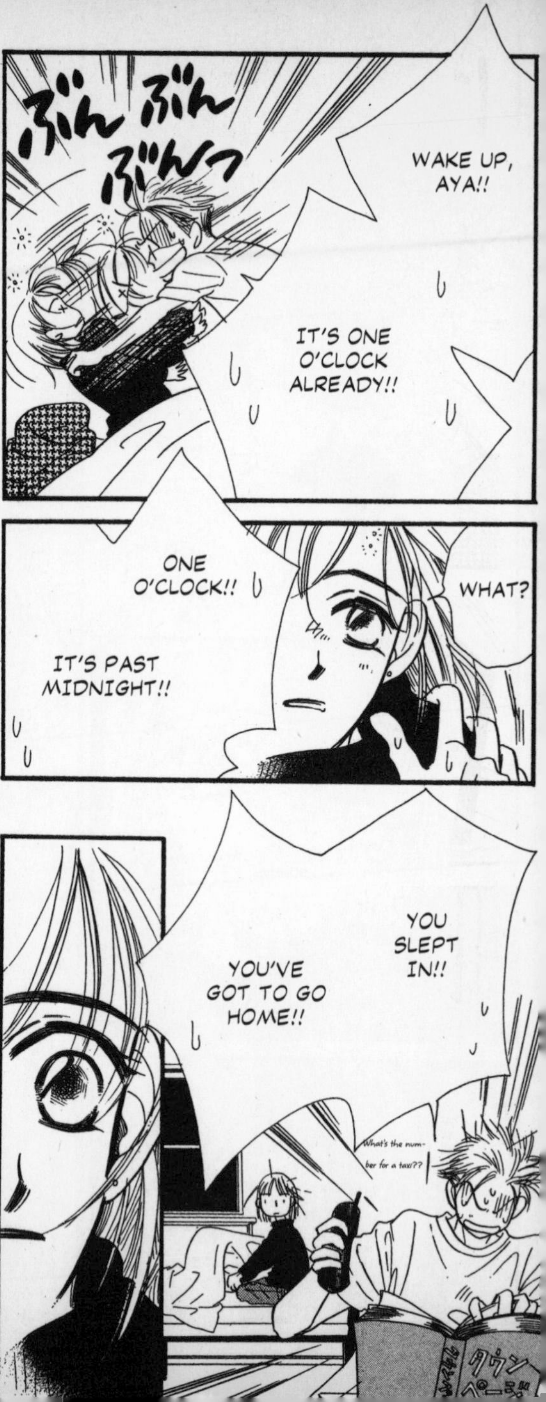

ぶんぶん
ぶんっ
WAKE UP, AYA!!
IT'S ONE O'CLOCK ALREADY!!
WHAT?
ONE O'CLOCK!!
IT'S PAST MIDNIGHT!!
YOU SLEPT IN!!
YOU'VE GOT TO GO HOME!!
What's the number for a taxi??

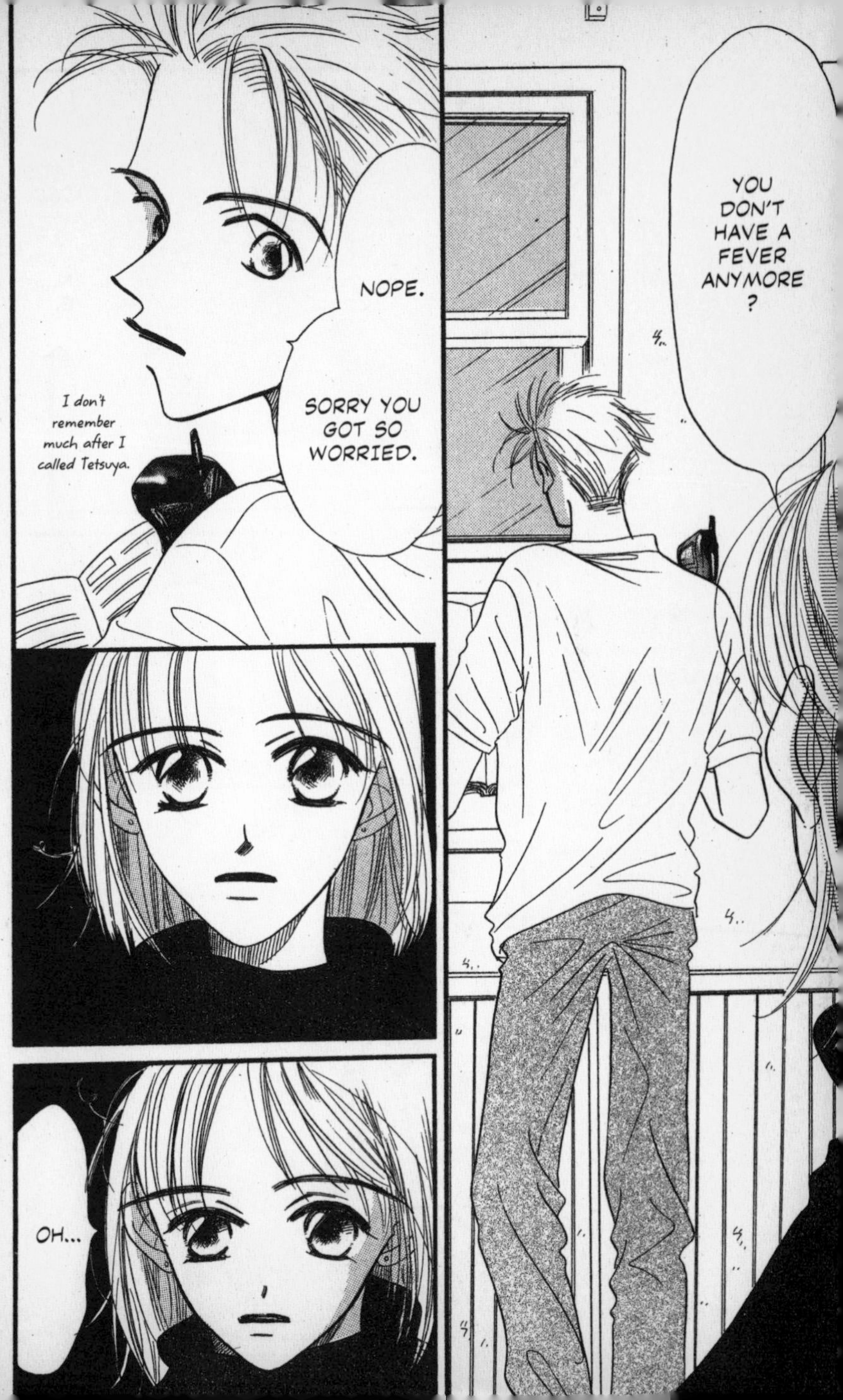
YOU DON'T HAVE A FEVER ANYMORE?
NOPE.
SORRY YOU GOT SO WORRIED.
I don't remember much after I called Tetsuya.
OH...

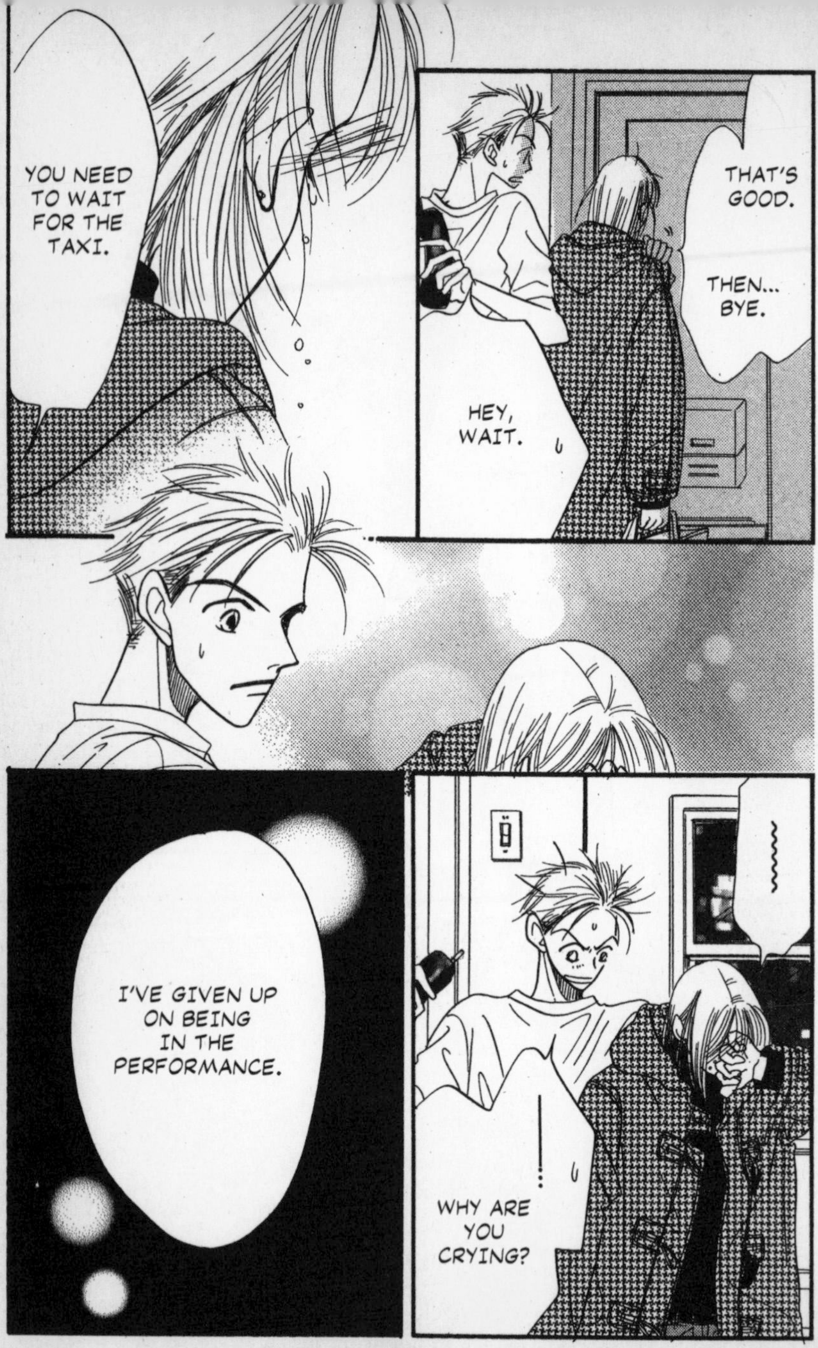
THAT'S GOOD.
THEN... BYE.
HEY, WAIT.
YOU NEED TO WAIT FOR THE TAXI.
...!
WHY ARE YOU CRYING?
I'VE GIVEN UP ON BEING IN THE PERFORMANCE.

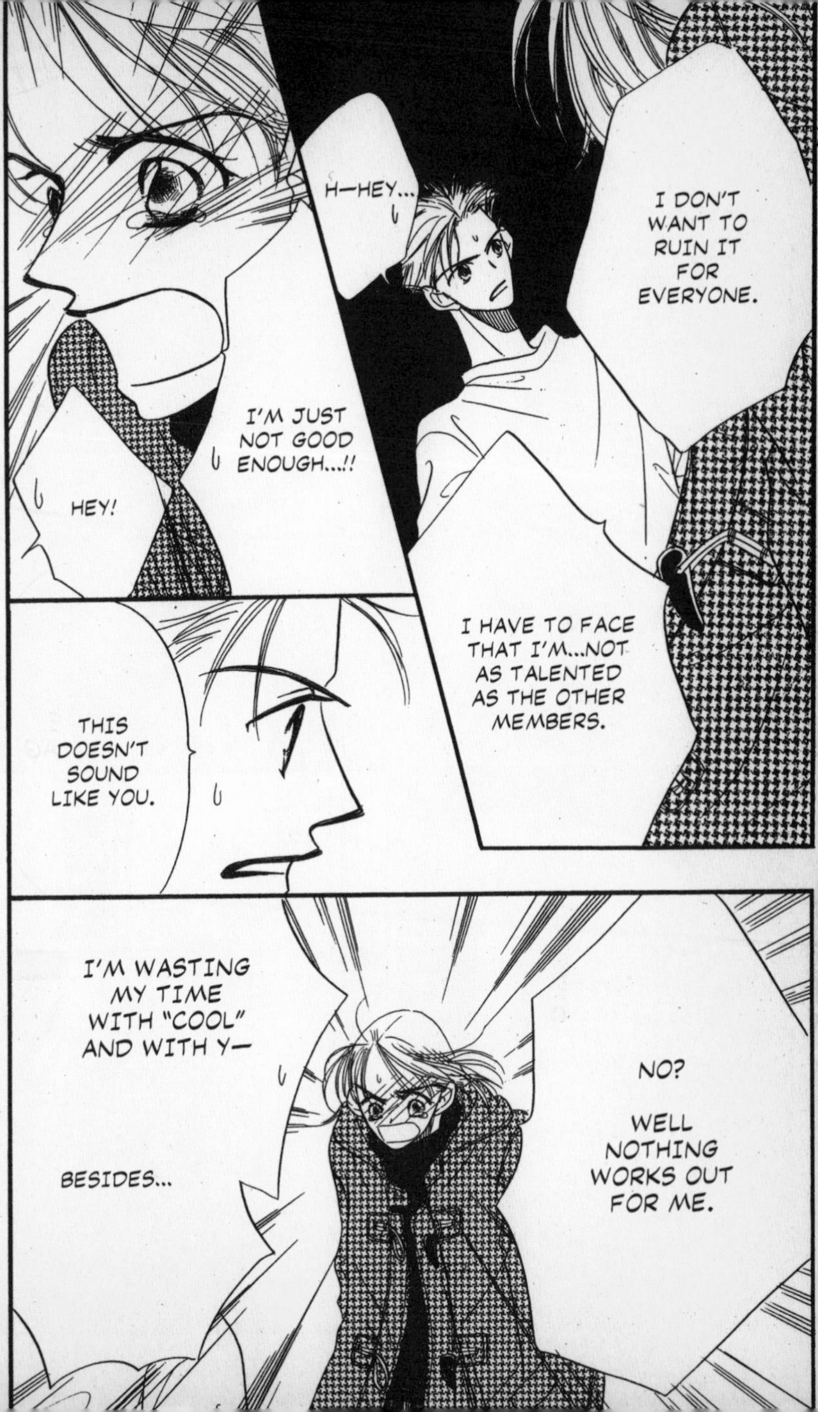
I DON'T WANT TO RUIN IT FOR EVERYONE.
H—HEY...
I HAVE TO FACE THAT I'M...NOT AS TALENTED AS THE OTHER MEMBERS.
I'M JUST NOT GOOD ENOUGH...!!
HEY!
THIS DOESN'T SOUND LIKE YOU.
NO?
WELL NOTHING WORKS OUT FOR ME.
I'M WASTING MY TIME WITH "COOL" AND WITH Y—
BESIDES...

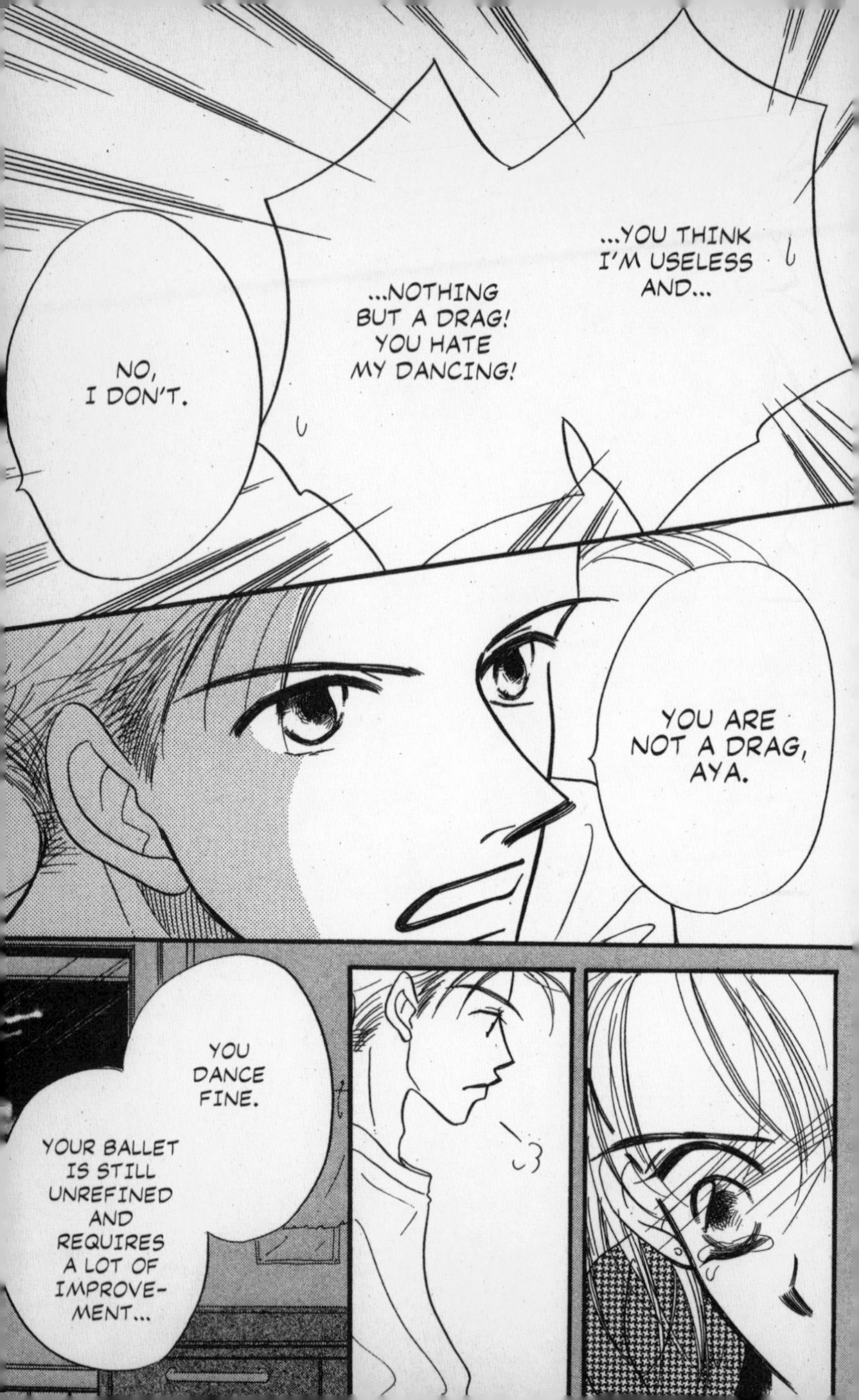
...YOU THINK I'M USELESS AND...
...NOTHING BUT A DRAG! YOU HATE MY DANCING!
NO, I DON'T.
YOU ARE NOT A DRAG, AYA.
YOU DANCE FINE.
YOUR BALLET IS STILL UNREFINED AND REQUIRES A LOT OF IMPROVEMENT...

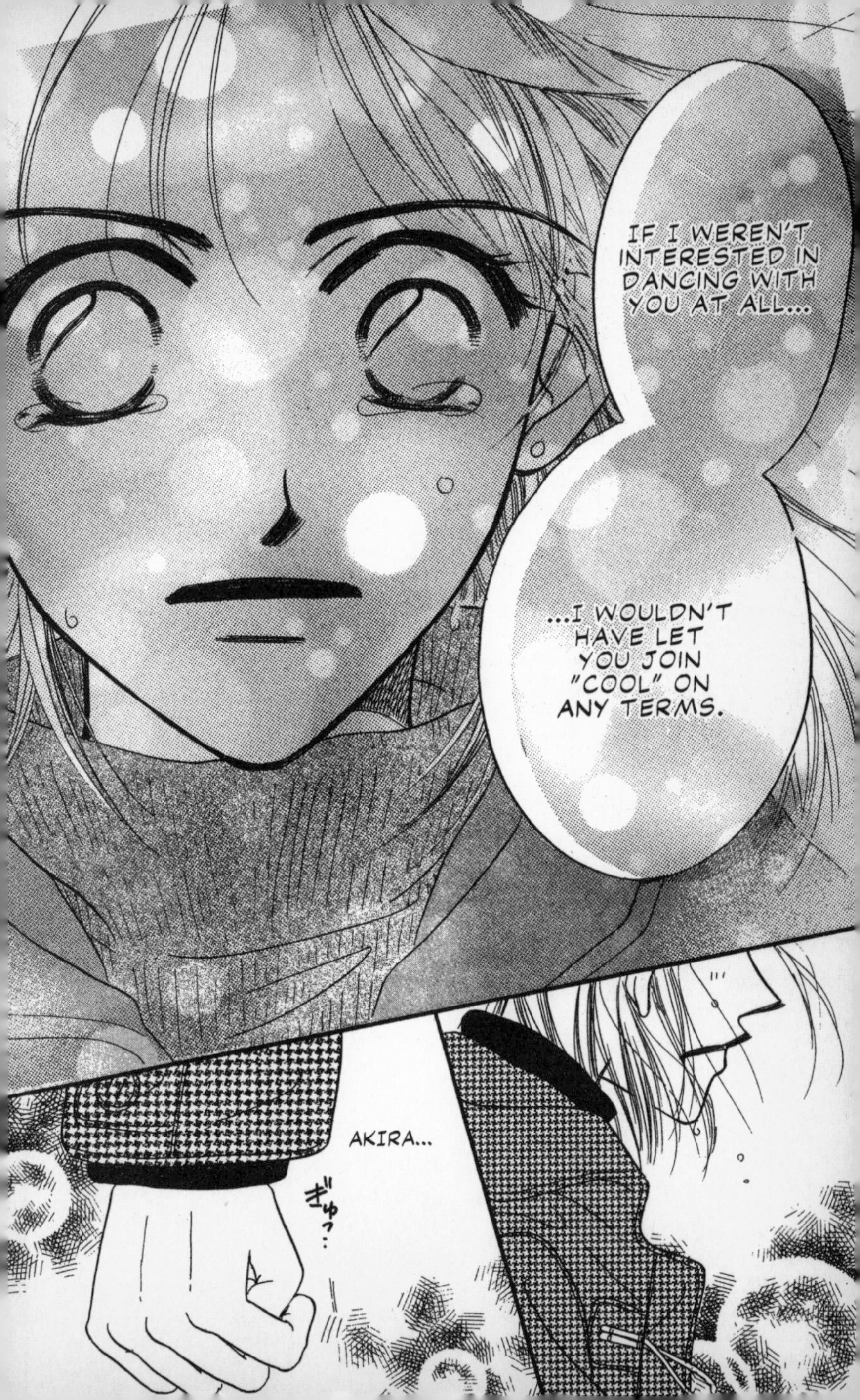
IF I WEREN'T INTERESTED IN DANCING WITH YOU AT ALL...
...I WOULDN'T HAVE LET YOU JOIN "COOL" ON ANY TERMS.
AKIRA...
ぎゅっ

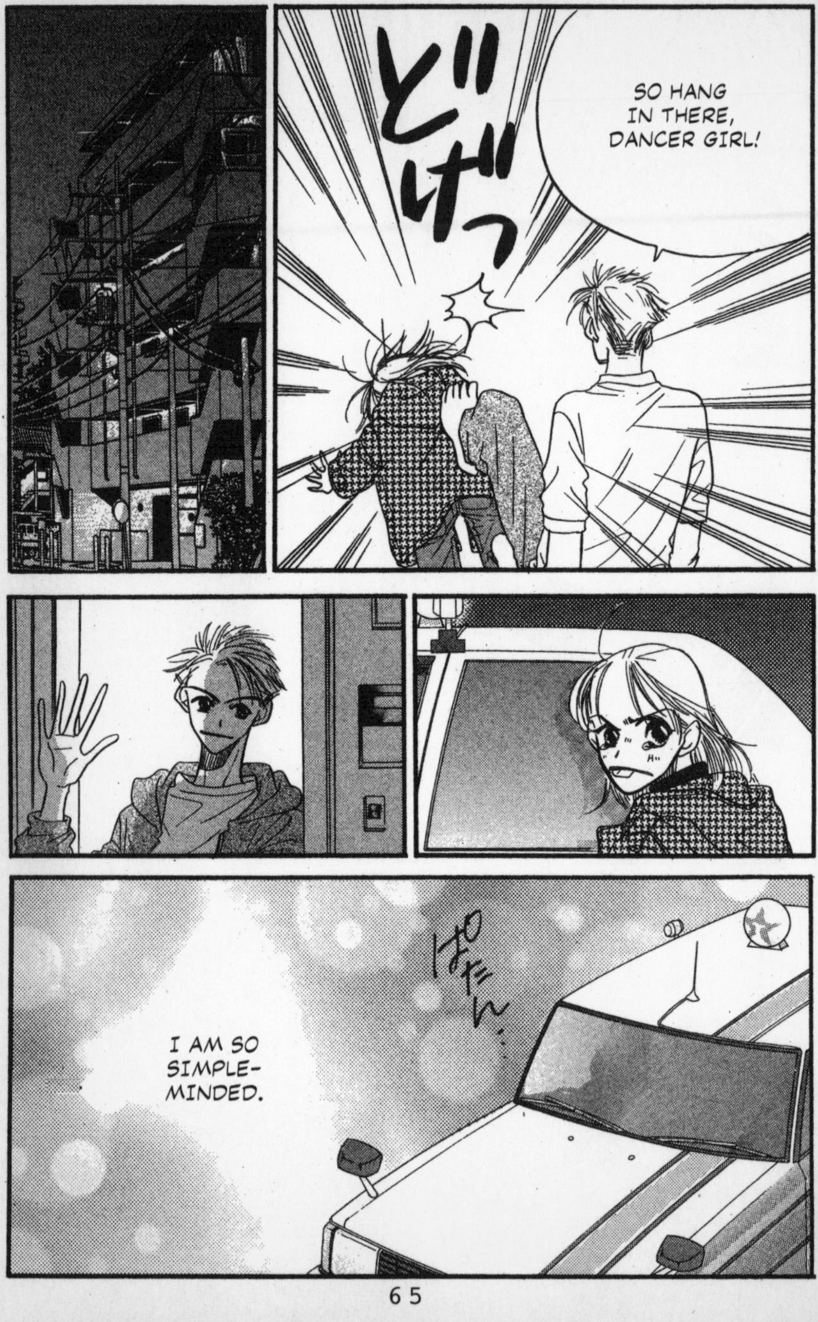
SO HANG IN THERE, DANCER GIRL!
どげっ
ぱたん…
I AM SO SIMPLE-MINDED.

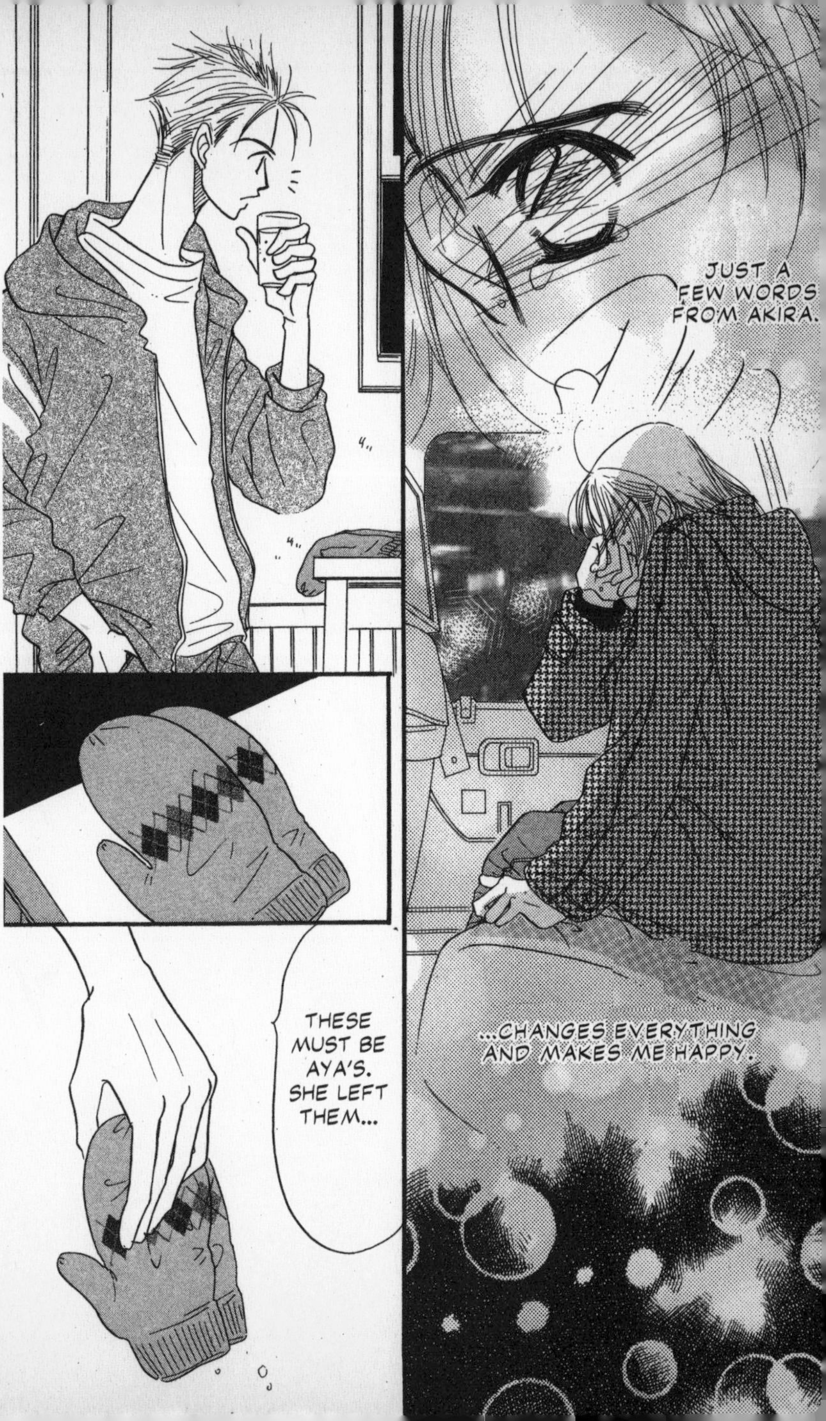
JUST A FEW WORDS FROM AKIRA.
...CHANGES EVERYTHING AND MAKES ME HAPPY.
THESE MUST BE AYA'S. SHE LEFT THEM...

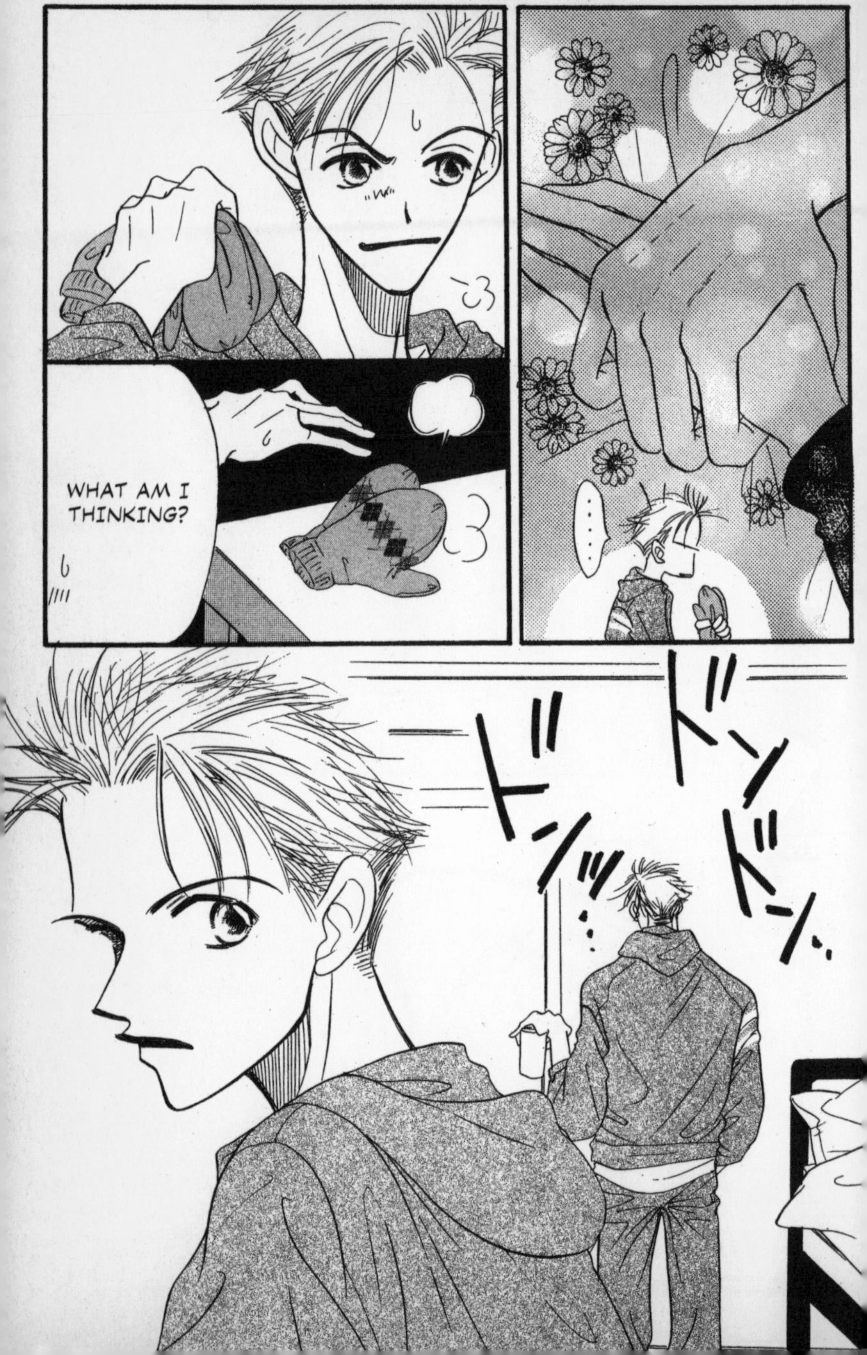

....
WHAT AM I THINKING?

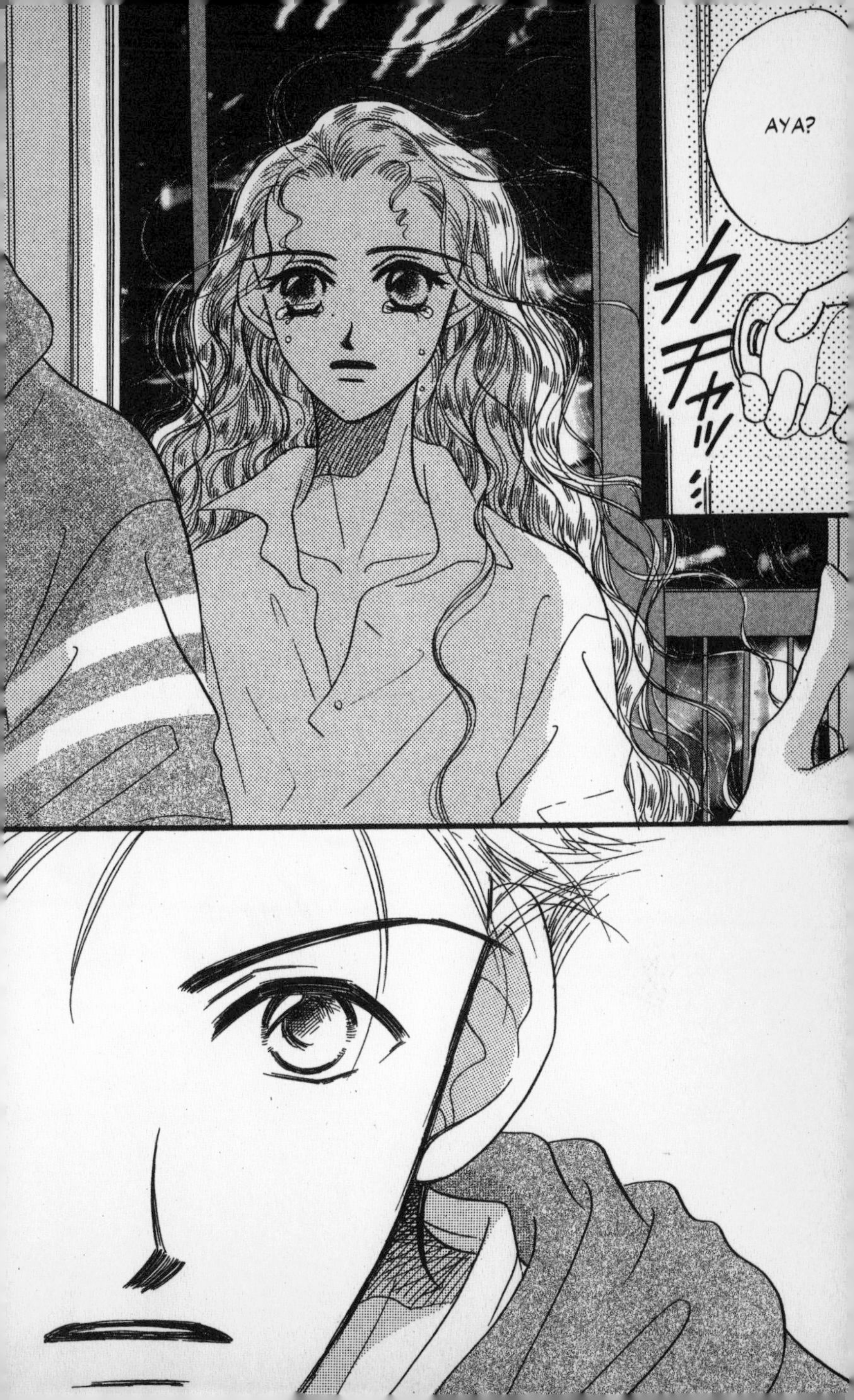
AYA?
カチャッ

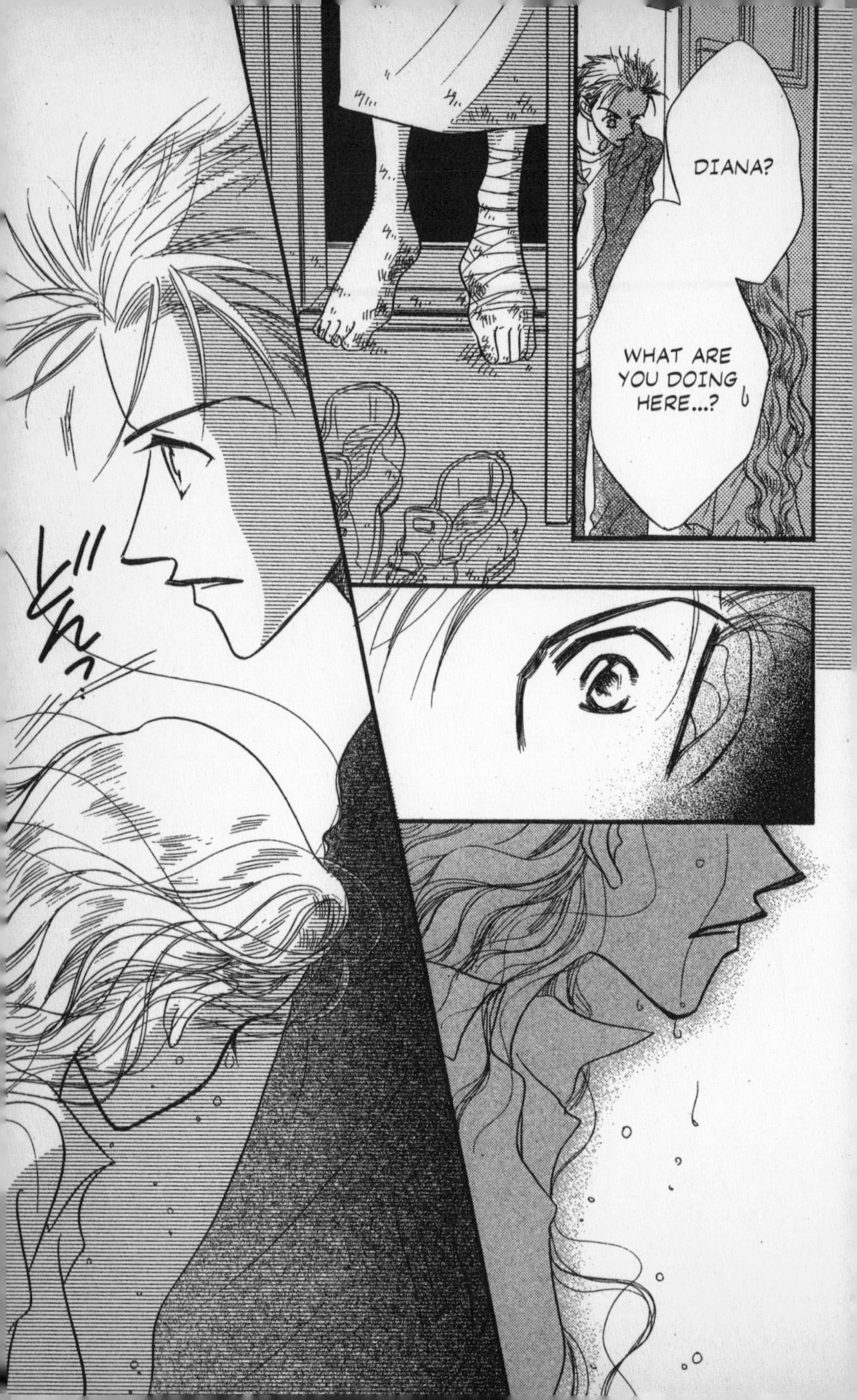
DIANA?
WHAT ARE YOU DOING HERE...?

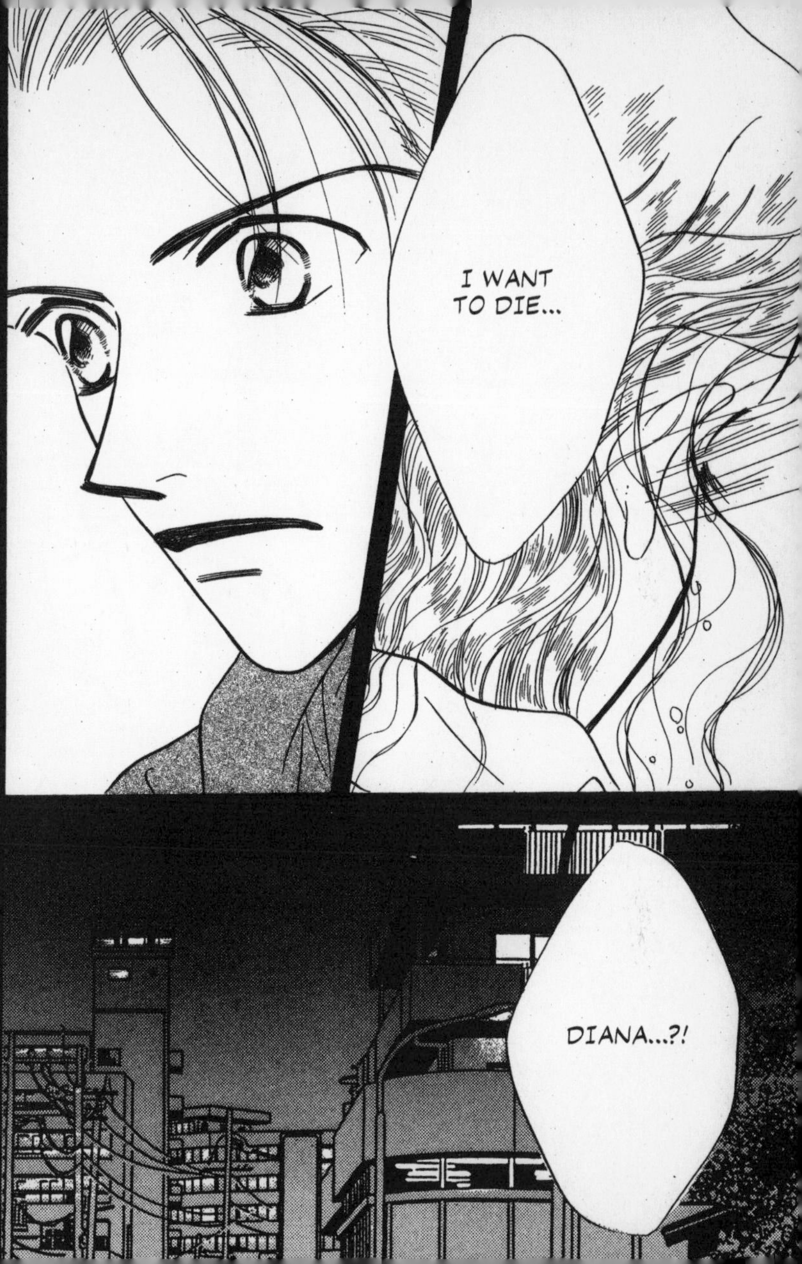
I WANT TO DIE...
DIANA...?!

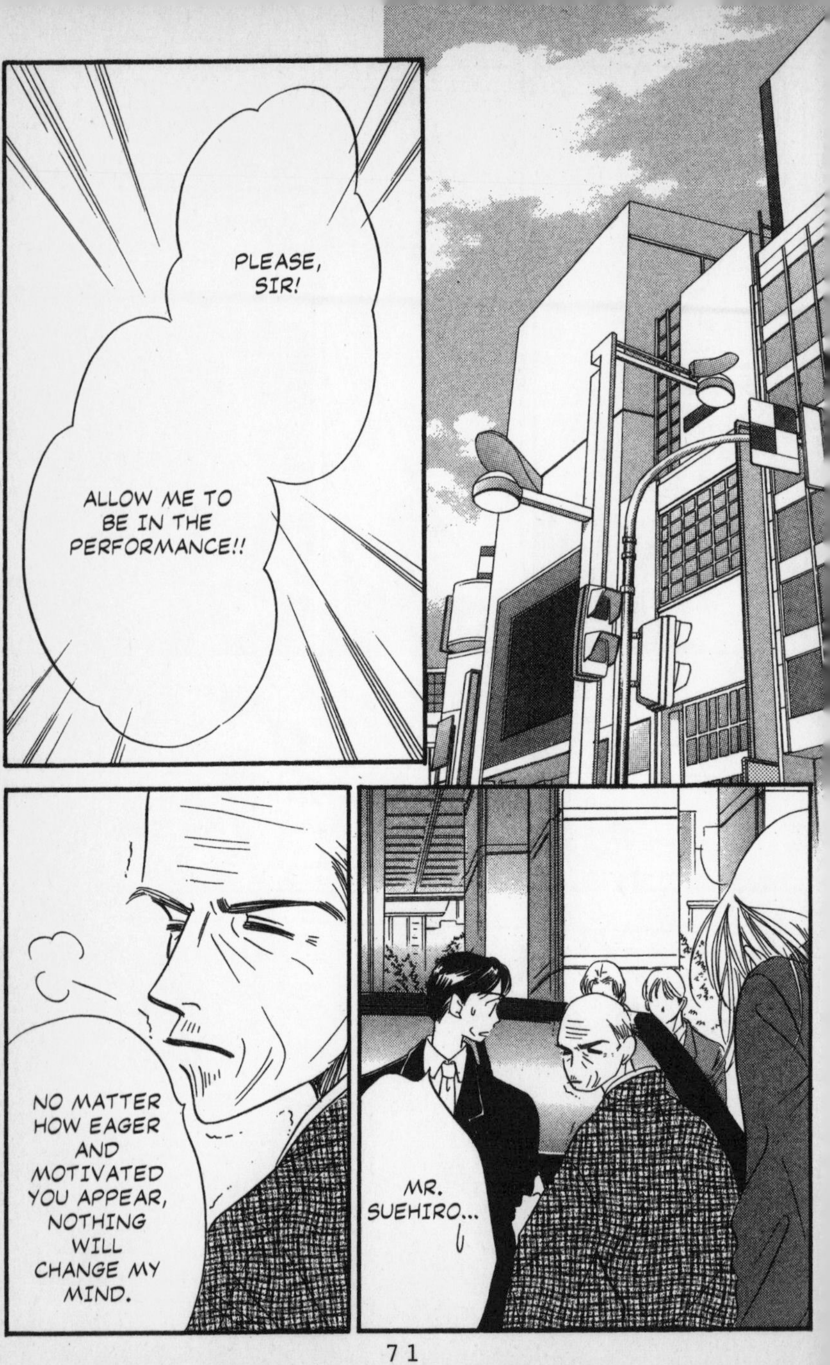
PLEASE, SIR!
ALLOW ME TO BE IN THE PERFORMANCE!!
MR. SUEHIRO...
NO MATTER HOW EAGER AND MOTIVATED YOU APPEAR, NOTHING WILL CHANGE MY MIND.

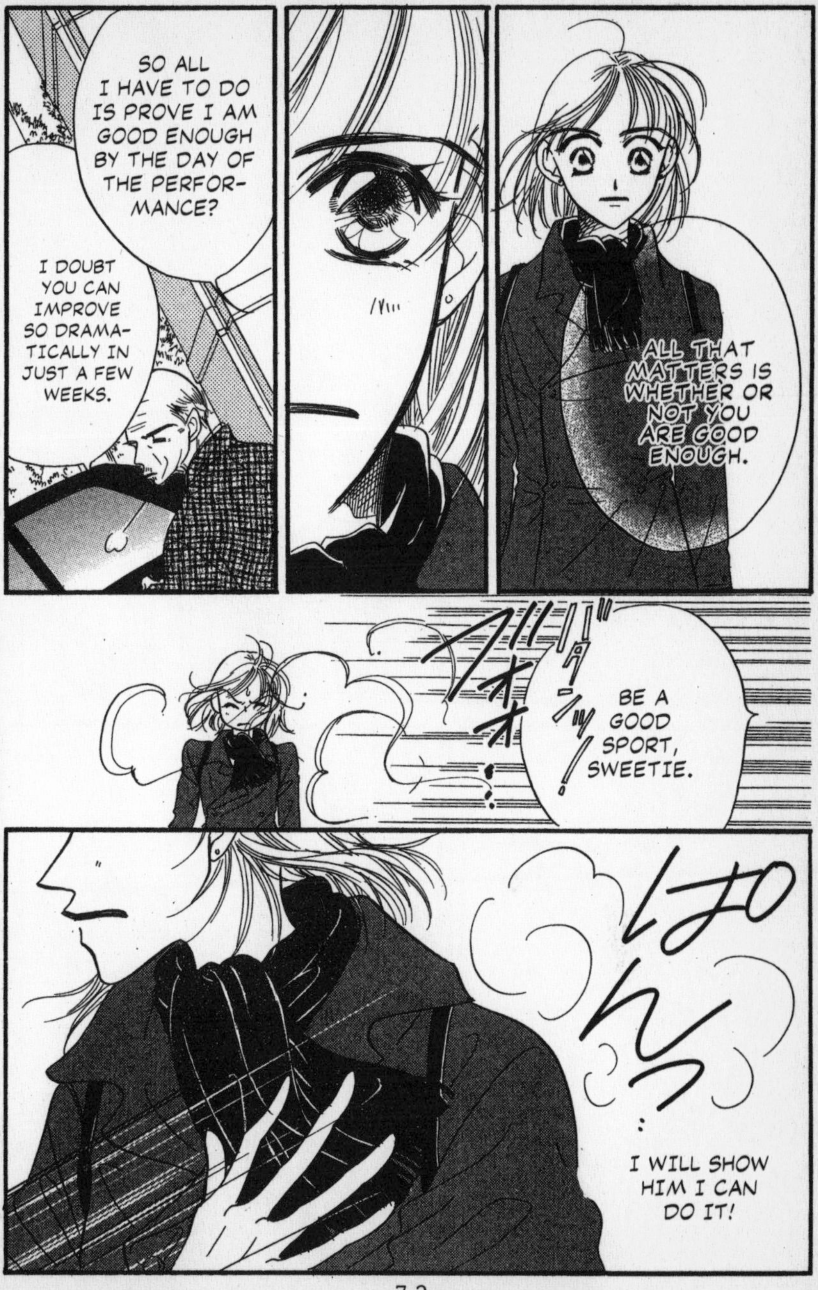
ALL THAT MATTERS IS WHETHER OR NOT YOU ARE GOOD ENOUGH.
SO ALL I HAVE TO DO IS PROVE I AM GOOD ENOUGH BY THE DAY OF THE PERFOR-MANCE?
I DOUBT YOU CAN IMPROVE SO DRAMA-TICALLY IN JUST A FEW WEEKS.
BE A GOOD SPORT, SWEETIE.
I WILL SHOW HIM I CAN DO IT!

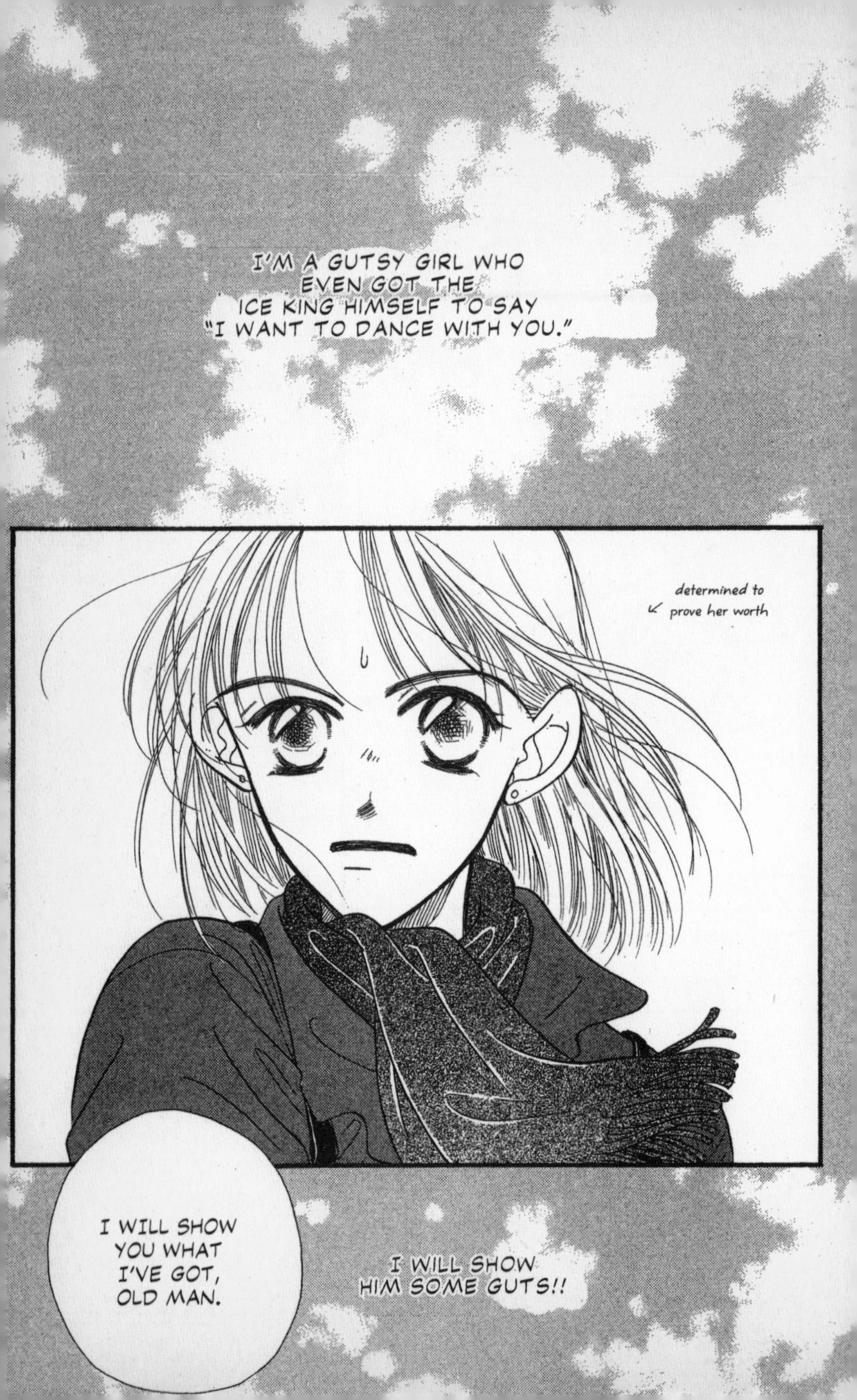
I'M A GUTSY GIRL WHO EVEN GOT THE ICE KING HIMSELF TO SAY "I WANT TO DANCE WITH YOU."
determined to prove her worth
I WILL SHOW YOU WHAT I'VE GOT, OLD MAN.
I WILL SHOW HIM SOME GUTS!!

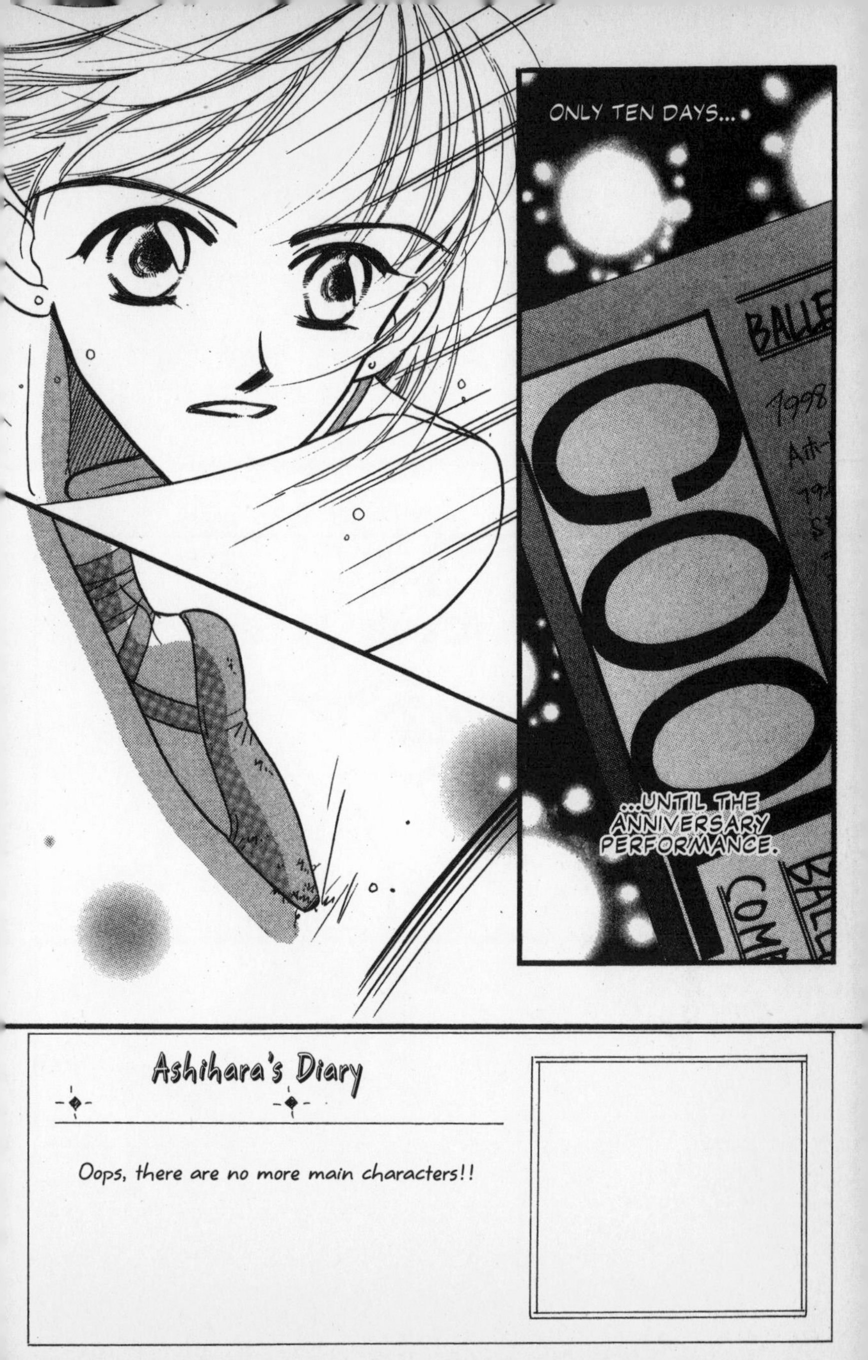
ONLY TEN DAYS...
...UNTIL THE ANNIVERSARY PERFORMANCE.

Ashihara's Diary

Oops, there are no more main characters!!

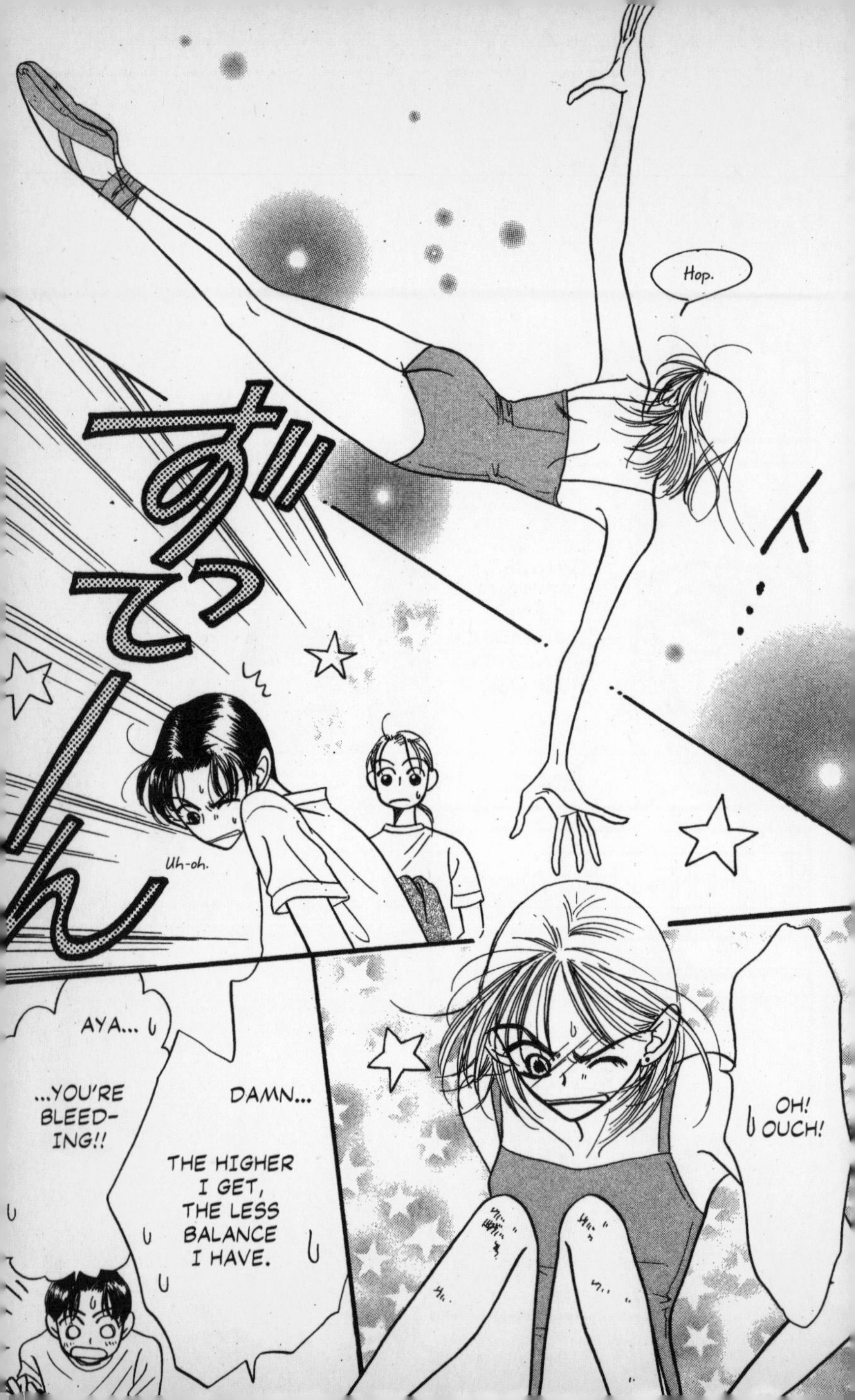
Hop.
ト…
ずってーん
Uh-oh.
OH! OUCH!
DAMN...
THE HIGHER I GET, THE LESS BALANCE I HAVE.
AYA...
...YOU'RE BLEED-ING!!

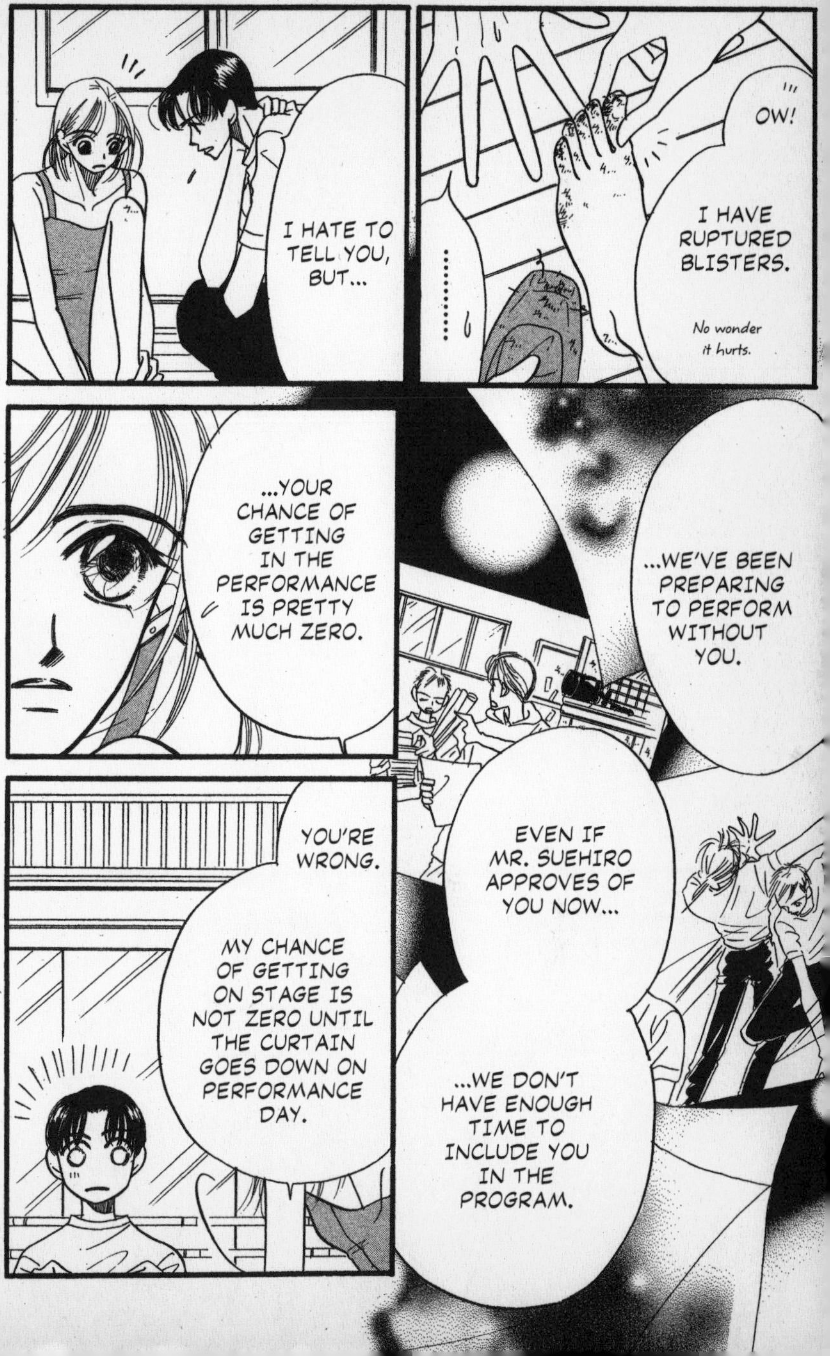
OW!
I HAVE RUPTURED BLISTERS.
No wonder it hurts.
......
I HATE TO TELL YOU, BUT...
...WE'VE BEEN PREPARING TO PERFORM WITHOUT YOU.
EVEN IF MR. SUEHIRO APPROVES OF YOU NOW...
...WE DON'T HAVE ENOUGH TIME TO INCLUDE YOU IN THE PROGRAM.
...YOUR CHANCE OF GETTING IN THE PERFORMANCE IS PRETTY MUCH ZERO.
YOU'RE WRONG.
MY CHANCE OF GETTING ON STAGE IS NOT ZERO UNTIL THE CURTAIN GOES DOWN ON PERFORMANCE DAY.

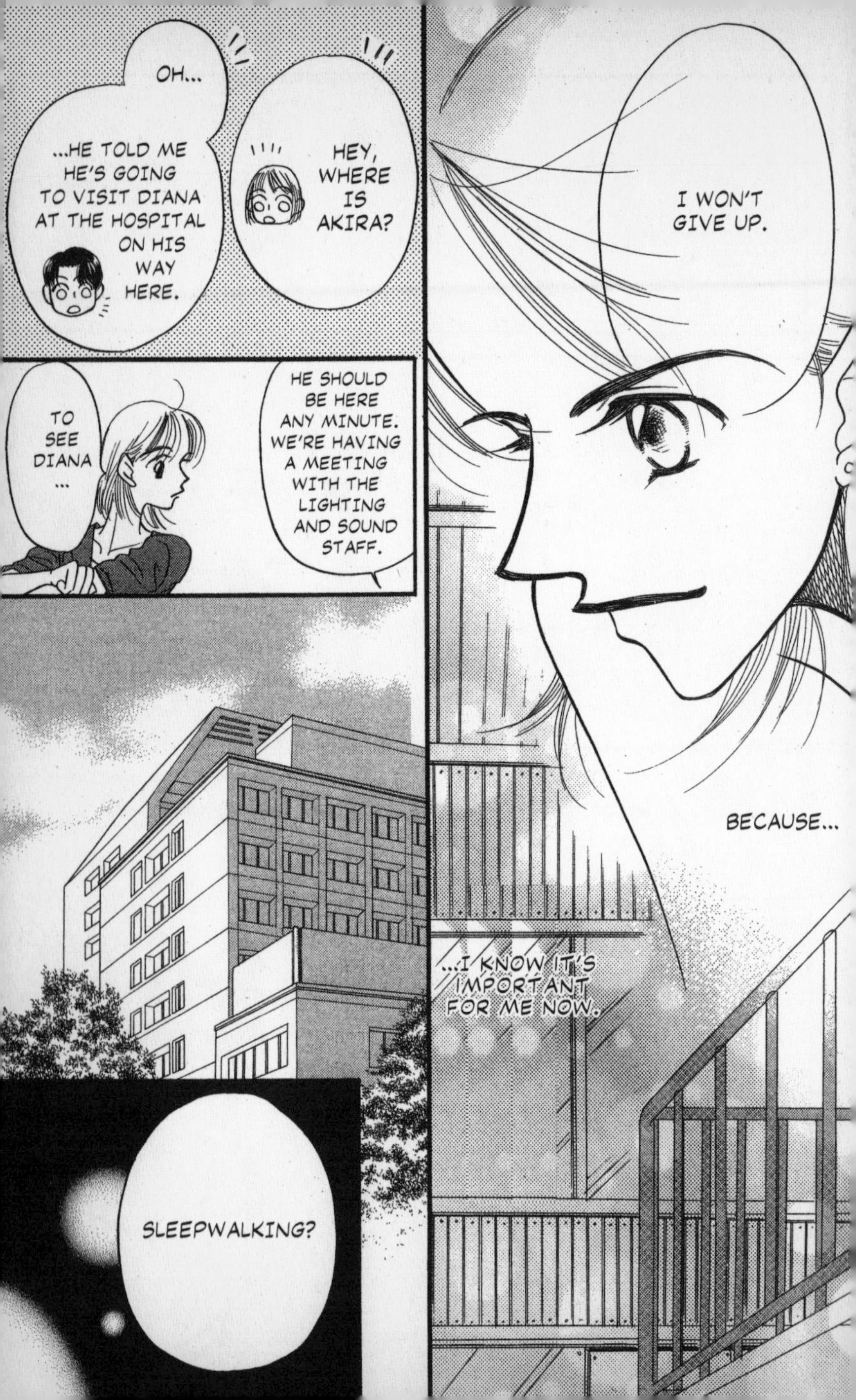
I WON'T GIVE UP.
BECAUSE...
...I KNOW IT'S IMPORTANT FOR ME NOW.
HEY, WHERE IS AKIRA?
OH...
...HE TOLD ME HE'S GOING TO VISIT DIANA AT THE HOSPITAL ON HIS WAY HERE.
HE SHOULD BE HERE ANY MINUTE. WE'RE HAVING A MEETING WITH THE LIGHTING AND SOUND STAFF.
TO SEE DIANA ...
SLEEPWALKING?

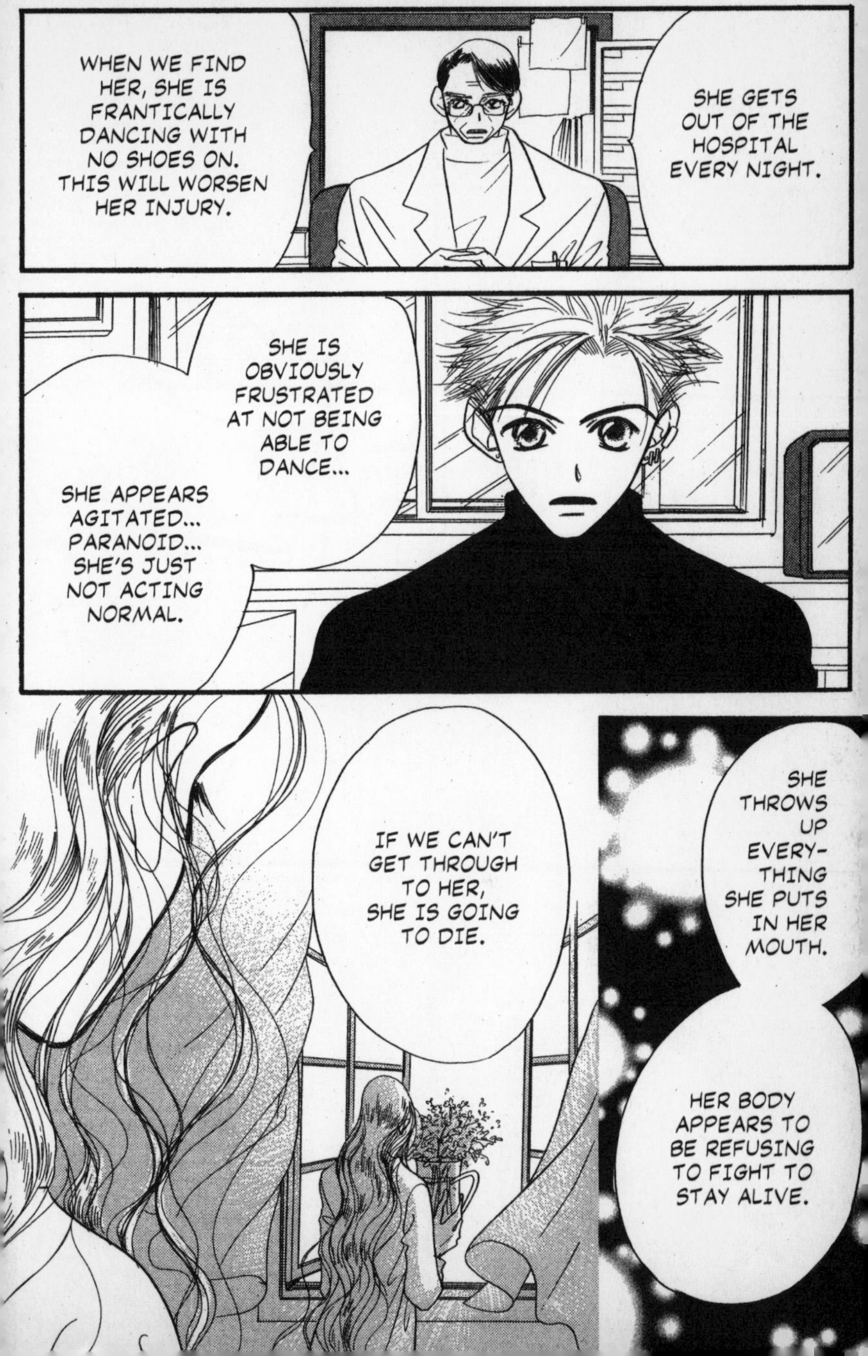
SHE GETS OUT OF THE HOSPITAL EVERY NIGHT.
WHEN WE FIND HER, SHE IS FRANTICALLY DANCING WITH NO SHOES ON. THIS WILL WORSEN HER INJURY.
SHE IS OBVIOUSLY FRUSTRATED AT NOT BEING ABLE TO DANCE...
SHE APPEARS AGITATED... PARANOID... SHE'S JUST NOT ACTING NORMAL.
SHE THROWS UP EVERY-THING SHE PUTS IN HER MOUTH.
HER BODY APPEARS TO BE REFUSING TO FIGHT TO STAY ALIVE.
IF WE CAN'T GET THROUGH TO HER, SHE IS GOING TO DIE.

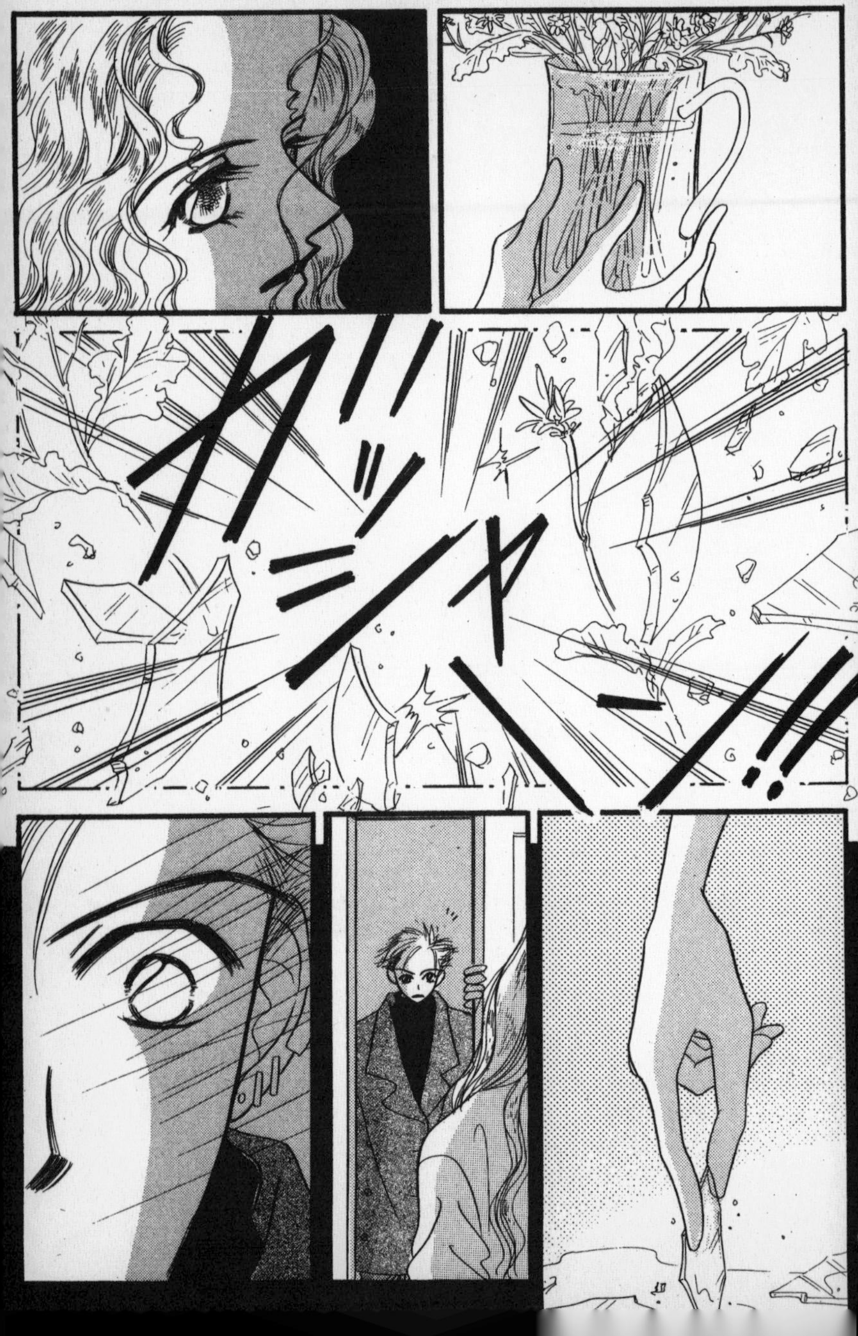
ガッシャーン!!

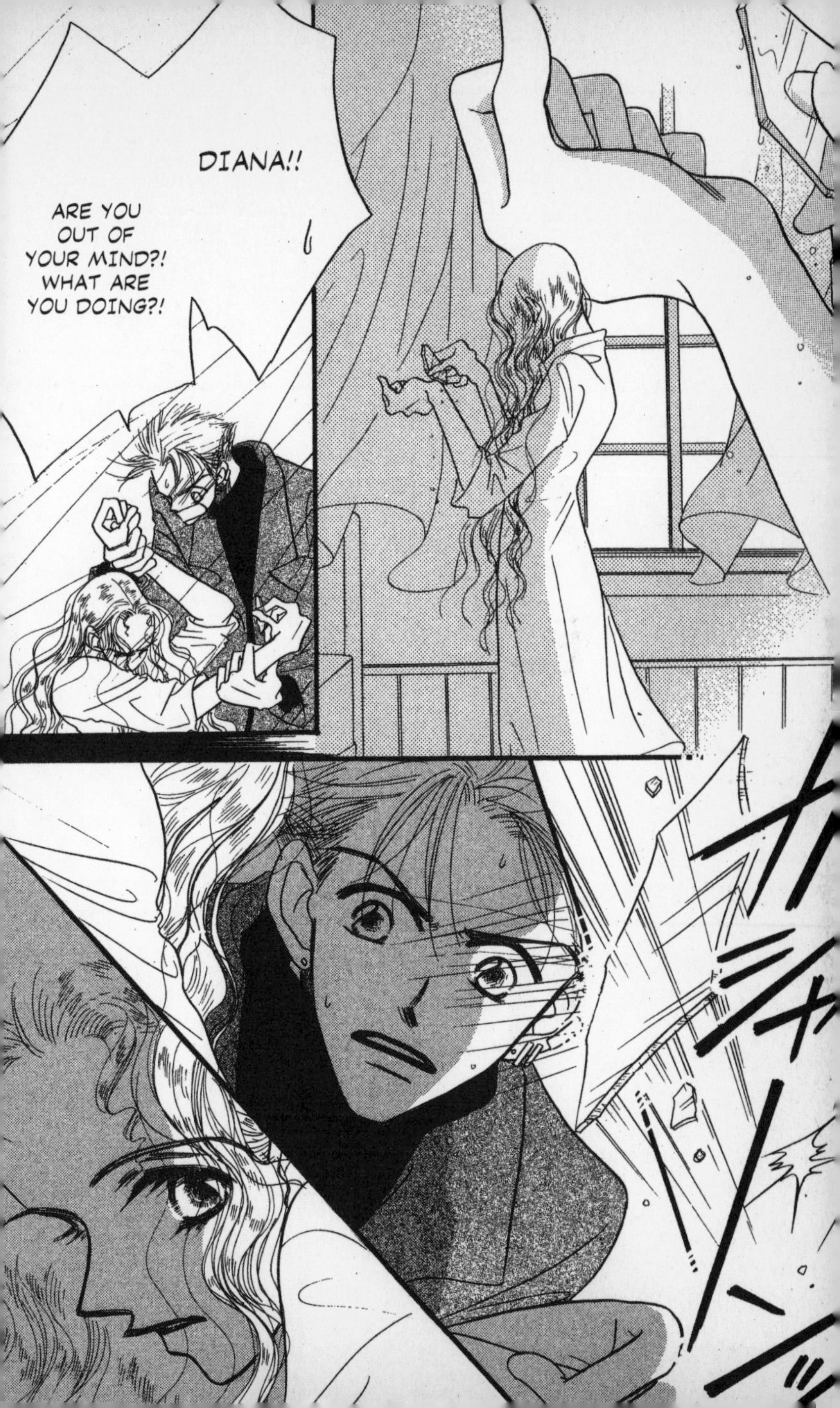
DIANA!!
ARE YOU OUT OF YOUR MIND?! WHAT ARE YOU DOING?!

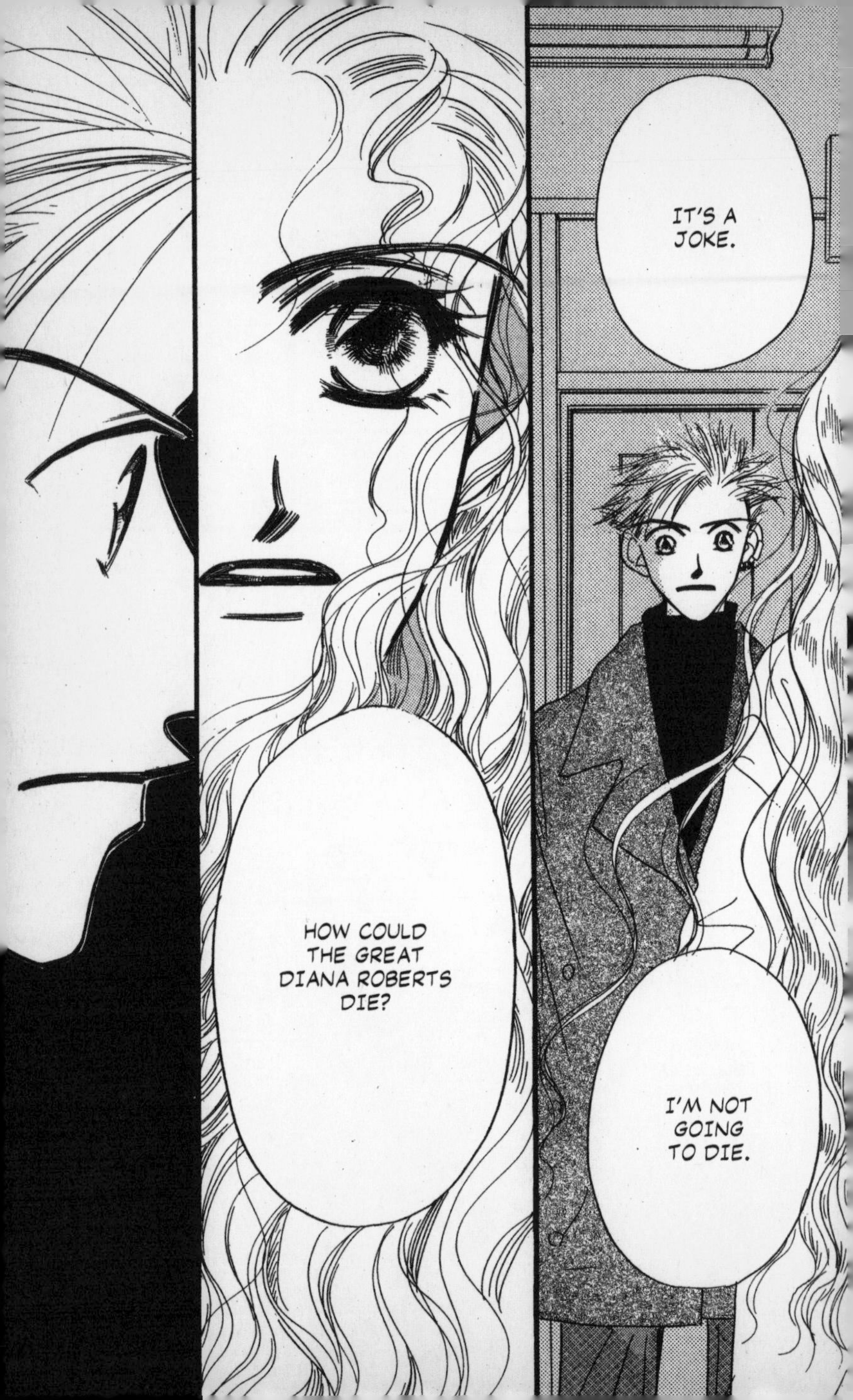
IT'S A JOKE.
I'M NOT GOING TO DIE.
HOW COULD THE GREAT DIANA ROBERTS DIE?

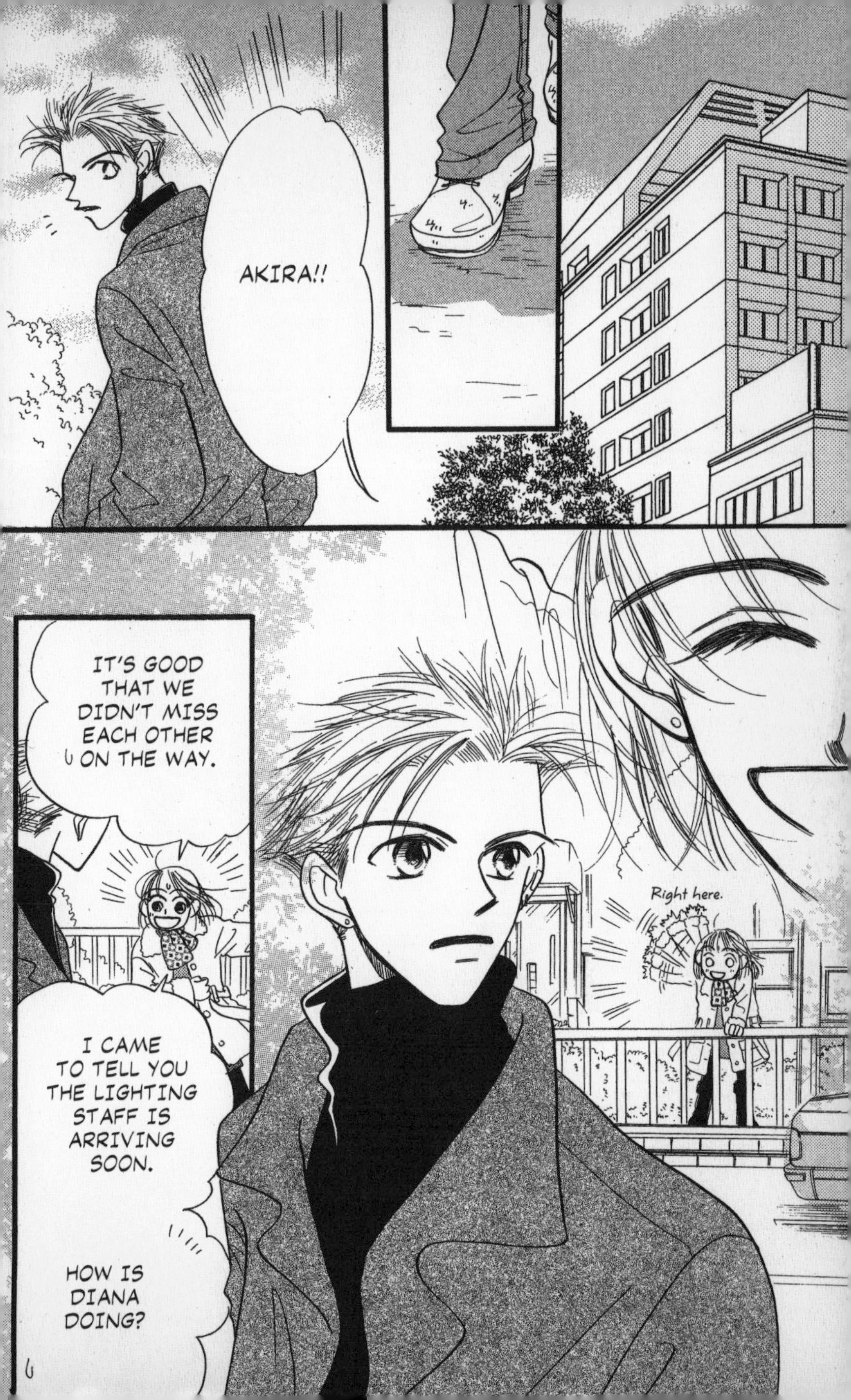
AKIRA!!
Right here.
IT'S GOOD THAT WE DIDN'T MISS EACH OTHER ON THE WAY.
I CAME TO TELL YOU THE LIGHTING STAFF IS ARRIVING SOON.
HOW IS DIANA DOING?

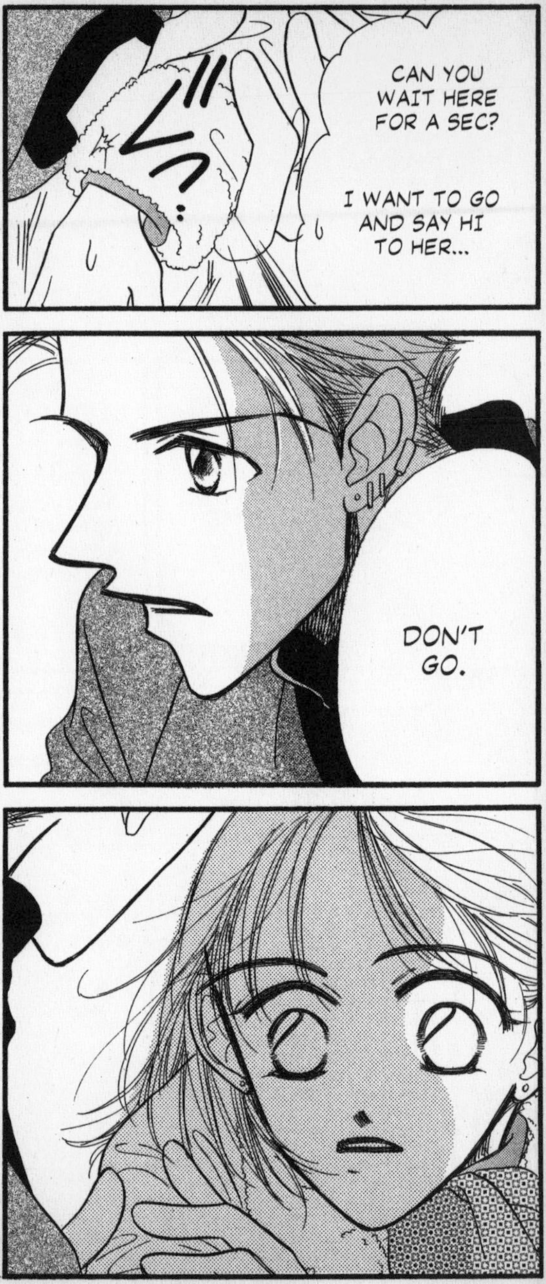
CAN YOU WAIT HERE FOR A SEC?
I WANT TO GO AND SAY HI TO HER...
DON'T GO.

Ashihara's Diary

-◆- No. 3 -◆-

A friend of mine asked me if I would like to take a trip to England with her. Of course I gave her a positive response. This unexpected plan turned out to be such a nice trip. I was so excited to be there, I even forgot to take pictures of some places I needed for the story. It's part of my good memories of England now.

*

"Princess Line" was published in Bessho Shojo Comics DX while Forbidden Dance was still going on. I have never worked on a one-issue story while writing a series at the same time. I had such a tight schedule with two stories going on. I was under a lot of stress, especially the three months before Princess Line was due.

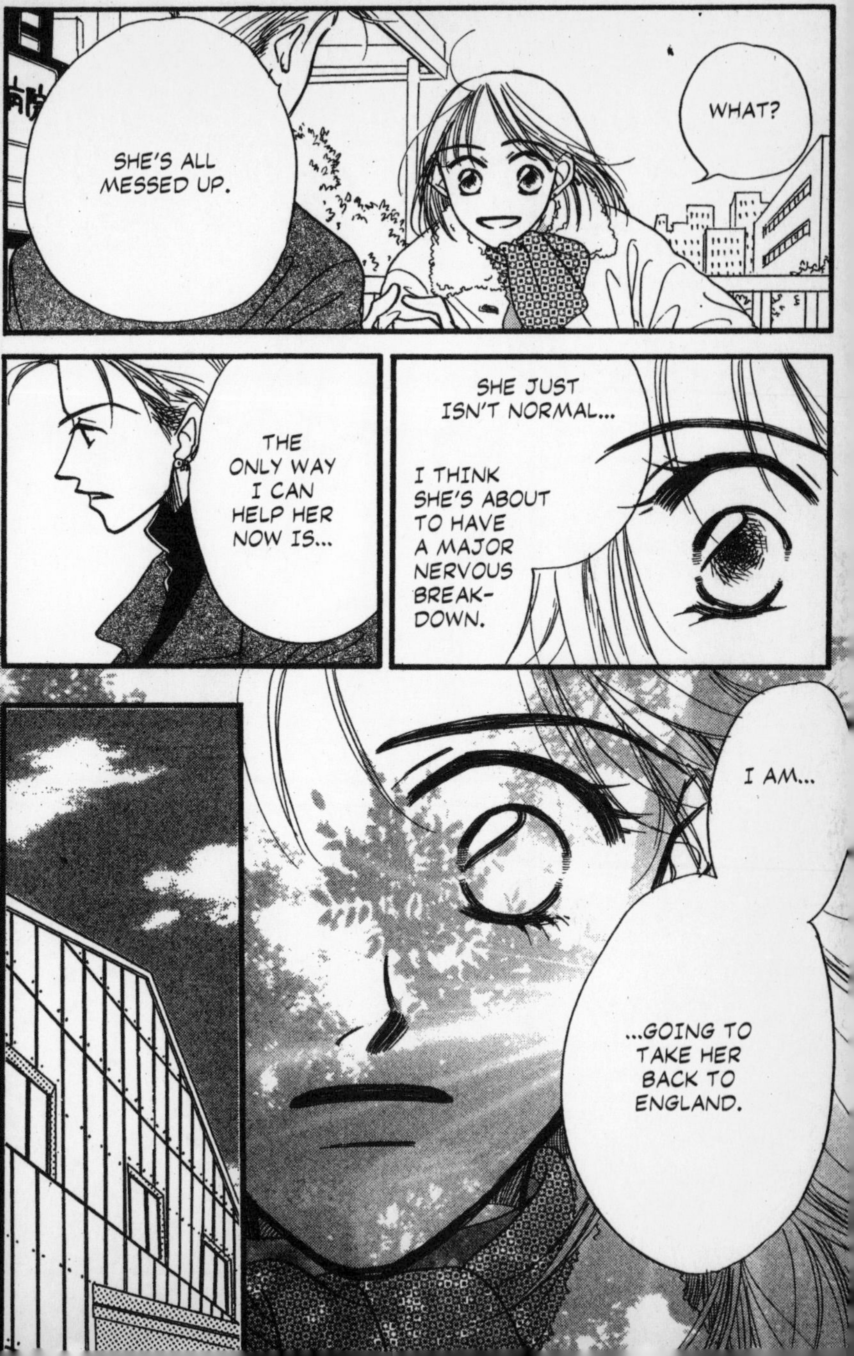
WHAT?
SHE'S ALL MESSED UP.
SHE JUST ISN'T NORMAL...
I THINK SHE'S ABOUT TO HAVE A MAJOR NERVOUS BREAK-DOWN.
THE ONLY WAY I CAN HELP HER NOW IS...
I AM...
...GOING TO TAKE HER BACK TO ENGLAND.

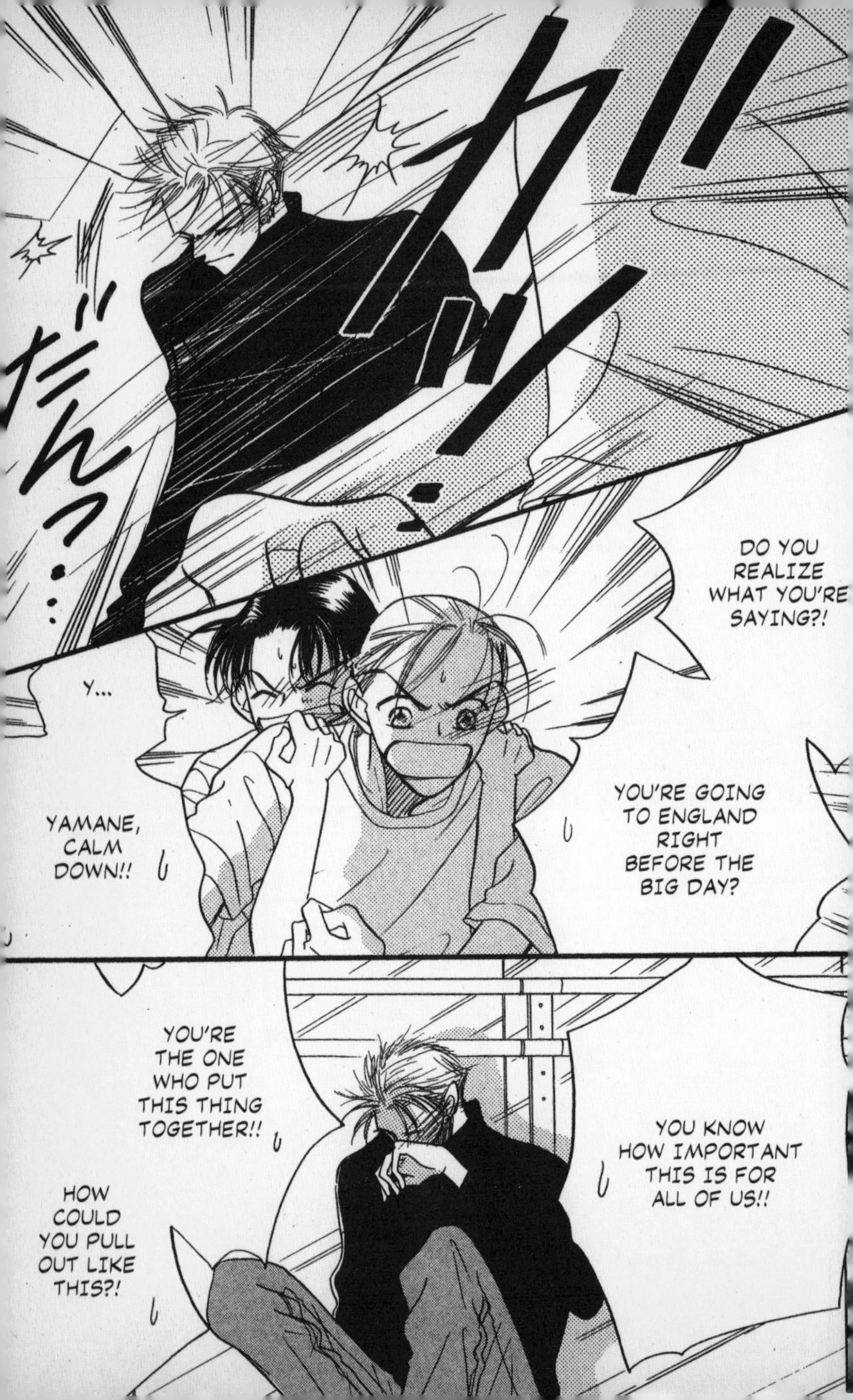
ガッ
だんっ…
DO YOU REALIZE WHAT YOU'RE SAYING?!
YOU'RE GOING TO ENGLAND RIGHT BEFORE THE BIG DAY?
Y...
YAMANE, CALM DOWN!!
YOU KNOW HOW IMPORTANT THIS IS FOR ALL OF US!!
YOU'RE THE ONE WHO PUT THIS THING TOGETHER!!
HOW COULD YOU PULL OUT LIKE THIS?!

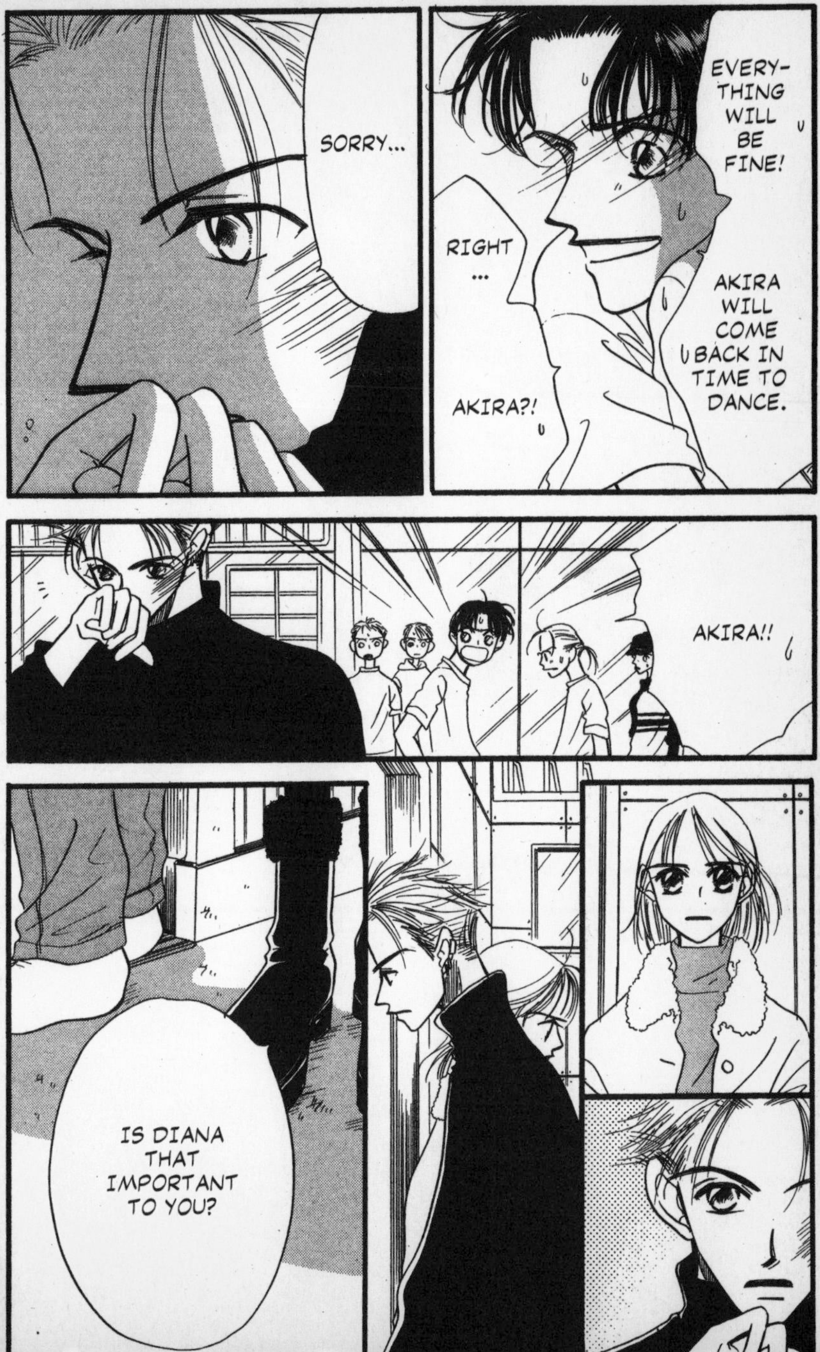
EVERY-THING WILL BE FINE!
AKIRA WILL COME BACK IN TIME TO DANCE.
RIGHT ...
AKIRA?!
SORRY...
AKIRA!!
IS DIANA THAT IMPORTANT TO YOU?

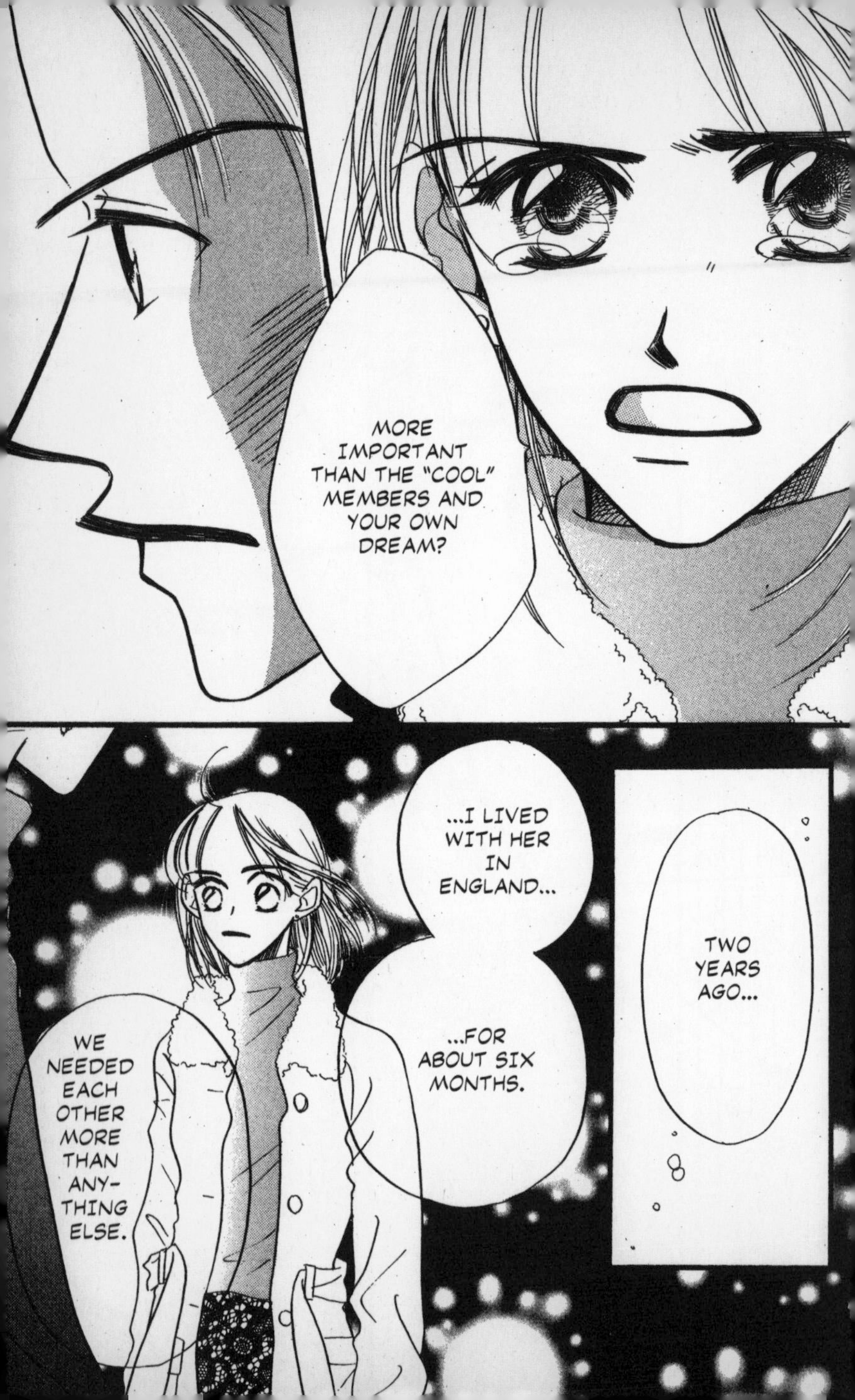
MORE IMPORTANT THAN THE "COOL" MEMBERS AND YOUR OWN DREAM?
TWO YEARS AGO...
...I LIVED WITH HER IN ENGLAND...
...FOR ABOUT SIX MONTHS.
WE NEEDED EACH OTHER MORE THAN ANY-THING ELSE.

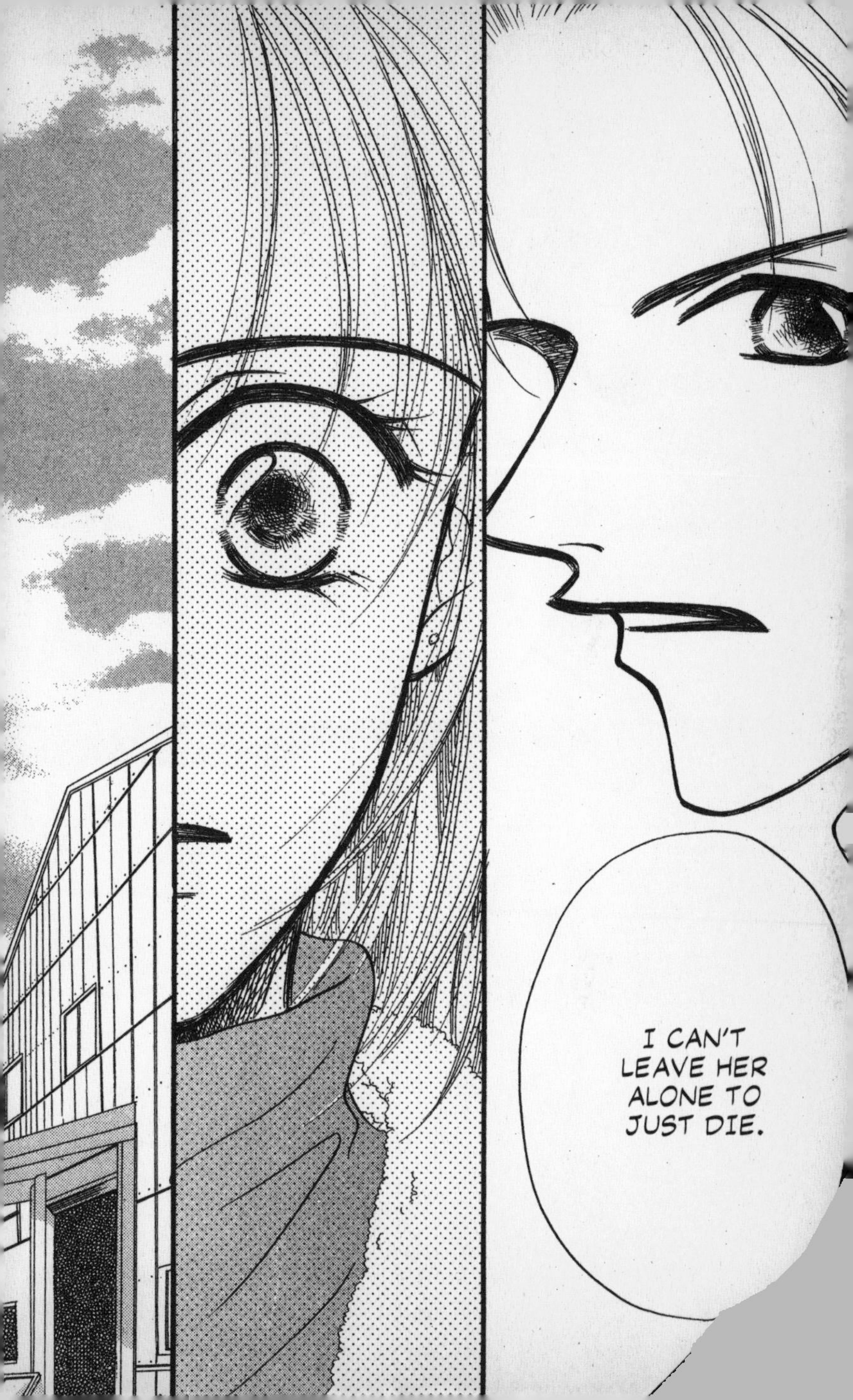
I CAN'T LEAVE HER ALONE TO JUST DIE.

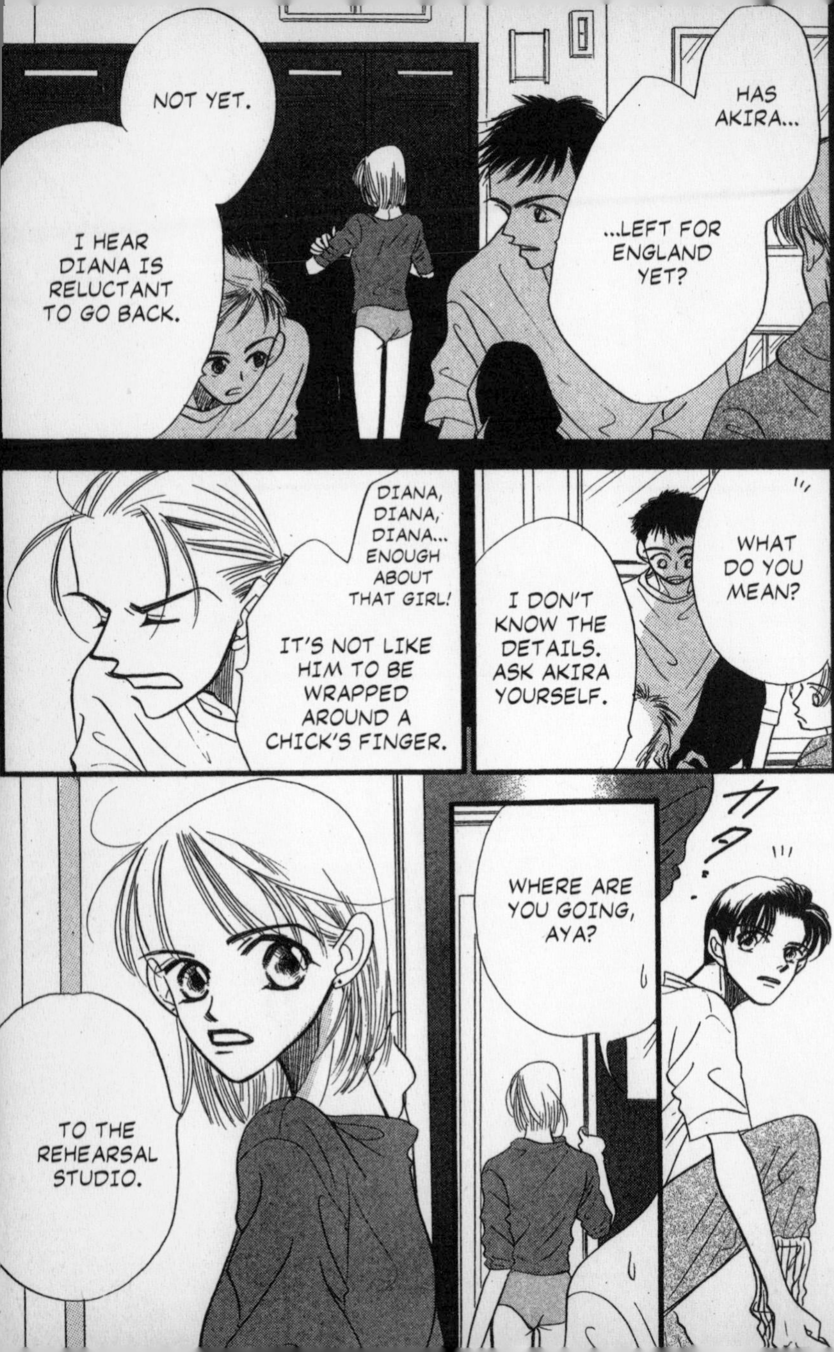
HAS AKIRA...
...LEFT FOR ENGLAND YET?
NOT YET.
I HEAR DIANA IS RELUCTANT TO GO BACK.
WHAT DO YOU MEAN?
I DON'T KNOW THE DETAILS. ASK AKIRA YOURSELF.
DIANA, DIANA, DIANA... ENOUGH ABOUT THAT GIRL!
IT'S NOT LIKE HIM TO BE WRAPPED AROUND A CHICK'S FINGER.
カタ
WHERE ARE YOU GOING, AYA?
TO THE REHEARSAL STUDIO.

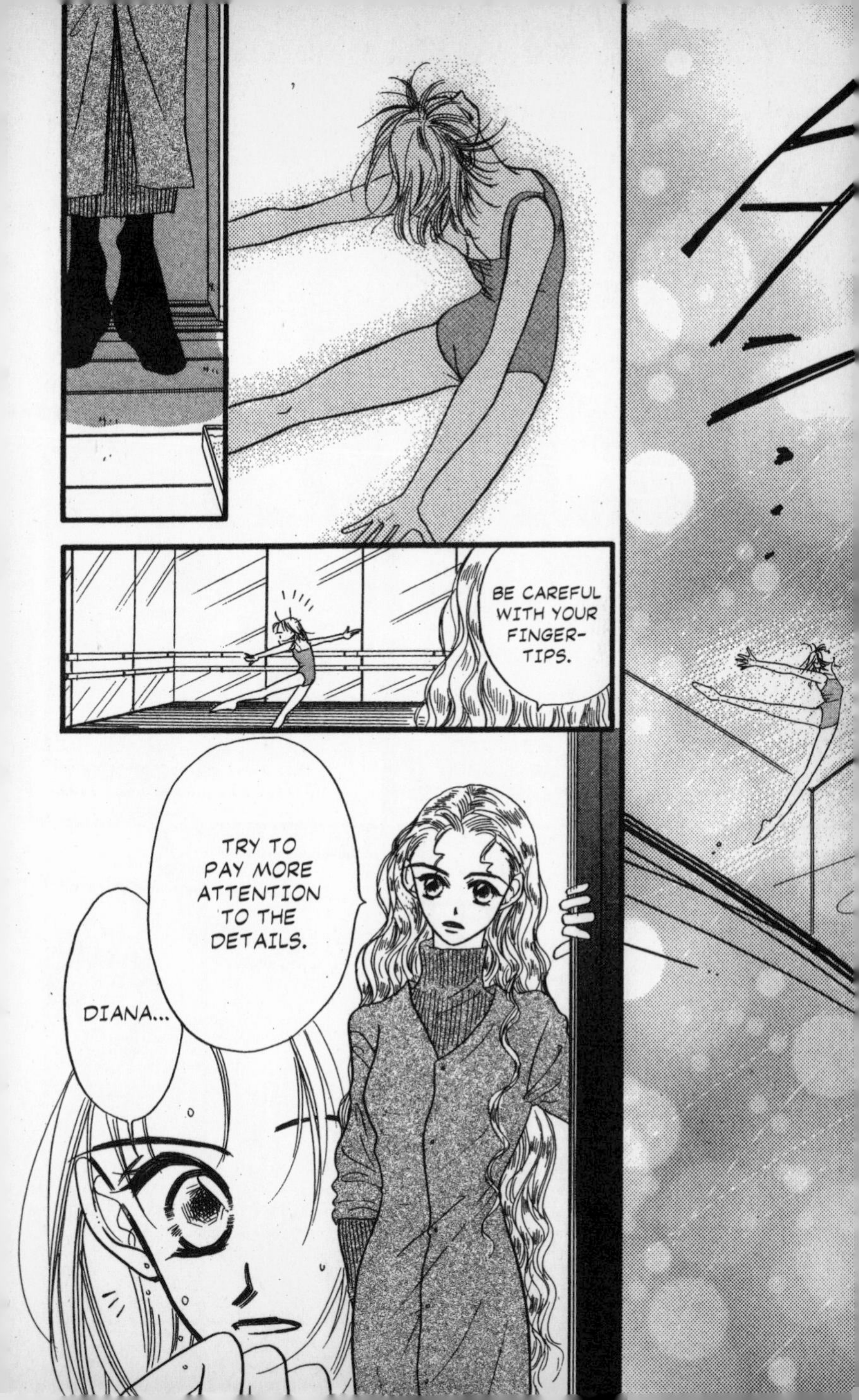
BE CAREFUL WITH YOUR FINGER-TIPS.
TRY TO PAY MORE ATTENTION TO THE DETAILS.
DIANA...

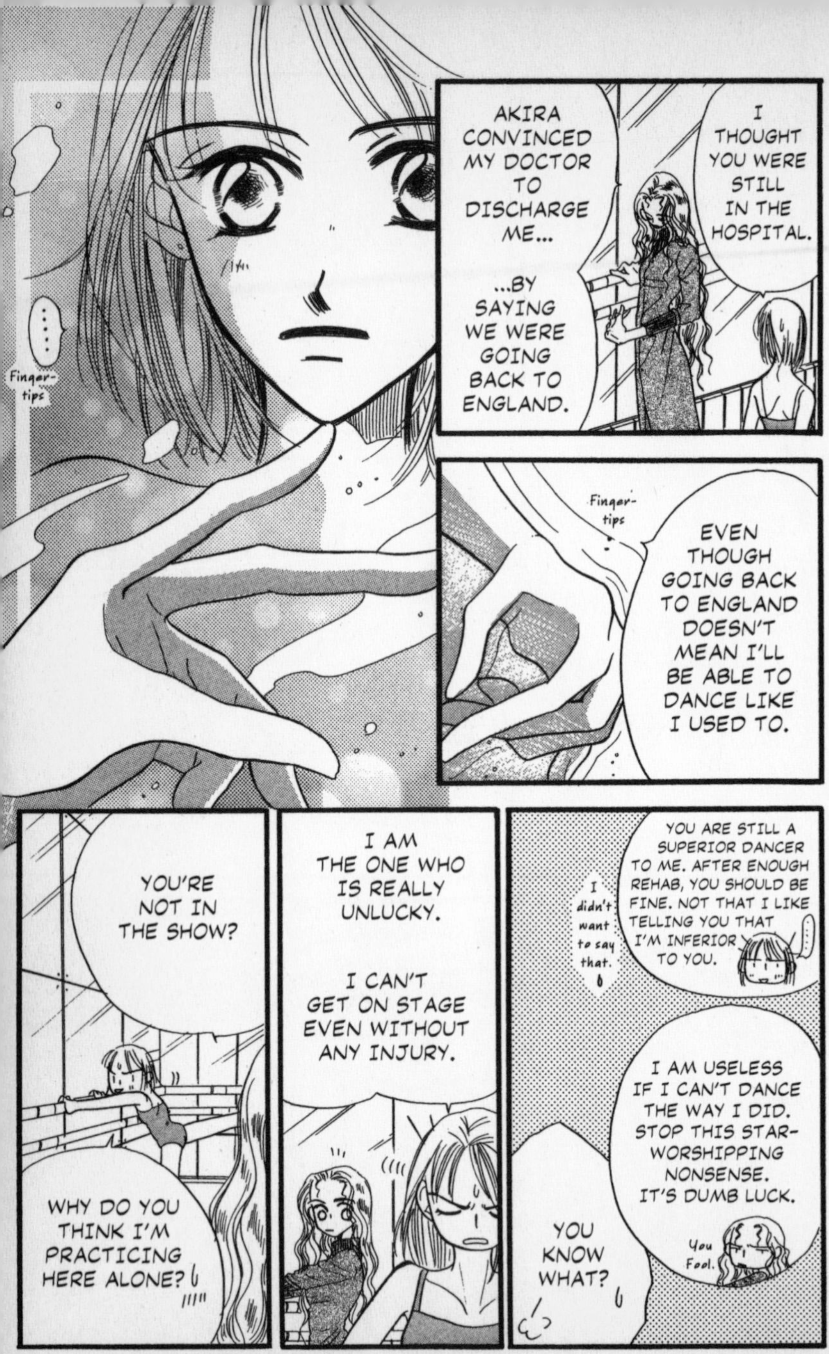

I THOUGHT YOU WERE STILL IN THE HOSPITAL.
AKIRA CONVINCED MY DOCTOR TO DISCHARGE ME...
...BY SAYING WE WERE GOING BACK TO ENGLAND.
Finger-tips
EVEN THOUGH GOING BACK TO ENGLAND DOESN'T MEAN I'LL BE ABLE TO DANCE LIKE I USED TO.
.....
Finger-tips
YOU ARE STILL A SUPERIOR DANCER TO ME. AFTER ENOUGH REHAB, YOU SHOULD BE FINE. NOT THAT I LIKE TELLING YOU THAT I'M INFERIOR TO YOU.
I didn't want to say that.
I AM USELESS IF I CAN'T DANCE THE WAY I DID. STOP THIS STAR-WORSHIPPING NONSENSE. IT'S DUMB LUCK.
You Fool.
YOU KNOW WHAT?
I AM THE ONE WHO IS REALLY UNLUCKY.
I CAN'T GET ON STAGE EVEN WITHOUT ANY INJURY.
YOU'RE NOT IN THE SHOW?
WHY DO YOU THINK I'M PRACTICING HERE ALONE?

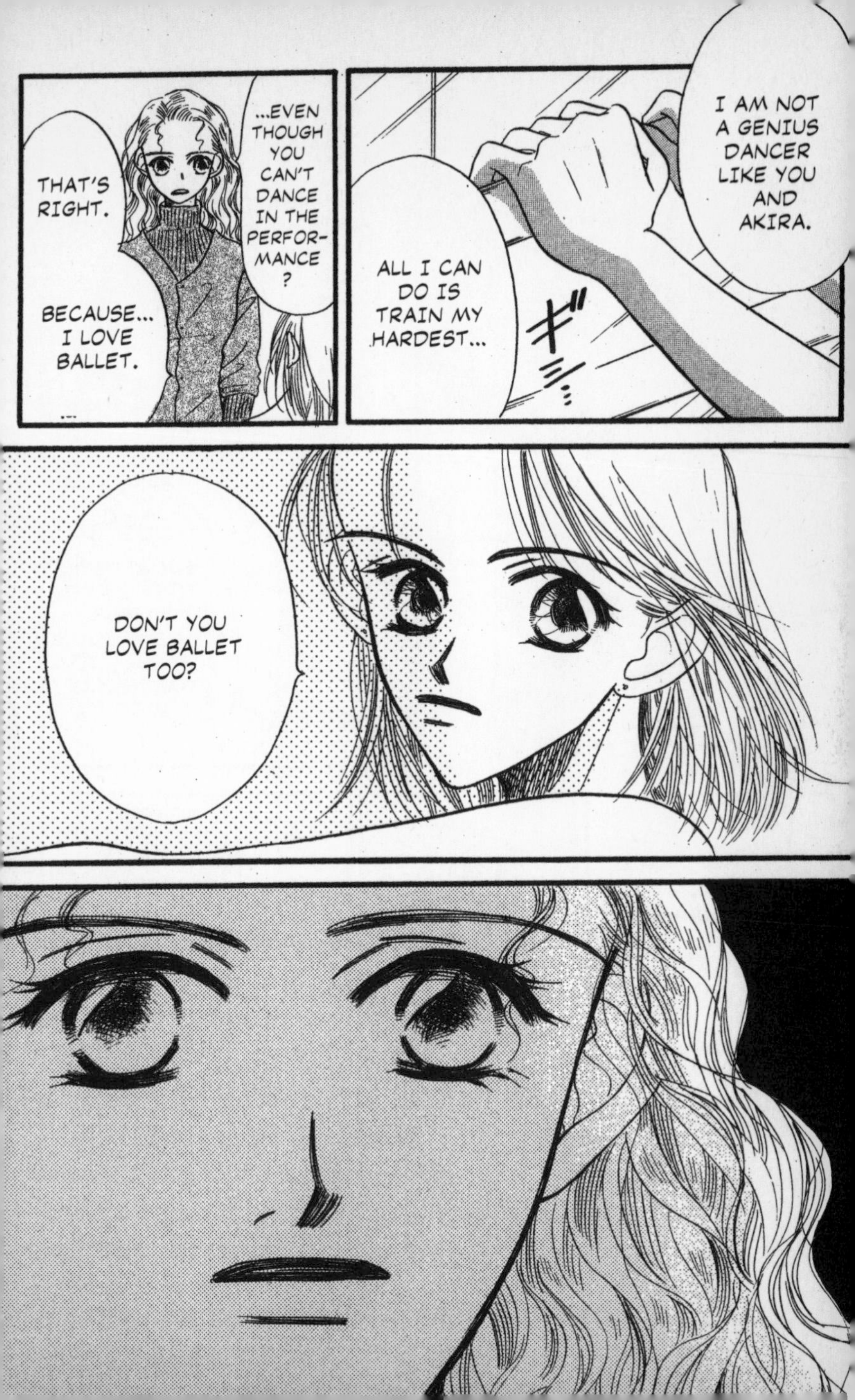
I AM NOT A GENIUS DANCER LIKE YOU AND AKIRA.
ALL I CAN DO IS TRAIN MY HARDEST...
...EVEN THOUGH YOU CAN'T DANCE IN THE PERFORMANCE?
THAT'S RIGHT.
BECAUSE... I LOVE BALLET.
DON'T YOU LOVE BALLET TOO?

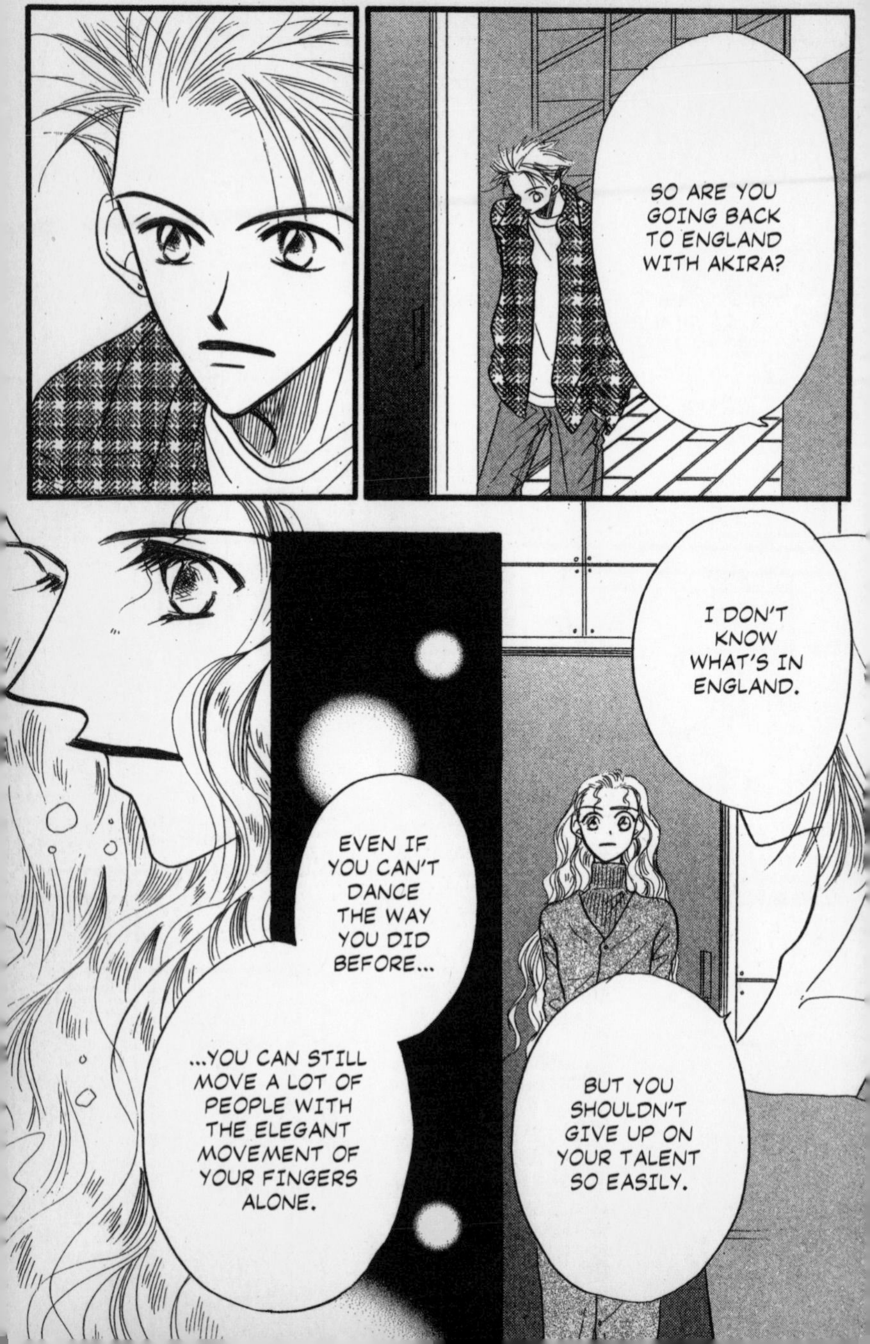
SO ARE YOU GOING BACK TO ENGLAND WITH AKIRA?
I DON'T KNOW WHAT'S IN ENGLAND.
BUT YOU SHOULDN'T GIVE UP ON YOUR TALENT SO EASILY.
EVEN IF YOU CAN'T DANCE THE WAY YOU DID BEFORE...
...YOU CAN STILL MOVE A LOT OF PEOPLE WITH THE ELEGANT MOVEMENT OF YOUR FINGERS ALONE.

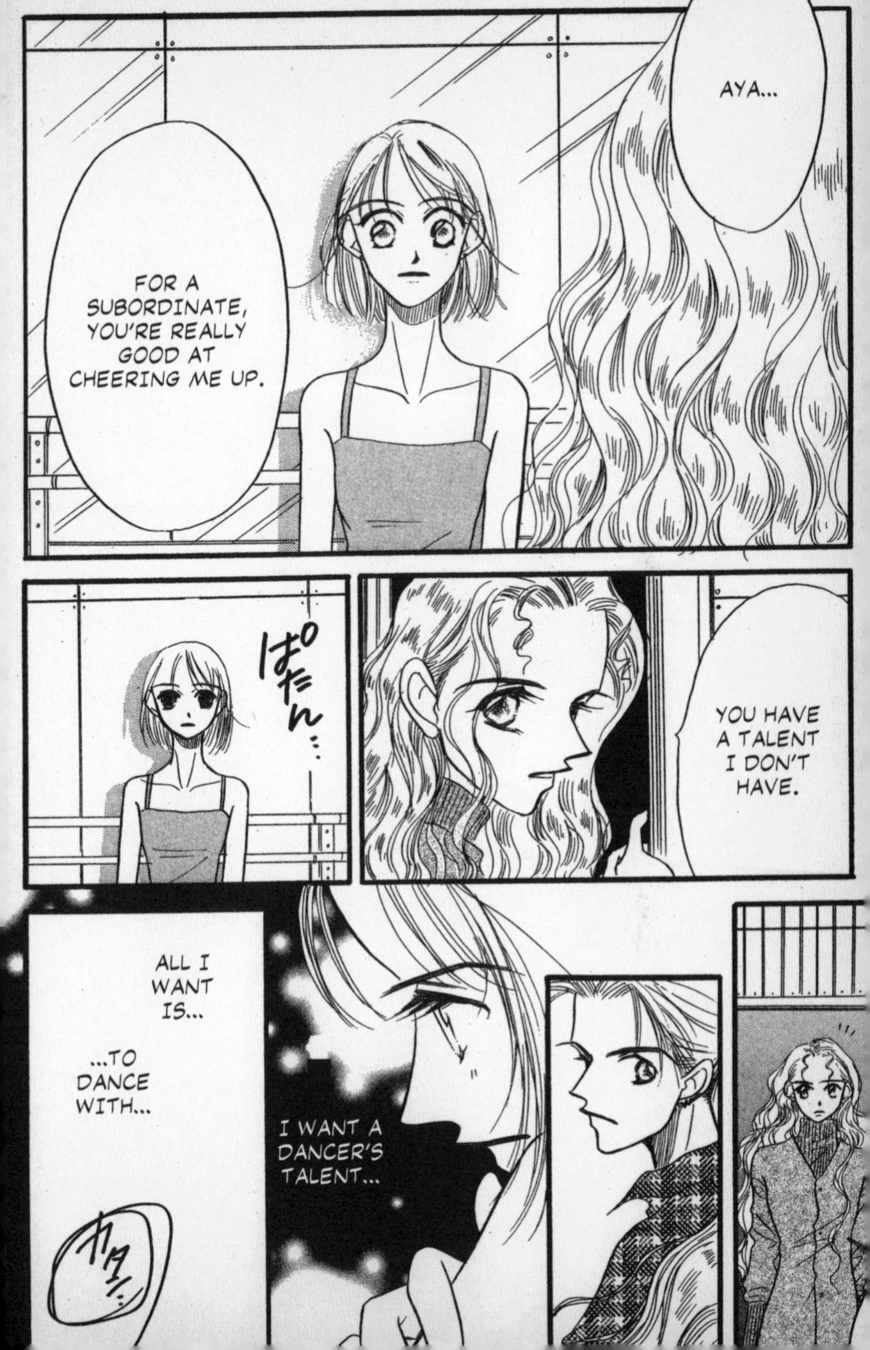
AYA...
FOR A SUBORDINATE, YOU'RE REALLY GOOD AT CHEERING ME UP.
YOU HAVE A TALENT I DON'T HAVE.
ぱたん...
I WANT A DANCER'S TALENT...
ALL I WANT IS...
...TO DANCE WITH...
カタン...

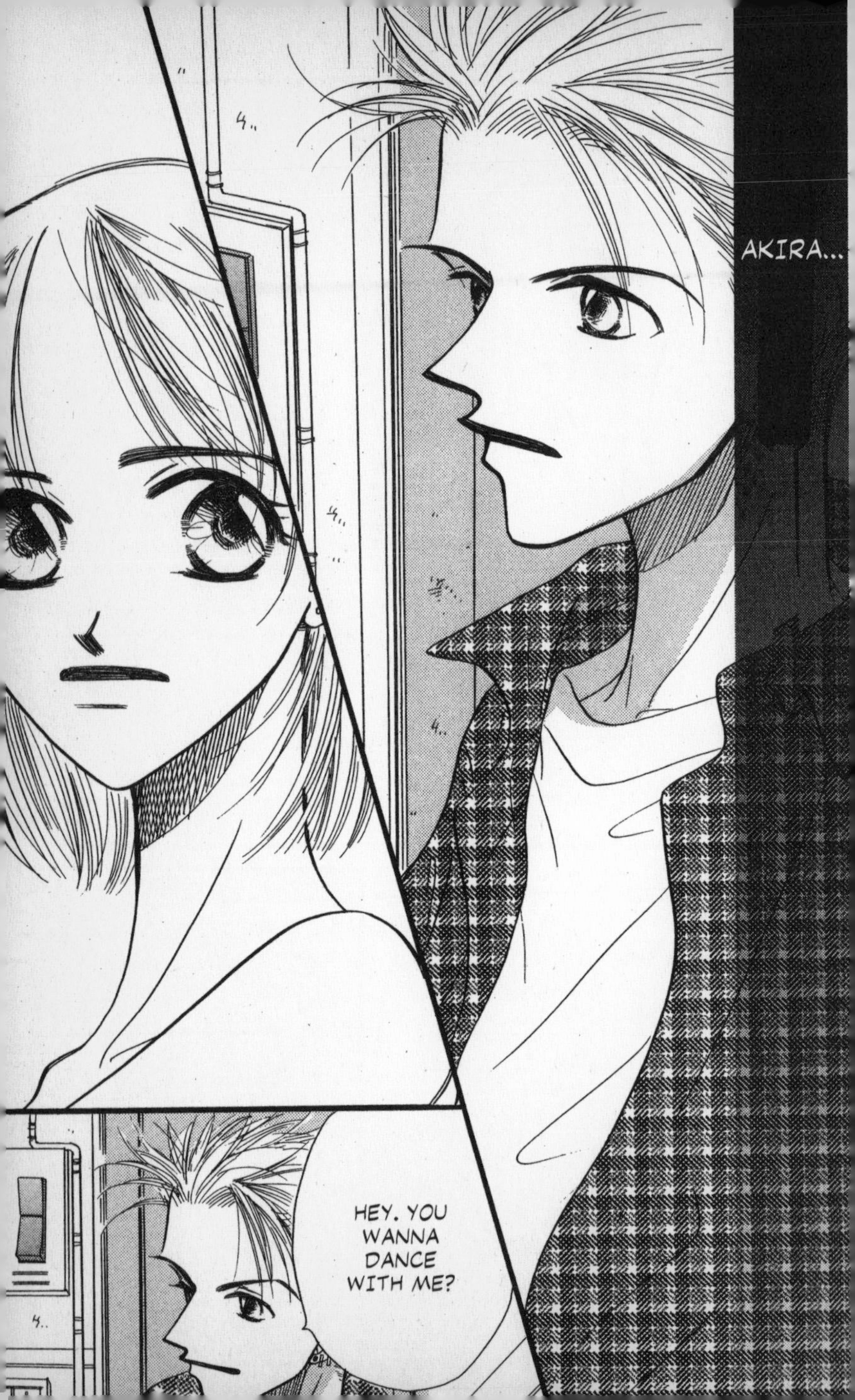
AKIRA...
HEY. YOU WANNA DANCE WITH ME?

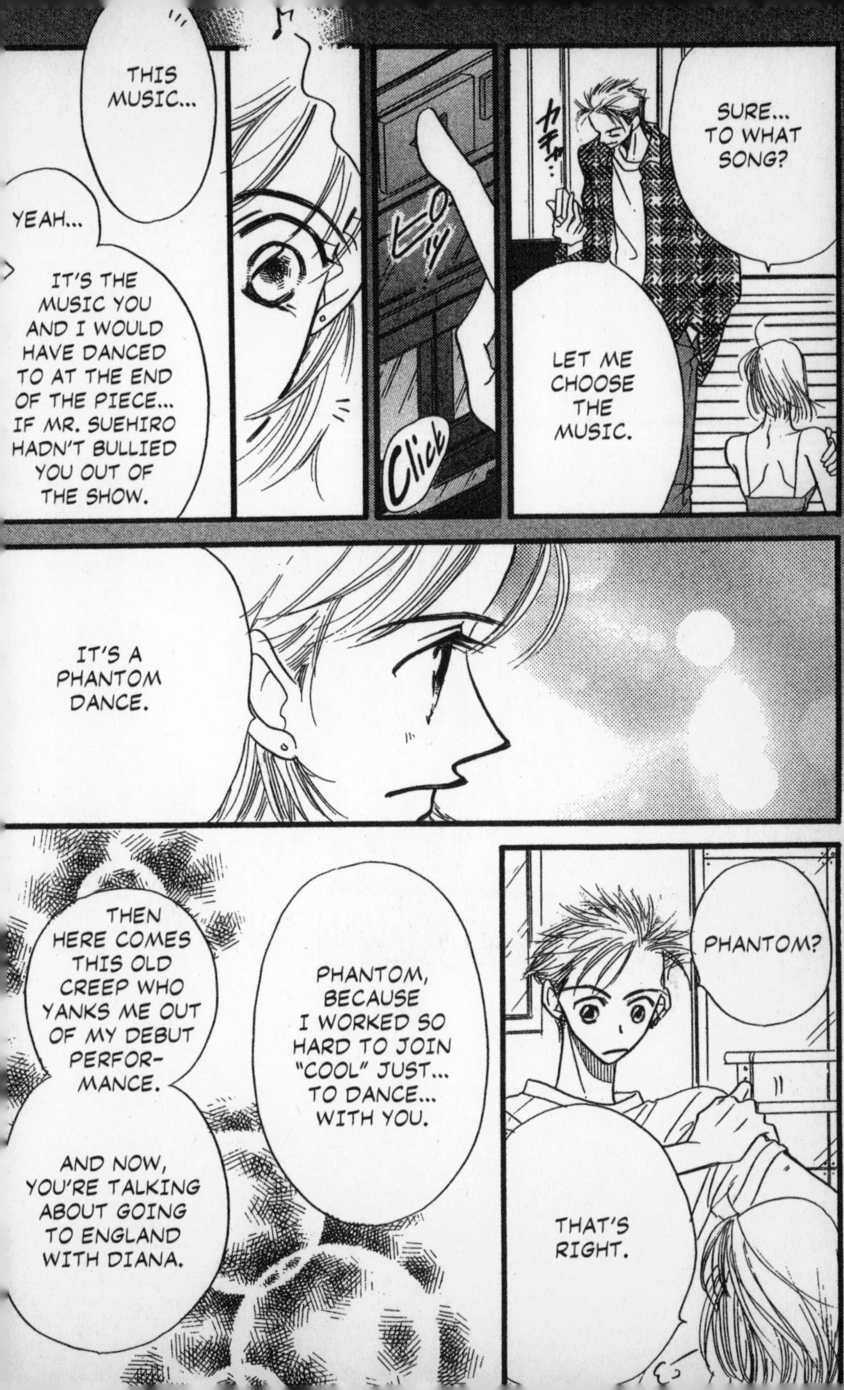
SURE... TO WHAT SONG?
カチャ…
LET ME CHOOSE THE MUSIC.
Click
THIS MUSIC...
YEAH...
IT'S THE MUSIC YOU AND I WOULD HAVE DANCED TO AT THE END OF THE PIECE... IF MR. SUEHIRO HADN'T BULLIED YOU OUT OF THE SHOW.
IT'S A PHANTOM DANCE.
PHANTOM?
THAT'S RIGHT.
PHANTOM, BECAUSE I WORKED SO HARD TO JOIN "COOL" JUST... TO DANCE... WITH YOU.
THEN HERE COMES THIS OLD CREEP WHO YANKS ME OUT OF MY DEBUT PERFORMANCE.
AND NOW, YOU'RE TALKING ABOUT GOING TO ENGLAND WITH DIANA.

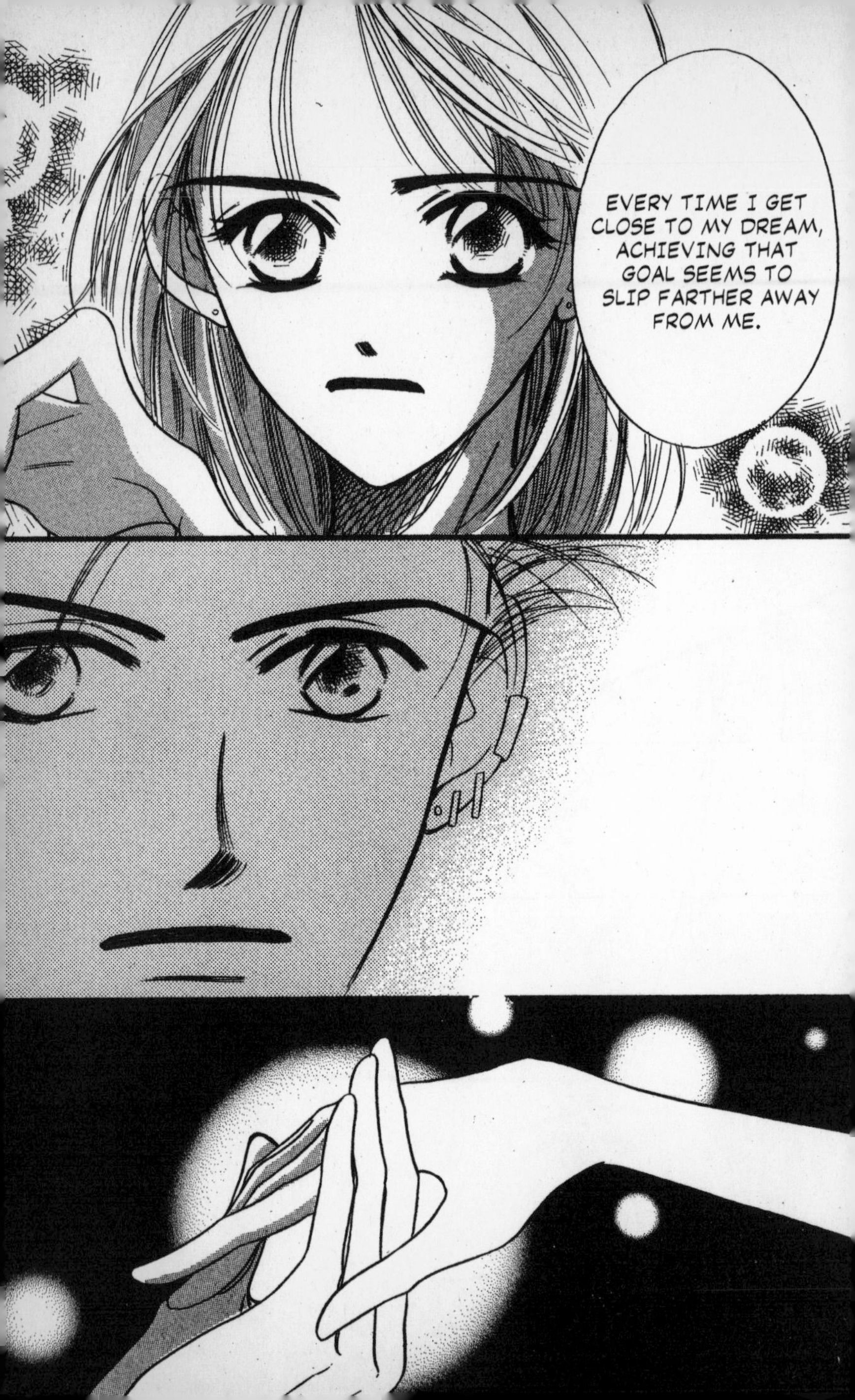
EVERY TIME I GET CLOSE TO MY DREAM, ACHIEVING THAT GOAL SEEMS TO SLIP FARTHER AWAY FROM ME.

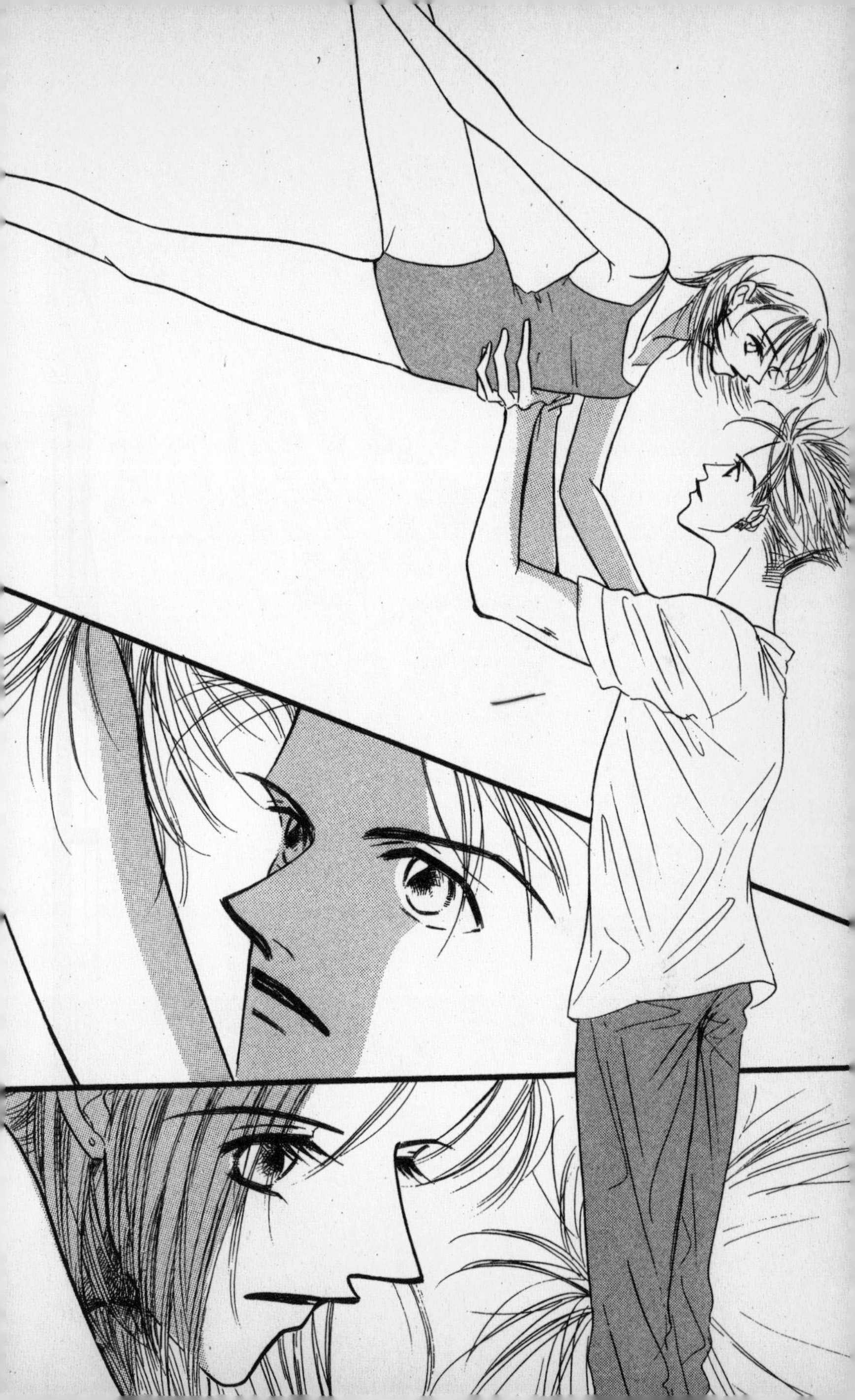

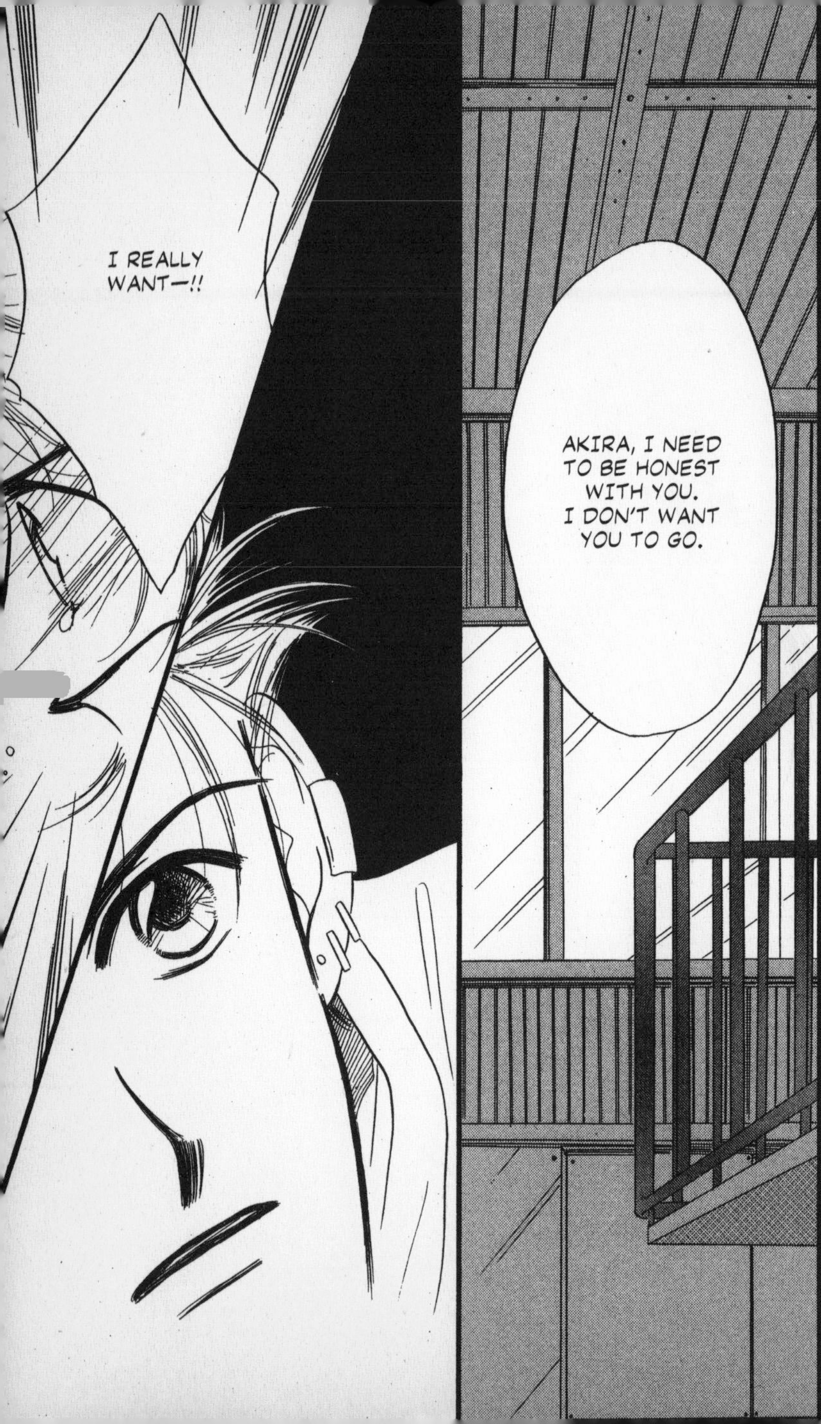
AKIRA, I NEED TO BE HONEST WITH YOU. I DON'T WANT YOU TO GO.
I REALLY WANT—!!

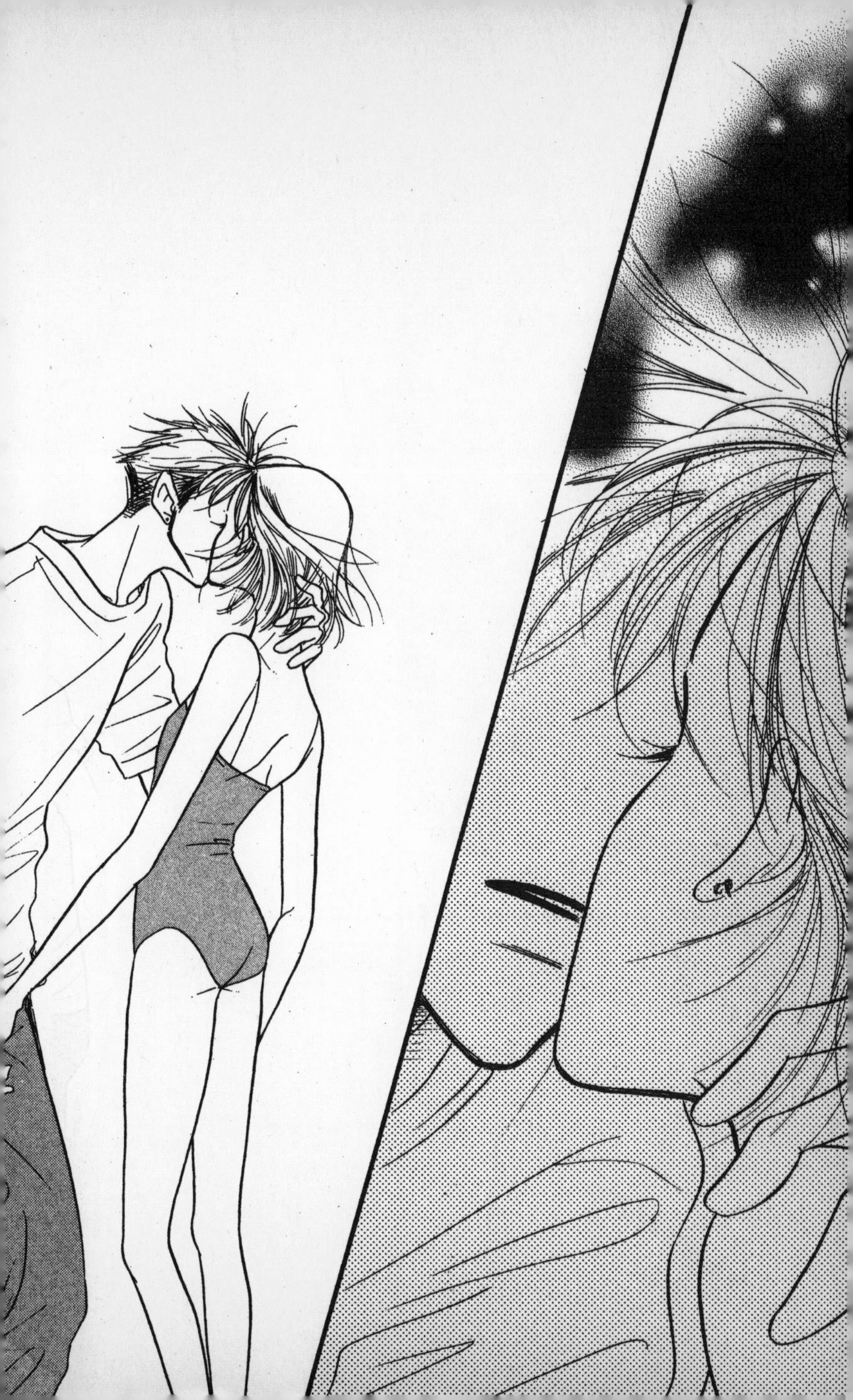

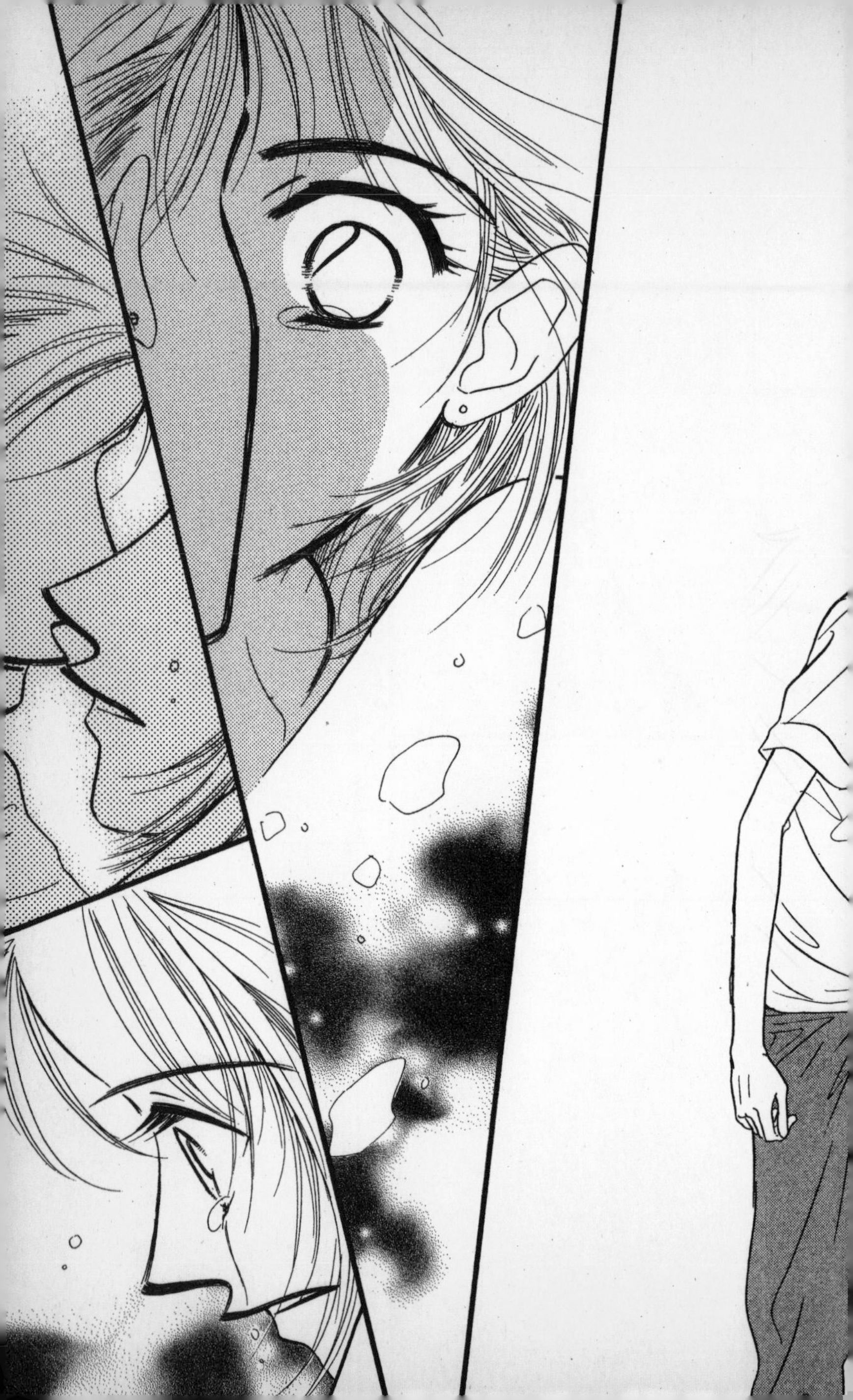

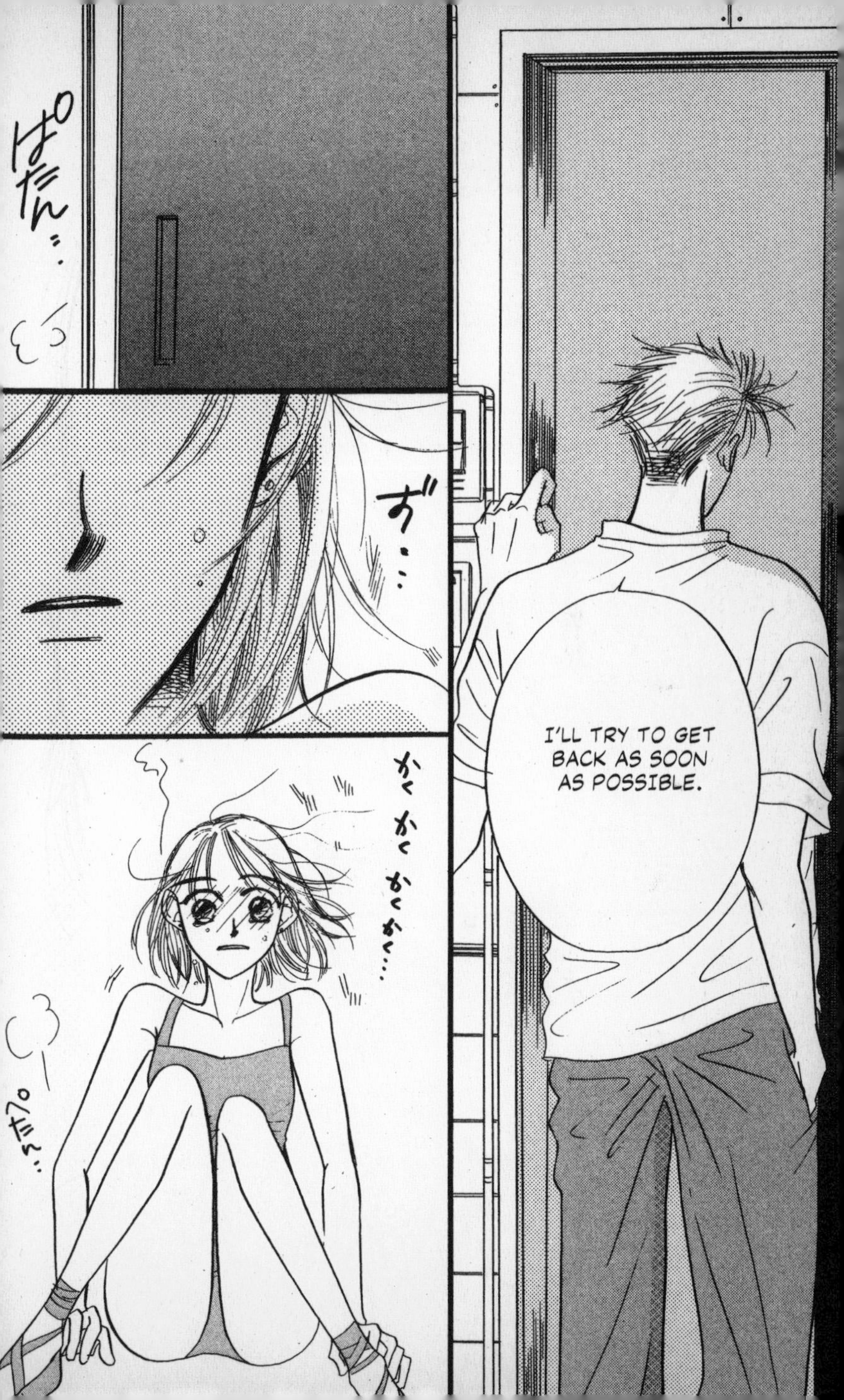
I'LL TRY TO GET BACK AS SOON AS POSSIBLE.
ぱたん…
かく かく かく かく…

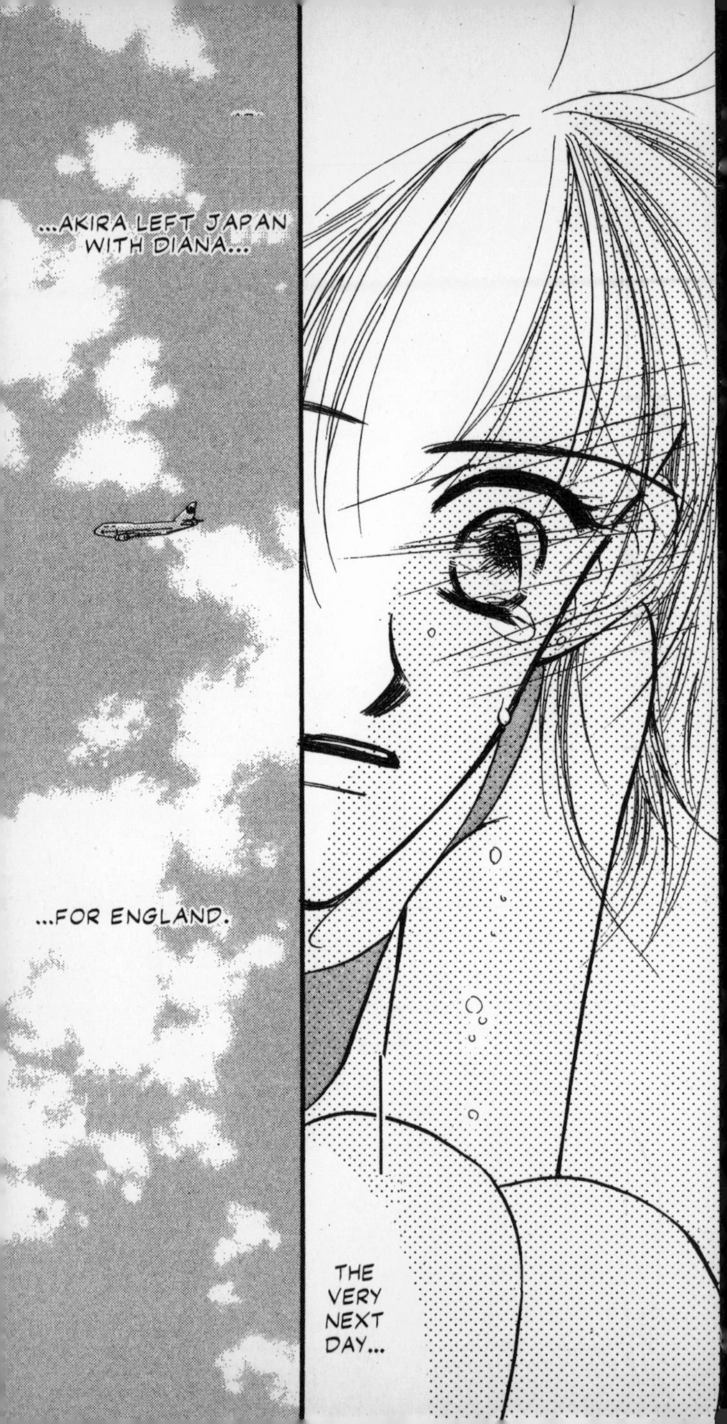
THE VERY NEXT DAY...
...AKIRA LEFT JAPAN WITH DIANA...
...FOR ENGLAND.

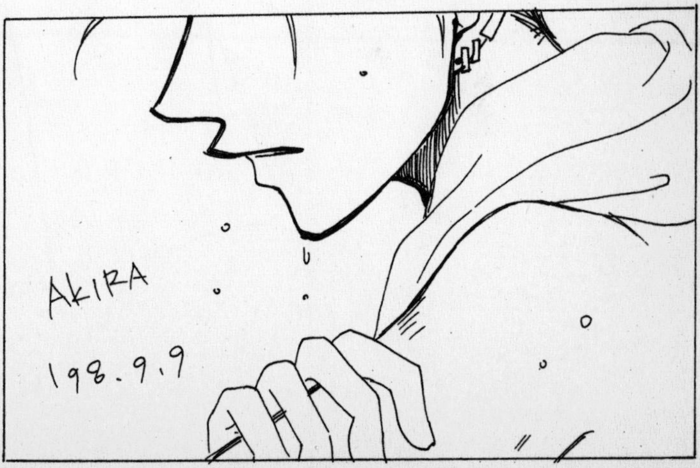
AKIRA
198.9.9

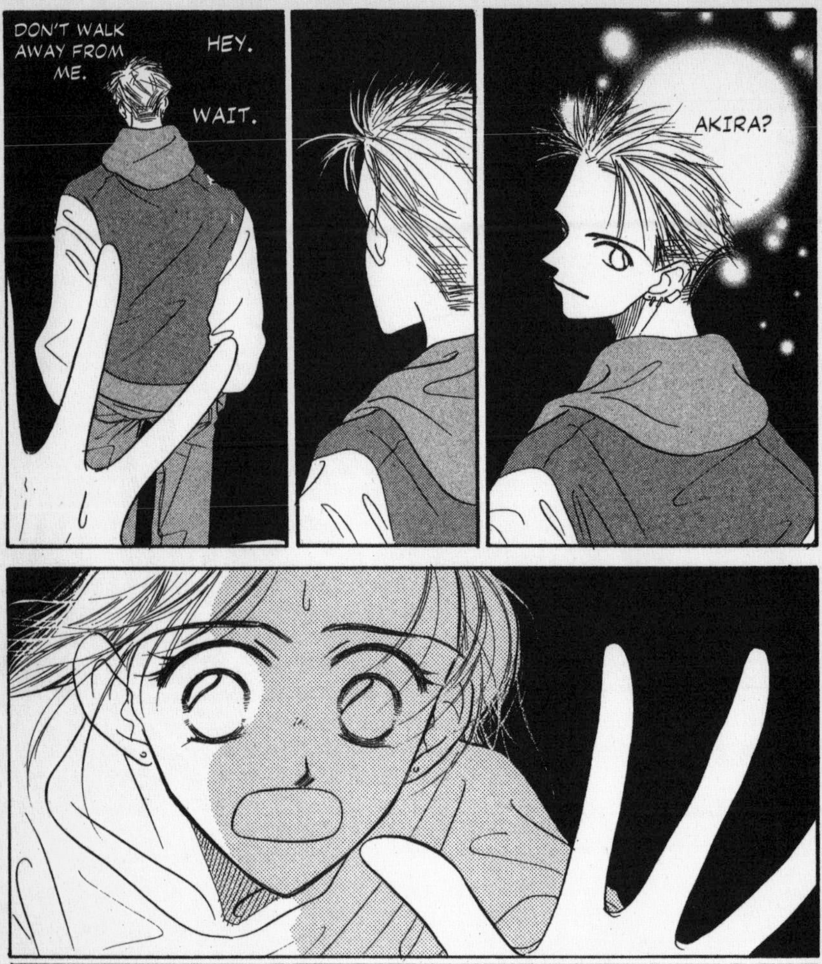
AKIRA?
HEY.
WAIT.
DON'T WALK AWAY FROM ME.

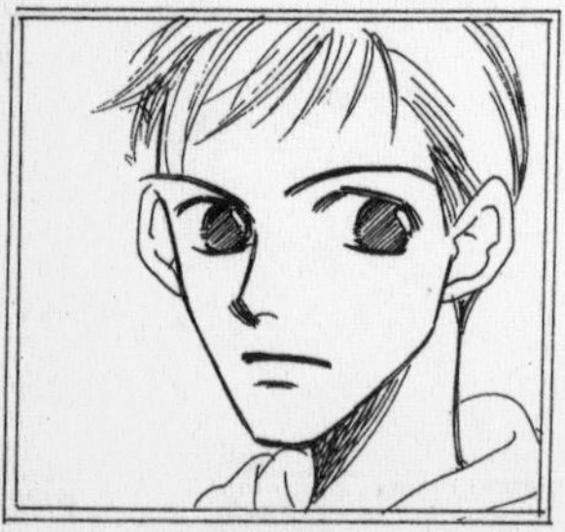

Ashihara's Diary

-◆- "Cool" member No.1 -◆- Age approximately 19

He is a troublesome member who often fights with Yamane. If you take some time to look for him, you can see that he makes a frequent appearance in the series. Why? Because his hairdo is easy to draw... A friend of mine noticed he has the same hair style as Sahara, the boy in "Princess Line." Oh well.

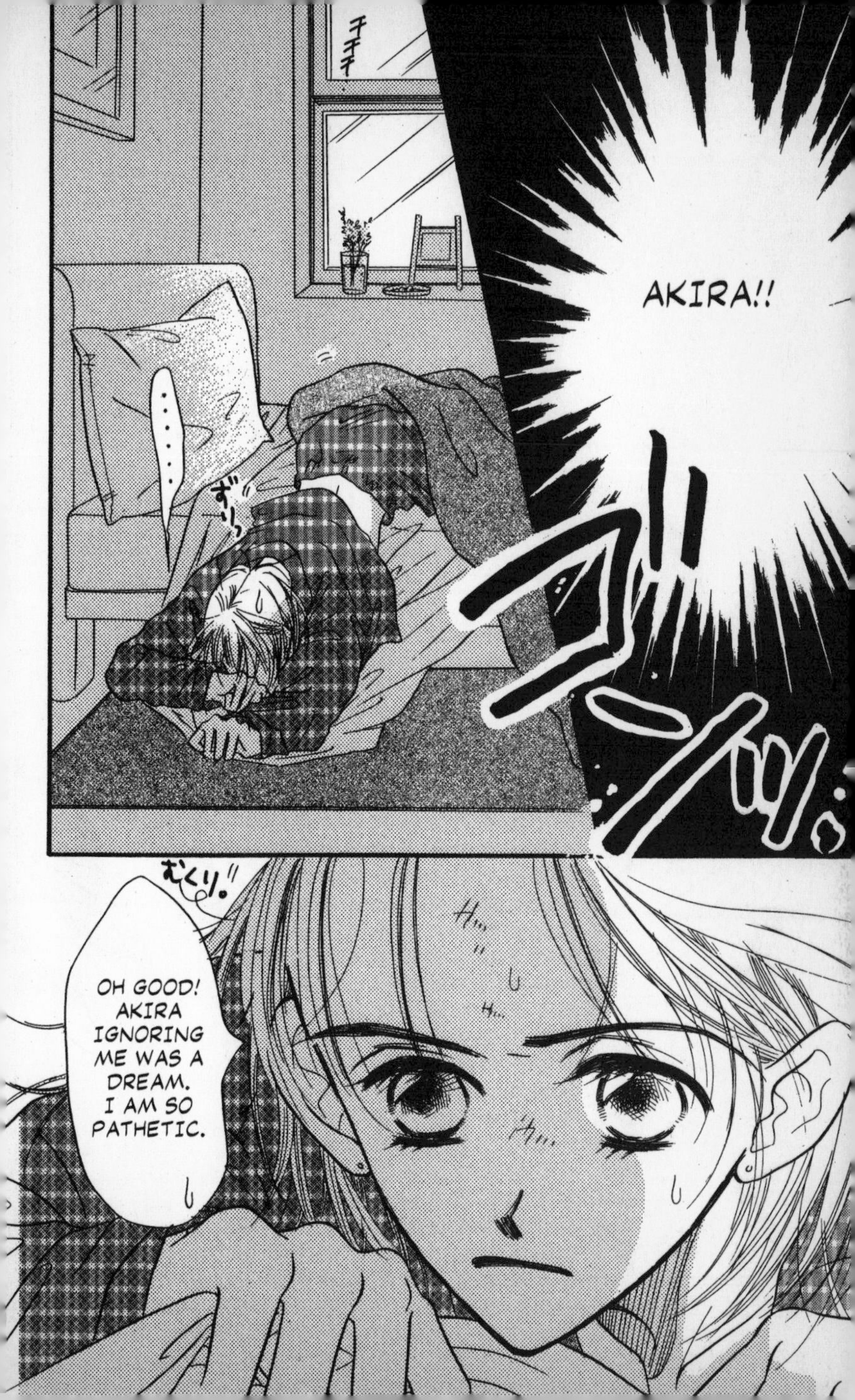
AKIRA!!
チチチ
......
ずりっ
むくり。
OH GOOD! AKIRA IGNORING ME WAS A DREAM. I AM SO PATHETIC.

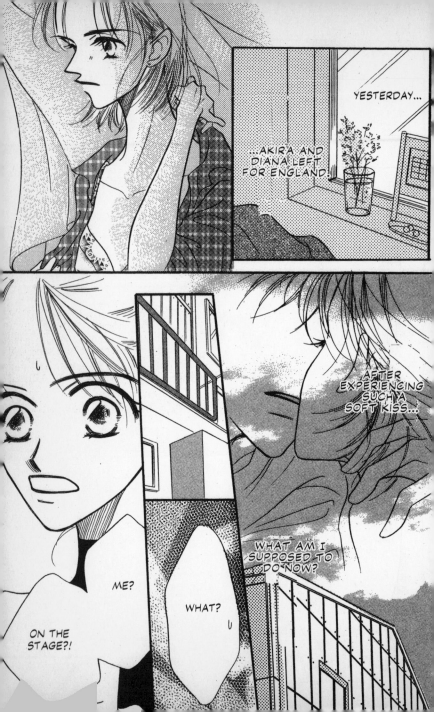

YESTERDAY...

...AKIRA AND DIANA LEFT FOR ENGLAND.

AFTER EXPERIENCING SUCH A SOFT KISS...

WHAT AM I SUPPOSED TO DO NOW?

ME?

WHAT?

ON THE STAGE?!

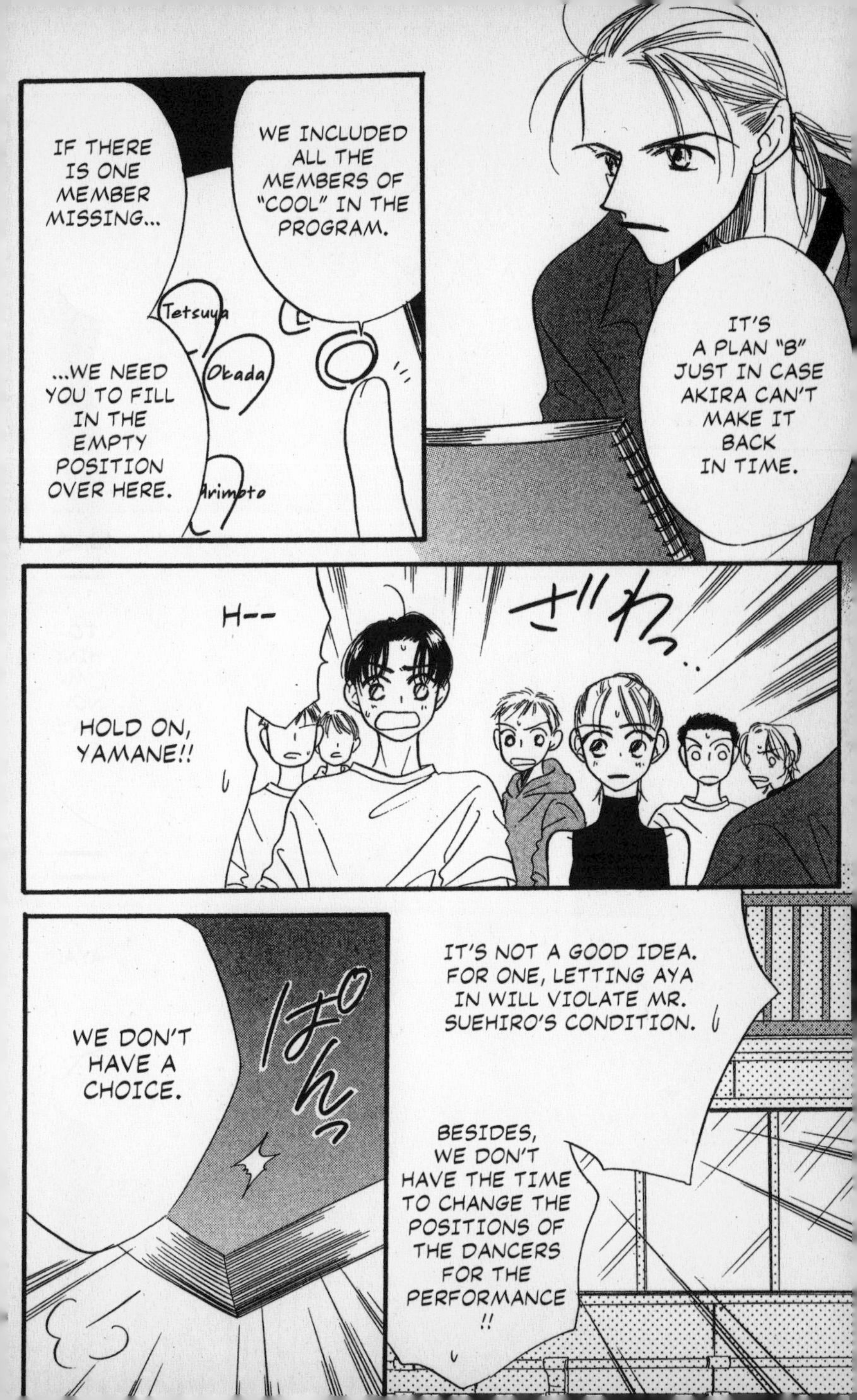
IT'S A PLAN "B" JUST IN CASE AKIRA CAN'T MAKE IT BACK IN TIME.
WE INCLUDED ALL THE MEMBERS OF "COOL" IN THE PROGRAM.
IF THERE IS ONE MEMBER MISSING...
Tetsuya
Okada
Arimoto
...WE NEED YOU TO FILL IN THE EMPTY POSITION OVER HERE.
ざわっ…
H--
HOLD ON, YAMANE!!
IT'S NOT A GOOD IDEA. FOR ONE, LETTING AYA IN WILL VIOLATE MR. SUEHIRO'S CONDITION.
BESIDES, WE DON'T HAVE THE TIME TO CHANGE THE POSITIONS OF THE DANCERS FOR THE PERFORMANCE!!
ぱんっ
WE DON'T HAVE A CHOICE.

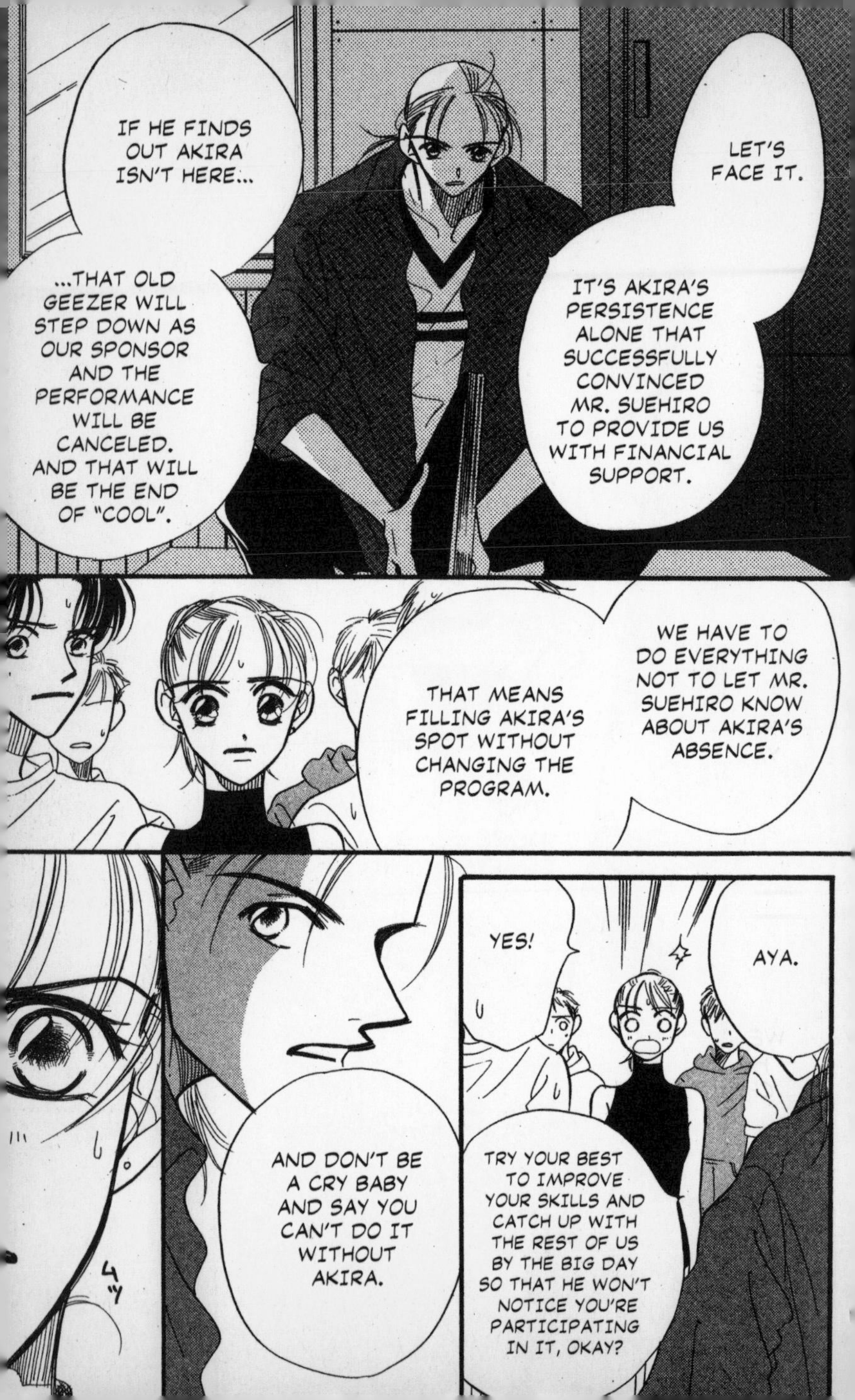
LET'S FACE IT.
IT'S AKIRA'S PERSISTENCE ALONE THAT SUCCESSFULLY CONVINCED MR. SUEHIRO TO PROVIDE US WITH FINANCIAL SUPPORT.
IF HE FINDS OUT AKIRA ISN'T HERE...
...THAT OLD GEEZER WILL STEP DOWN AS OUR SPONSOR AND THE PERFORMANCE WILL BE CANCELED. AND THAT WILL BE THE END OF "COOL".
WE HAVE TO DO EVERYTHING NOT TO LET MR. SUEHIRO KNOW ABOUT AKIRA'S ABSENCE.
THAT MEANS FILLING AKIRA'S SPOT WITHOUT CHANGING THE PROGRAM.
AYA.
YES!
TRY YOUR BEST TO IMPROVE YOUR SKILLS AND CATCH UP WITH THE REST OF US BY THE BIG DAY SO THAT HE WON'T NOTICE YOU'RE PARTICIPATING IN IT, OKAY?
AND DON'T BE A CRY BABY AND SAY YOU CAN'T DO IT WITHOUT AKIRA.
ムッ

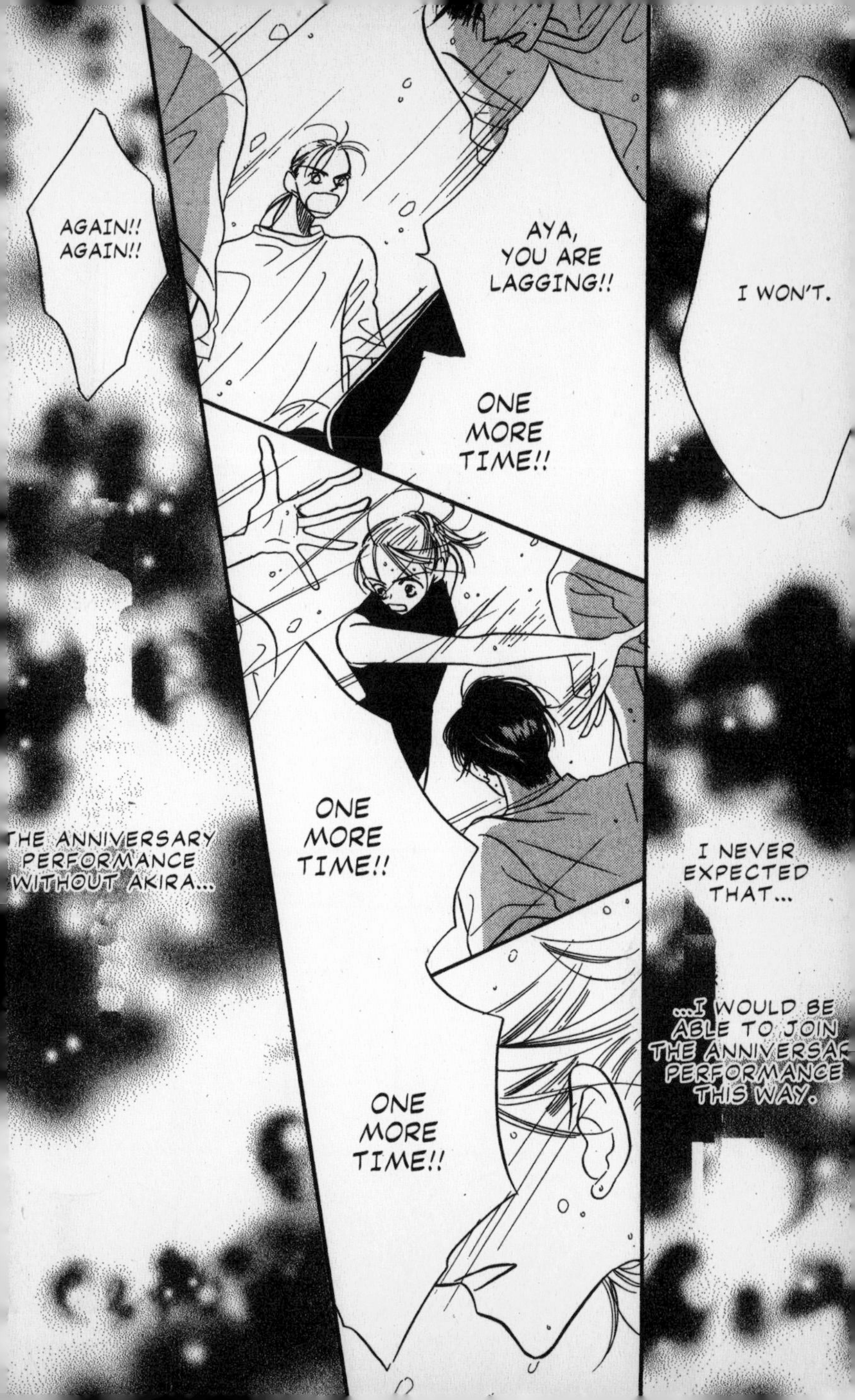
I WON'T.
I NEVER EXPECTED THAT...
...I WOULD BE ABLE TO JOIN THE ANNIVERSARY PERFORMANCE THIS WAY.
AYA, YOU ARE LAGGING!!
ONE MORE TIME!!
ONE MORE TIME!!
ONE MORE TIME!!
AGAIN!! AGAIN!!
THE ANNIVERSARY PERFORMANCE WITHOUT AKIRA...

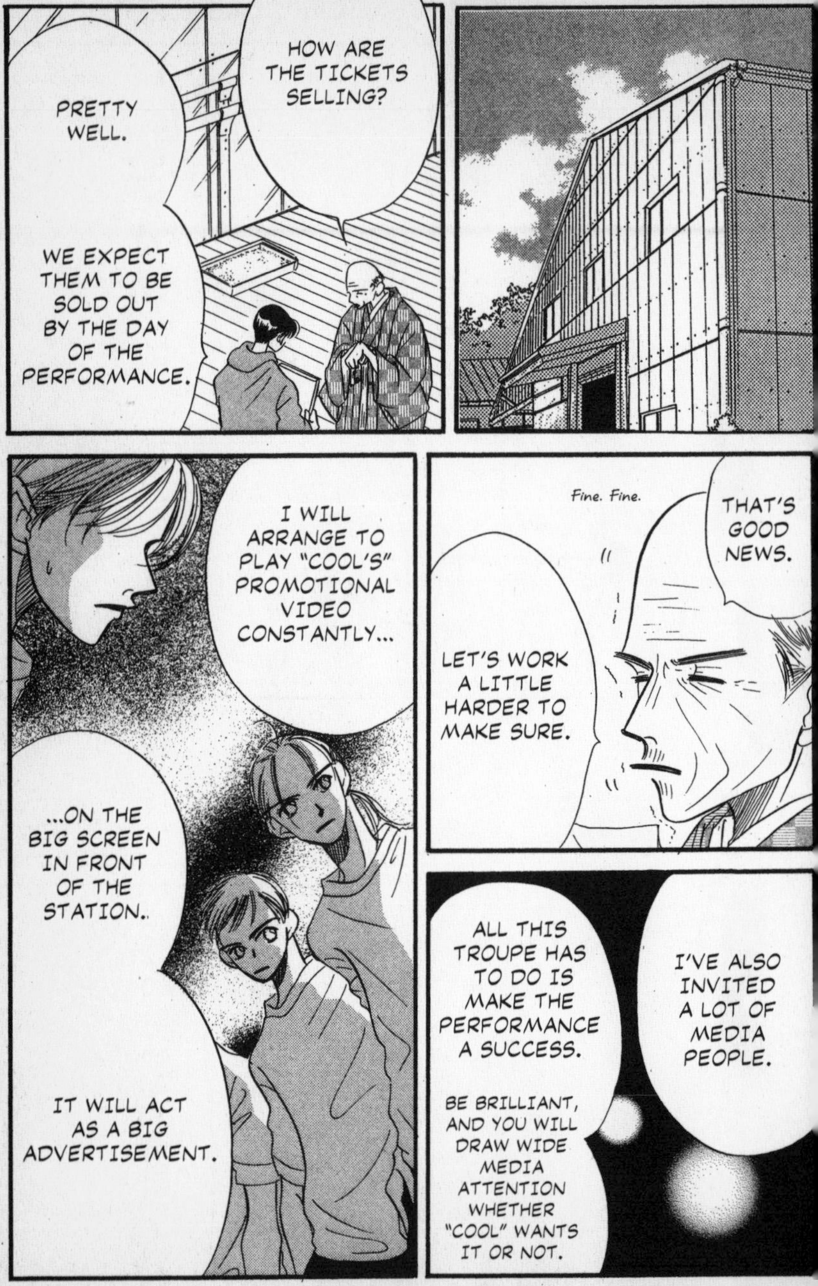
HOW ARE THE TICKETS SELLING?
PRETTY WELL.
WE EXPECT THEM TO BE SOLD OUT BY THE DAY OF THE PERFORMANCE.
Fine. Fine.
THAT'S GOOD NEWS.
LET'S WORK A LITTLE HARDER TO MAKE SURE.
I'VE ALSO INVITED A LOT OF MEDIA PEOPLE.
ALL THIS TROUPE HAS TO DO IS MAKE THE PERFORMANCE A SUCCESS.
BE BRILLIANT, AND YOU WILL DRAW WIDE MEDIA ATTENTION WHETHER "COOL" WANTS IT OR NOT.
I WILL ARRANGE TO PLAY "COOL'S" PROMOTIONAL VIDEO CONSTANTLY...
...ON THE BIG SCREEN IN FRONT OF THE STATION..
IT WILL ACT AS A BIG ADVERTISEMENT.

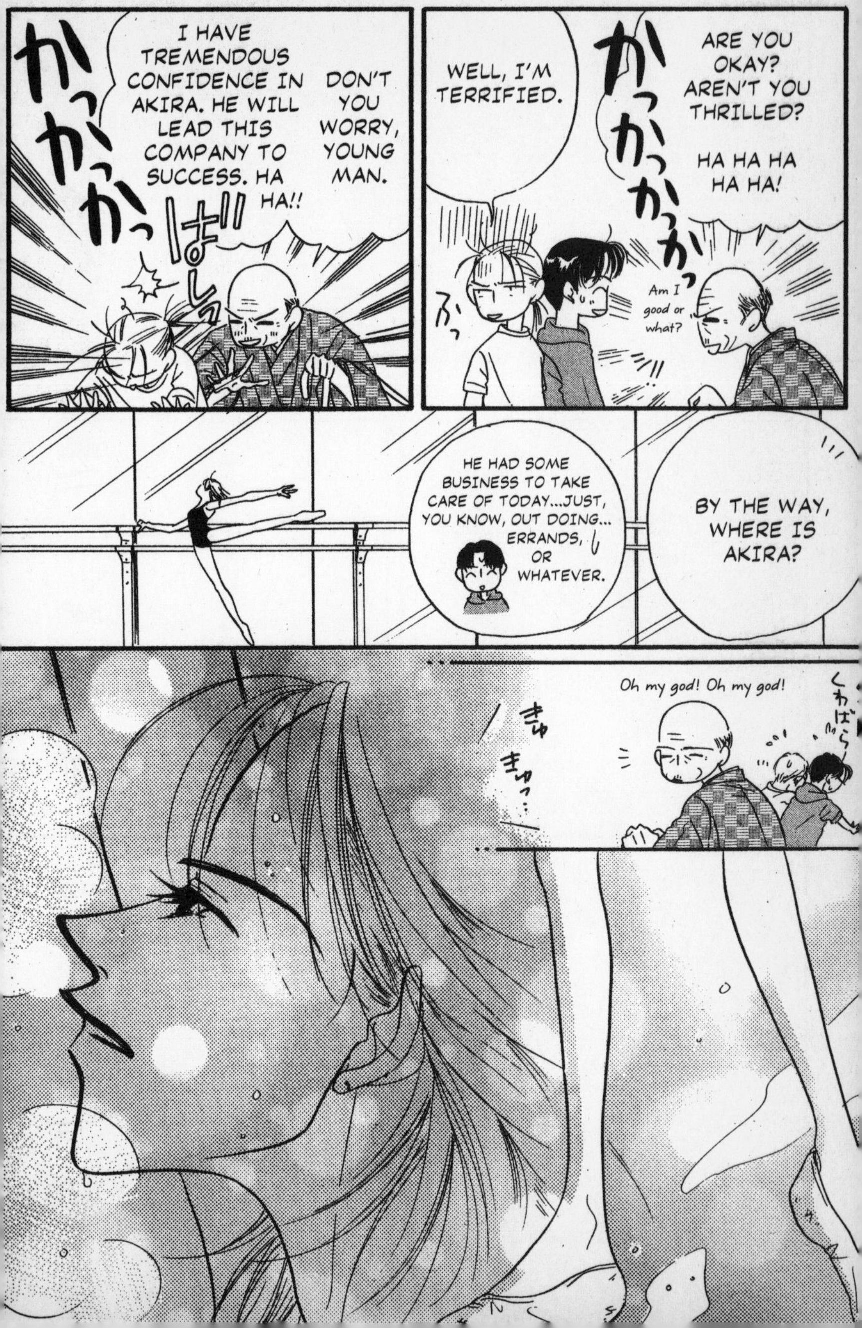

ARE YOU OKAY? AREN'T YOU THRILLED?
HA HA HA HA HA!
かっかっかっ
WELL, I'M TERRIFIED.
Am I good or what?
ふっ
DON'T YOU WORRY, YOUNG MAN.
I HAVE TREMENDOUS CONFIDENCE IN AKIRA. HE WILL LEAD THIS COMPANY TO SUCCESS. HA HA!!
かっかっかっ
ばしっ
BY THE WAY, WHERE IS AKIRA?
HE HAD SOME BUSINESS TO TAKE CARE OF TODAY...JUST, YOU KNOW, OUT DOING... ERRANDS, OR WHATEVER.
くわばら
Oh my god! Oh my god!
きゅきゅっ...

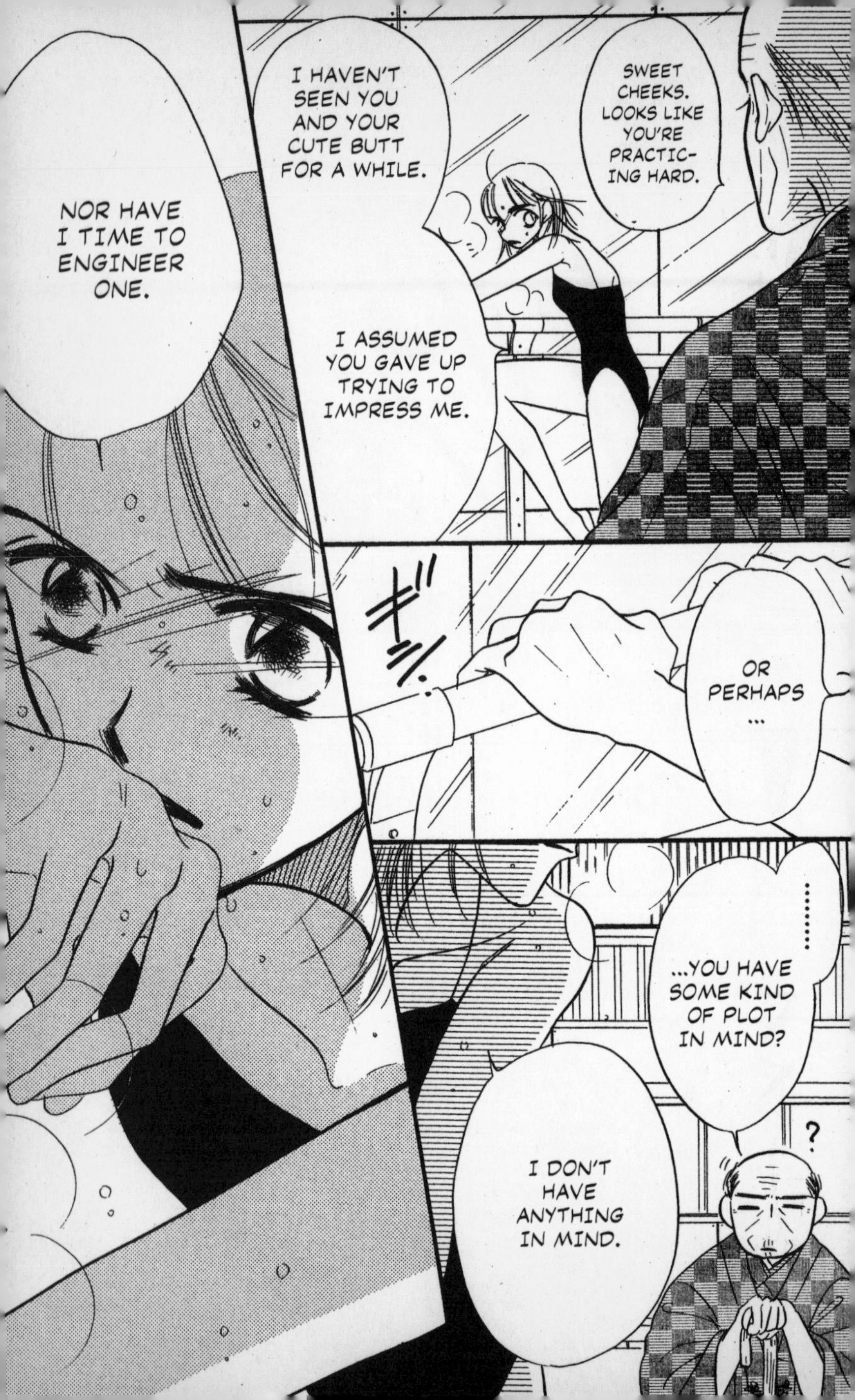
SWEET CHEEKS. LOOKS LIKE YOU'RE PRACTIC-ING HARD.
I HAVEN'T SEEN YOU AND YOUR CUTE BUTT FOR A WHILE.
I ASSUMED YOU GAVE UP TRYING TO IMPRESS ME.
OR PERHAPS ...
......
...YOU HAVE SOME KIND OF PLOT IN MIND?
?
I DON'T HAVE ANYTHING IN MIND.
NOR HAVE I TIME TO ENGINEER ONE.

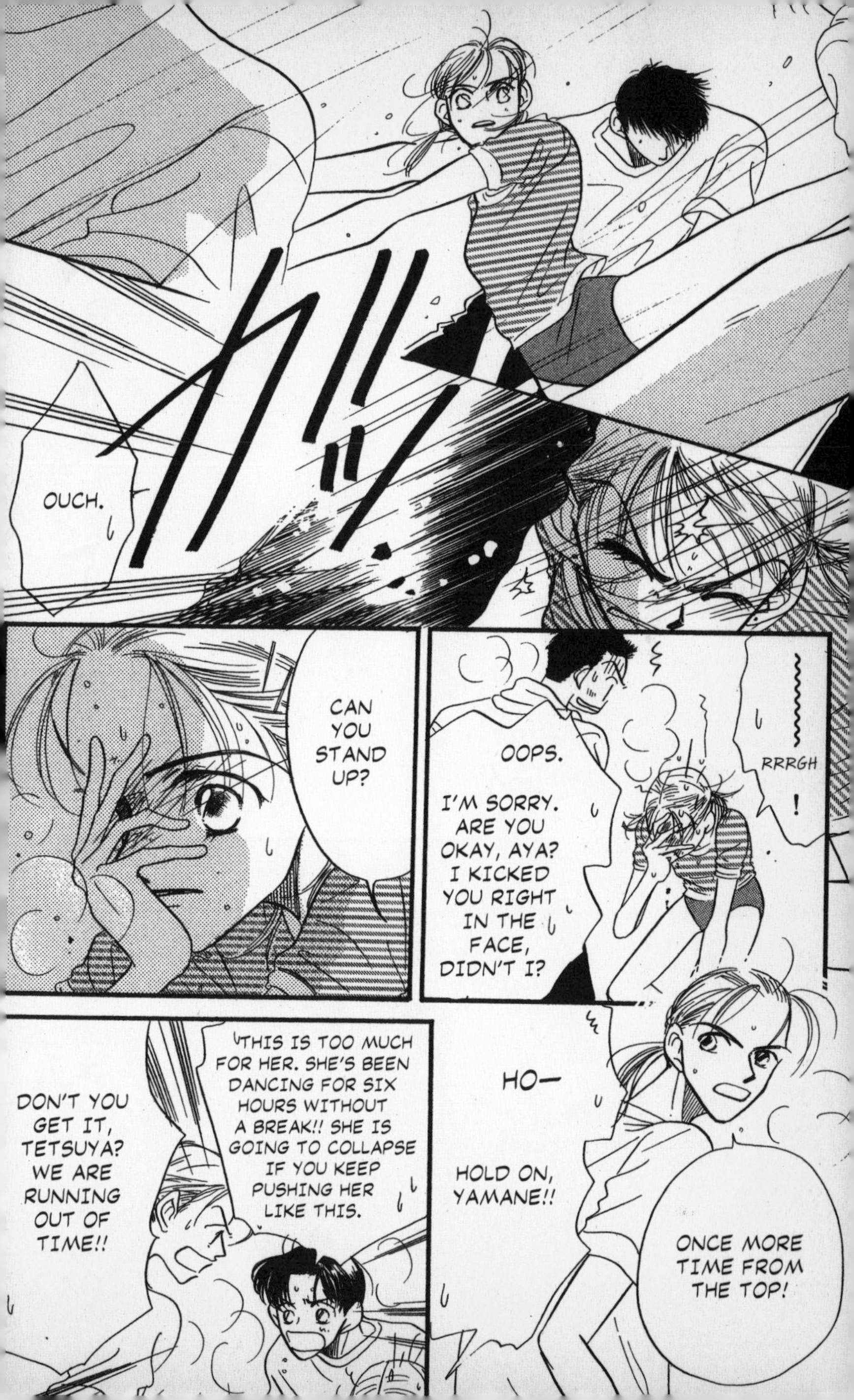
ガッ
OUCH.
RRRGH!
OOPS.
I'M SORRY. ARE YOU OKAY, AYA? I KICKED YOU RIGHT IN THE FACE, DIDN'T I?
CAN YOU STAND UP?
ONCE MORE TIME FROM THE TOP!
HO—
HOLD ON, YAMANE!!
THIS IS TOO MUCH FOR HER. SHE'S BEEN DANCING FOR SIX HOURS WITHOUT A BREAK!! SHE IS GOING TO COLLAPSE IF YOU KEEP PUSHING HER LIKE THIS.
DON'T YOU GET IT, TETSUYA? WE ARE RUNNING OUT OF TIME!!

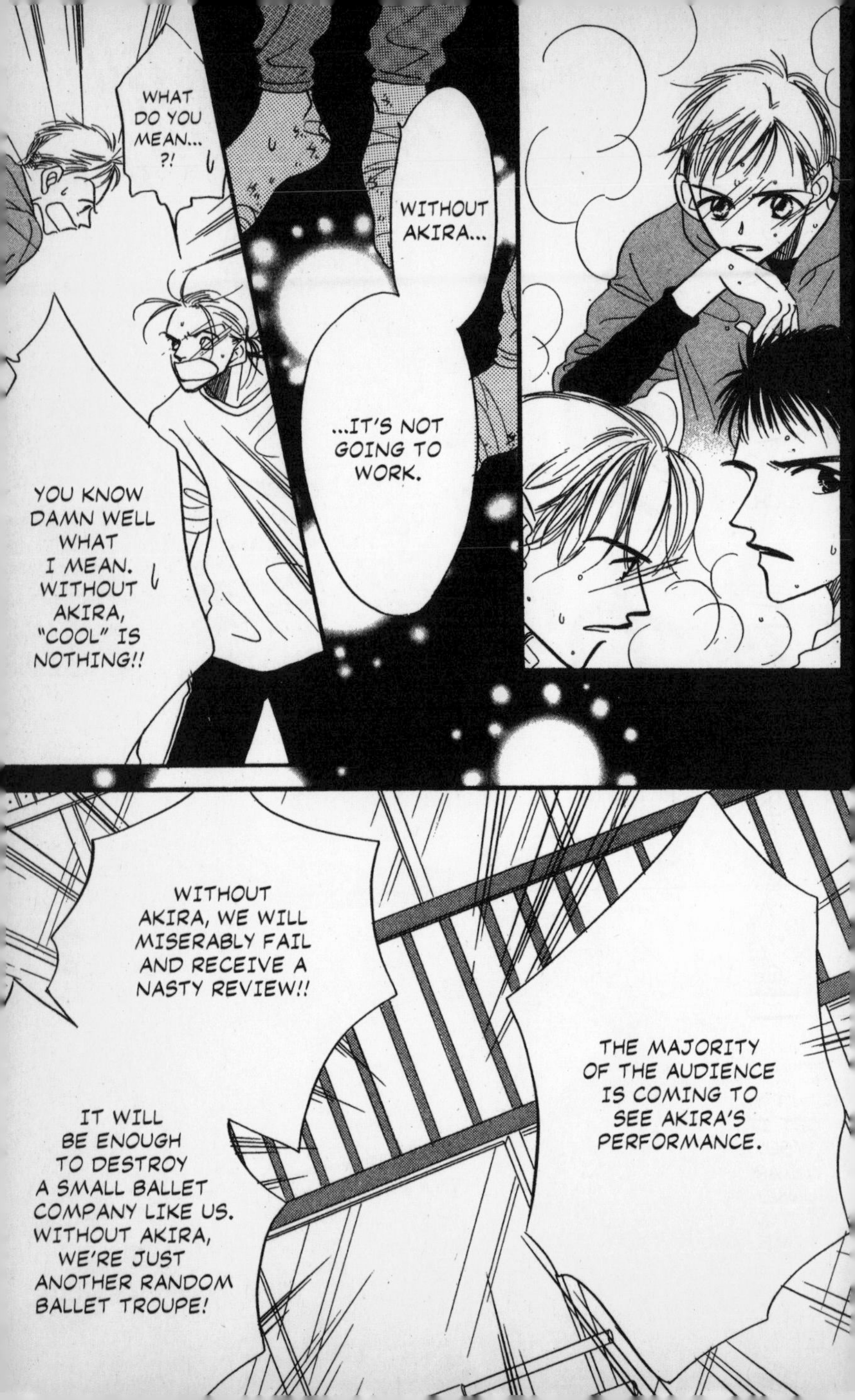
WITHOUT AKIRA...
...IT'S NOT GOING TO WORK.
WHAT DO YOU MEAN...?!
YOU KNOW DAMN WELL WHAT I MEAN. WITHOUT AKIRA, "COOL" IS NOTHING!!
THE MAJORITY OF THE AUDIENCE IS COMING TO SEE AKIRA'S PERFORMANCE.
WITHOUT AKIRA, WE WILL MISERABLY FAIL AND RECEIVE A NASTY REVIEW!!
IT WILL BE ENOUGH TO DESTROY A SMALL BALLET COMPANY LIKE US. WITHOUT AKIRA, WE'RE JUST ANOTHER RANDOM BALLET TROUPE!

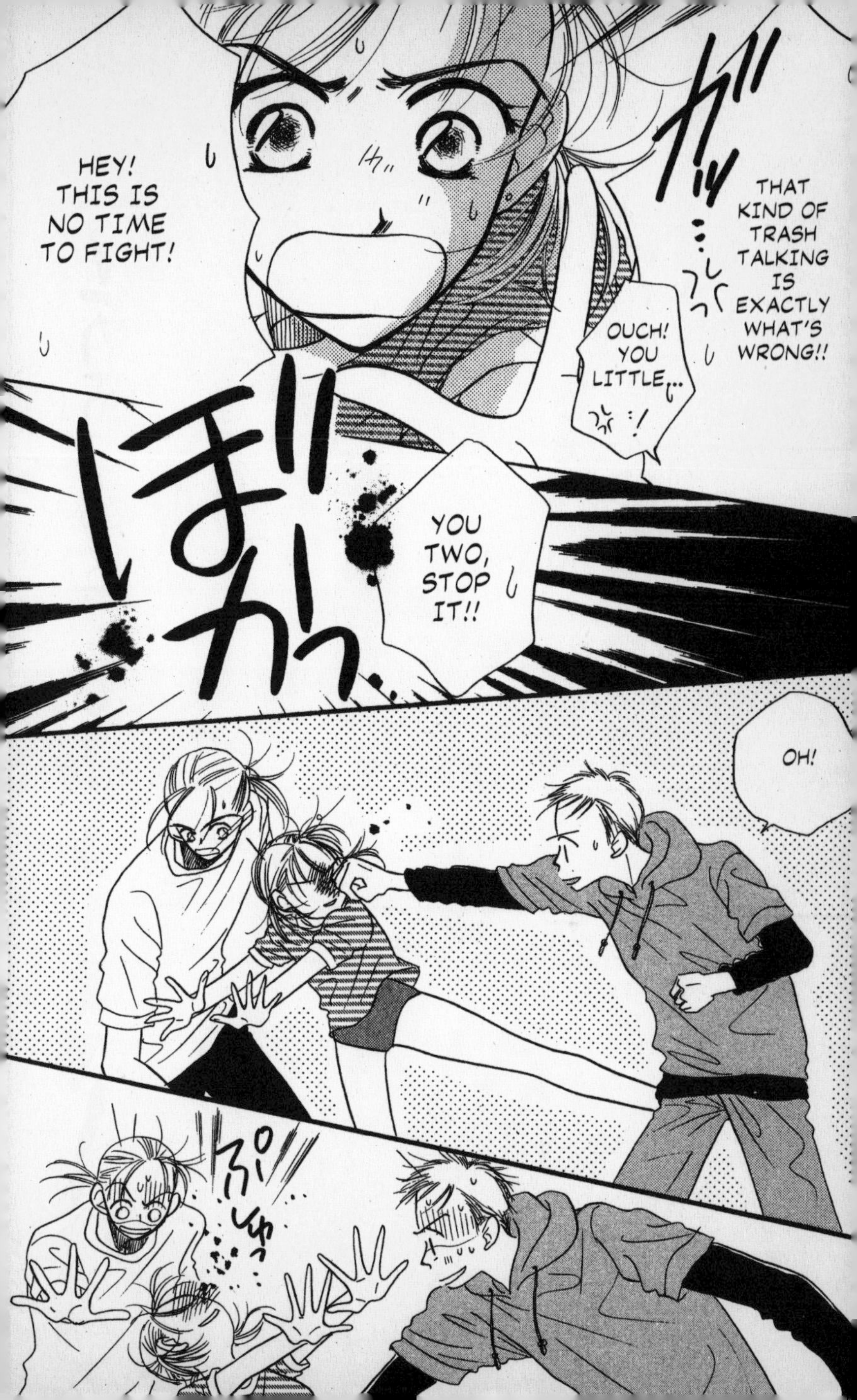
THAT KIND OF TRASH TALKING IS EXACTLY WHAT'S WRONG!!
OUCH! YOU LITTLE...
HEY! THIS IS NO TIME TO FIGHT!
YOU TWO, STOP IT!!
OH!

Ashihara's Diary

-No. 4-

No matter how hard it was, I am satisfied with how "Princess Line" turned out. I haven't written a high school romance for a while, and I enjoyed working on it. The high school I went to also had a night school attached to it. After 5 o'clock in the evening, the atmosphere changes in the building. Such old memories helped me create the image of some scenes. I asked a friend of mine, who is a graduate student in pharmacological science, to do some research on drugs for me. I promised her I would buy her a dinner. I haven't got around to doing so yet. Sorry! Next time, when I have a chance!

*

I will see you all in the last volume!!

Hinako Ashihara
September 9, 1998

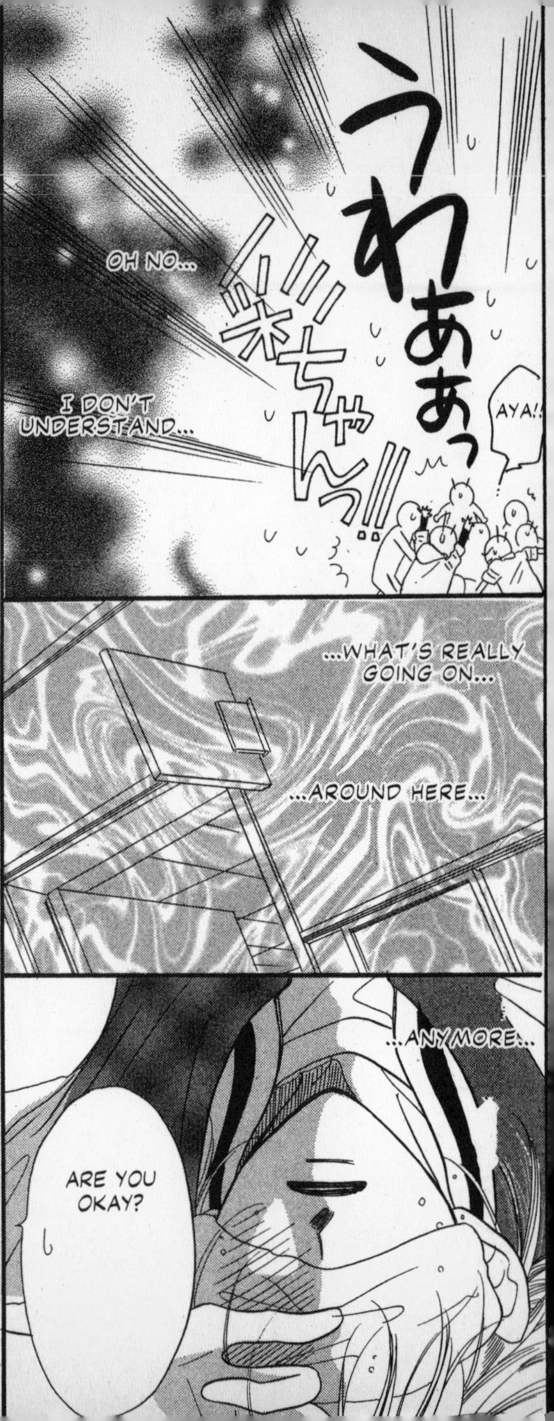
うわああっ
彩ちゃんっ!!
AYA!!
OH NO...
I DON'T UNDERSTAND...
...WHAT'S REALLY GOING ON...
...AROUND HERE...
...ANYMORE...
ARE YOU OKAY?

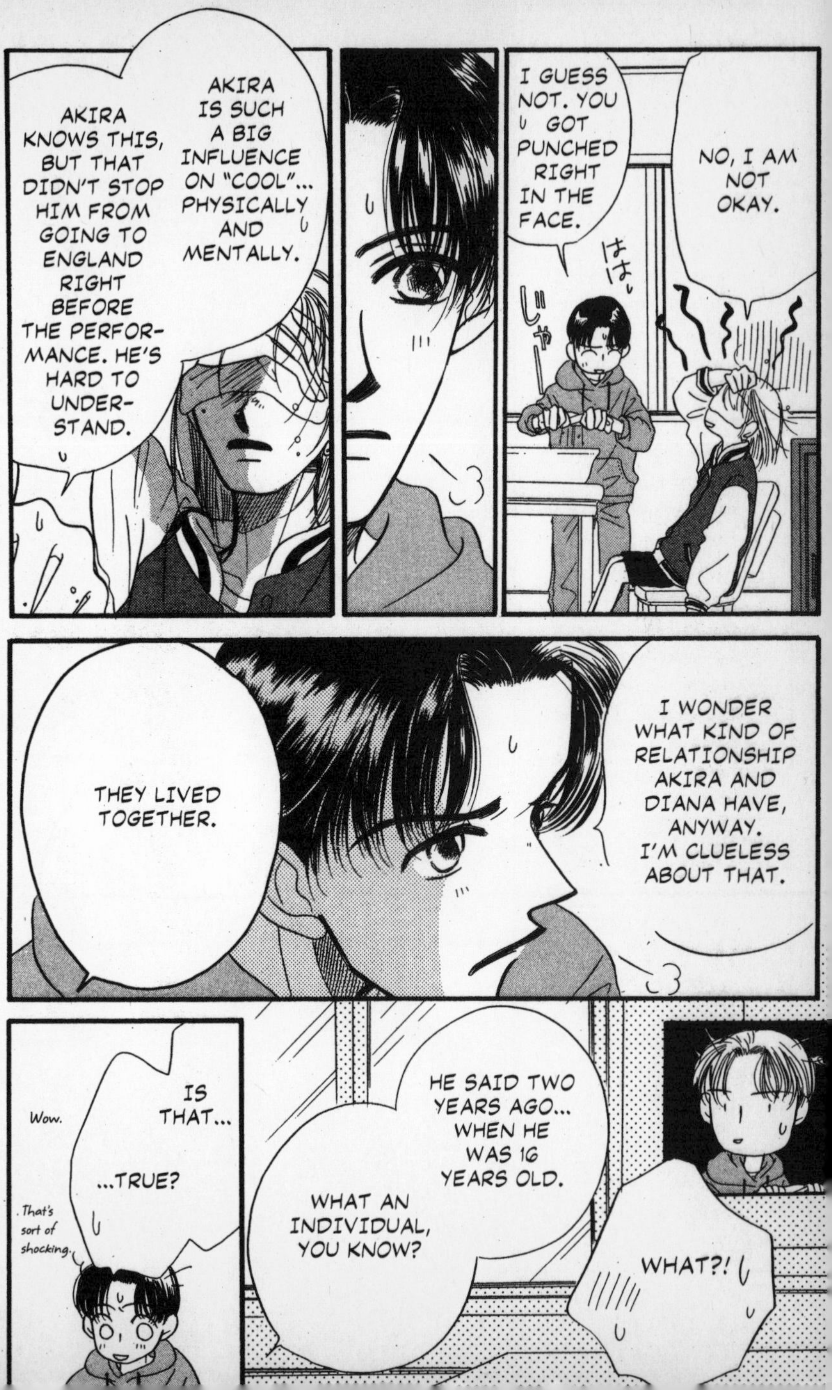
NO, I AM NOT OKAY.
I GUESS NOT. YOU GOT PUNCHED RIGHT IN THE FACE.
はは
じゃ
AKIRA IS SUCH A BIG INFLUENCE ON "COOL"... PHYSICALLY AND MENTALLY.
AKIRA KNOWS THIS, BUT THAT DIDN'T STOP HIM FROM GOING TO ENGLAND RIGHT BEFORE THE PERFORMANCE. HE'S HARD TO UNDERSTAND.
I WONDER WHAT KIND OF RELATIONSHIP AKIRA AND DIANA HAVE, ANYWAY. I'M CLUELESS ABOUT THAT.
THEY LIVED TOGETHER.
WHAT?!
HE SAID TWO YEARS AGO... WHEN HE WAS 16 YEARS OLD.
WHAT AN INDIVIDUAL, YOU KNOW?
IS THAT...
...TRUE?
Wow.
That's sort of shocking.

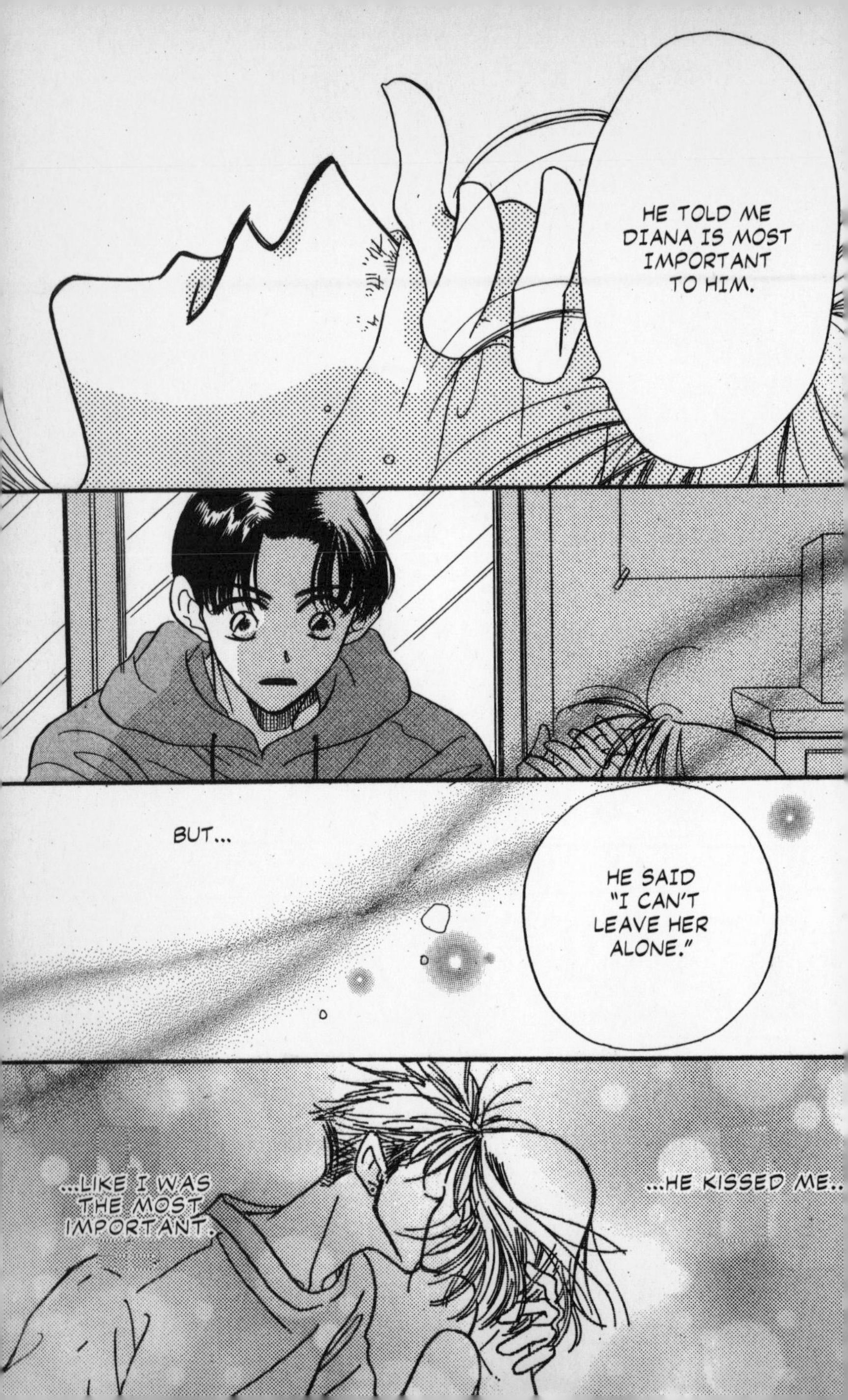
HE TOLD ME DIANA IS MOST IMPORTANT TO HIM.
HE SAID "I CAN'T LEAVE HER ALONE."
BUT...
...HE KISSED ME...
...LIKE I WAS THE MOST IMPORTANT.

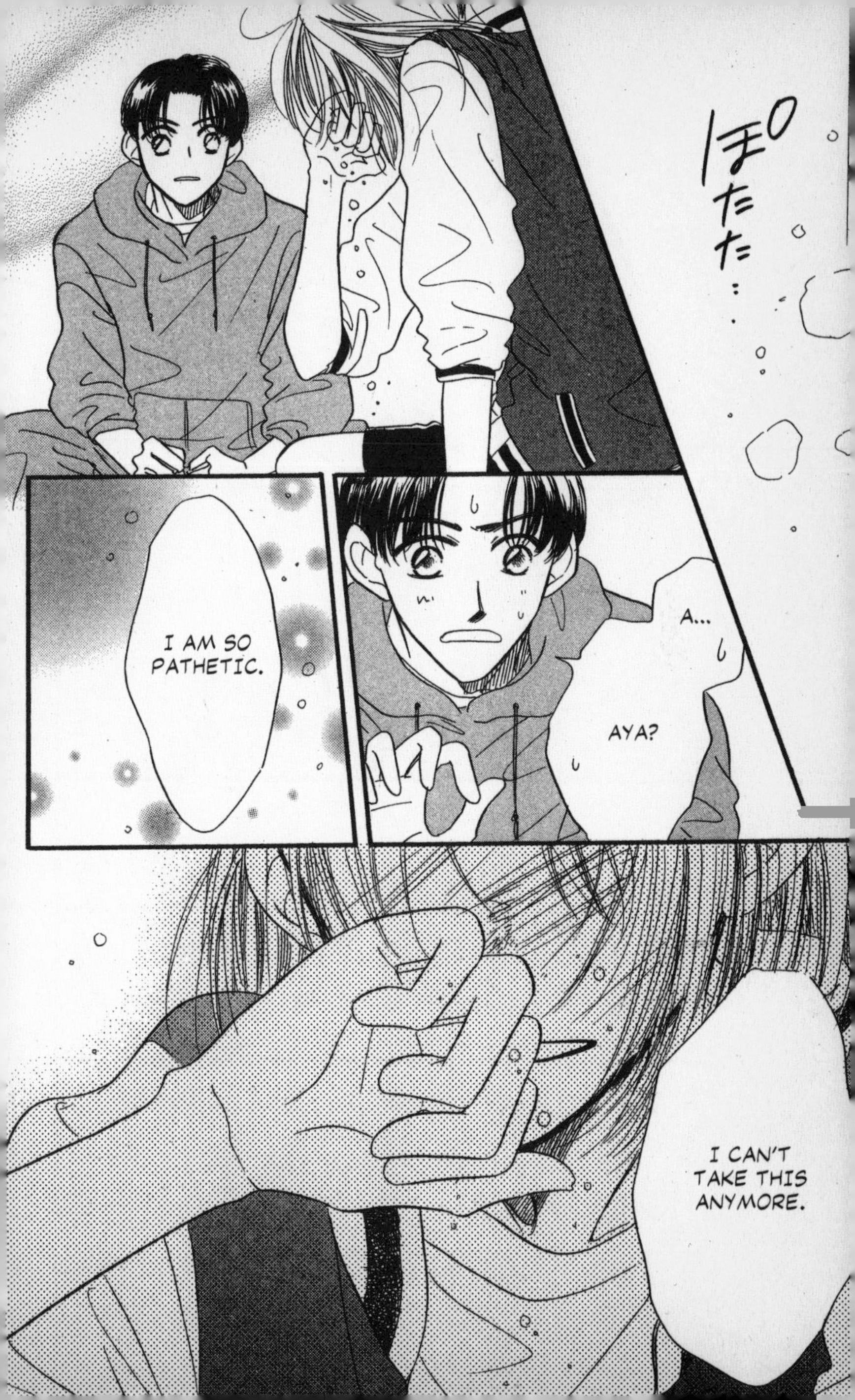
ぽたた…
A...
AYA?
I AM SO PATHETIC.
I CAN'T TAKE THIS ANYMORE.

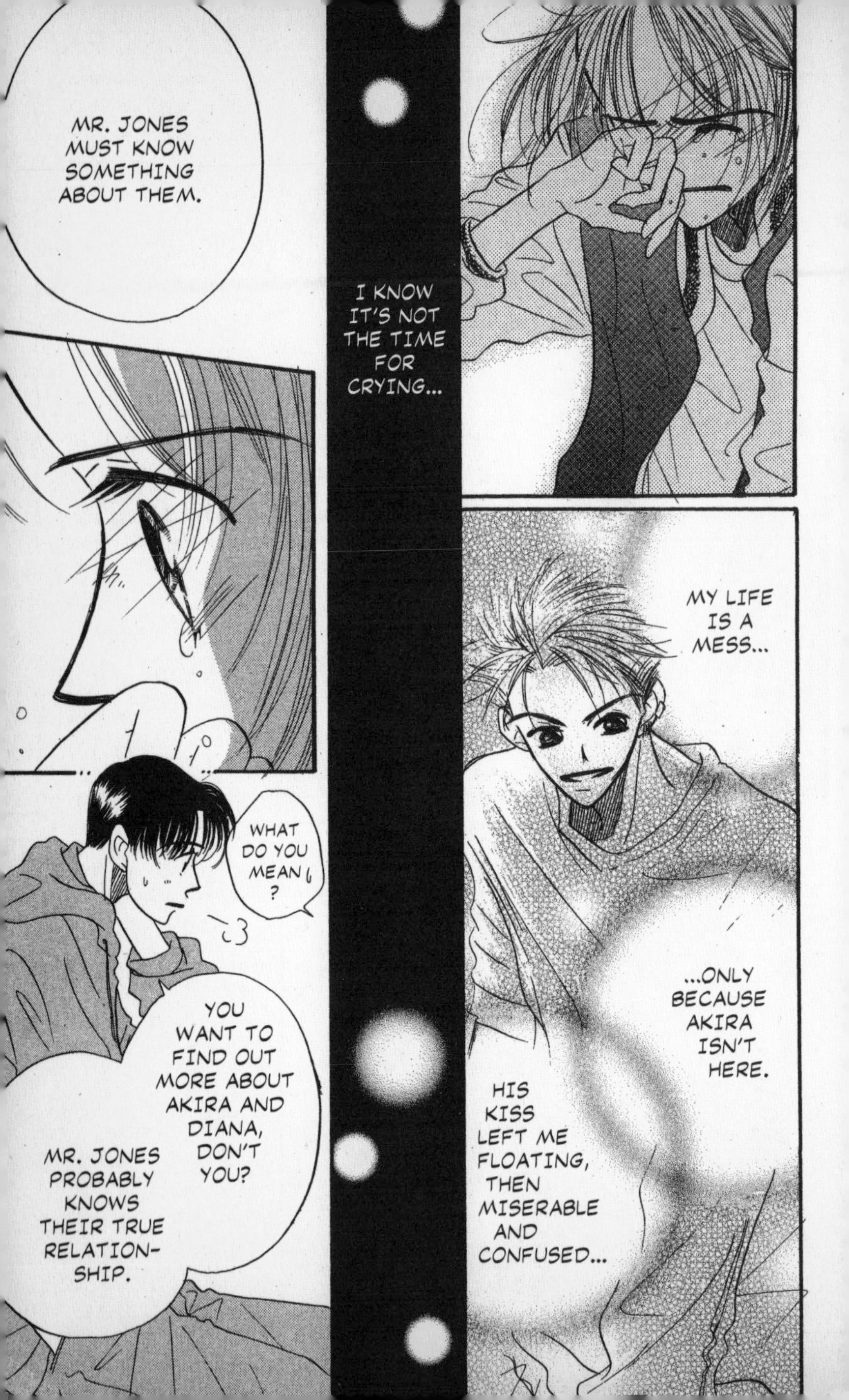
I KNOW IT'S NOT THE TIME FOR CRYING...
MY LIFE IS A MESS...
...ONLY BECAUSE AKIRA ISN'T HERE.
HIS KISS LEFT ME FLOATING, THEN MISERABLE AND CONFUSED...
MR. JONES MUST KNOW SOMETHING ABOUT THEM.
WHAT DO YOU MEAN ?
YOU WANT TO FIND OUT MORE ABOUT AKIRA AND DIANA, DON'T YOU?
MR. JONES PROBABLY KNOWS THEIR TRUE RELATIONSHIP.

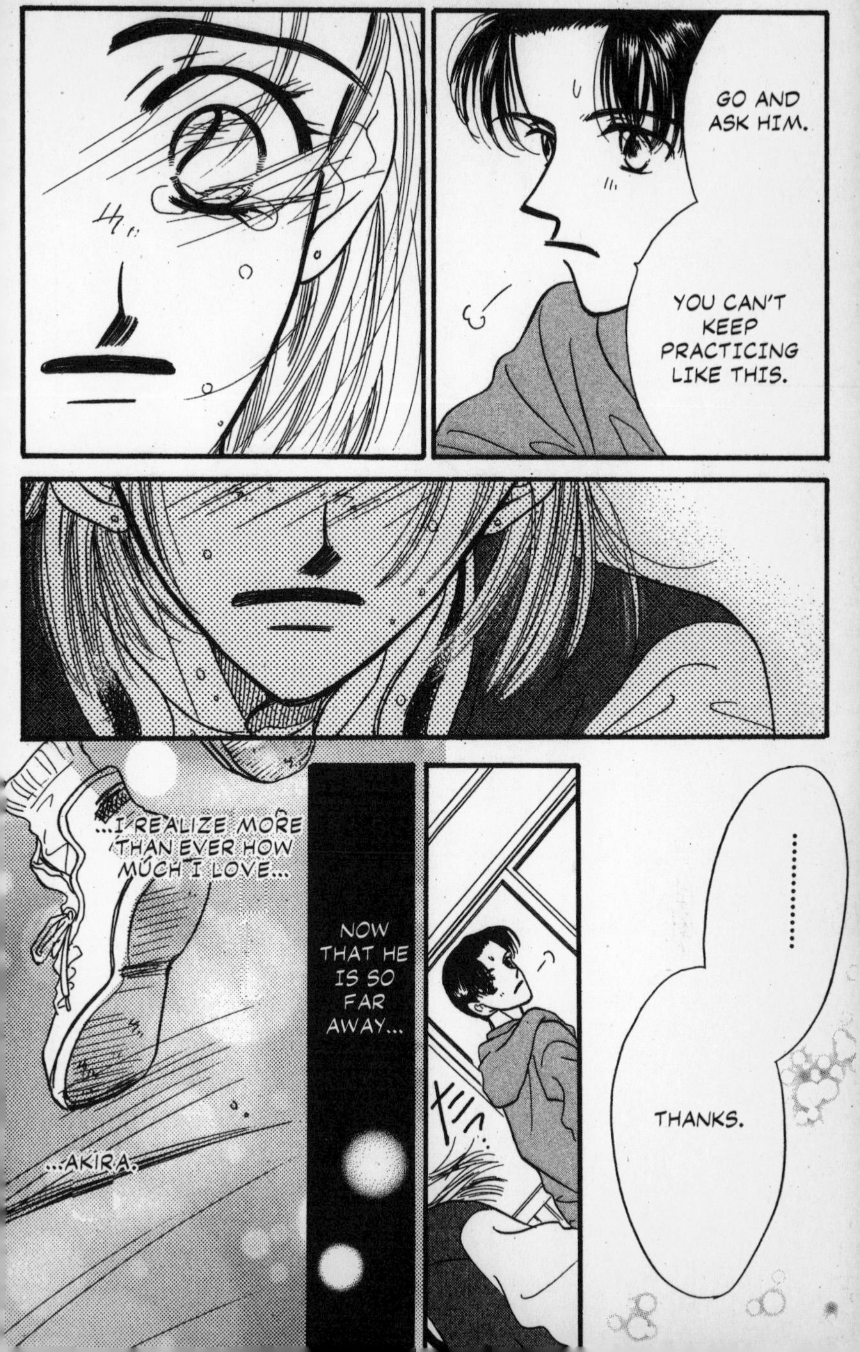
GO AND ASK HIM.
YOU CAN'T KEEP PRACTICING LIKE THIS.
....
THANKS.
NOW THAT HE IS SO FAR AWAY...
...I REALIZE MORE THAN EVER HOW MUCH I LOVE...
...AKIRA.

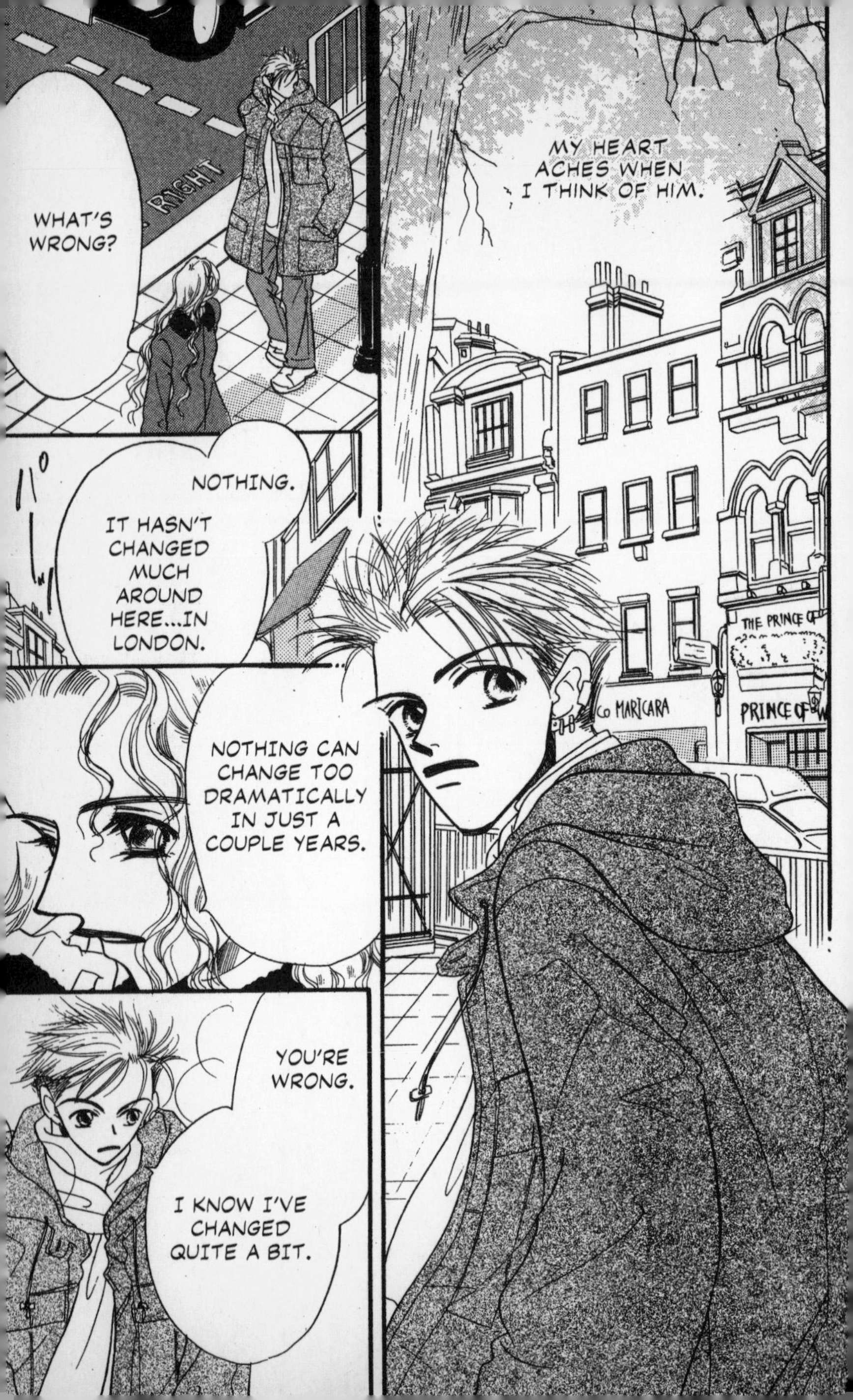
MY HEART ACHES WHEN I THINK OF HIM.
THE PRINCE OF
MARICARA
WHAT'S WRONG?
RIGHT
NOTHING.
IT HASN'T CHANGED MUCH AROUND HERE...IN LONDON.
NOTHING CAN CHANGE TOO DRAMATICALLY IN JUST A COUPLE YEARS.
YOU'RE WRONG.
I KNOW I'VE CHANGED QUITE A BIT.

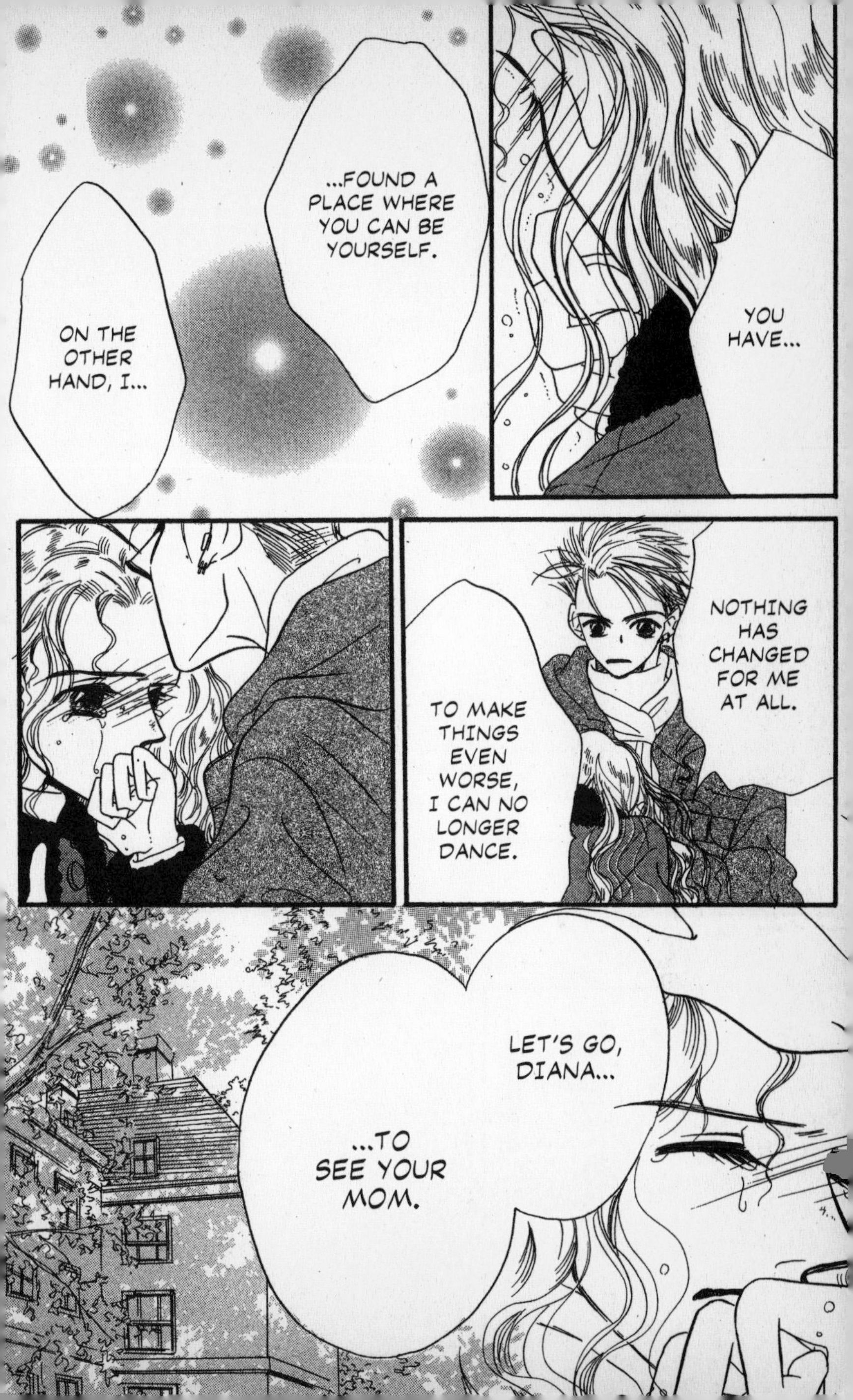
YOU HAVE...
...FOUND A PLACE WHERE YOU CAN BE YOURSELF.
ON THE OTHER HAND, I...
NOTHING HAS CHANGED FOR ME AT ALL.
TO MAKE THINGS EVEN WORSE, I CAN NO LONGER DANCE.
LET'S GO, DIANA...
...TO SEE YOUR MOM.

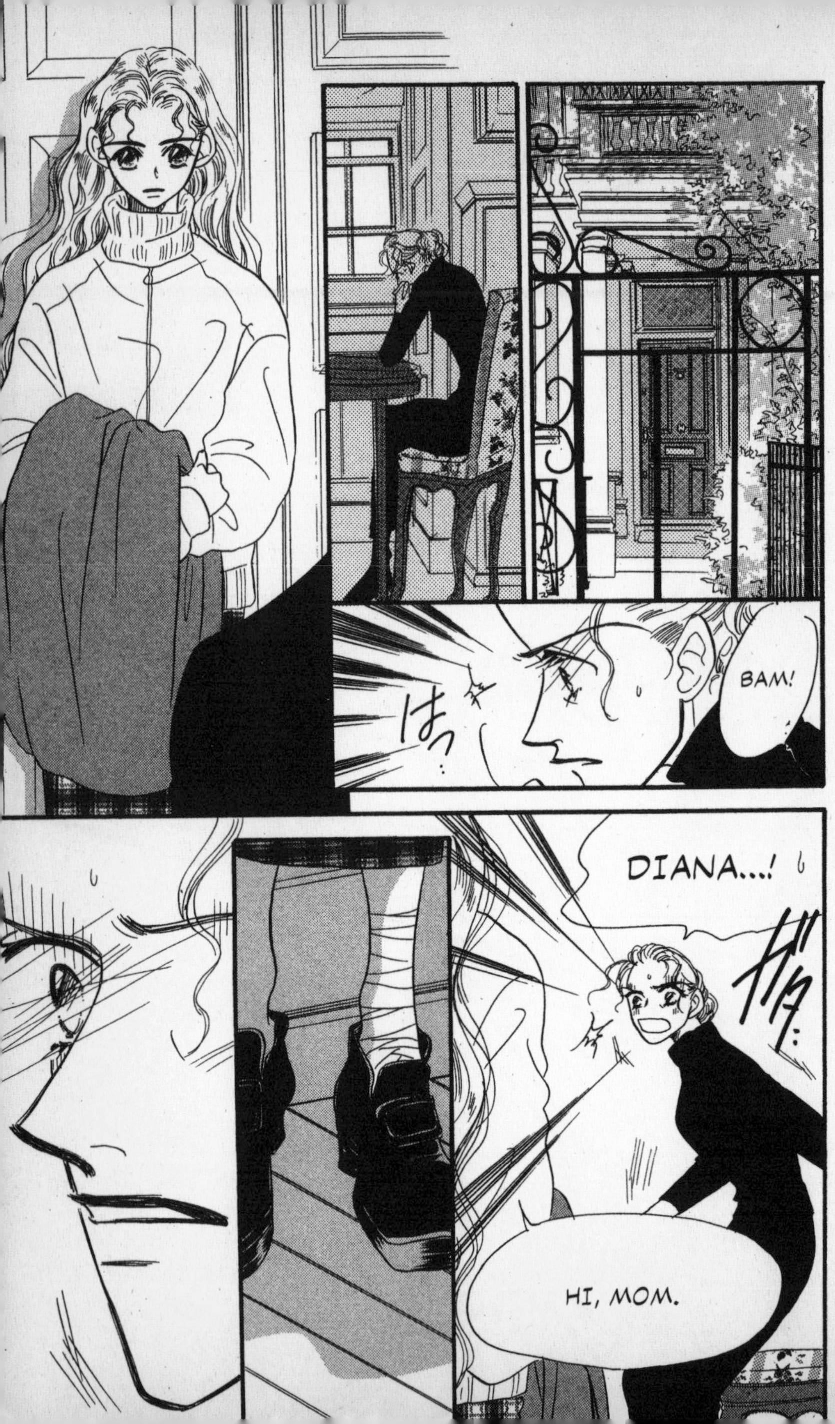
BAM!
はっ
DIANA...!
ガタ
HI, MOM.

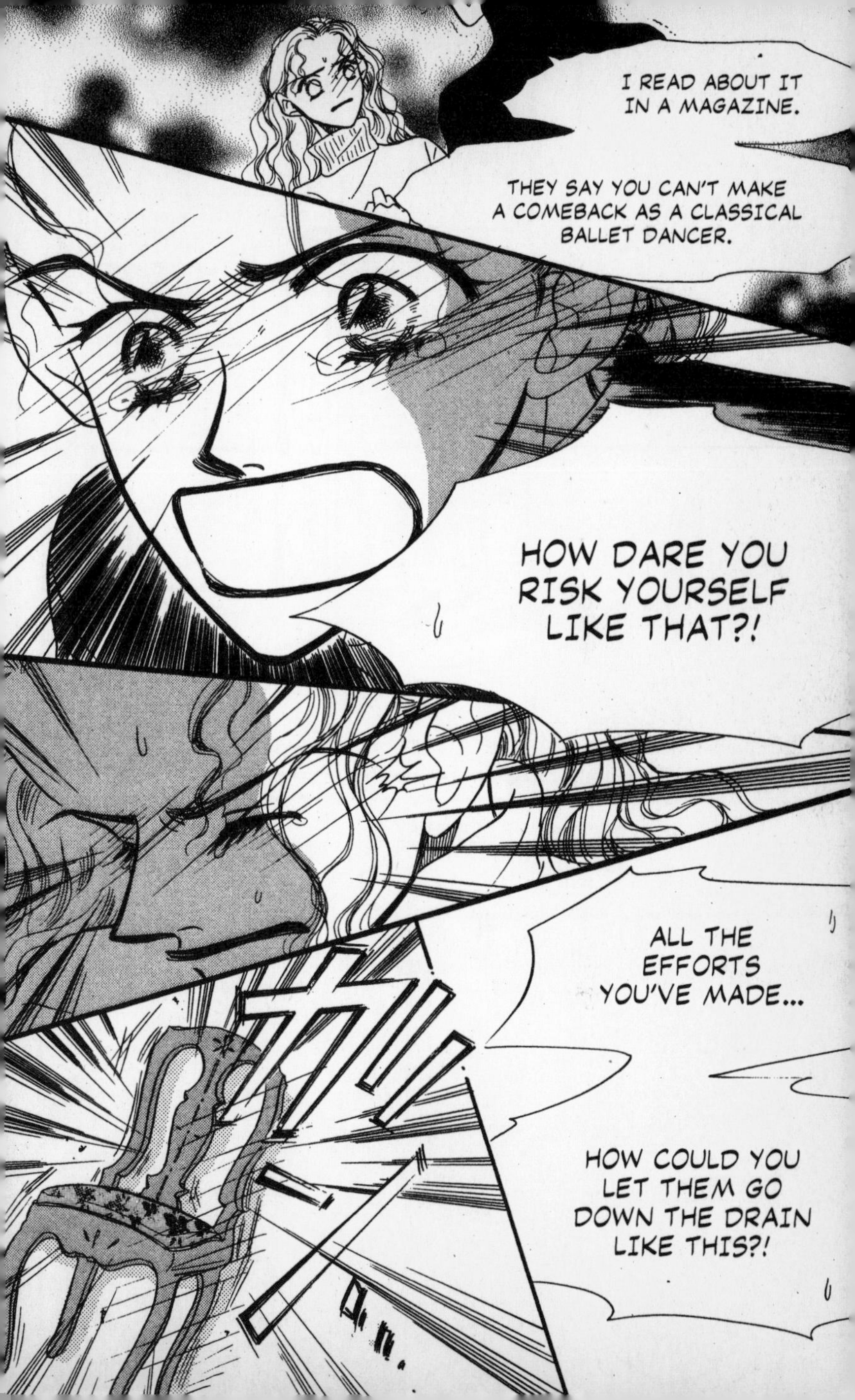
I READ ABOUT IT IN A MAGAZINE.
THEY SAY YOU CAN'T MAKE A COMEBACK AS A CLASSICAL BALLET DANCER.
HOW DARE YOU RISK YOURSELF LIKE THAT?!
ALL THE EFFORTS YOU'VE MADE...
HOW COULD YOU LET THEM GO DOWN THE DRAIN LIKE THIS?!

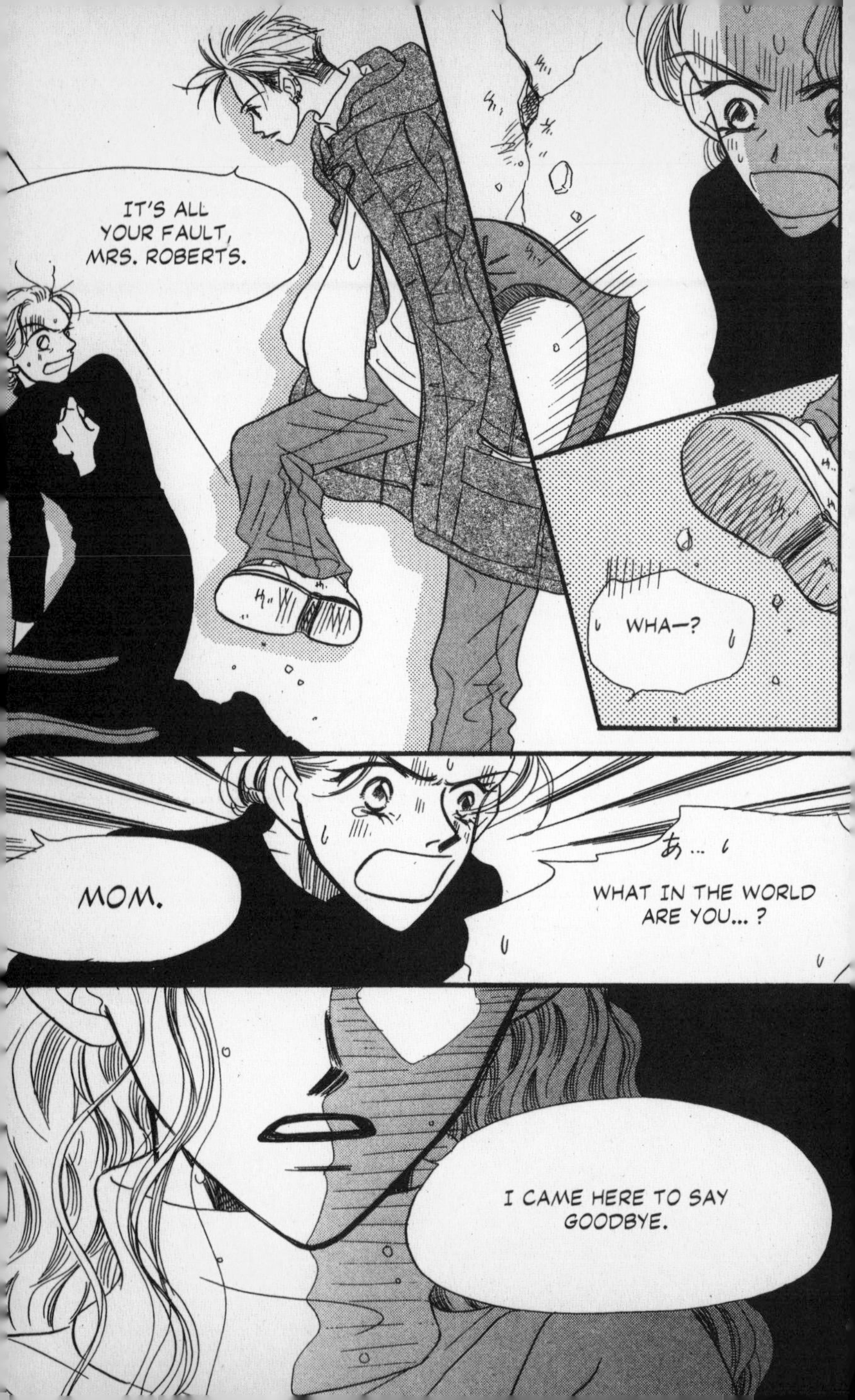
WHA—?
IT'S ALL YOUR FAULT, MRS. ROBERTS.
あ…
WHAT IN THE WORLD ARE YOU... ?
MOM.
I CAME HERE TO SAY GOODBYE.

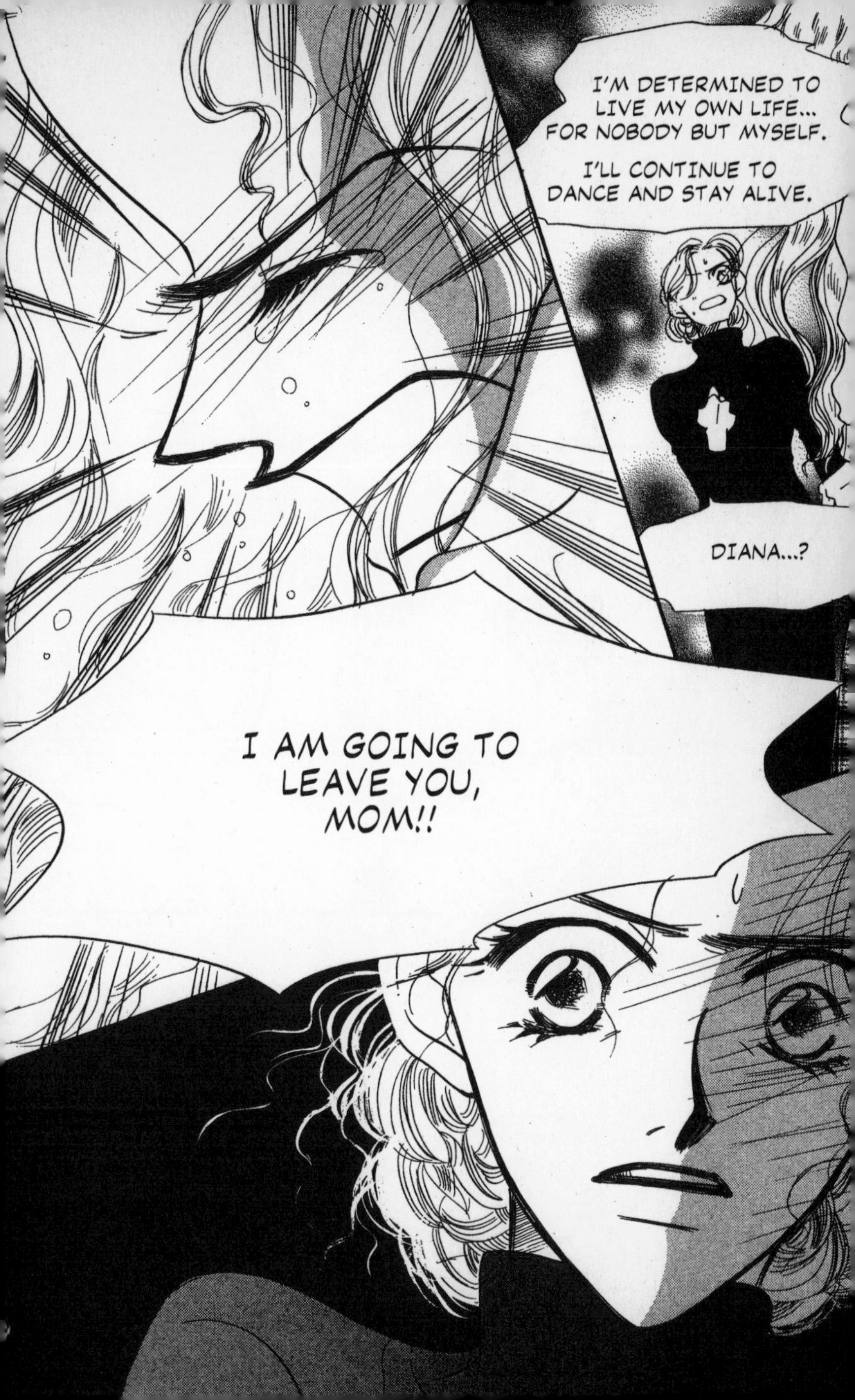
I'M DETERMINED TO LIVE MY OWN LIFE... FOR NOBODY BUT MYSELF.
I'LL CONTINUE TO DANCE AND STAY ALIVE.
DIANA...?
I AM GOING TO LEAVE YOU, MOM!!

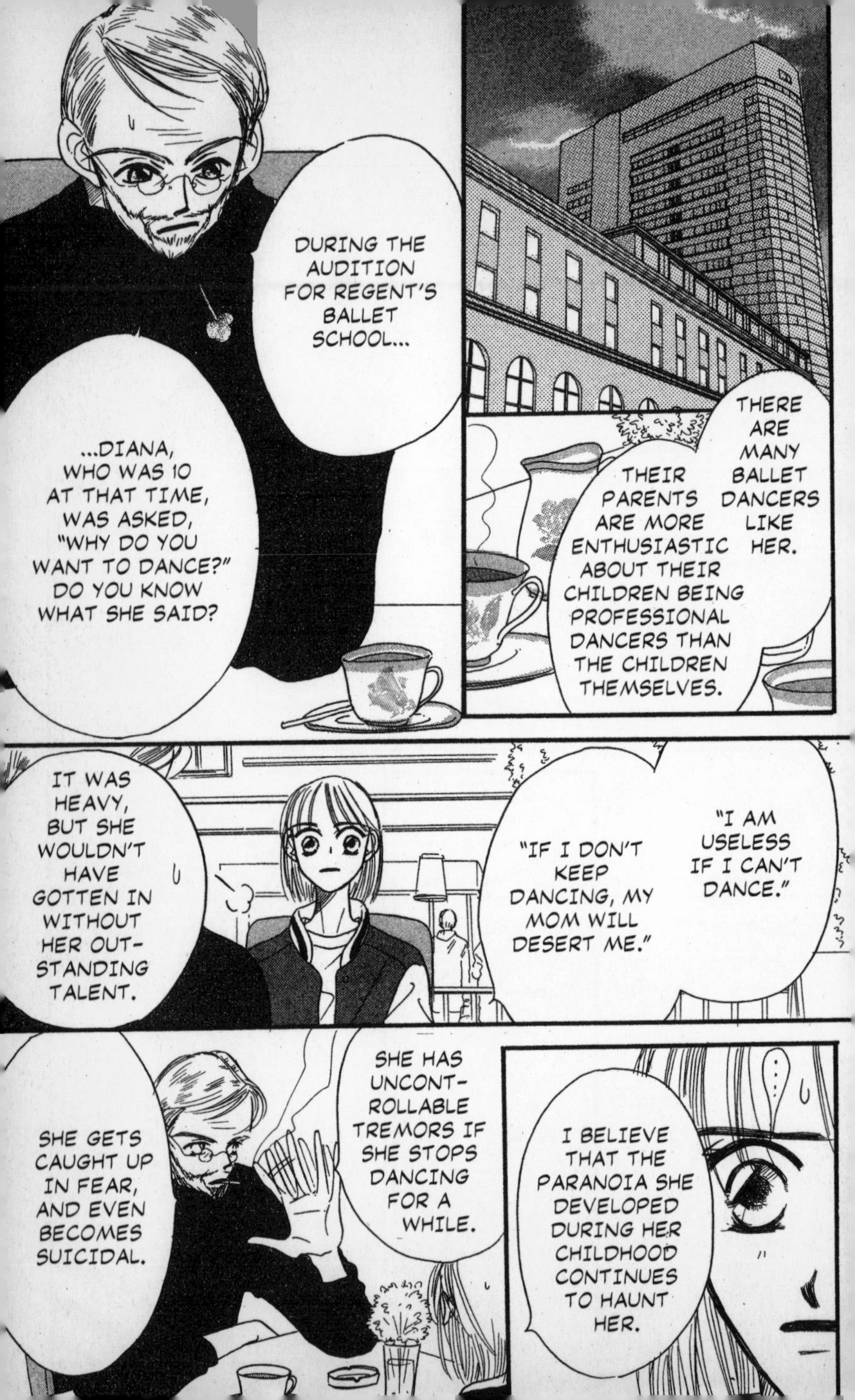
THERE ARE MANY BALLET DANCERS LIKE HER.
THEIR PARENTS ARE MORE ENTHUSIASTIC ABOUT THEIR CHILDREN BEING PROFESSIONAL DANCERS THAN THE CHILDREN THEMSELVES.
DURING THE AUDITION FOR REGENT'S BALLET SCHOOL...
...DIANA, WHO WAS 10 AT THAT TIME, WAS ASKED, "WHY DO YOU WANT TO DANCE?" DO YOU KNOW WHAT SHE SAID?
"I AM USELESS IF I CAN'T DANCE."
"IF I DON'T KEEP DANCING, MY MOM WILL DESERT ME."
IT WAS HEAVY, BUT SHE WOULDN'T HAVE GOTTEN IN WITHOUT HER OUT-STANDING TALENT.
I BELIEVE THAT THE PARANOIA SHE DEVELOPED DURING HER CHILDHOOD CONTINUES TO HAUNT HER.
SHE HAS UNCONT-ROLLABLE TREMORS IF SHE STOPS DANCING FOR A WHILE.
SHE GETS CAUGHT UP IN FEAR, AND EVEN BECOMES SUICIDAL.

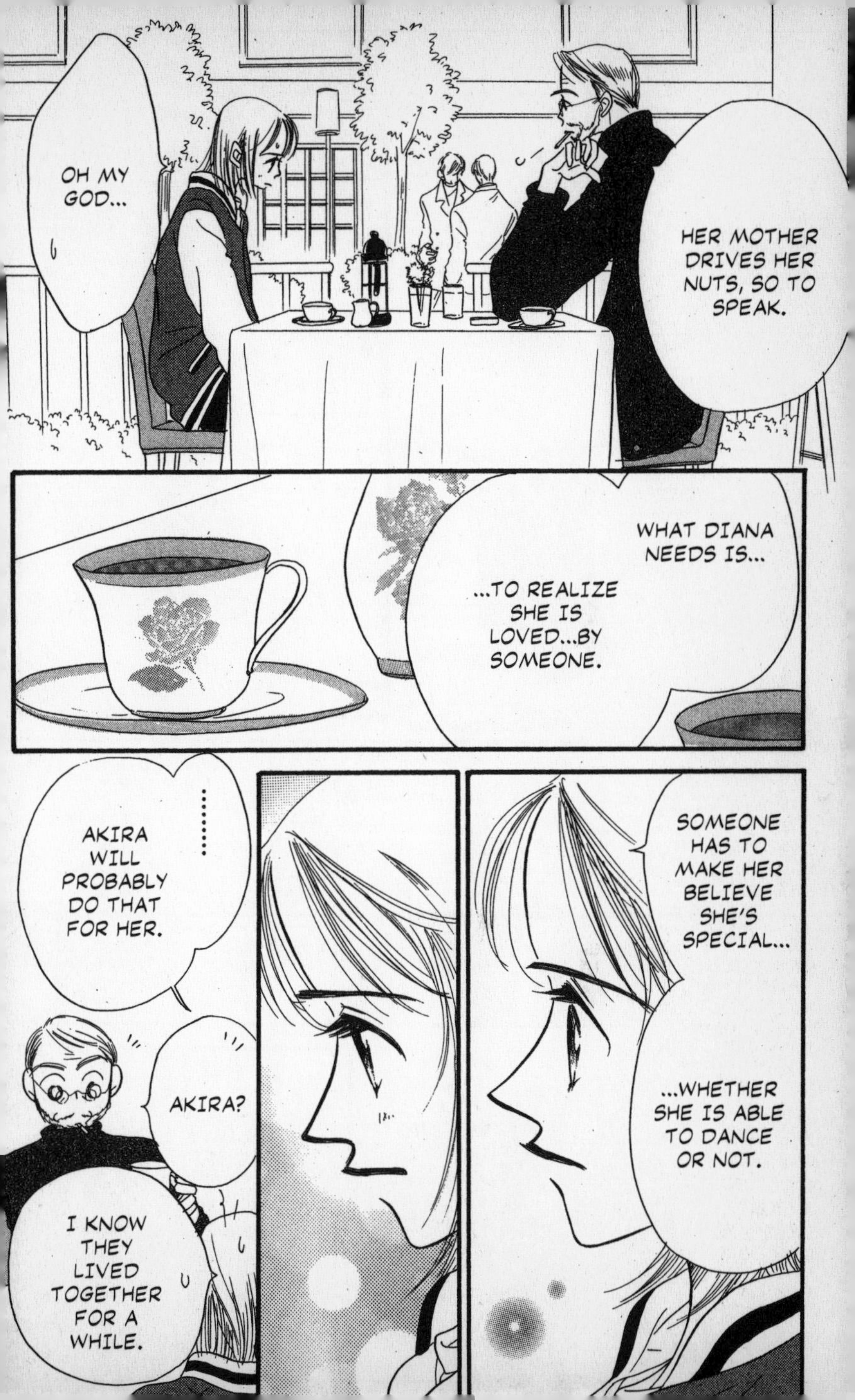
HER MOTHER DRIVES HER NUTS, SO TO SPEAK.
OH MY GOD...
WHAT DIANA NEEDS IS...
...TO REALIZE SHE IS LOVED...BY SOMEONE.
SOMEONE HAS TO MAKE HER BELIEVE SHE'S SPECIAL...
...WHETHER SHE IS ABLE TO DANCE OR NOT.
......
AKIRA WILL PROBABLY DO THAT FOR HER.
AKIRA?
I KNOW THEY LIVED TOGETHER FOR A WHILE.

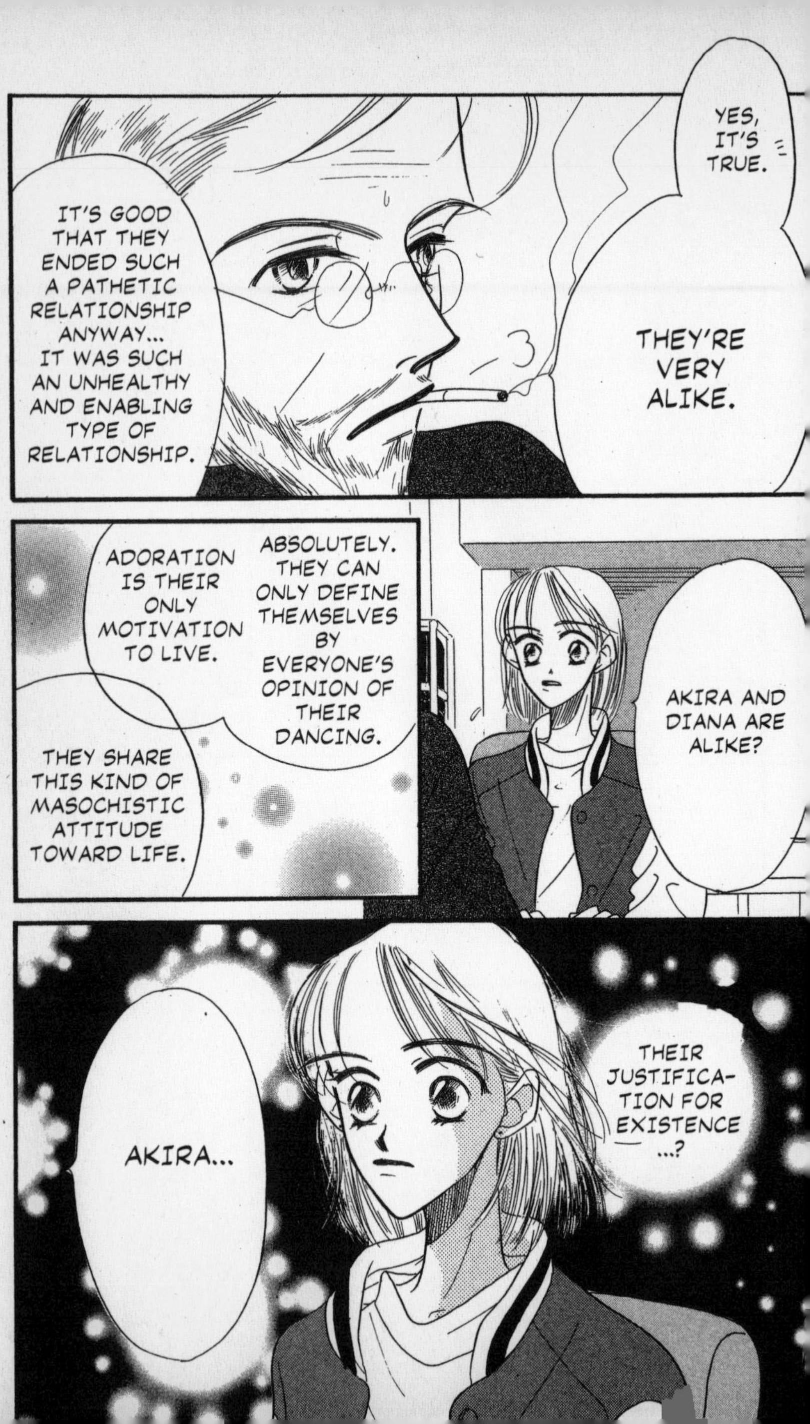
YES, IT'S TRUE.
THEY'RE VERY ALIKE.
IT'S GOOD THAT THEY ENDED SUCH A PATHETIC RELATIONSHIP ANYWAY... IT WAS SUCH AN UNHEALTHY AND ENABLING TYPE OF RELATIONSHIP.
AKIRA AND DIANA ARE ALIKE?
ABSOLUTELY. THEY CAN ONLY DEFINE THEMSELVES BY EVERYONE'S OPINION OF THEIR DANCING.
ADORATION IS THEIR ONLY MOTIVATION TO LIVE.
THEY SHARE THIS KIND OF MASOCHISTIC ATTITUDE TOWARD LIFE.
THEIR JUSTIFICA-TION FOR EXISTENCE ...?
AKIRA...

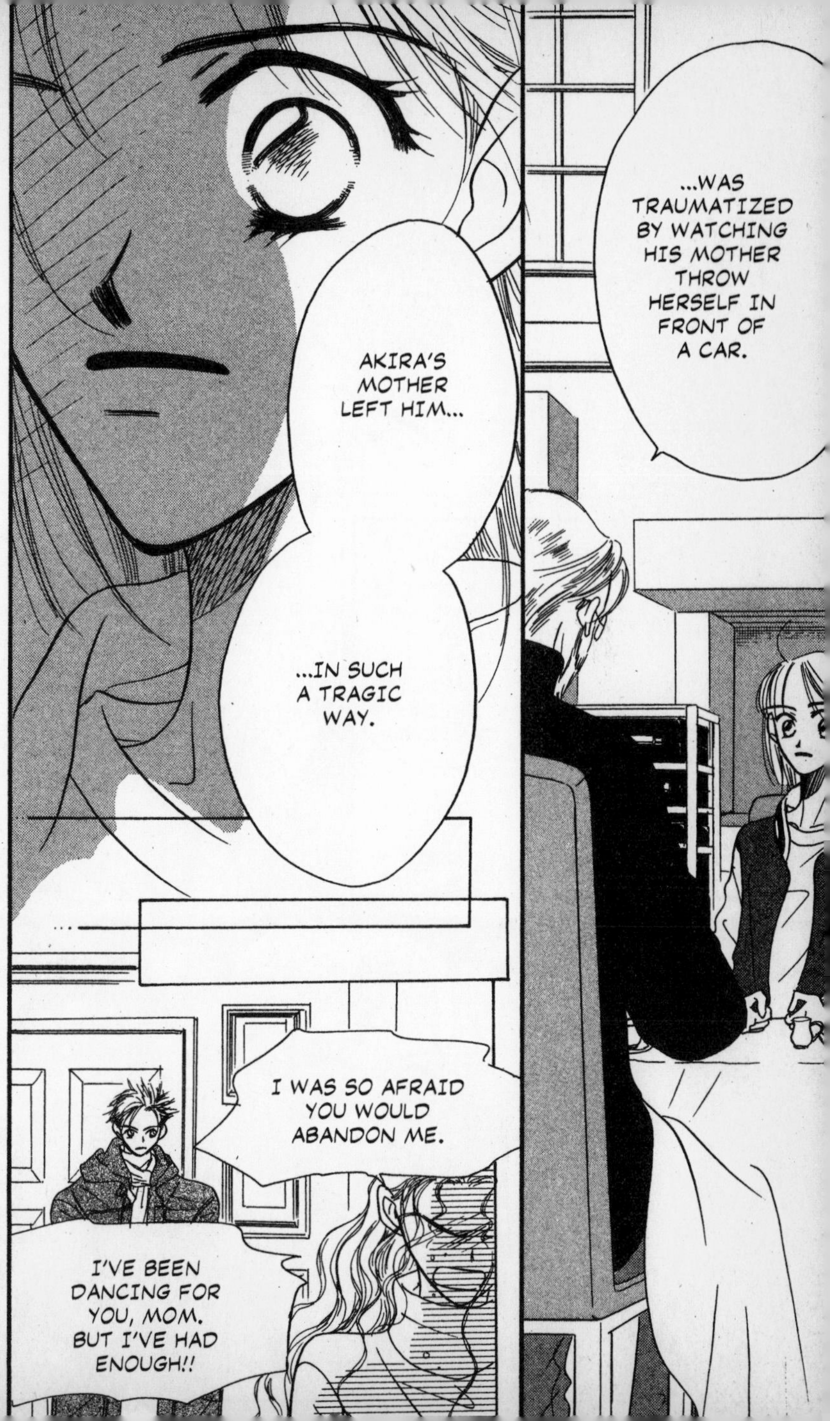
...WAS TRAUMATIZED BY WATCHING HIS MOTHER THROW HERSELF IN FRONT OF A CAR.
AKIRA'S MOTHER LEFT HIM...
...IN SUCH A TRAGIC WAY.
I WAS SO AFRAID YOU WOULD ABANDON ME.
I'VE BEEN DANCING FOR YOU, MOM. BUT I'VE HAD ENOUGH!!

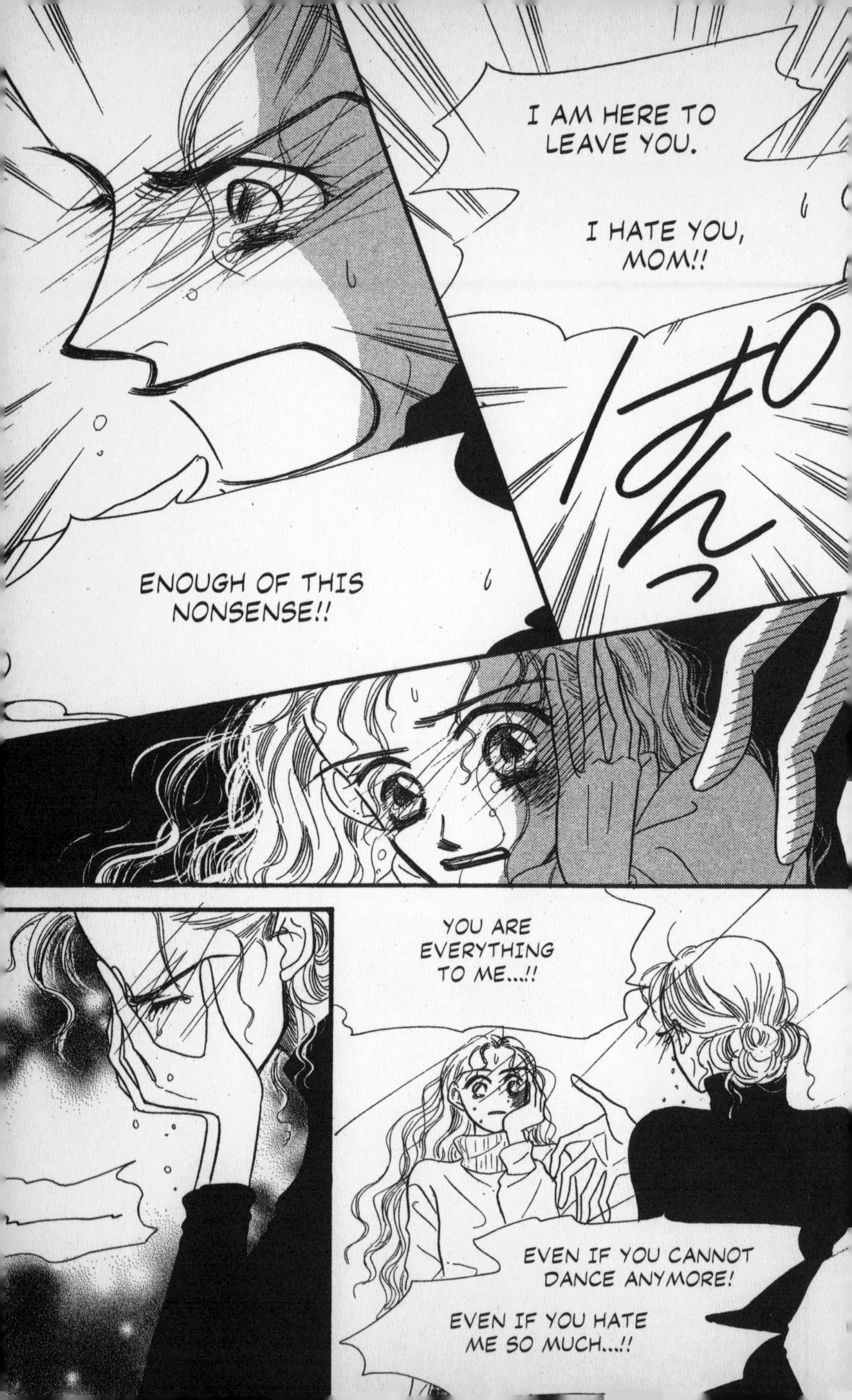
I AM HERE TO LEAVE YOU.
I HATE YOU, MOM!!
ENOUGH OF THIS NONSENSE!!
YOU ARE EVERYTHING TO ME...!!
EVEN IF YOU CANNOT DANCE ANYMORE!
EVEN IF YOU HATE ME SO MUCH...!!

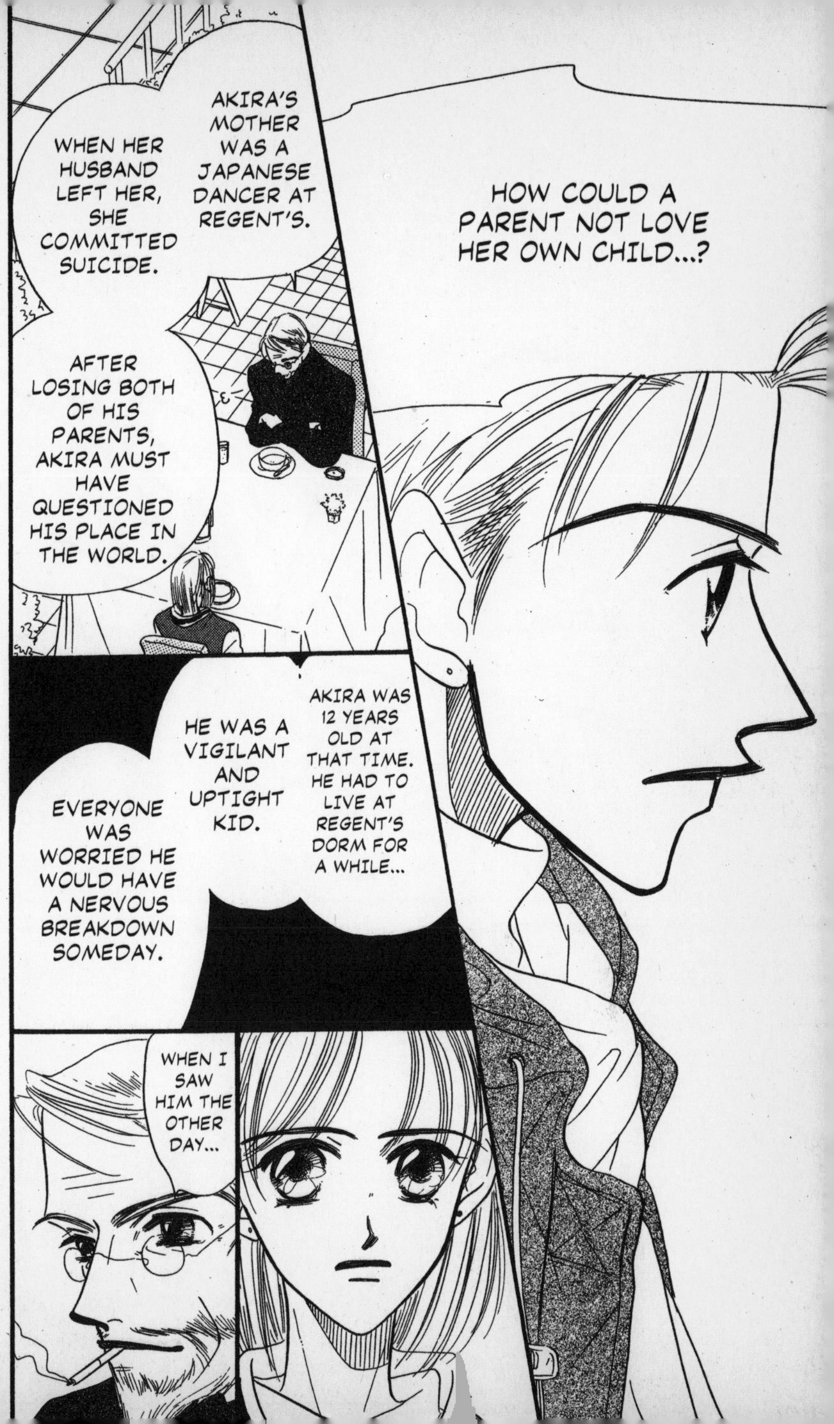
HOW COULD A PARENT NOT LOVE HER OWN CHILD...?
AKIRA'S MOTHER WAS A JAPANESE DANCER AT REGENT'S.
WHEN HER HUSBAND LEFT HER, SHE COMMITTED SUICIDE.
AFTER LOSING BOTH OF HIS PARENTS, AKIRA MUST HAVE QUESTIONED HIS PLACE IN THE WORLD.
AKIRA WAS 12 YEARS OLD AT THAT TIME. HE HAD TO LIVE AT REGENT'S DORM FOR A WHILE...
HE WAS A VIGILANT AND UPTIGHT KID.
EVERYONE WAS WORRIED HE WOULD HAVE A NERVOUS BREAKDOWN SOMEDAY.
WHEN I SAW HIM THE OTHER DAY...

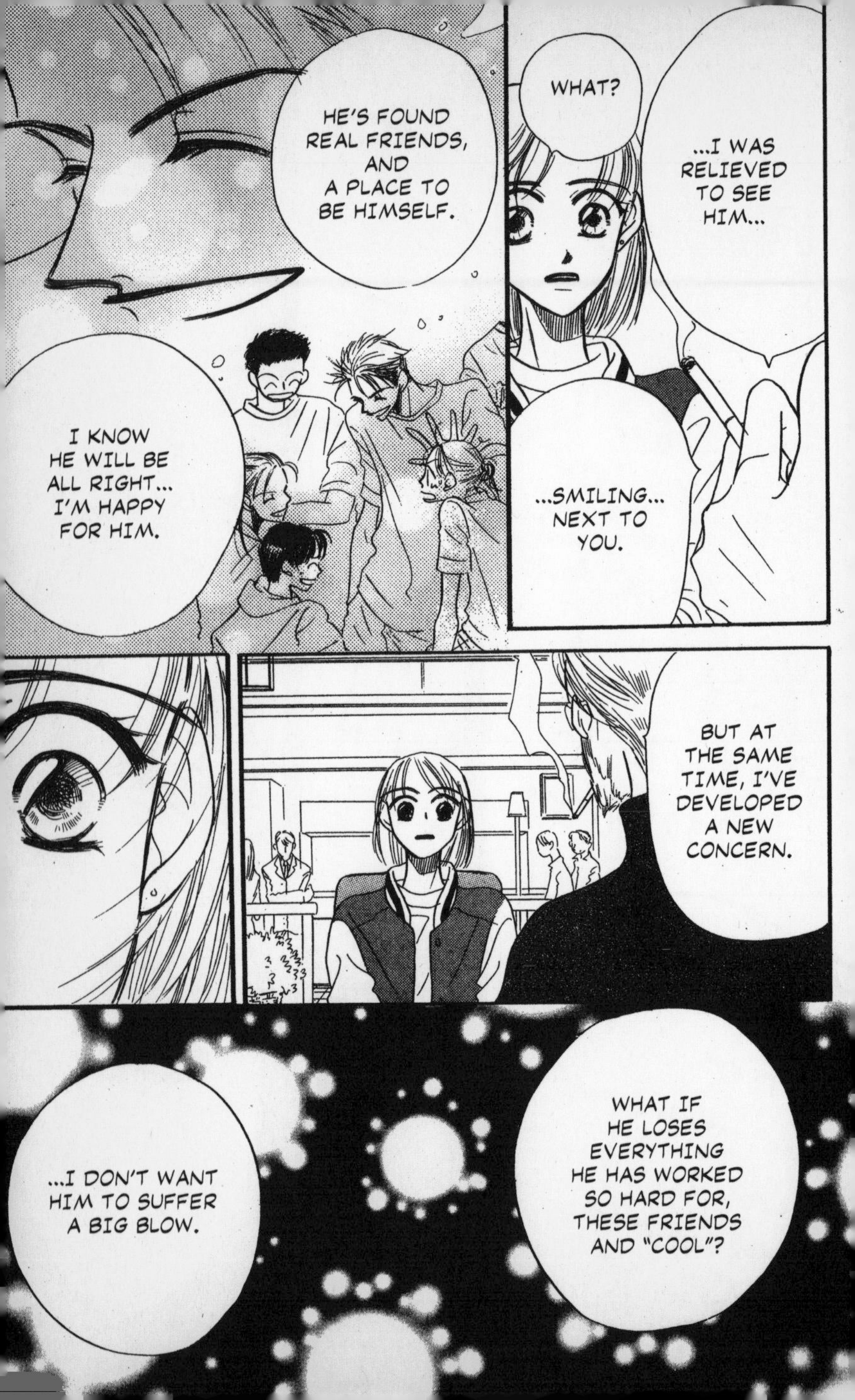
...I WAS RELIEVED TO SEE HIM...
WHAT?
...SMILING... NEXT TO YOU.
HE'S FOUND REAL FRIENDS, AND A PLACE TO BE HIMSELF.
I KNOW HE WILL BE ALL RIGHT... I'M HAPPY FOR HIM.
BUT AT THE SAME TIME, I'VE DEVELOPED A NEW CONCERN.
WHAT IF HE LOSES EVERYTHING HE HAS WORKED SO HARD FOR, THESE FRIENDS AND "COOL"?
...I DON'T WANT HIM TO SUFFER A BIG BLOW.

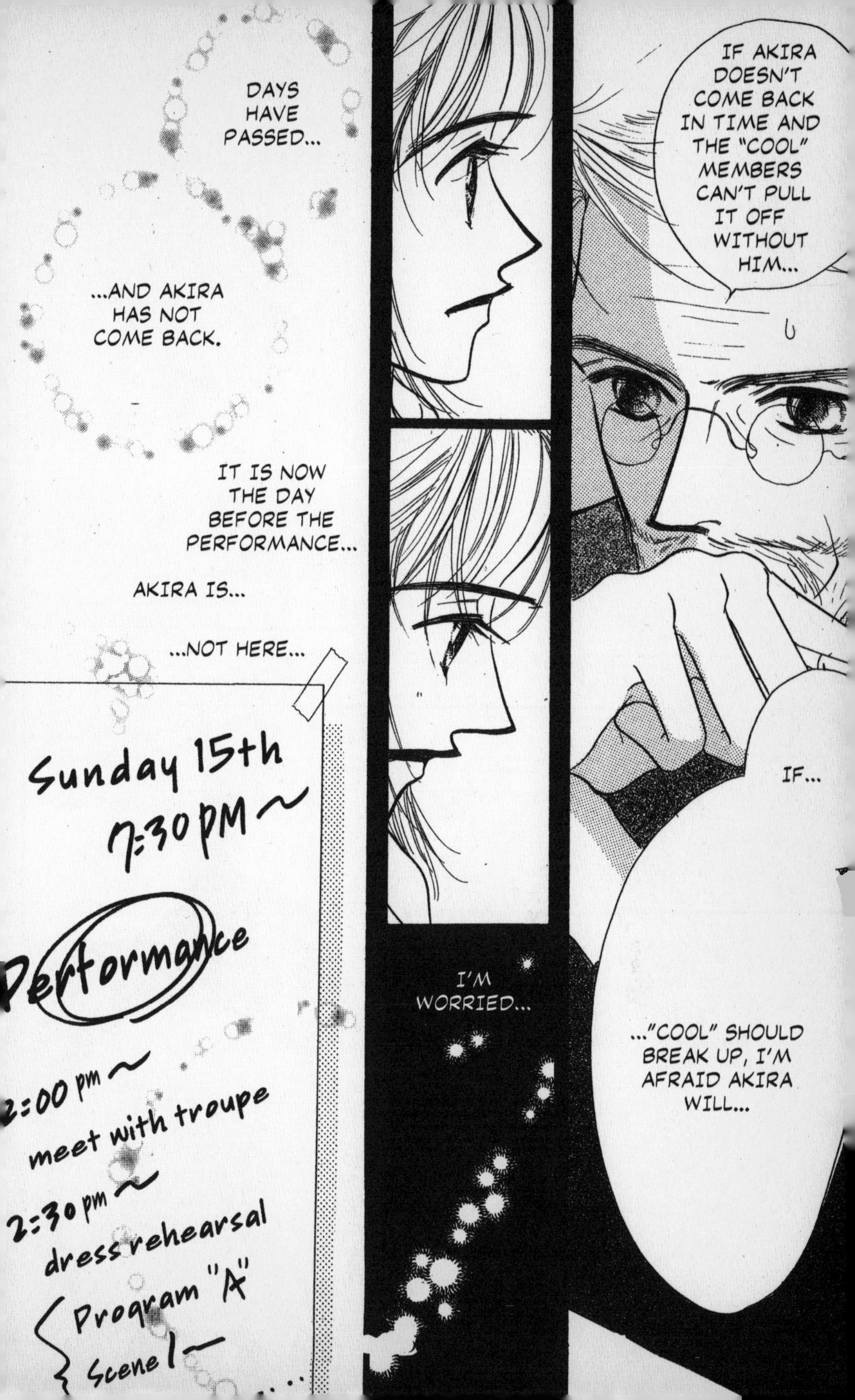
IF AKIRA DOESN'T COME BACK IN TIME AND THE "COOL" MEMBERS CAN'T PULL IT OFF WITHOUT HIM...
IF...
..."COOL" SHOULD BREAK UP, I'M AFRAID AKIRA WILL...
I'M WORRIED...
DAYS HAVE PASSED...
...AND AKIRA HAS NOT COME BACK.
IT IS NOW THE DAY BEFORE THE PERFORMANCE...
AKIRA IS...
...NOT HERE...
Sunday 15th
7:30 PM ~
Performance
2:00 pm ~
meet with troupe
2:30 pm ~
dress rehearsal
Program "A"
Scene 1 ~

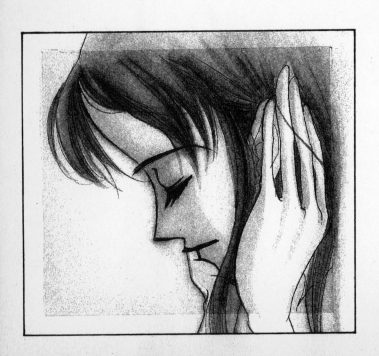

Princess Line

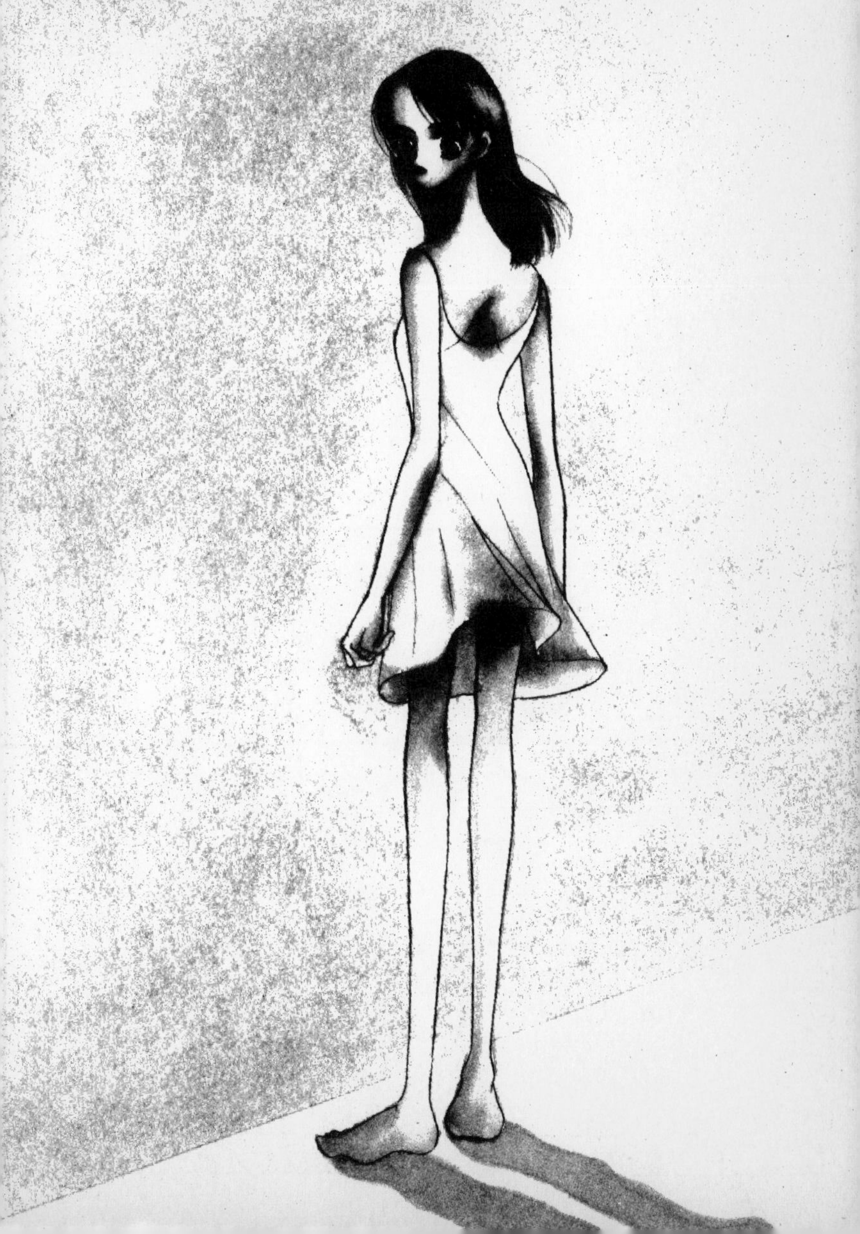

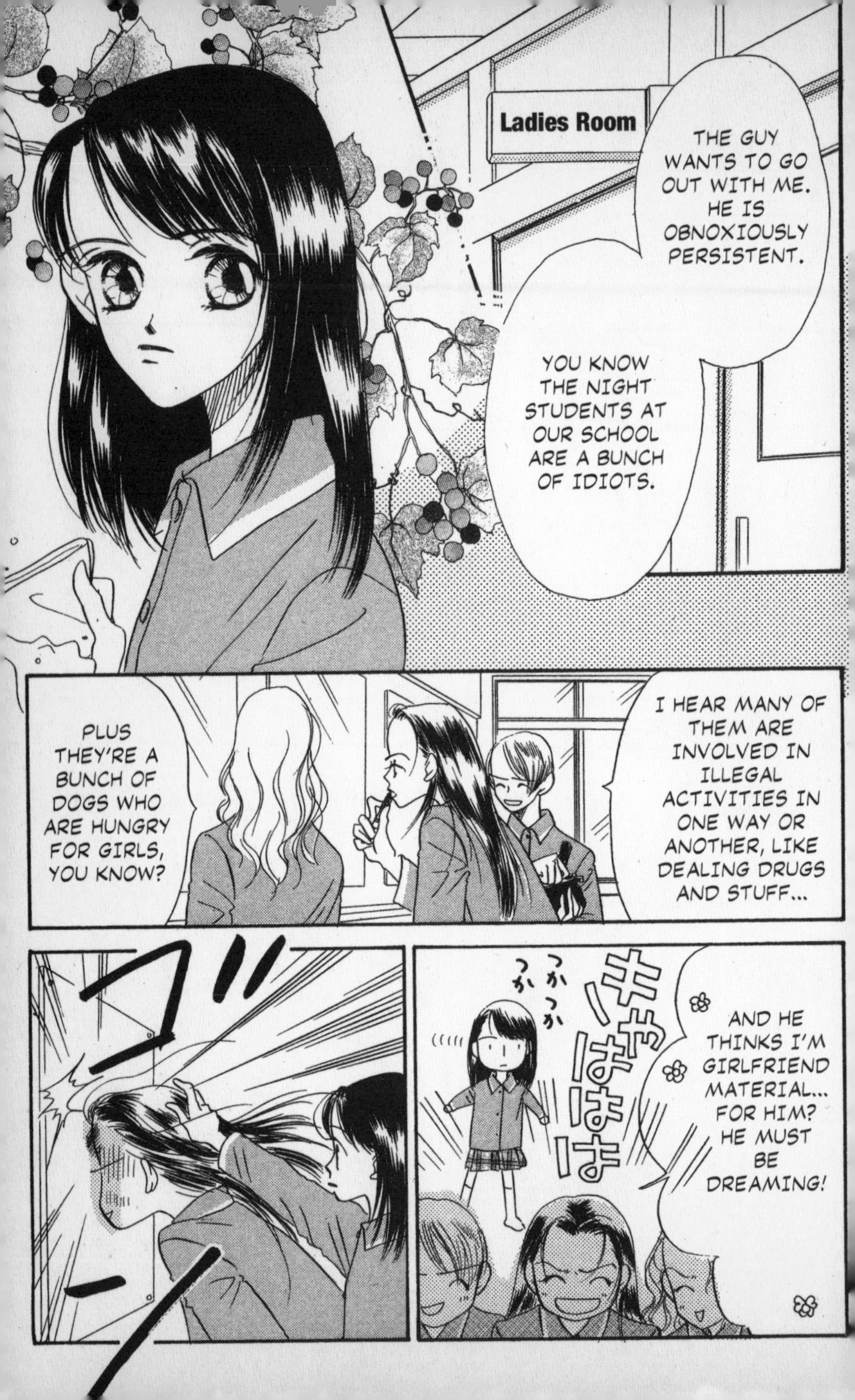

Ladies Room
THE GUY WANTS TO GO OUT WITH ME. HE IS OBNOXIOUSLY PERSISTENT.
YOU KNOW THE NIGHT STUDENTS AT OUR SCHOOL ARE A BUNCH OF IDIOTS.
I HEAR MANY OF THEM ARE INVOLVED IN ILLEGAL ACTIVITIES IN ONE WAY OR ANOTHER, LIKE DEALING DRUGS AND STUFF...
PLUS THEY'RE A BUNCH OF DOGS WHO ARE HUNGRY FOR GIRLS, YOU KNOW?
AND HE THINKS I'M GIRLFRIEND MATERIAL... FOR HIM? HE MUST BE DREAMING!
きゃははは
つかつか
つか
ゴ

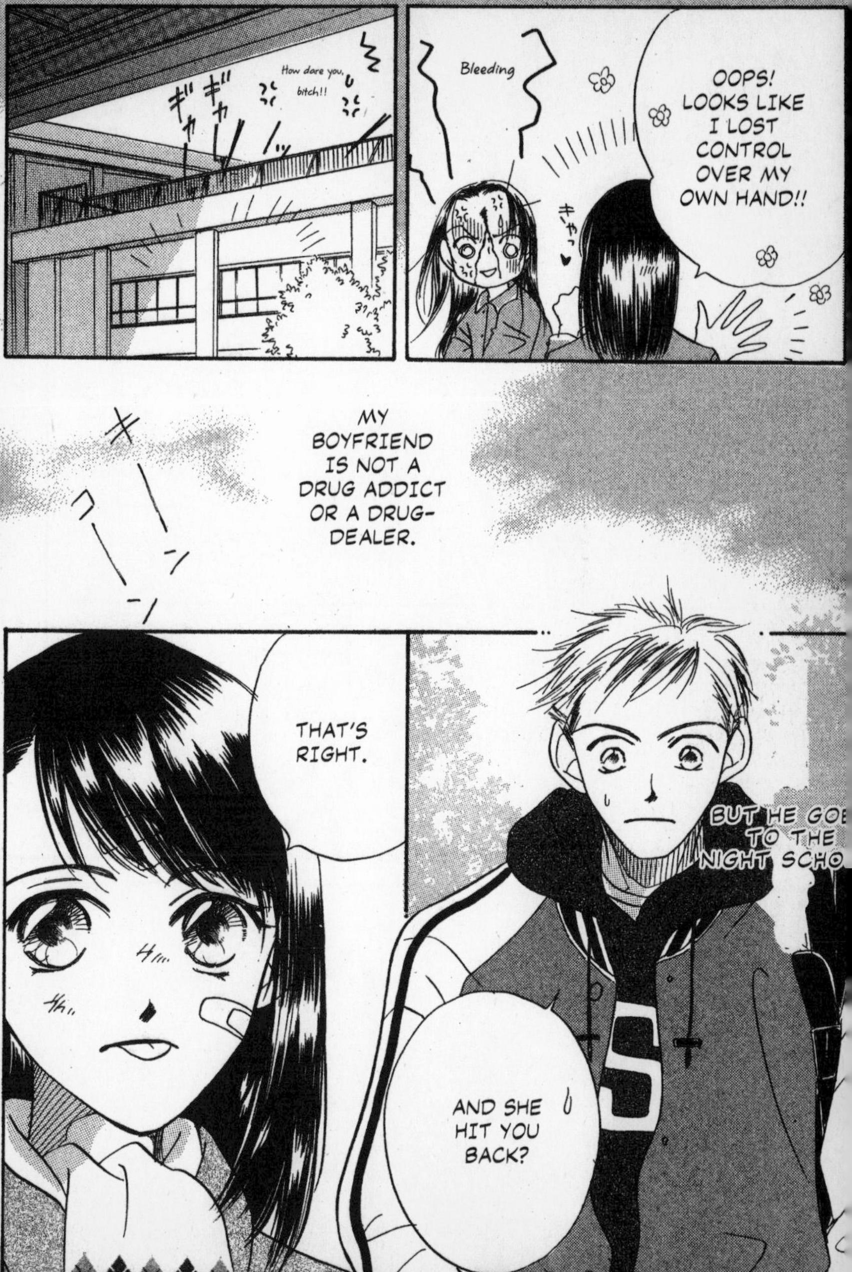

OOPS! LOOKS LIKE I LOST CONTROL OVER MY OWN HAND!!
Bleeding
How dare you, bitch!!
MY BOYFRIEND IS NOT A DRUG ADDICT OR A DRUG-DEALER.
BUT HE GOE TO THE NIGHT SCHO
AND SHE HIT YOU BACK?
THAT'S RIGHT.

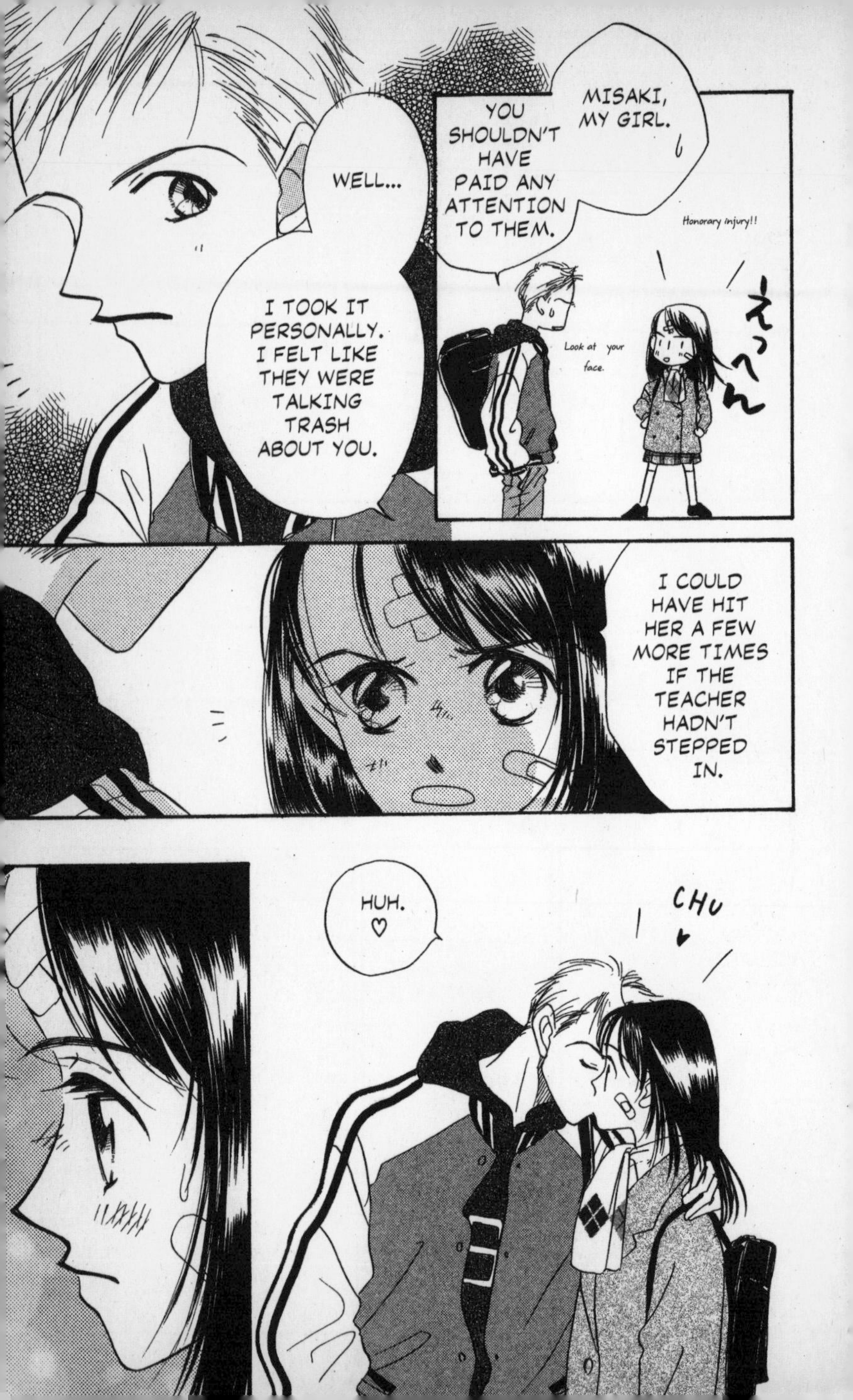
MISAKI, MY GIRL.
YOU SHOULDN'T HAVE PAID ANY ATTENTION TO THEM.
Honorary injury!!
えっへん
Look at your face.
WELL...
I TOOK IT PERSONALLY. I FELT LIKE THEY WERE TALKING TRASH ABOUT YOU.
I COULD HAVE HIT HER A FEW MORE TIMES IF THE TEACHER HADN'T STEPPED IN.
CHU ♥
HUH. ♡

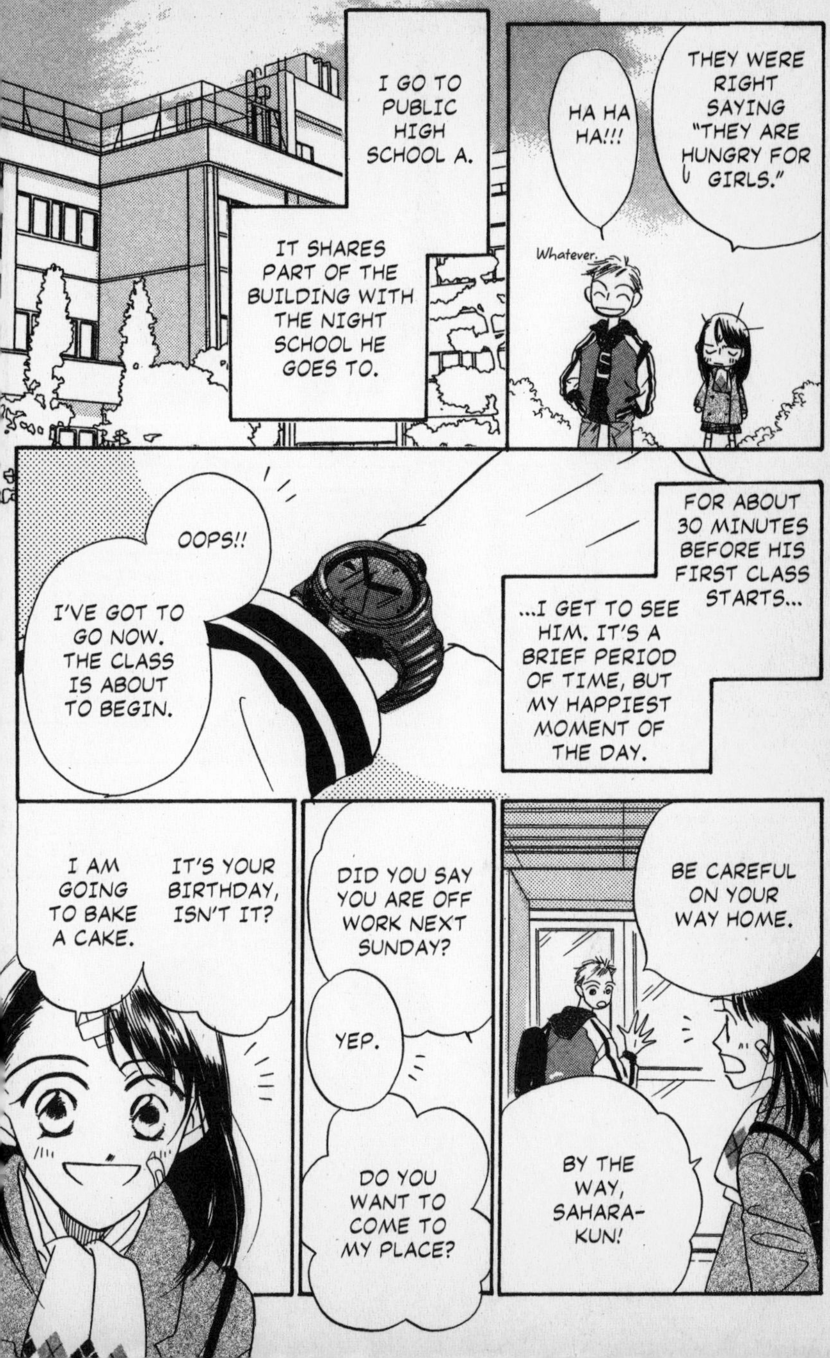
THEY WERE RIGHT SAYING "THEY ARE HUNGRY FOR GIRLS."
HA HA HA!!!
Whatever.
I GO TO PUBLIC HIGH SCHOOL A.
IT SHARES PART OF THE BUILDING WITH THE NIGHT SCHOOL HE GOES TO.
FOR ABOUT 30 MINUTES BEFORE HIS FIRST CLASS STARTS...
...I GET TO SEE HIM. IT'S A BRIEF PERIOD OF TIME, BUT MY HAPPIEST MOMENT OF THE DAY.
OOPS!!
I'VE GOT TO GO NOW. THE CLASS IS ABOUT TO BEGIN.
BE CAREFUL ON YOUR WAY HOME.
BY THE WAY, SAHARA-KUN!
DID YOU SAY YOU ARE OFF WORK NEXT SUNDAY?
YEP.
DO YOU WANT TO COME TO MY PLACE?
IT'S YOUR BIRTHDAY, ISN'T IT?
I AM GOING TO BAKE A CAKE.

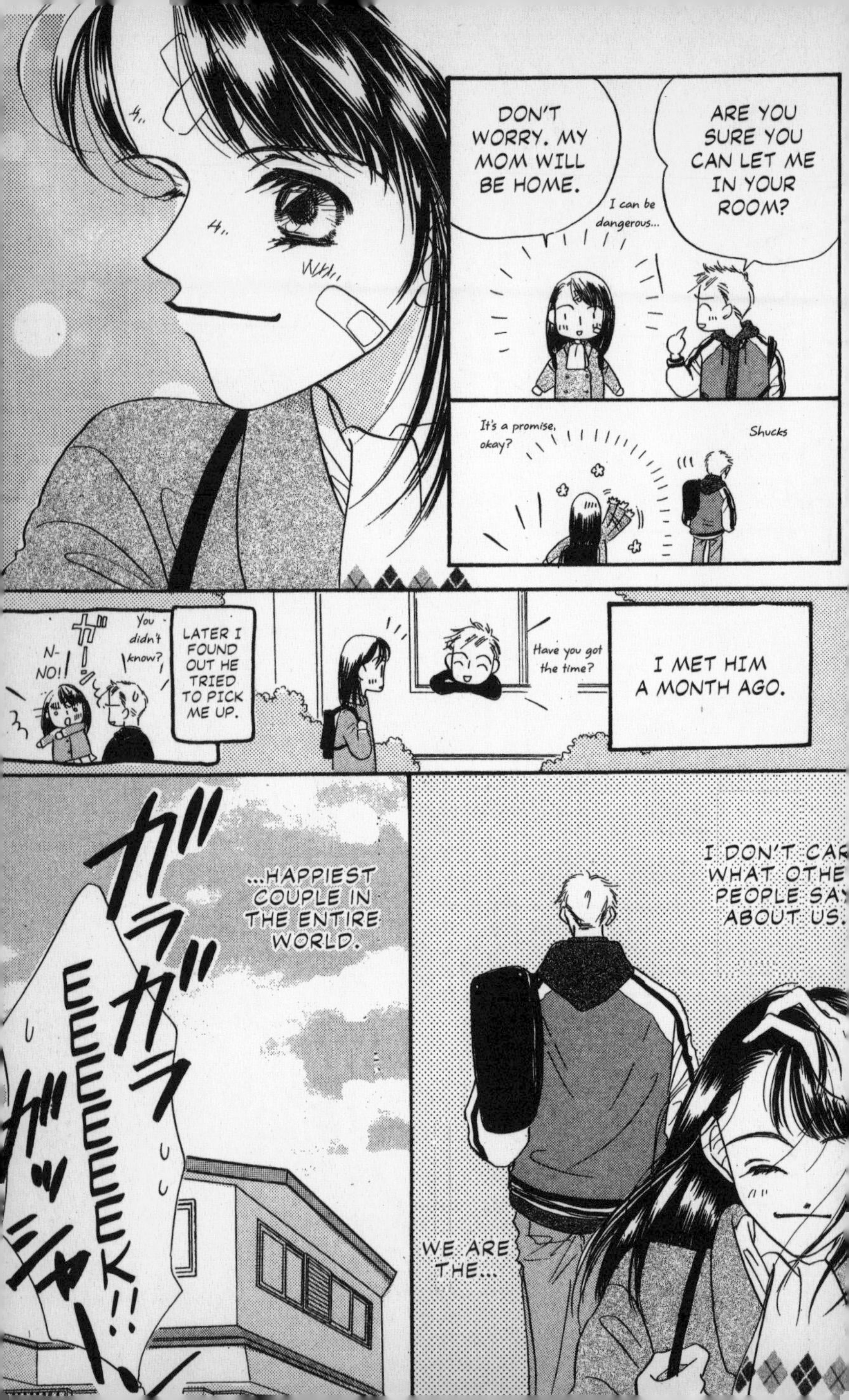
ARE YOU SURE YOU CAN LET ME IN YOUR ROOM?
I can be dangerous...
DON'T WORRY. MY MOM WILL BE HOME.
Shucks
It's a promise, okay?
I MET HIM A MONTH AGO.
Have you got the time?
LATER I FOUND OUT HE TRIED TO PICK ME UP.
You didn't know?
N- NO!
I DON'T CAR WHAT OTHE PEOPLE SA ABOUT US.
WE ARE THE...
...HAPPIEST COUPLE IN THE ENTIRE WORLD.
ガラガラ
EEEEEEEK!!
ガッシャー

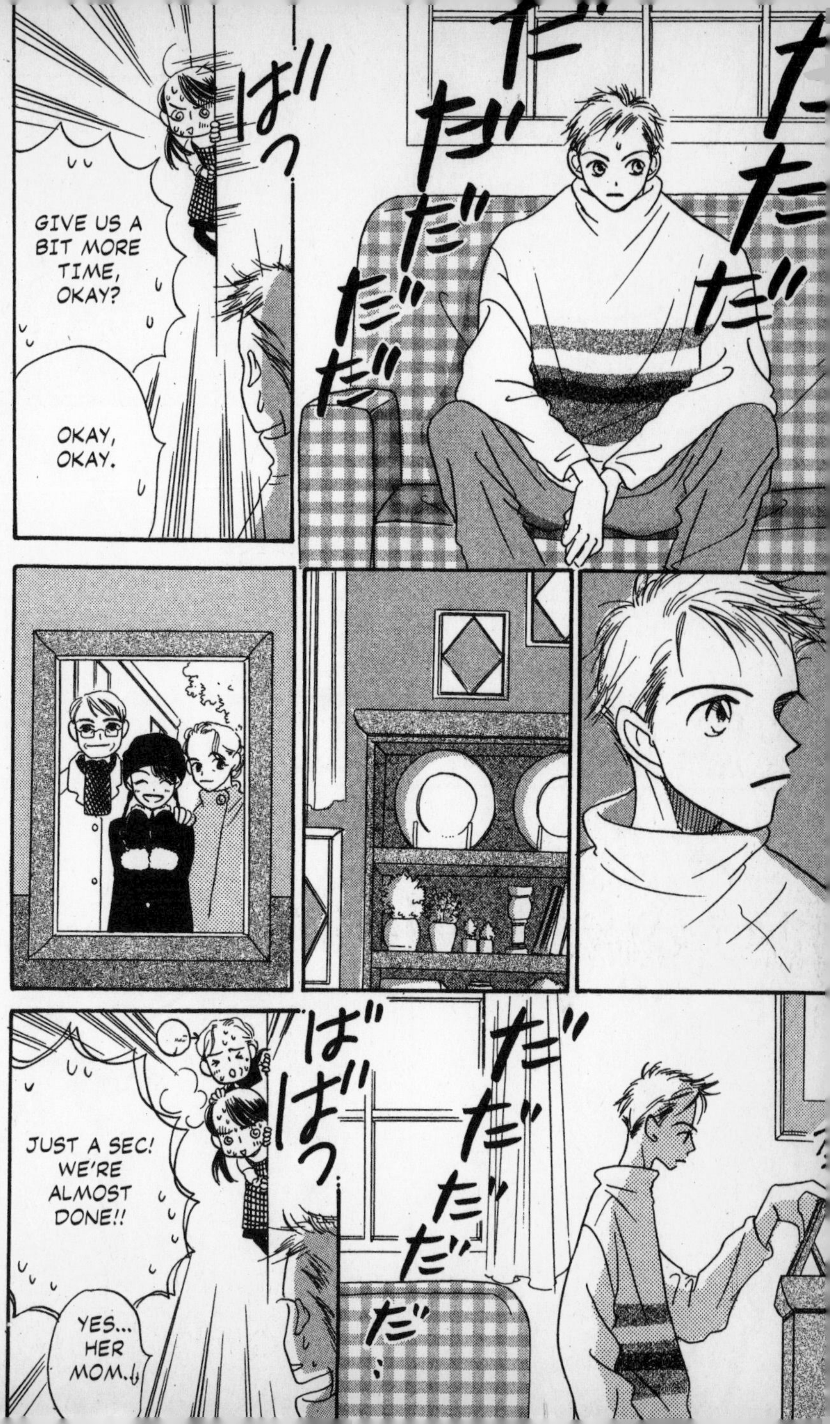
たただ
だだだだだだ
ばっ
GIVE US A BIT MORE TIME, OKAY?
OKAY, OKAY.
ただだだだ
ばばっ
JUST A SEC! WE'RE ALMOST DONE!!
YES... HER MOM.

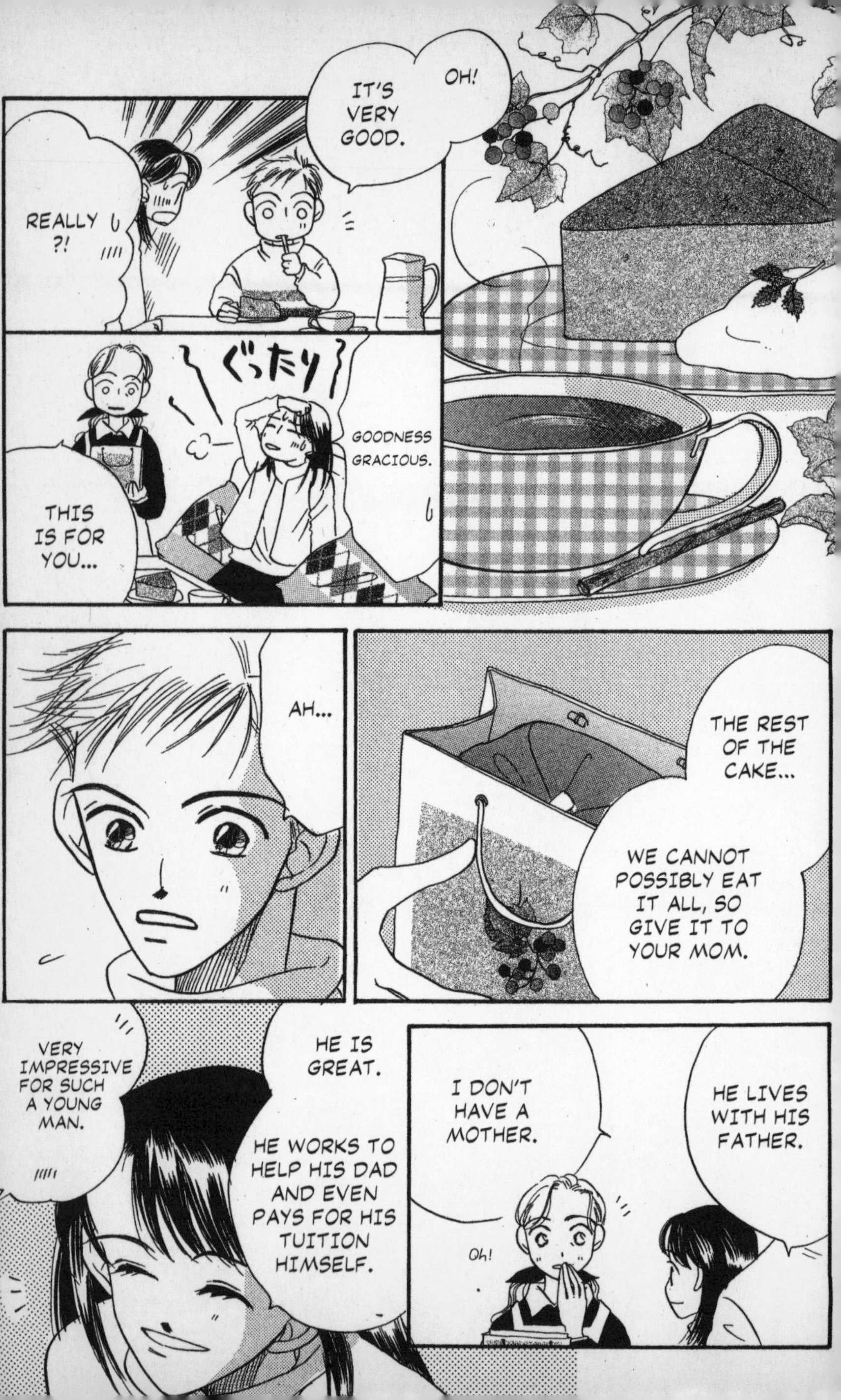
OH! IT'S VERY GOOD.
REALLY ?!
ぐったり
GOODNESS GRACIOUS.
THIS IS FOR YOU...
THE REST OF THE CAKE...
WE CANNOT POSSIBLY EAT IT ALL, SO GIVE IT TO YOUR MOM.
AH...
HE LIVES WITH HIS FATHER.
I DON'T HAVE A MOTHER.
Oh!
HE IS GREAT.
HE WORKS TO HELP HIS DAD AND EVEN PAYS FOR HIS TUITION HIMSELF.
VERY IMPRESSIVE FOR SUCH A YOUNG MAN.

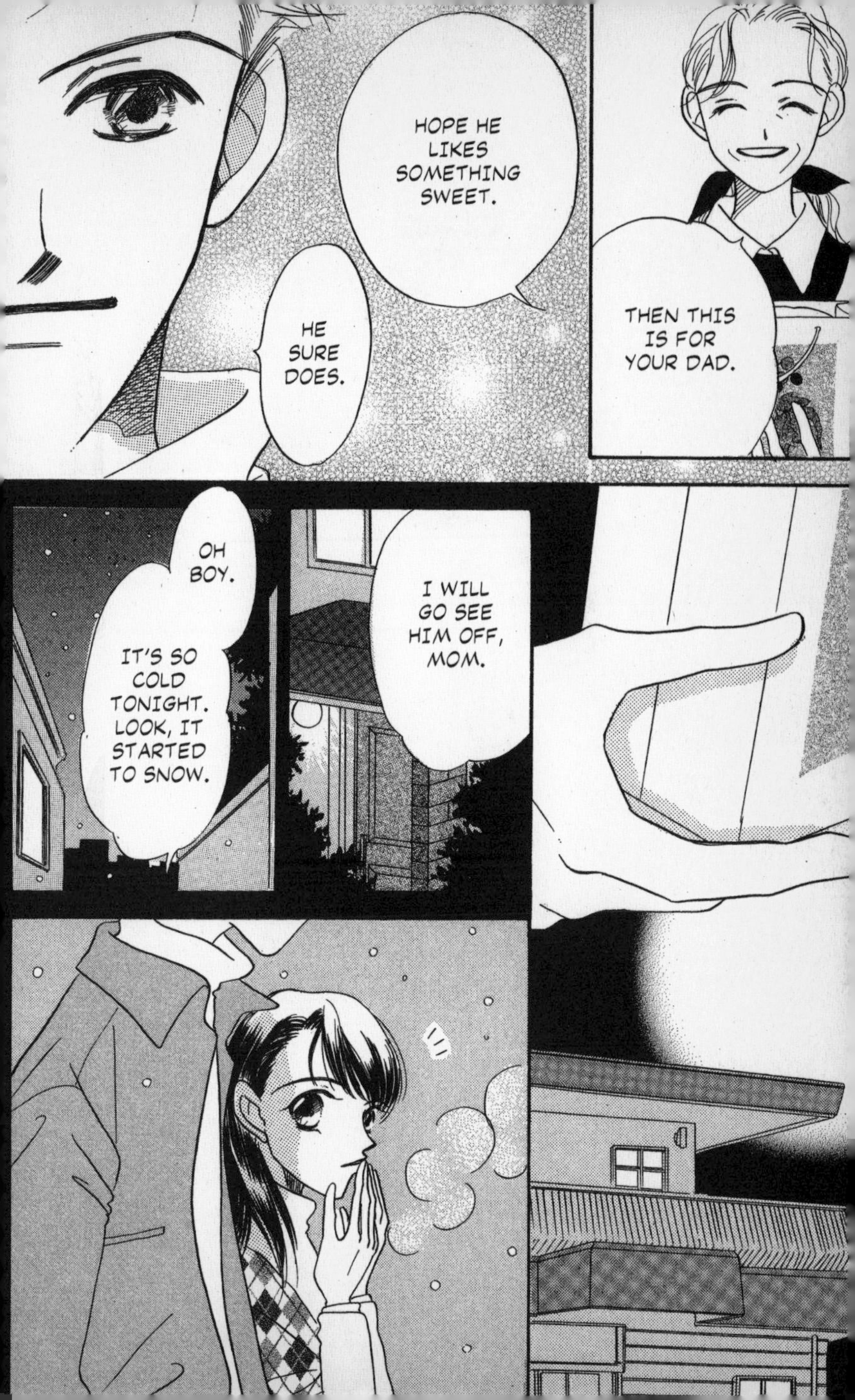
THEN THIS IS FOR YOUR DAD.
HOPE HE LIKES SOMETHING SWEET.
HE SURE DOES.
I WILL GO SEE HIM OFF, MOM.
OH BOY.
IT'S SO COLD TONIGHT. LOOK, IT STARTED TO SNOW.

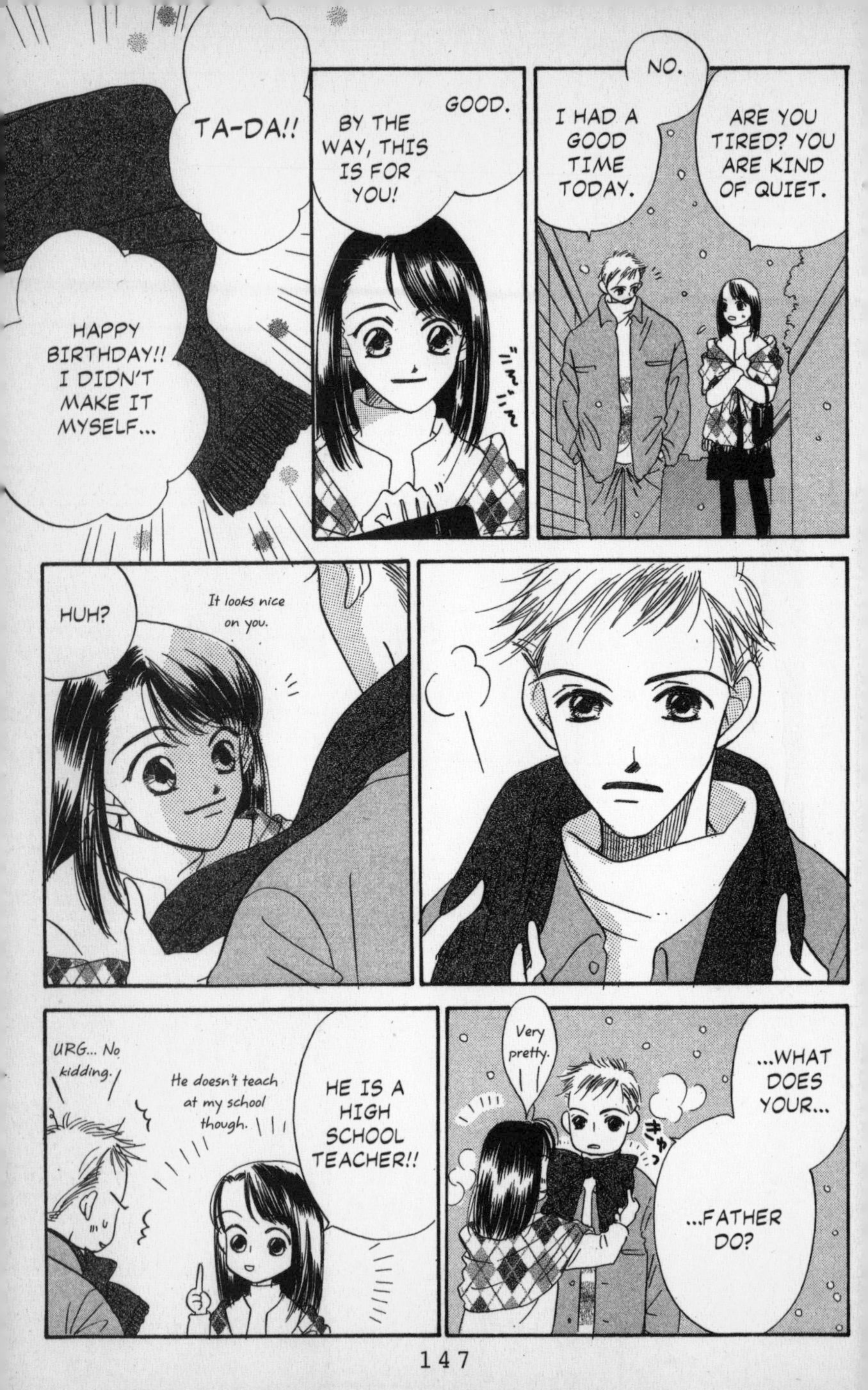
ARE YOU TIRED? YOU ARE KIND OF QUIET.
NO.
I HAD A GOOD TIME TODAY.
GOOD.
BY THE WAY, THIS IS FOR YOU!
TA-DA!!
HAPPY BIRTHDAY!! I DIDN'T MAKE IT MYSELF...
It looks nice on you.
HUH?
...WHAT DOES YOUR...
...FATHER DO?
Very pretty.
HE IS A HIGH SCHOOL TEACHER!!
He doesn't teach at my school though.
URG... No kidding.

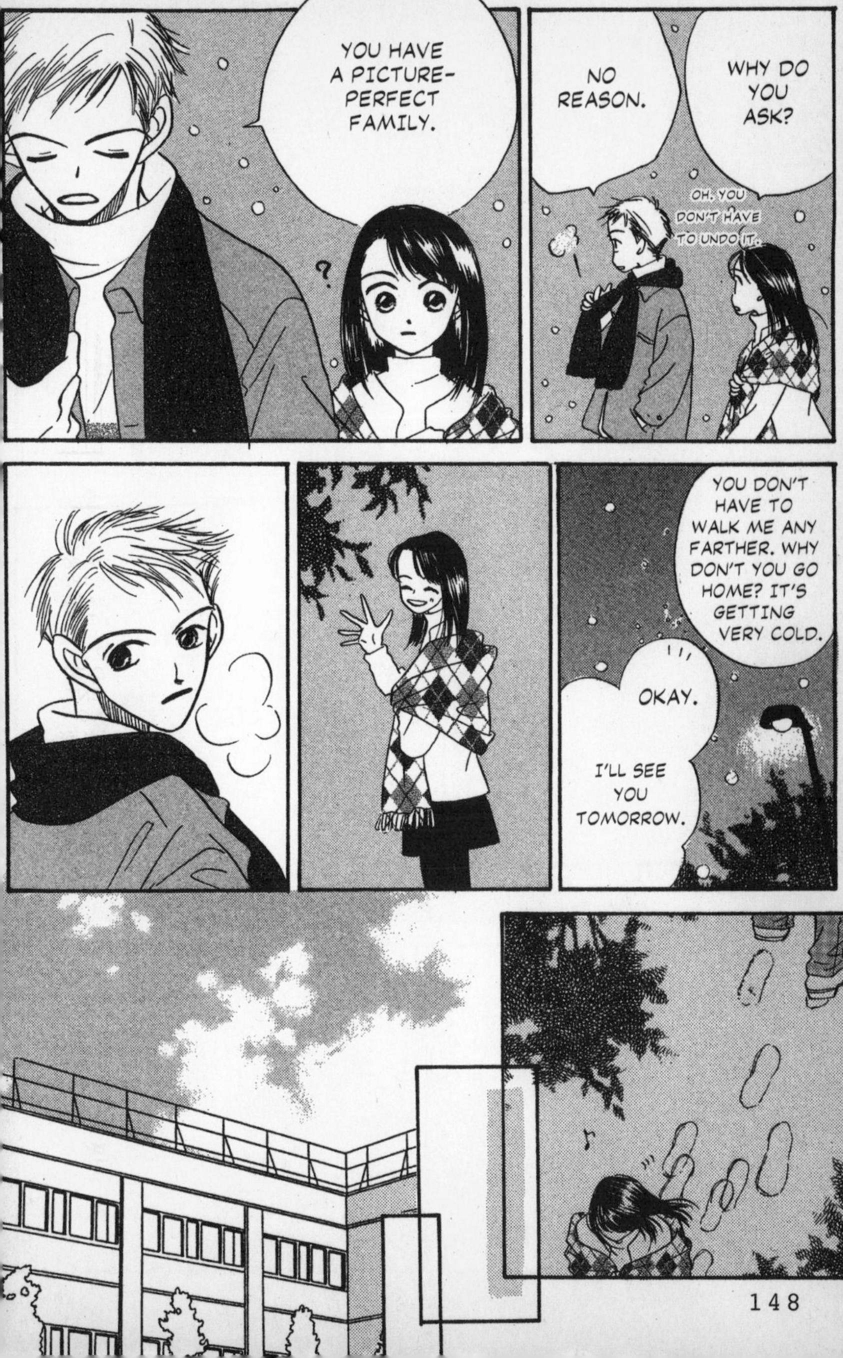
WHY DO YOU ASK?
NO REASON.
OH. YOU DON'T HAVE TO UNDO IT.
YOU HAVE A PICTURE-PERFECT FAMILY.
YOU DON'T HAVE TO WALK ME ANY FARTHER. WHY DON'T YOU GO HOME? IT'S GETTING VERY COLD.
OKAY.
I'LL SEE YOU TOMORROW.

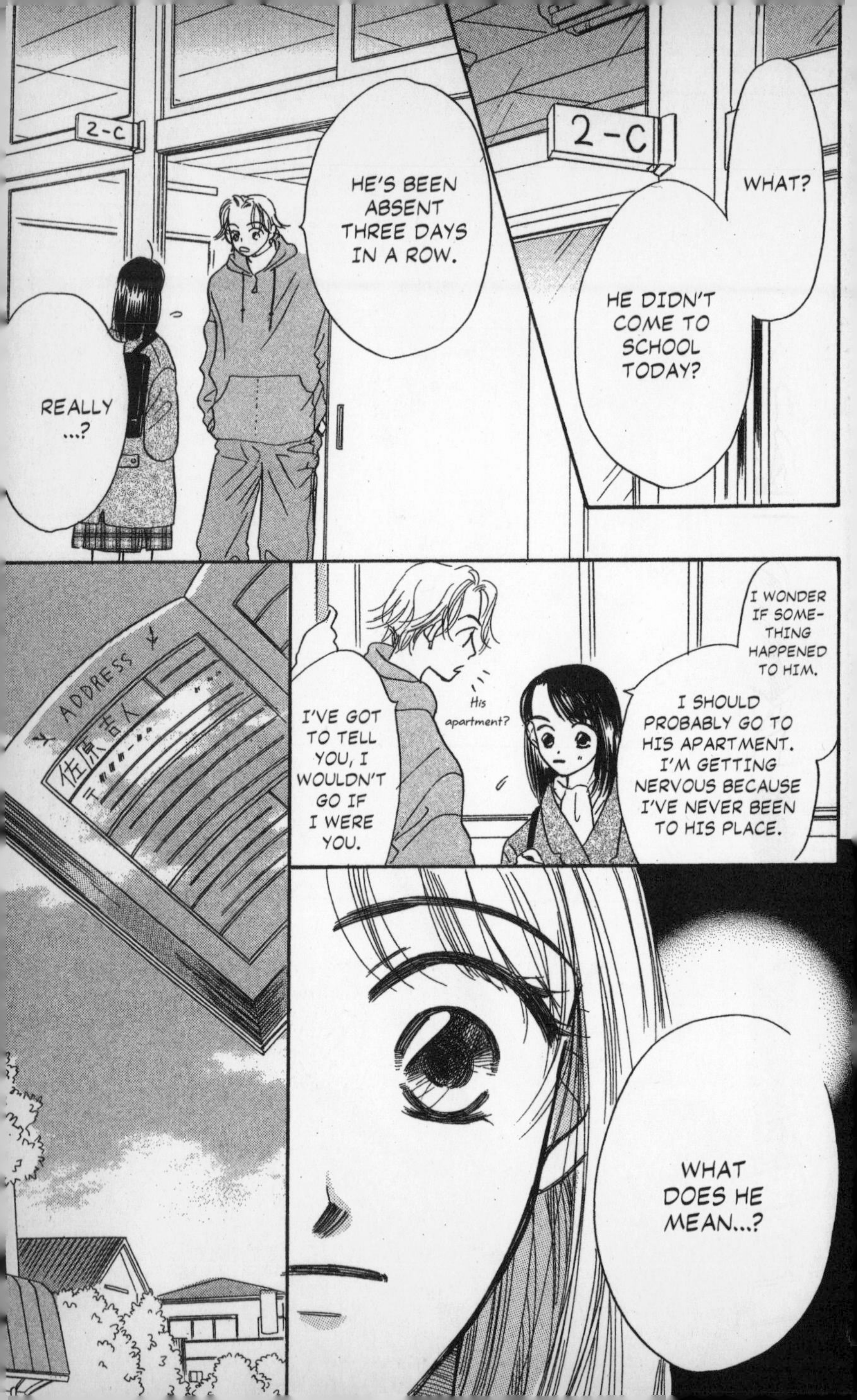
2-C
WHAT?
HE DIDN'T COME TO SCHOOL TODAY?
2-C
HE'S BEEN ABSENT THREE DAYS IN A ROW.
REALLY ...?
I WONDER IF SOME-THING HAPPENED TO HIM.
I SHOULD PROBABLY GO TO HIS APARTMENT. I'M GETTING NERVOUS BECAUSE I'VE NEVER BEEN TO HIS PLACE.
His apartment?
I'VE GOT TO TELL YOU, I WOULDN'T GO IF I WERE YOU.
WHAT DOES HE MEAN...?
ADDRESS

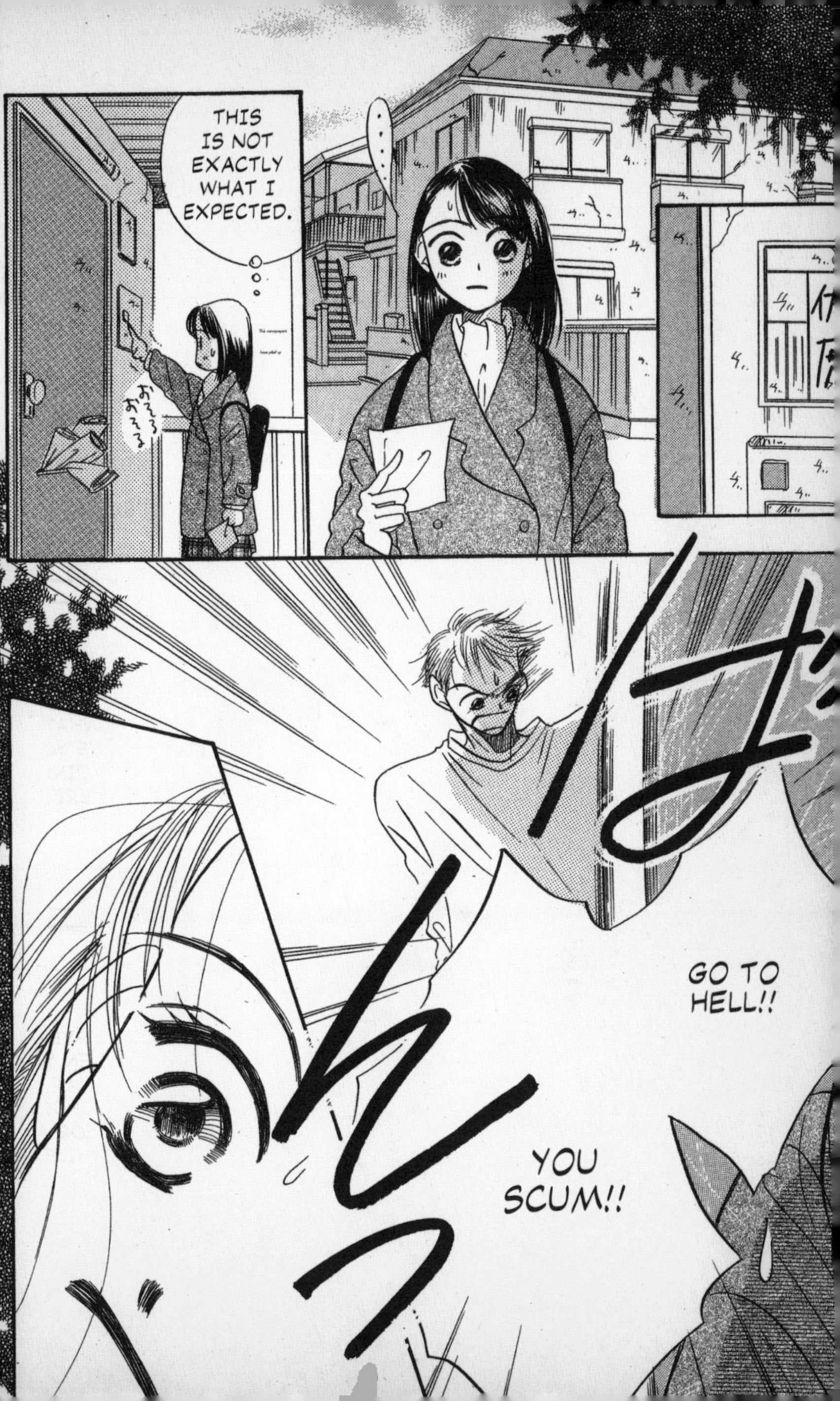
...
THIS IS NOT EXACTLY WHAT I EXPECTED.
GO TO HELL!!
YOU SCUM!!

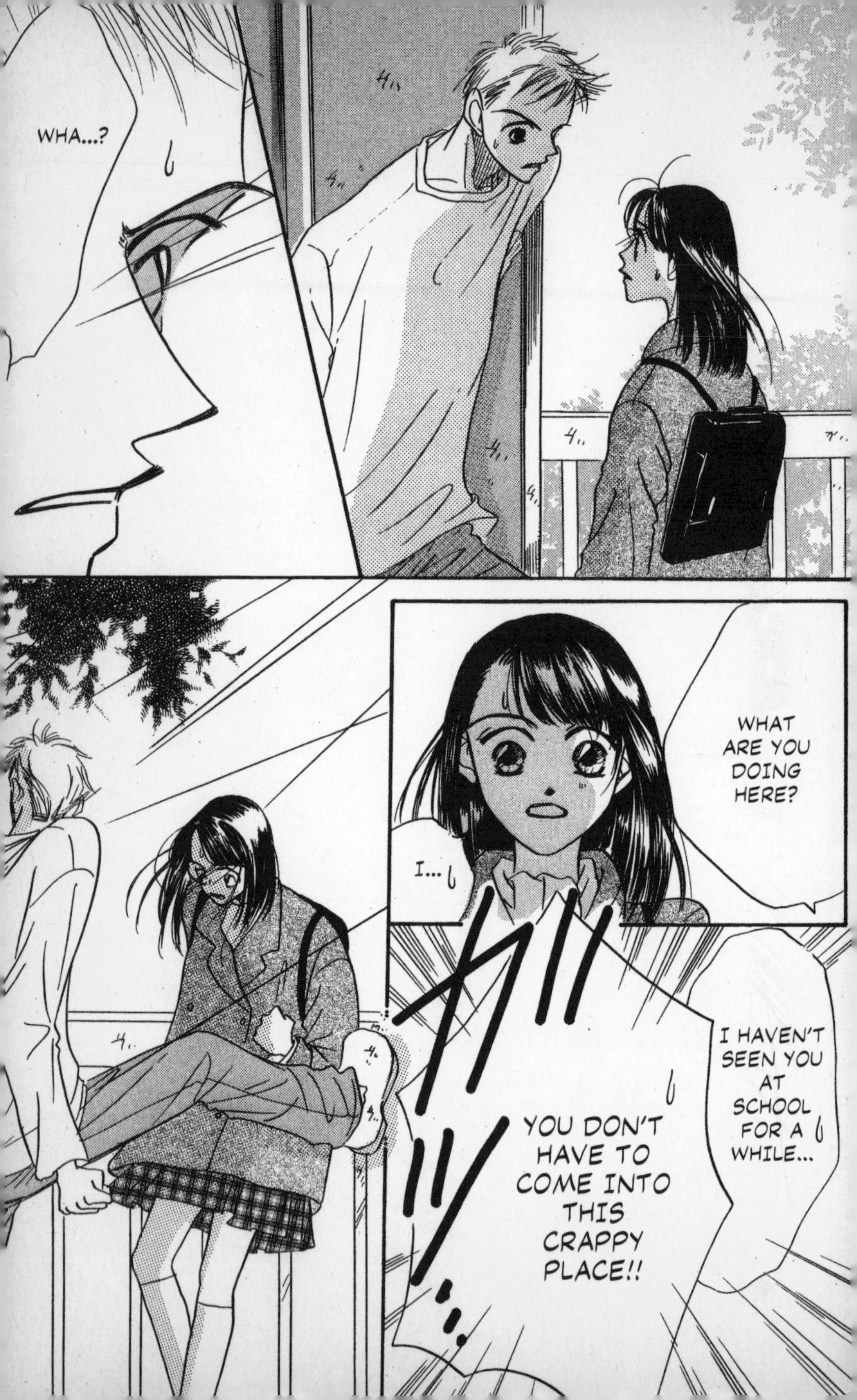
WHA...?
WHAT ARE YOU DOING HERE?
I...
I HAVEN'T SEEN YOU AT SCHOOL FOR A WHILE...
YOU DON'T HAVE TO COME INTO THIS CRAPPY PLACE!!

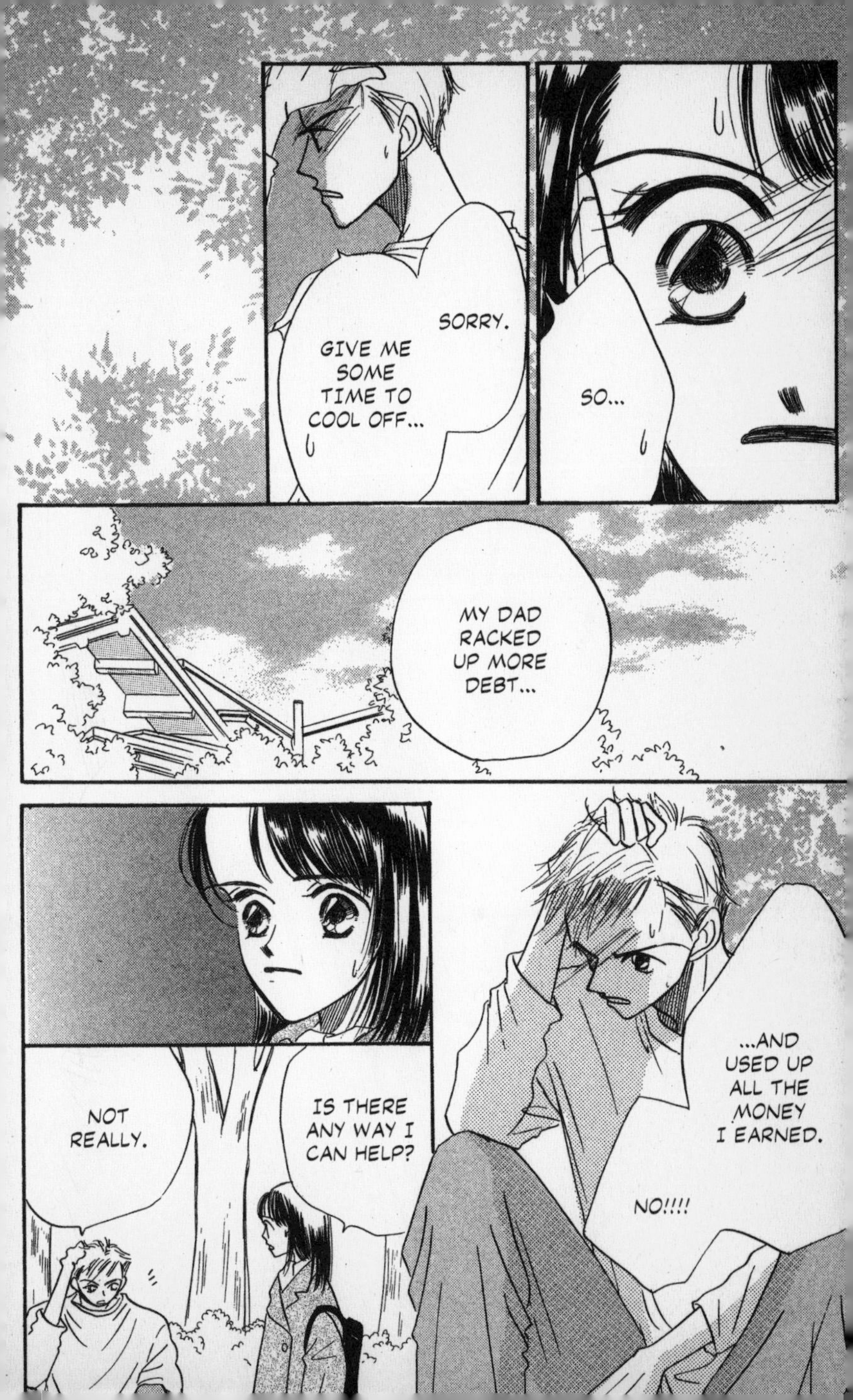
SO...
SORRY.
GIVE ME SOME TIME TO COOL OFF...
MY DAD RACKED UP MORE DEBT...
...AND USED UP ALL THE MONEY I EARNED.
NO!!!!
IS THERE ANY WAY I CAN HELP?
NOT REALLY.

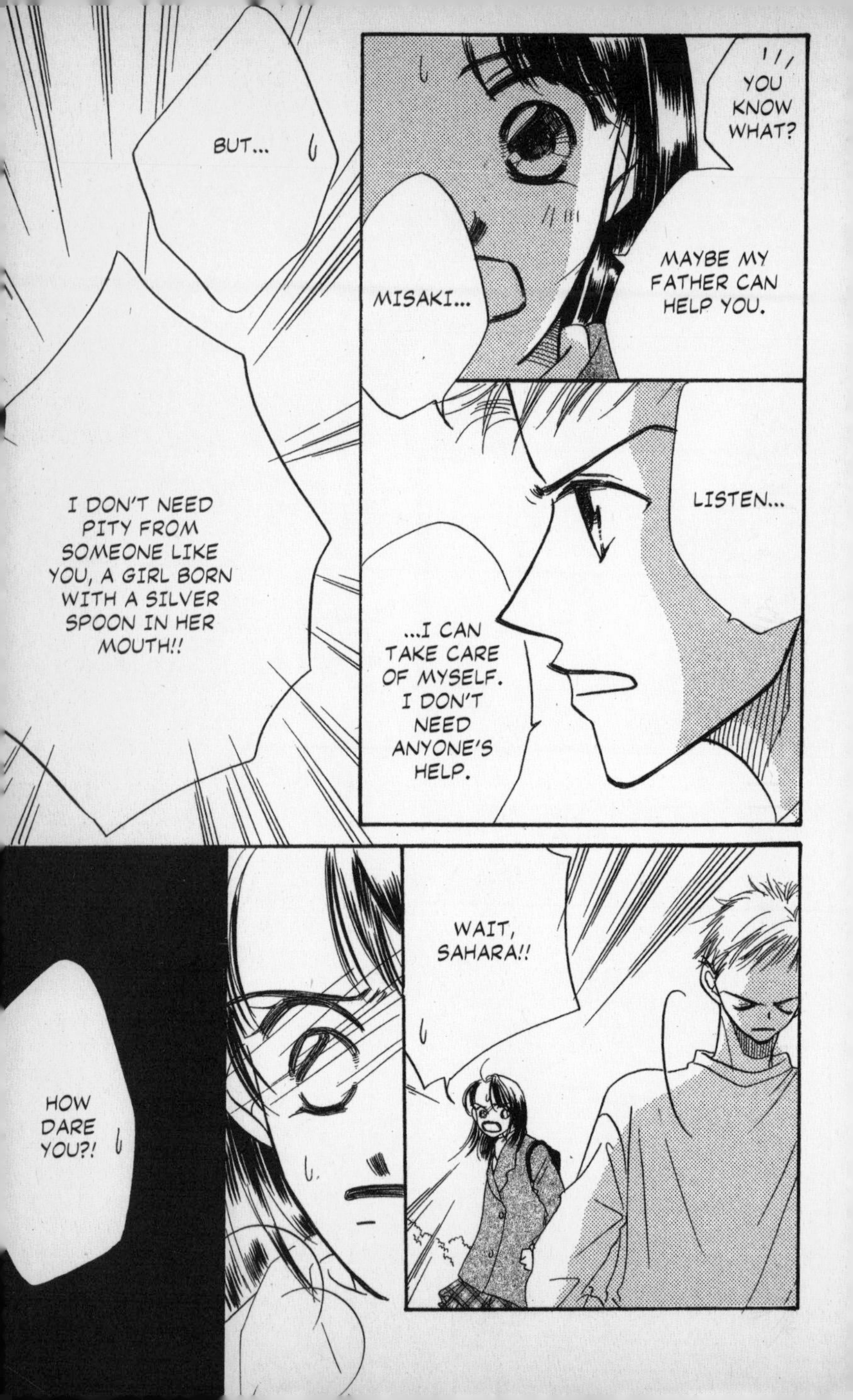

YOU KNOW WHAT?
MAYBE MY FATHER CAN HELP YOU.
MISAKI...
LISTEN...
...I CAN TAKE CARE OF MYSELF. I DON'T NEED ANYONE'S HELP.
BUT...
I DON'T NEED PITY FROM SOMEONE LIKE YOU, A GIRL BORN WITH A SILVER SPOON IN HER MOUTH!!
WAIT, SAHARA!!
HOW DARE YOU?!

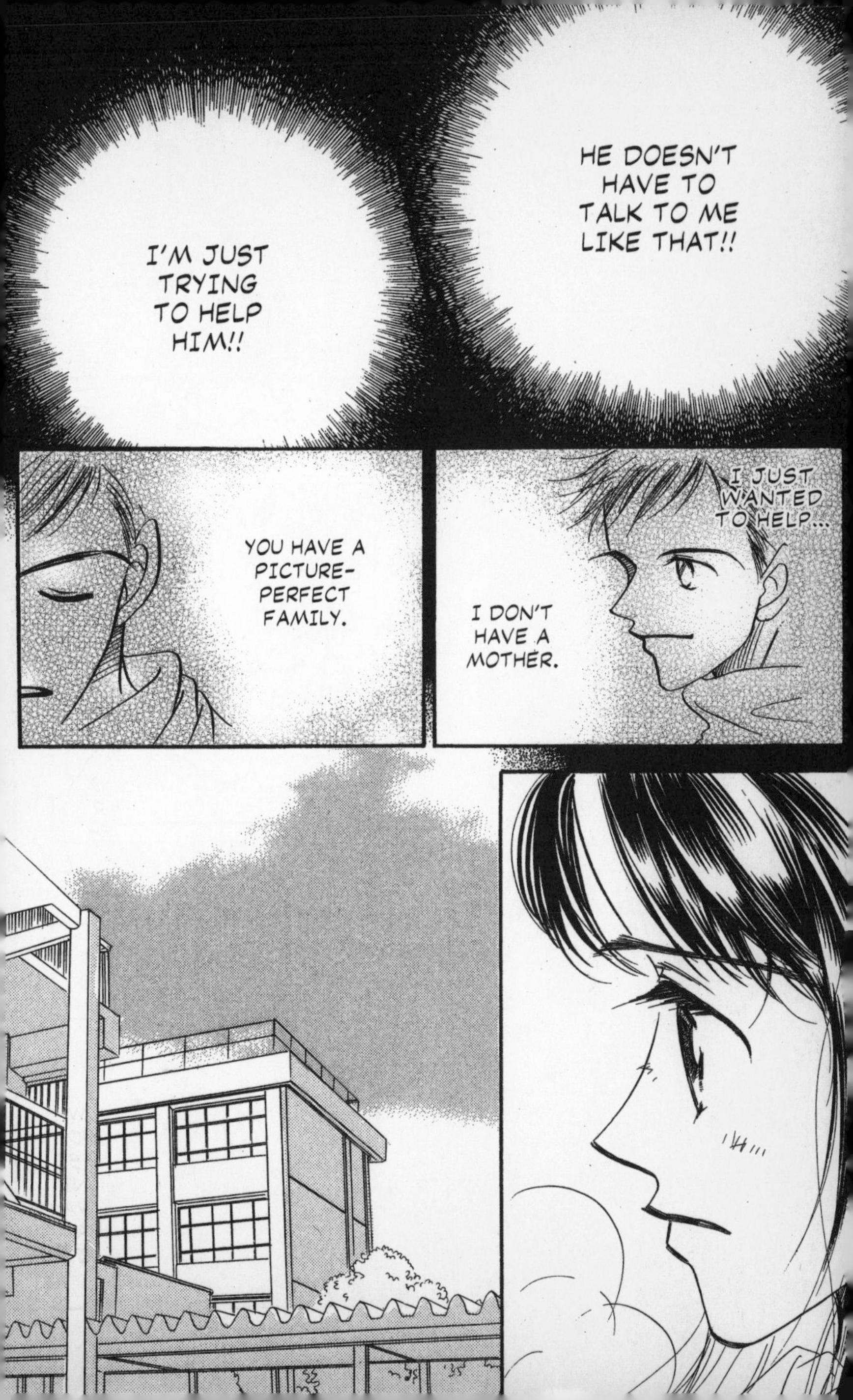
HE DOESN'T HAVE TO TALK TO ME LIKE THAT!!
I'M JUST TRYING TO HELP HIM!!
I JUST WANTED TO HELP...
I DON'T HAVE A MOTHER.
YOU HAVE A PICTURE-PERFECT FAMILY.

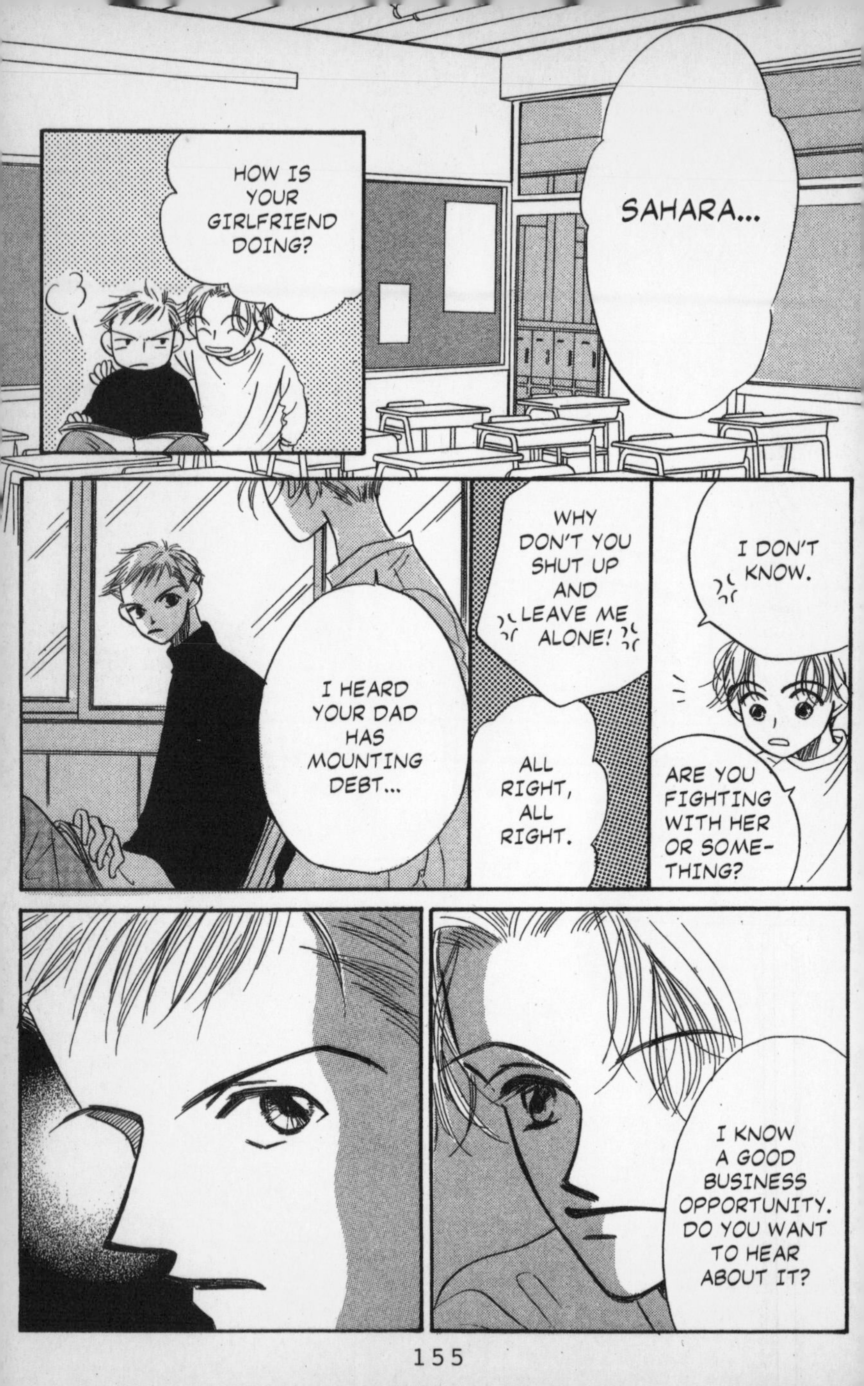
SAHARA...
HOW IS YOUR GIRLFRIEND DOING?
I DON'T KNOW.
ARE YOU FIGHTING WITH HER OR SOMETHING?
WHY DON'T YOU SHUT UP AND LEAVE ME ALONE!
ALL RIGHT, ALL RIGHT.
I HEARD YOUR DAD HAS MOUNTING DEBT...
I KNOW A GOOD BUSINESS OPPORTUNITY. DO YOU WANT TO HEAR ABOUT IT?

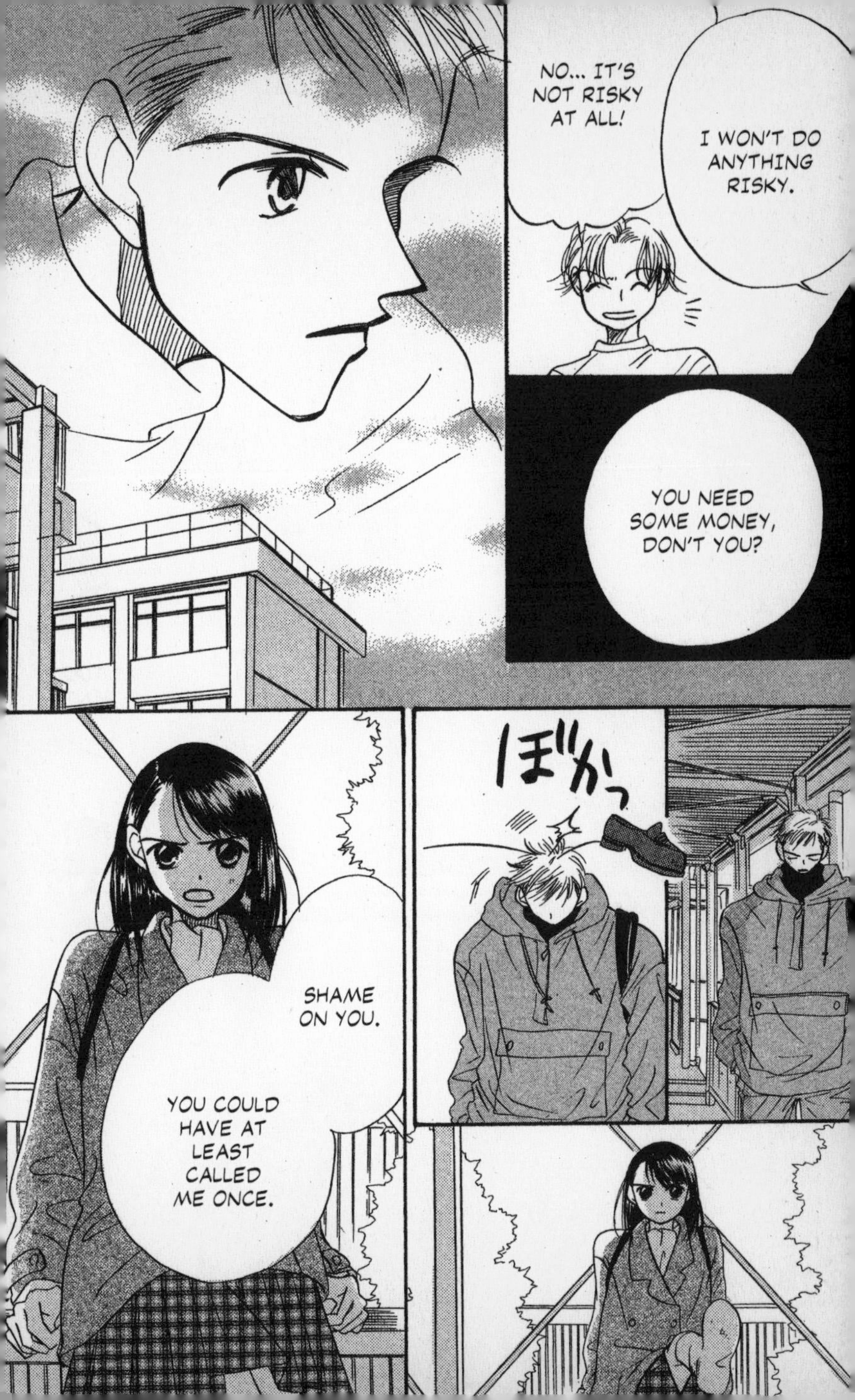
I WON'T DO ANYTHING RISKY.
NO... IT'S NOT RISKY AT ALL!
YOU NEED SOME MONEY, DON'T YOU?
ぼかっ
SHAME ON YOU.
YOU COULD HAVE AT LEAST CALLED ME ONCE.

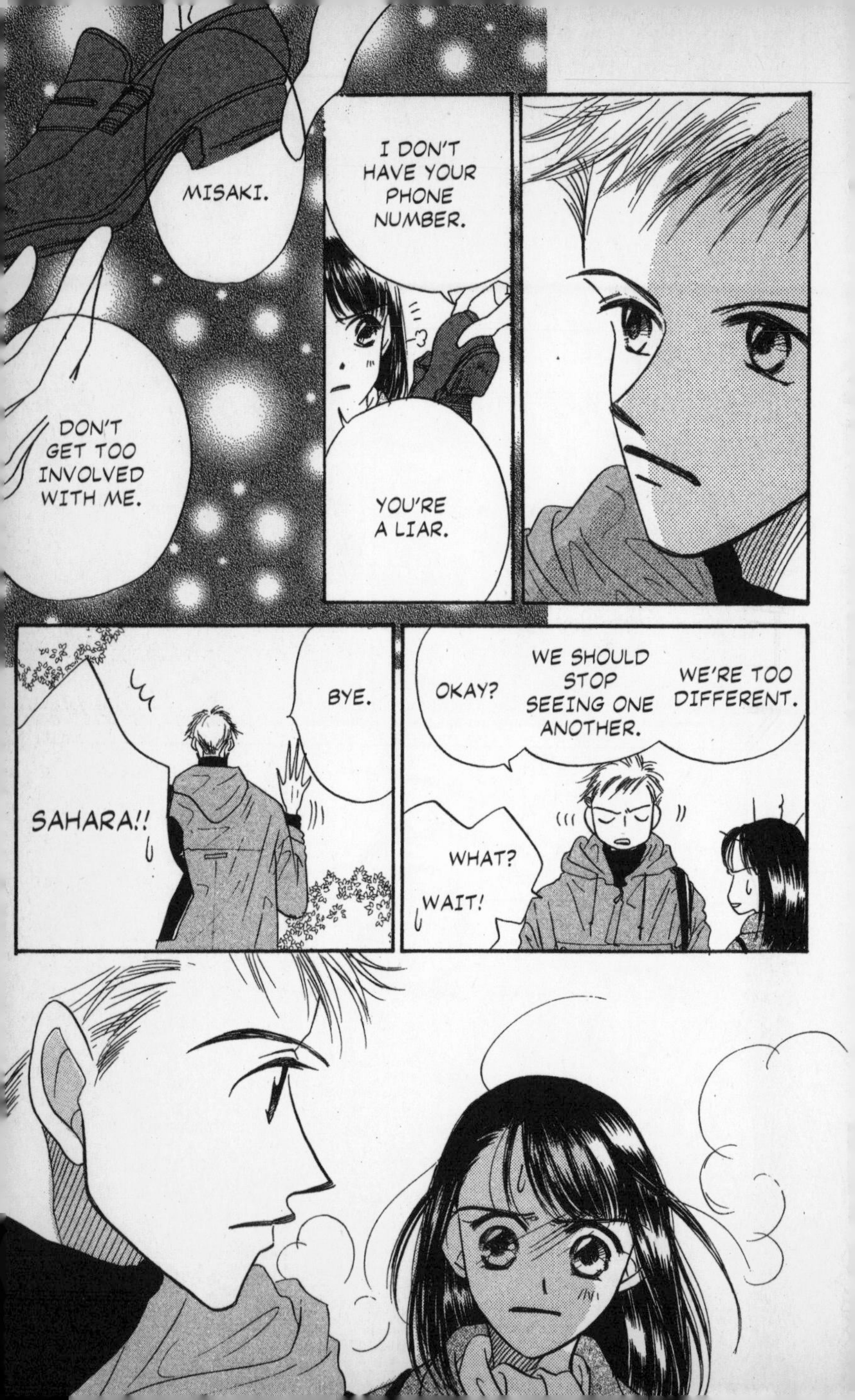
I DON'T HAVE YOUR PHONE NUMBER.
YOU'RE A LIAR.
MISAKI.
DON'T GET TOO INVOLVED WITH ME.
WE'RE TOO DIFFERENT.
WE SHOULD STOP SEEING ONE ANOTHER.
OKAY?
WHAT?
WAIT!
BYE.
SAHARA!!

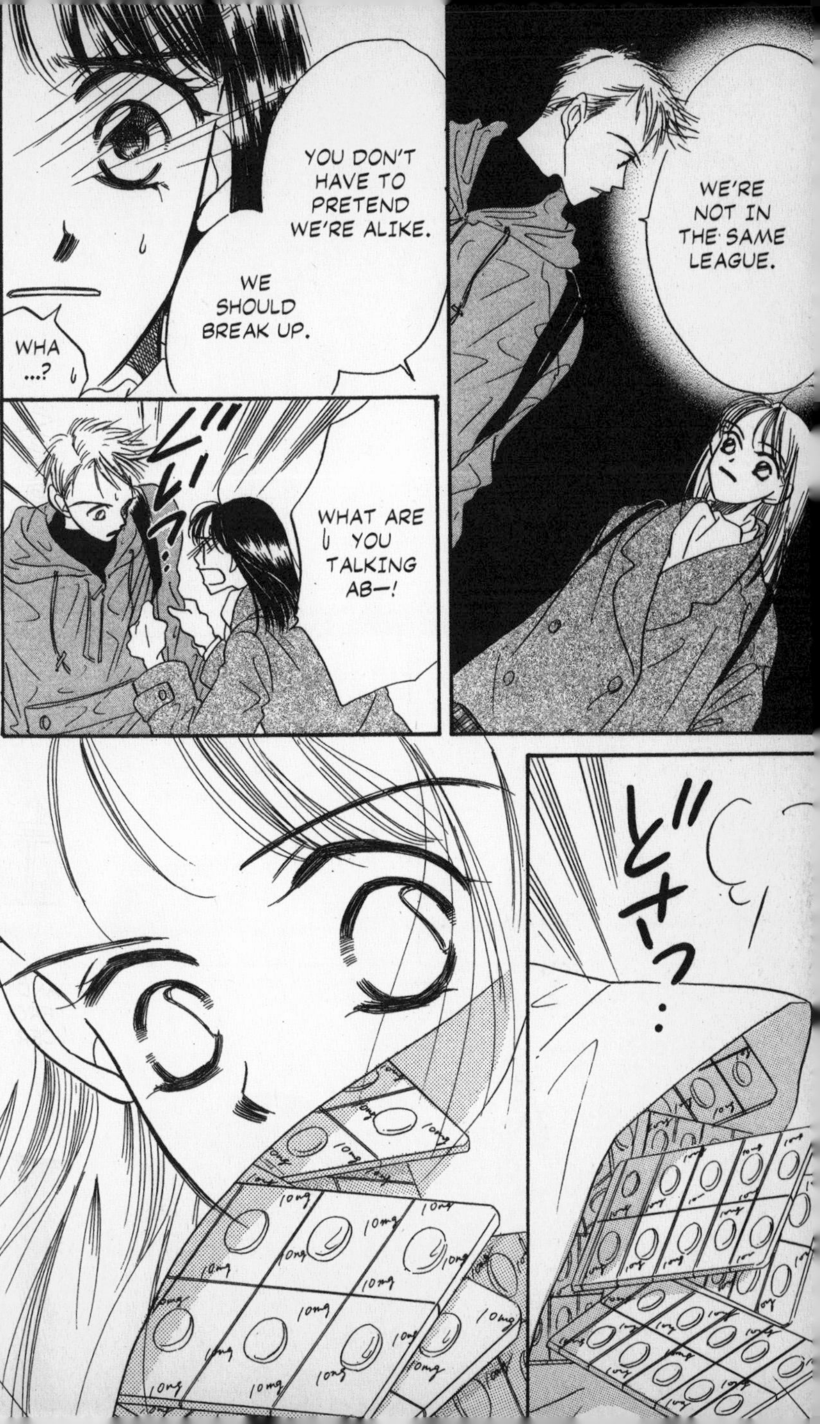
WE'RE NOT IN THE SAME LEAGUE.
YOU DON'T HAVE TO PRETEND WE'RE ALIKE.
WE SHOULD BREAK UP.
WHA ...?
WHAT ARE YOU TALKING AB—!
どさっ..

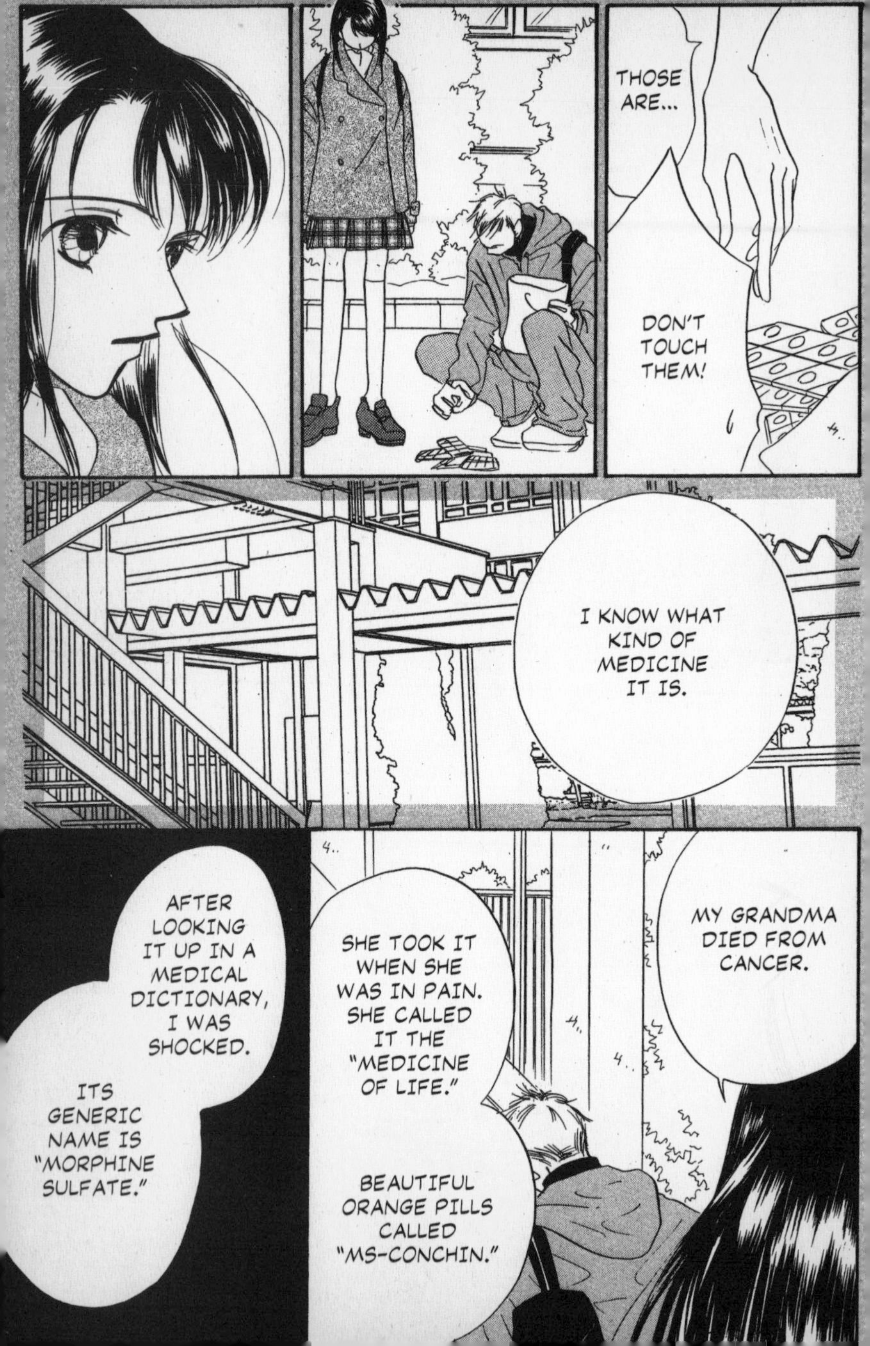
THOSE ARE...
DON'T TOUCH THEM!
I KNOW WHAT KIND OF MEDICINE IT IS.
MY GRANDMA DIED FROM CANCER.
SHE TOOK IT WHEN SHE WAS IN PAIN. SHE CALLED IT THE "MEDICINE OF LIFE."
BEAUTIFUL ORANGE PILLS CALLED "MS-CONCHIN."
AFTER LOOKING IT UP IN A MEDICAL DICTIONARY, I WAS SHOCKED.
ITS GENERIC NAME IS "MORPHINE SULFATE."

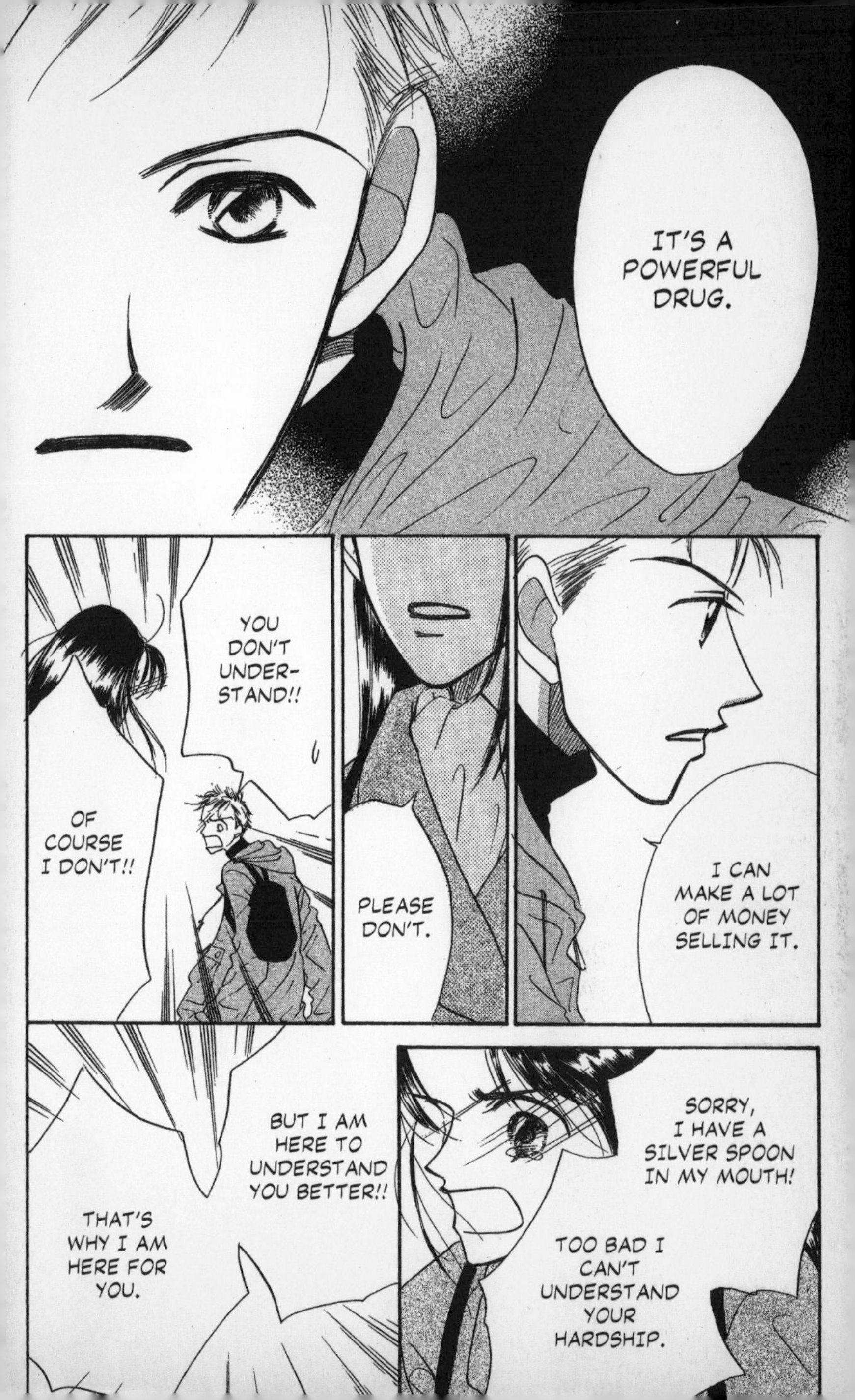
IT'S A POWERFUL DRUG.
I CAN MAKE A LOT OF MONEY SELLING IT.
PLEASE DON'T.
YOU DON'T UNDER-STAND!!
OF COURSE I DON'T!!
SORRY, I HAVE A SILVER SPOON IN MY MOUTH!
TOO BAD I CAN'T UNDERSTAND YOUR HARDSHIP.
BUT I AM HERE TO UNDERSTAND YOU BETTER!!
THAT'S WHY I AM HERE FOR YOU.

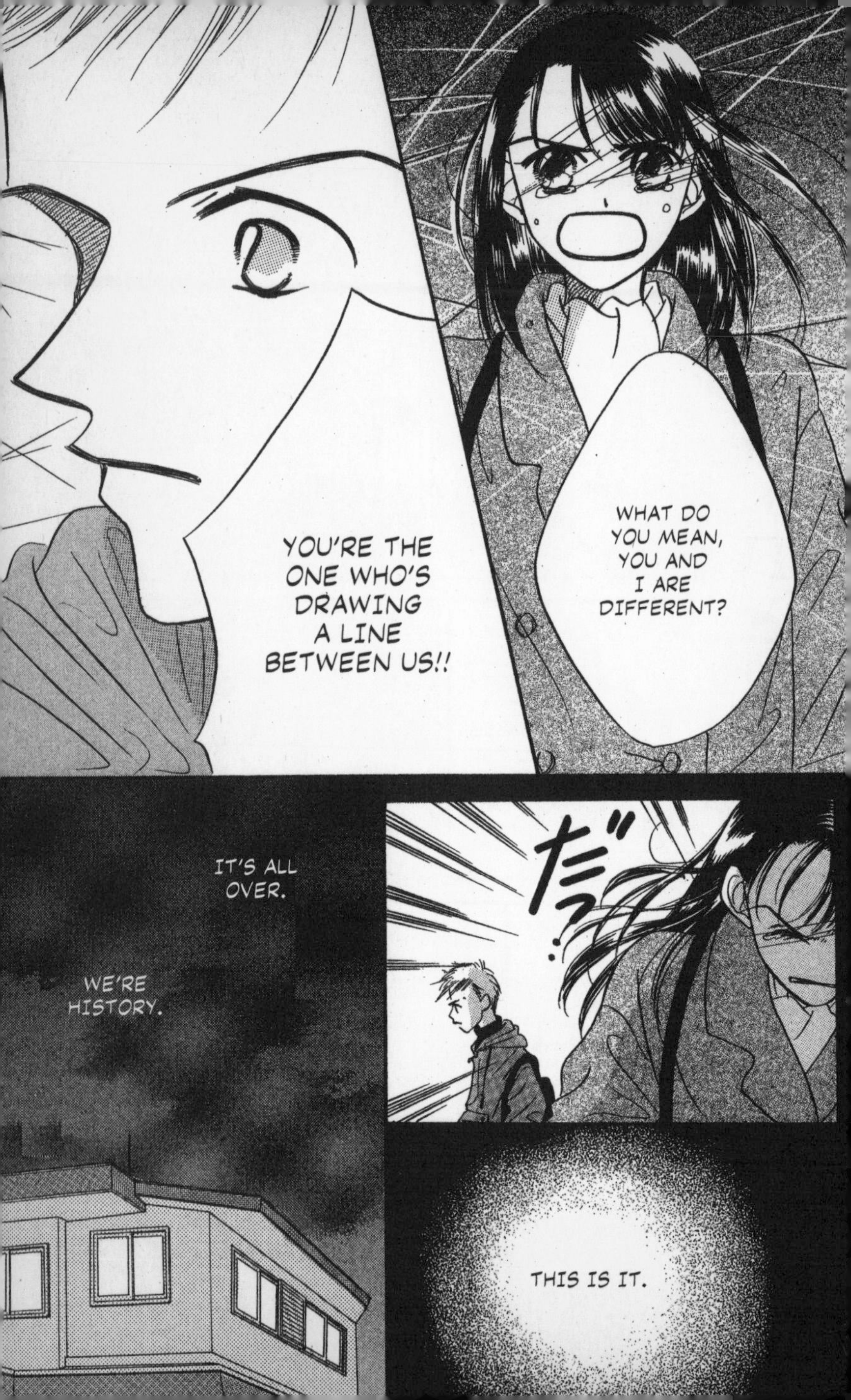
WHAT DO YOU MEAN, YOU AND I ARE DIFFERENT?
YOU'RE THE ONE WHO'S DRAWING A LINE BETWEEN US!!
だっ
THIS IS IT.
IT'S ALL OVER.
WE'RE HISTORY.

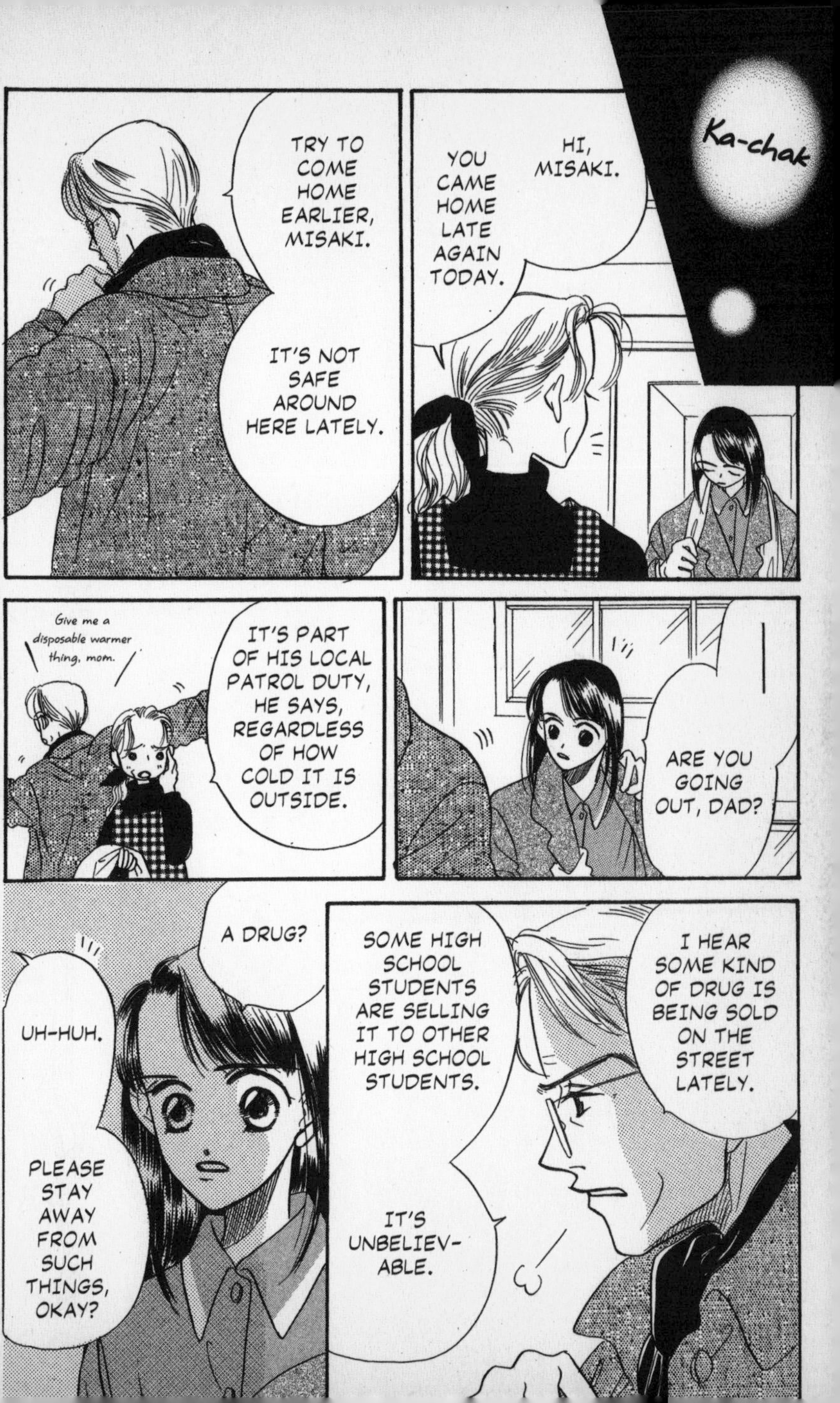
Ka-chak
HI, MISAKI.
YOU CAME HOME LATE AGAIN TODAY.
TRY TO COME HOME EARLIER, MISAKI.
IT'S NOT SAFE AROUND HERE LATELY.
ARE YOU GOING OUT, DAD?
IT'S PART OF HIS LOCAL PATROL DUTY, HE SAYS, REGARDLESS OF HOW COLD IT IS OUTSIDE.
Give me a disposable warmer thing, mom.
I HEAR SOME KIND OF DRUG IS BEING SOLD ON THE STREET LATELY.
SOME HIGH SCHOOL STUDENTS ARE SELLING IT TO OTHER HIGH SCHOOL STUDENTS.
IT'S UNBELIEV-ABLE.
A DRUG?
UH-HUH.
PLEASE STAY AWAY FROM SUCH THINGS, OKAY?

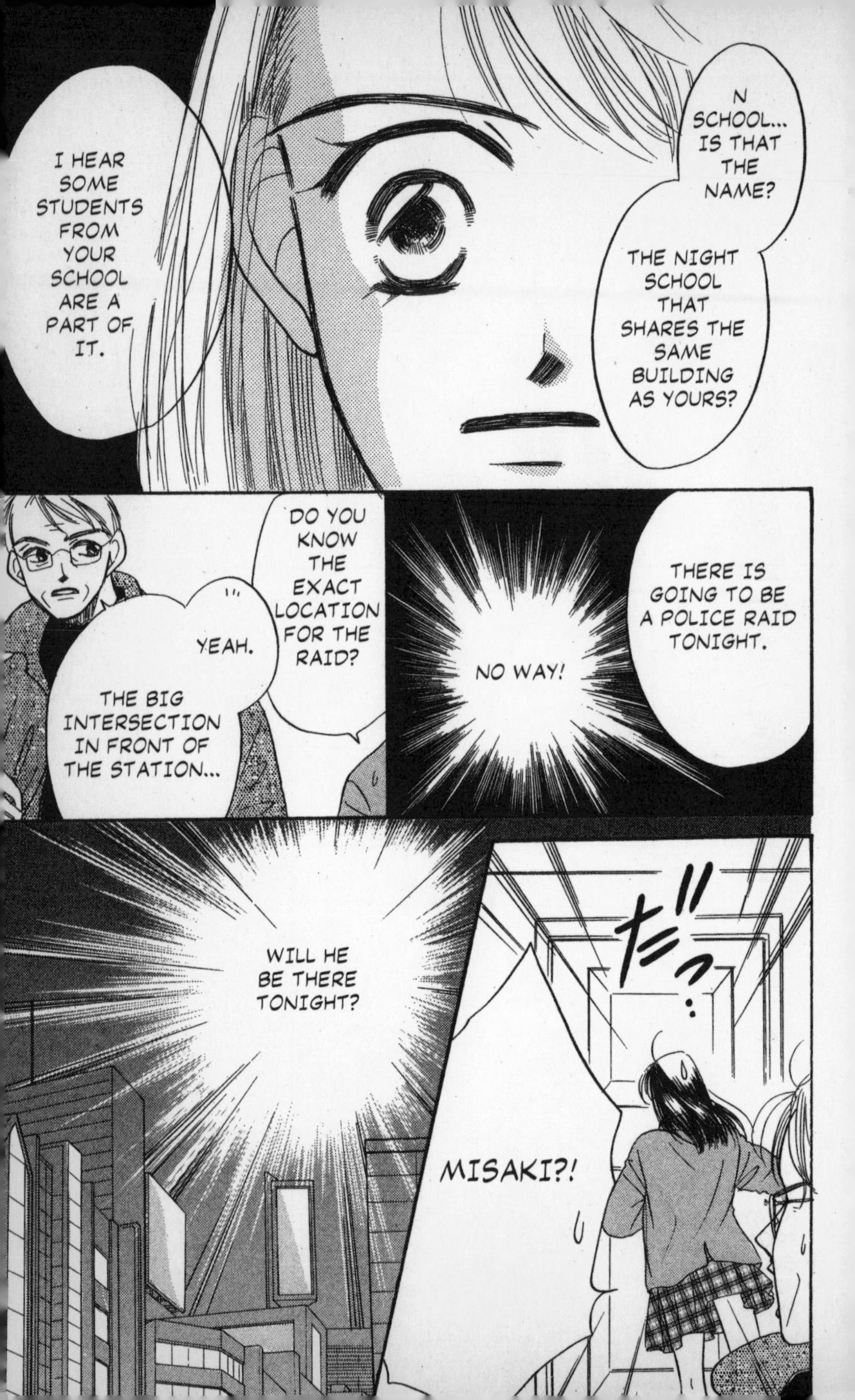
N SCHOOL... IS THAT THE NAME?
THE NIGHT SCHOOL THAT SHARES THE SAME BUILDING AS YOURS?
I HEAR SOME STUDENTS FROM YOUR SCHOOL ARE A PART OF IT.
THERE IS GOING TO BE A POLICE RAID TONIGHT.
NO WAY!
DO YOU KNOW THE EXACT LOCATION FOR THE RAID?
...
YEAH.
THE BIG INTERSECTION IN FRONT OF THE STATION...
だっ
MISAKI?!
WILL HE BE THERE TONIGHT?

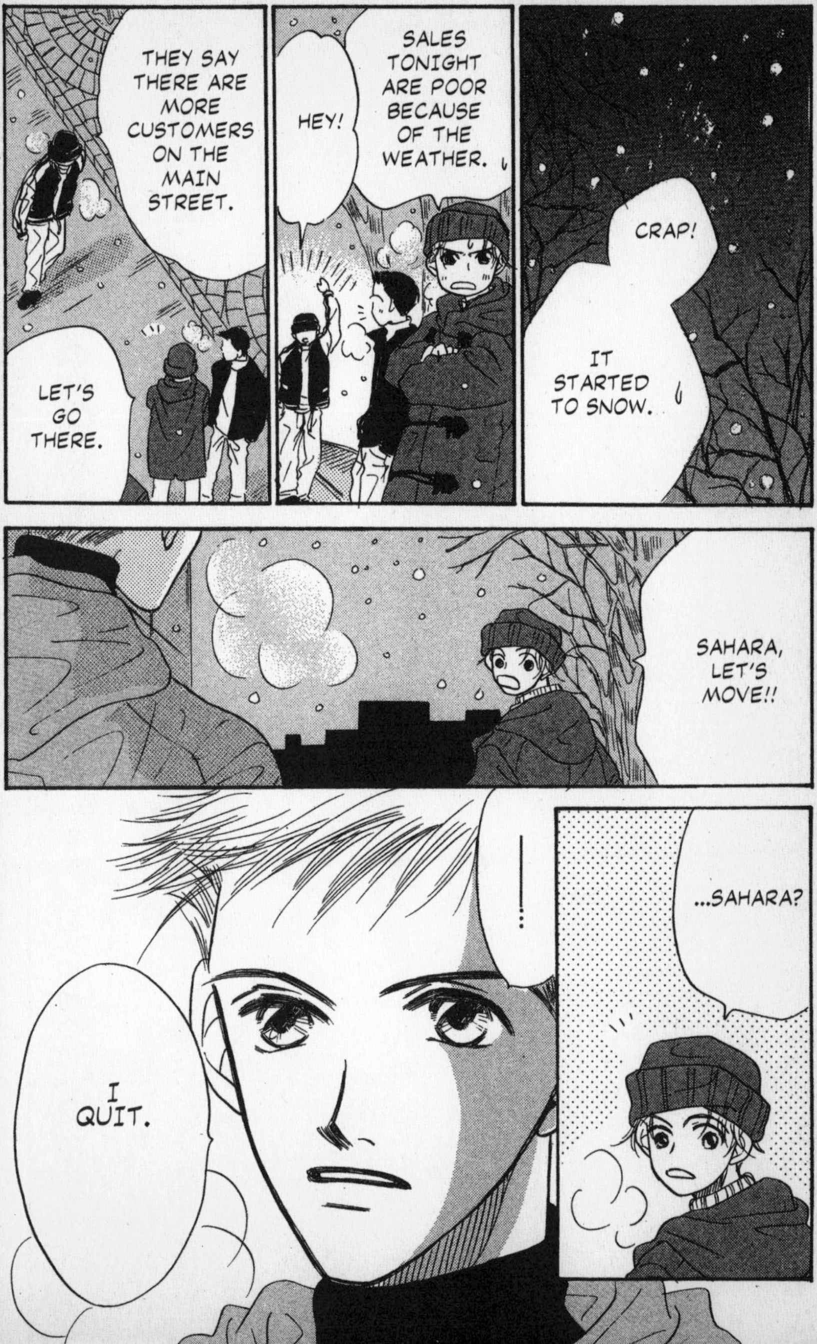
CRAP!
IT STARTED TO SNOW.
SALES TONIGHT ARE POOR BECAUSE OF THE WEATHER.
HEY!
THEY SAY THERE ARE MORE CUSTOMERS ON THE MAIN STREET.
LET'S GO THERE.
SAHARA, LET'S MOVE!!
...SAHARA?
I QUIT.

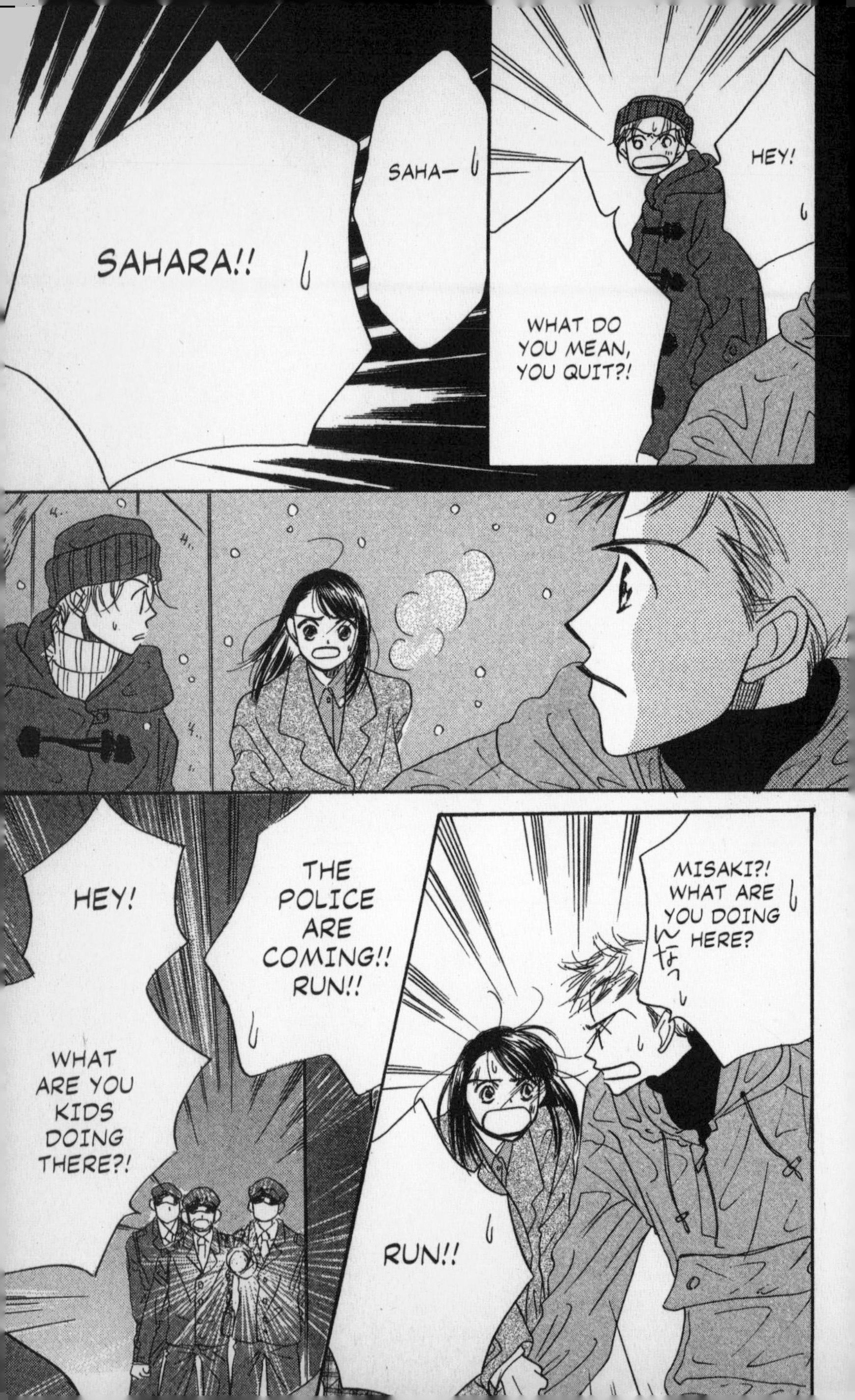
HEY!
WHAT DO YOU MEAN, YOU QUIT?!
SAHA—
SAHARA!!
MISAKI?! WHAT ARE YOU DOING HERE?
RUN!!
THE POLICE ARE COMING!! RUN!!
HEY!
WHAT ARE YOU KIDS DOING THERE?!

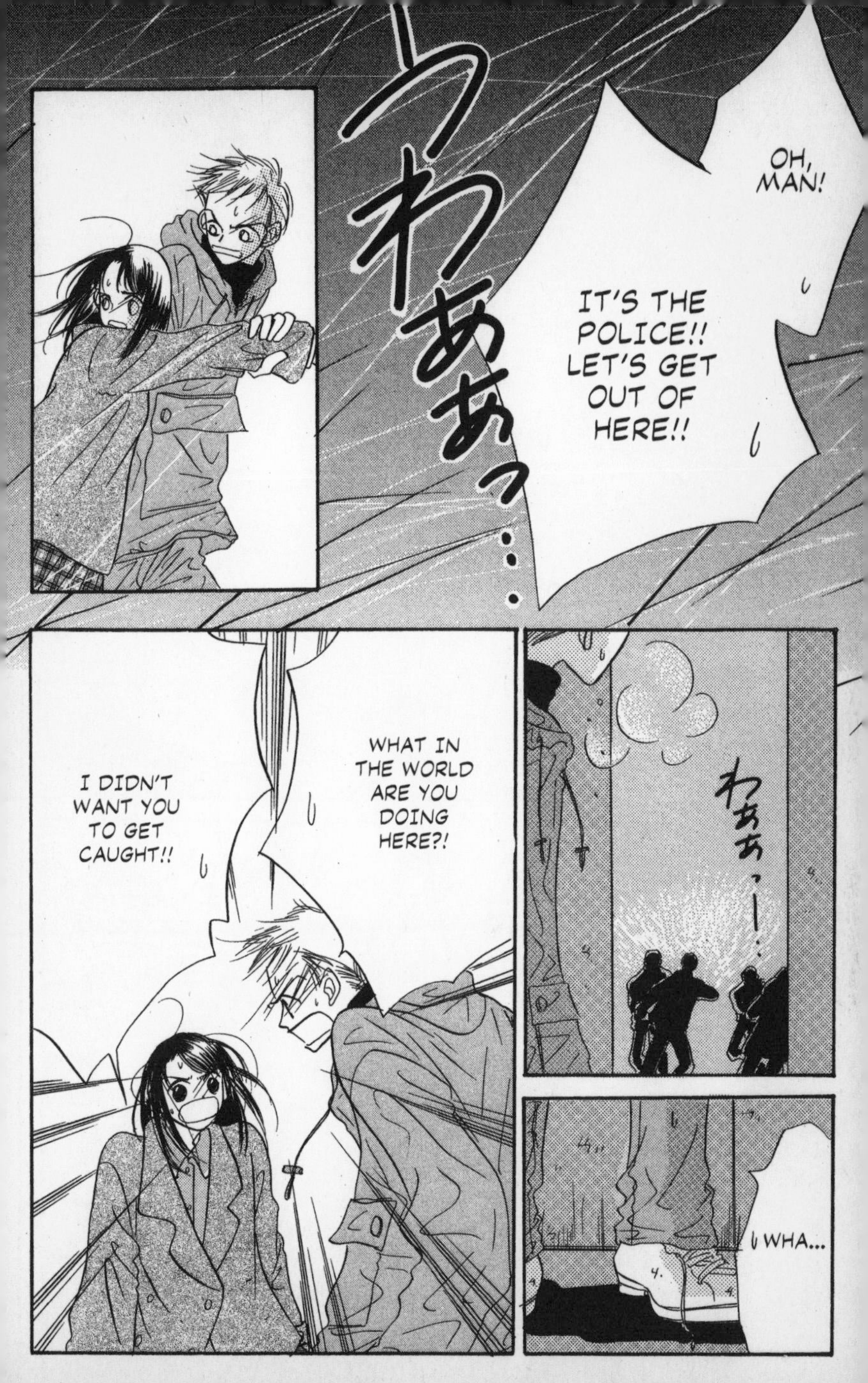
OH, MAN!
IT'S THE POLICE!! LET'S GET OUT OF HERE!!
わあぁっ…
わぁぁっー…
WHA...
WHAT IN THE WORLD ARE YOU DOING HERE?!
I DIDN'T WANT YOU TO GET CAUGHT!!

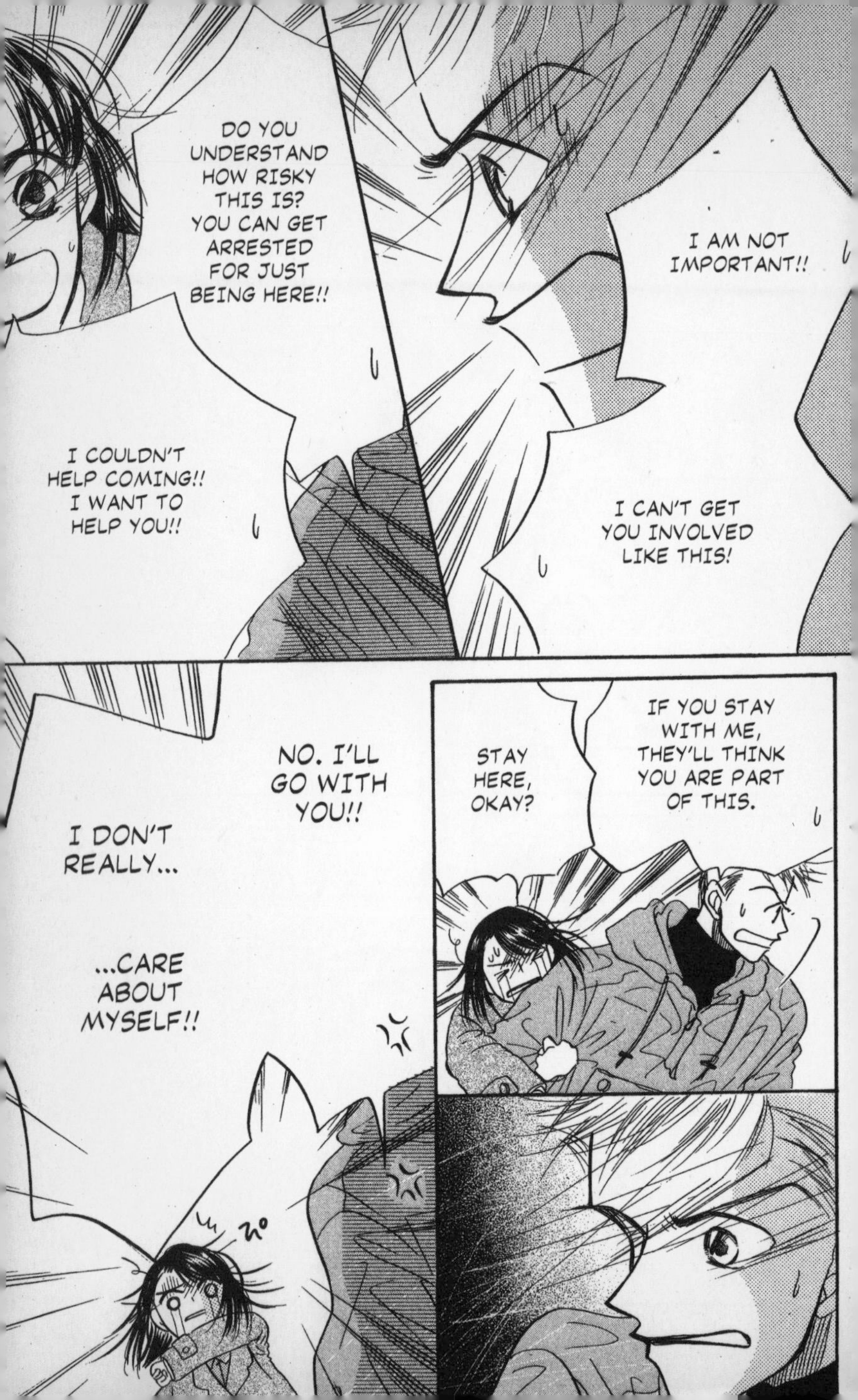
I AM NOT IMPORTANT!!
DO YOU UNDERSTAND HOW RISKY THIS IS? YOU CAN GET ARRESTED FOR JUST BEING HERE!!
I CAN'T GET YOU INVOLVED LIKE THIS!
I COULDN'T HELP COMING!! I WANT TO HELP YOU!!
IF YOU STAY WITH ME, THEY'LL THINK YOU ARE PART OF THIS.
STAY HERE, OKAY?
NO. I'LL GO WITH YOU!!
I DON'T REALLY...
...CARE ABOUT MYSELF!!

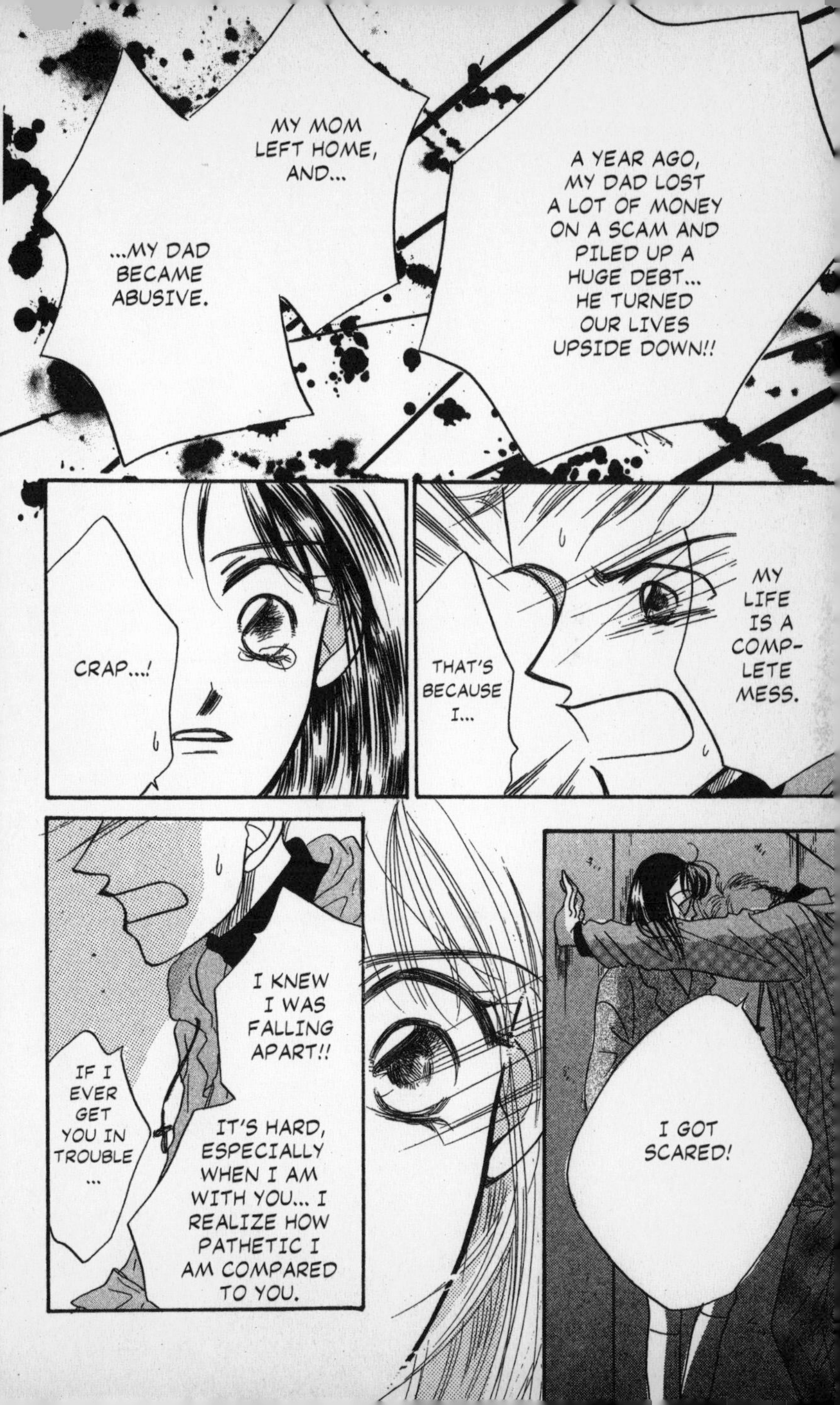
A YEAR AGO, MY DAD LOST A LOT OF MONEY ON A SCAM AND PILED UP A HUGE DEBT... HE TURNED OUR LIVES UPSIDE DOWN!!
MY MOM LEFT HOME, AND...
...MY DAD BECAME ABUSIVE.
MY LIFE IS A COMP-LETE MESS.
THAT'S BECAUSE I...
CRAP...!
I GOT SCARED!
I KNEW I WAS FALLING APART!!
IT'S HARD, ESPECIALLY WHEN I AM WITH YOU... I REALIZE HOW PATHETIC I AM COMPARED TO YOU.
IF I EVER GET YOU IN TROUBLE ...

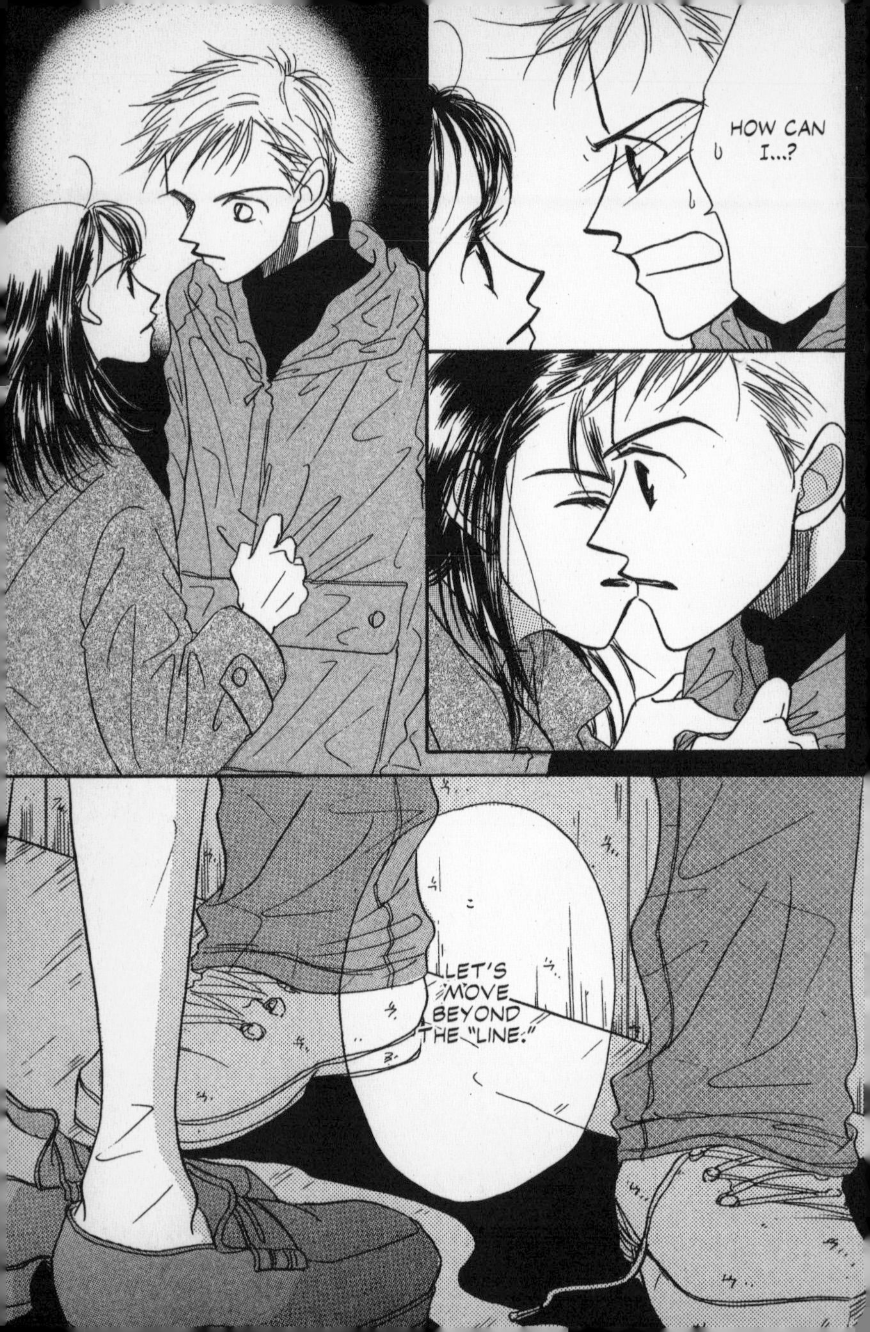
HOW CAN I...?
LET'S MOVE BEYOND THE "LINE."

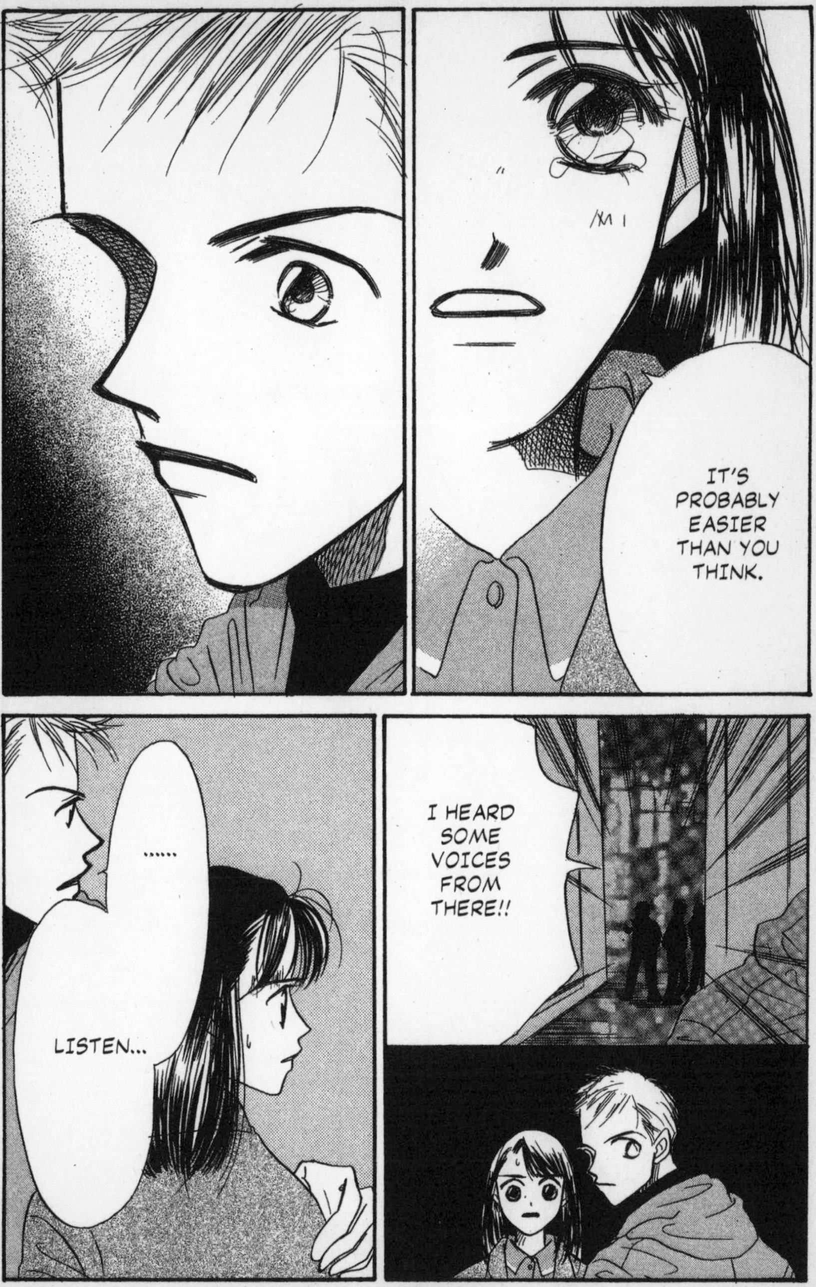
IT'S PROBABLY EASIER THAN YOU THINK.
I HEARD SOME VOICES FROM THERE!!
......
LISTEN...

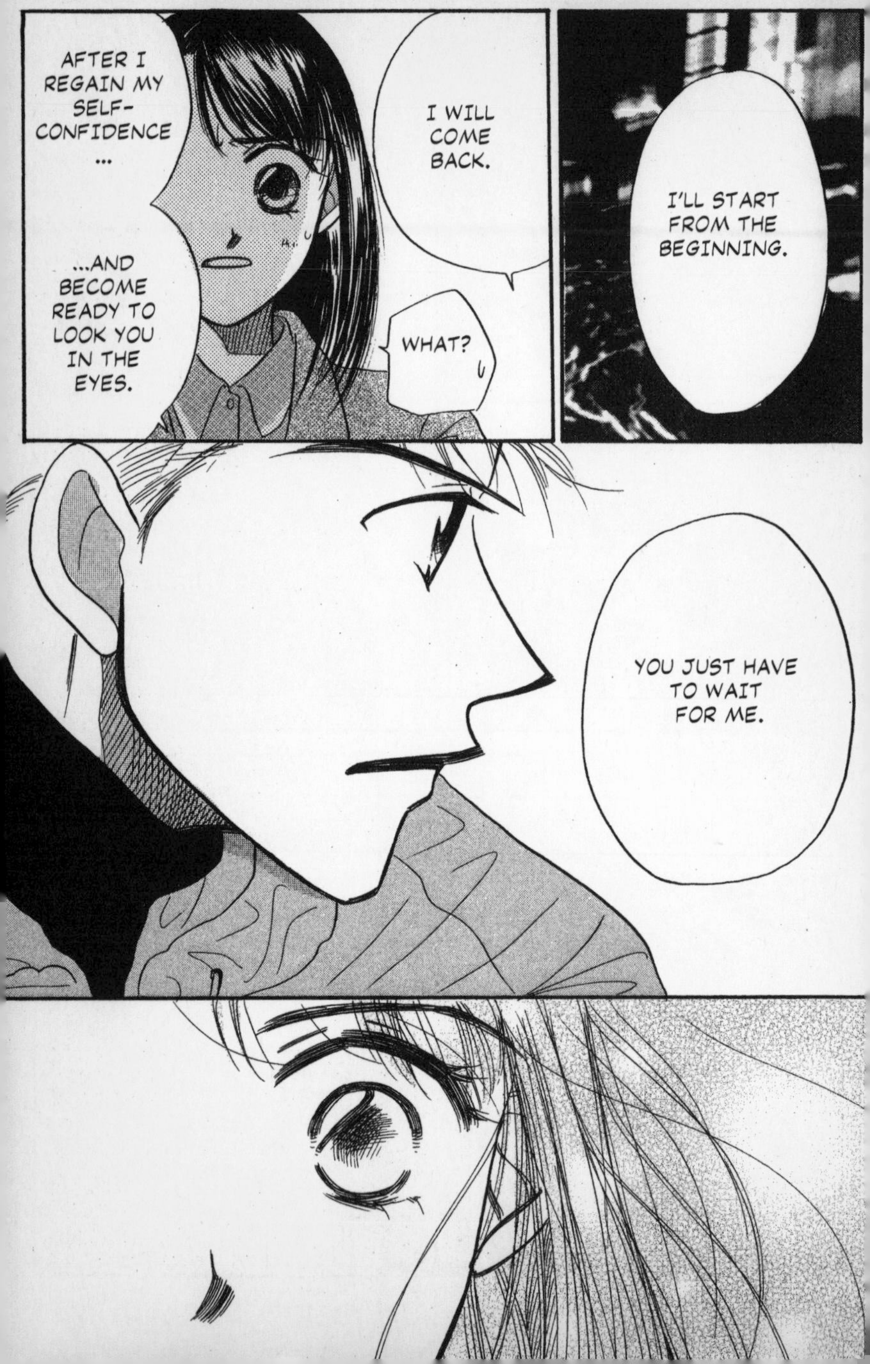
I'LL START FROM THE BEGINNING.
I WILL COME BACK.
AFTER I REGAIN MY SELF-CONFIDENCE ...
...AND BECOME READY TO LOOK YOU IN THE EYES.
WHAT?
YOU JUST HAVE TO WAIT FOR ME.

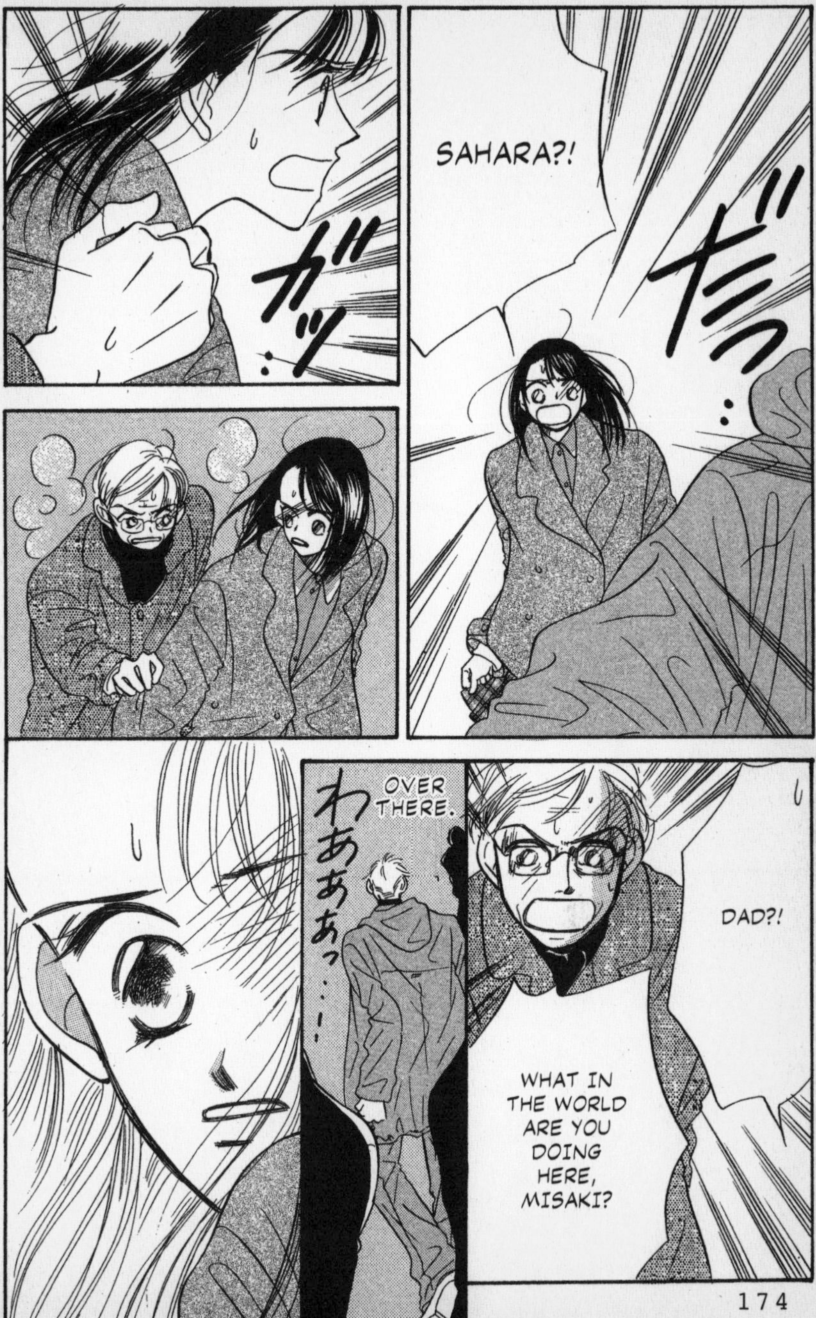
SAHARA?!
ダラ…
ガッ…
DAD?!
WHAT IN THE WORLD ARE YOU DOING HERE, MISAKI?
OVER THERE.
わあああっ…！

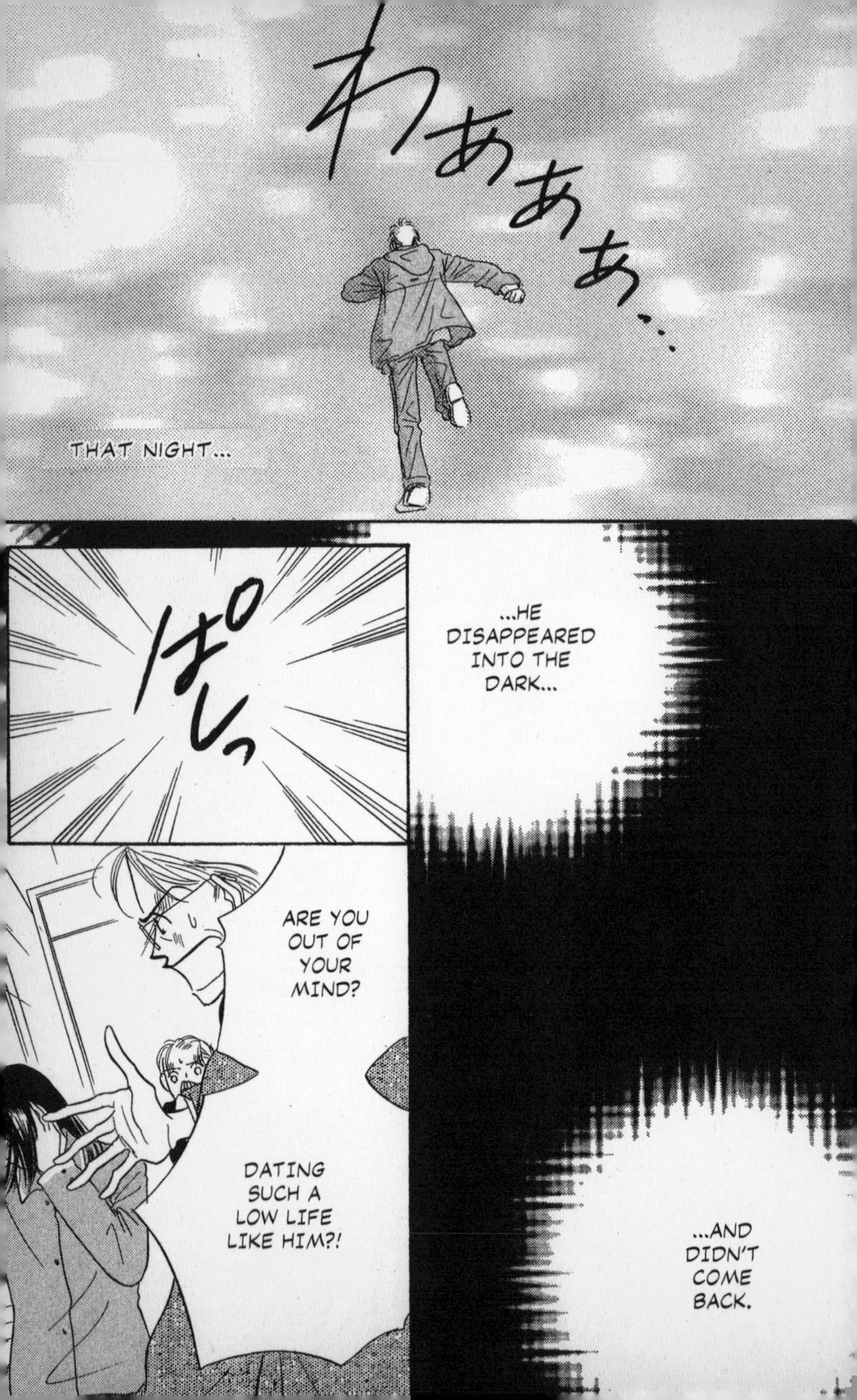
わあああ…
THAT NIGHT...
...HE DISAPPEARED INTO THE DARK...
...AND DIDN'T COME BACK.
ぱしっ
ARE YOU OUT OF YOUR MIND?
DATING SUCH A LOW LIFE LIKE HIM?!

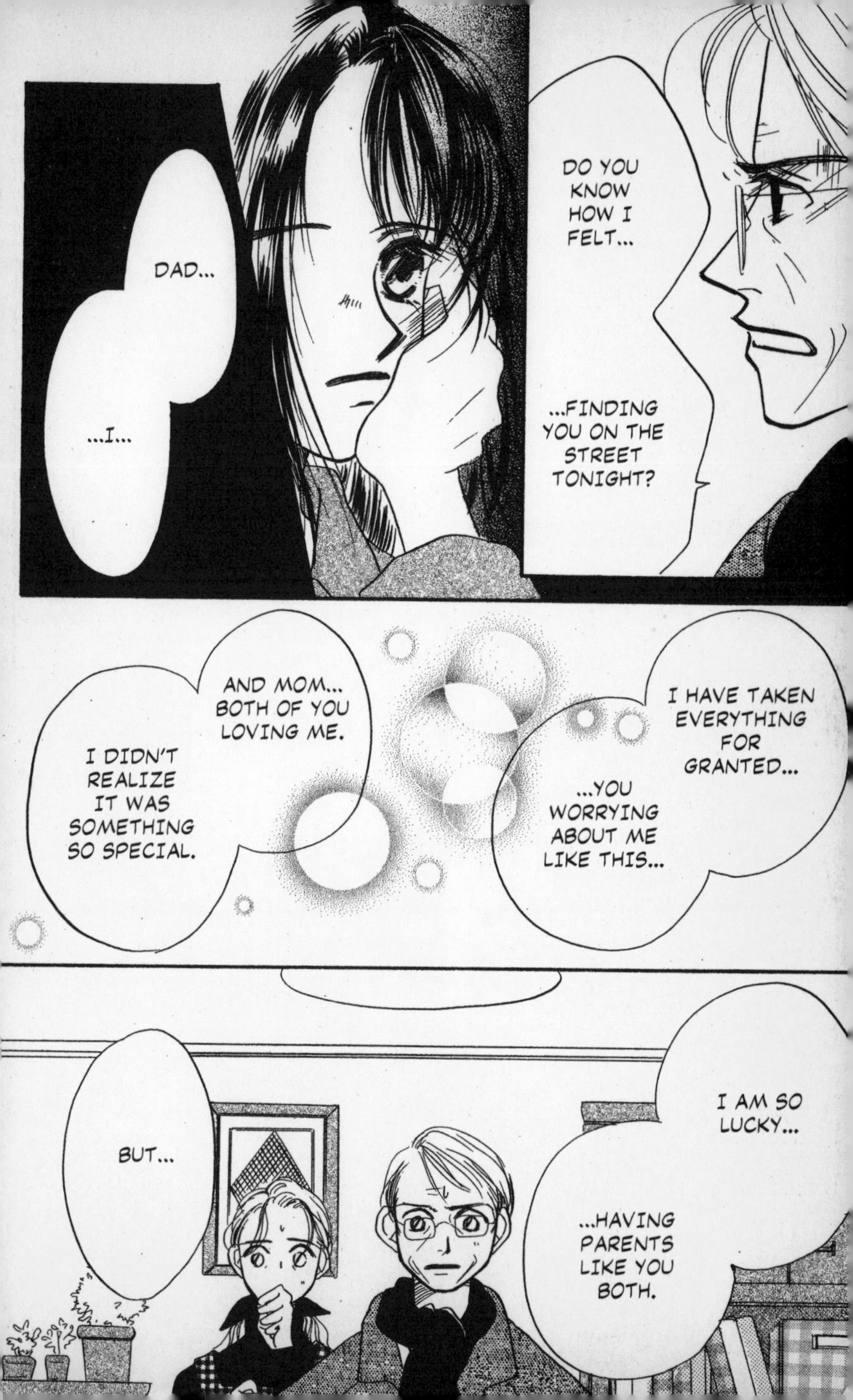
DO YOU KNOW HOW I FELT...
...FINDING YOU ON THE STREET TONIGHT?
DAD...
...I...
I HAVE TAKEN EVERYTHING FOR GRANTED...
...YOU WORRYING ABOUT ME LIKE THIS...
AND MOM... BOTH OF YOU LOVING ME.
I DIDN'T REALIZE IT WAS SOMETHING SO SPECIAL.
I AM SO LUCKY...
...HAVING PARENTS LIKE YOU BOTH.
BUT...

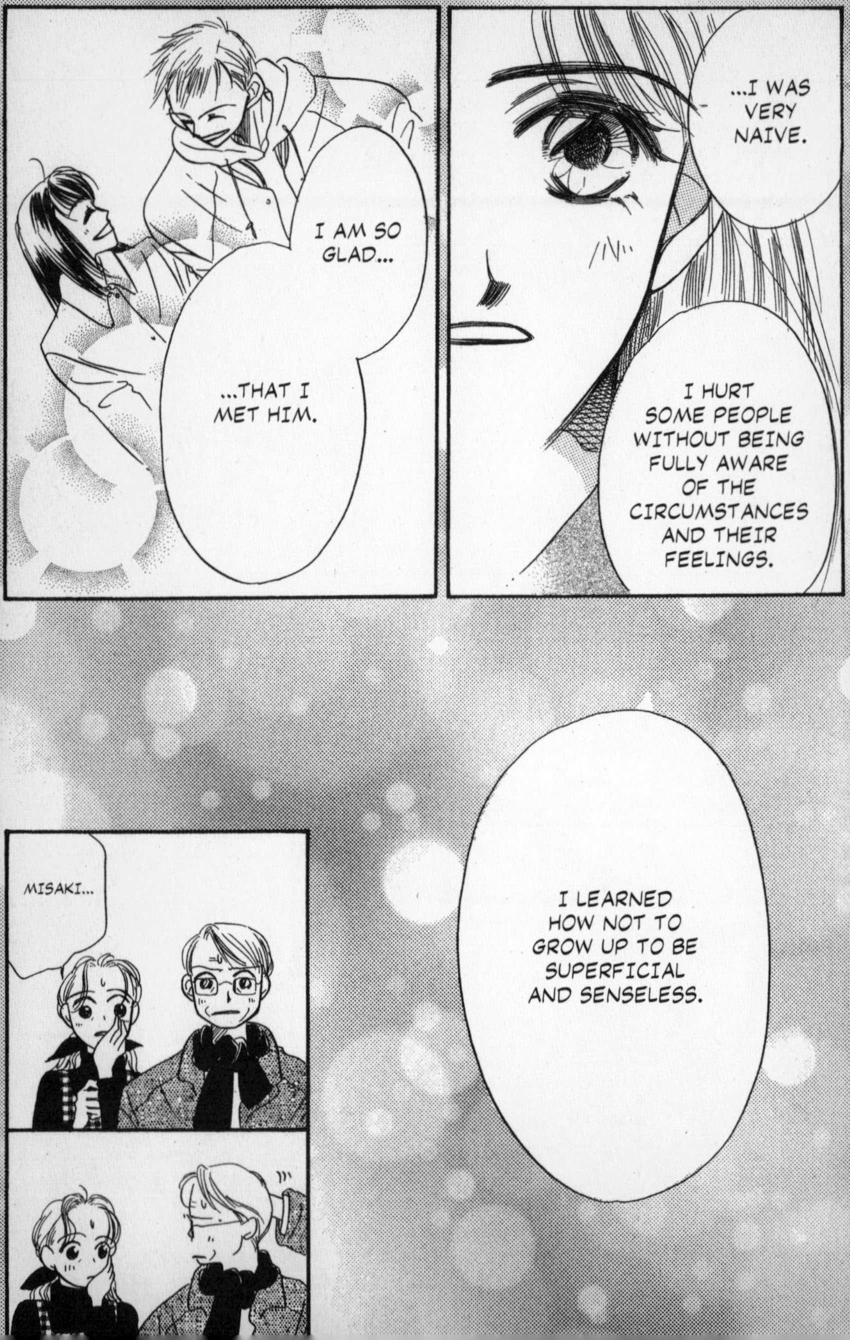
...I WAS VERY NAIVE.
I HURT SOME PEOPLE WITHOUT BEING FULLY AWARE OF THE CIRCUMSTANCES AND THEIR FEELINGS.
I AM SO GLAD...
...THAT I MET HIM.
I LEARNED HOW NOT TO GROW UP TO BE SUPERFICIAL AND SENSELESS.
MISAKI...

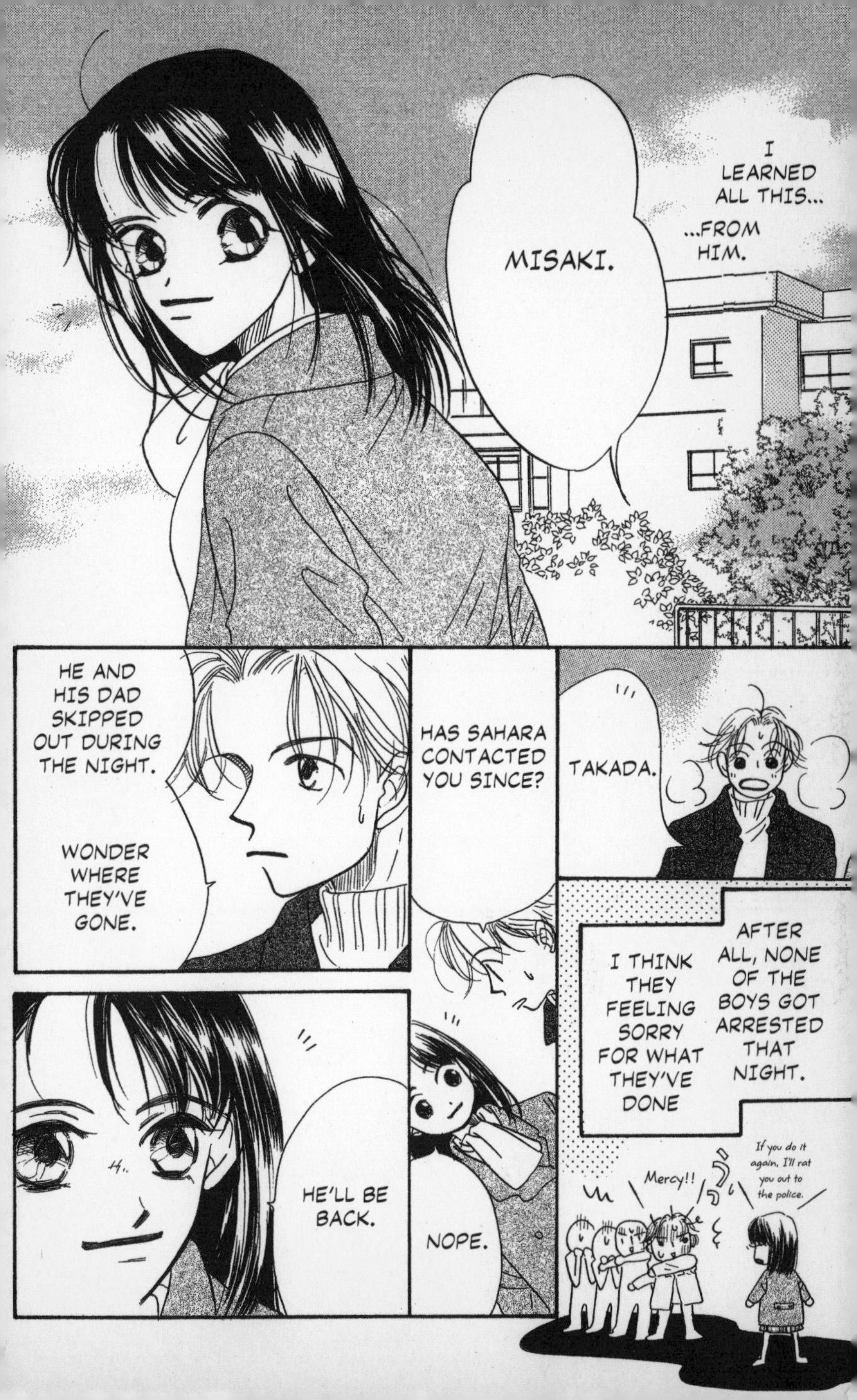
I LEARNED ALL THIS...
...FROM HIM.
MISAKI.
TAKADA.
AFTER ALL, NONE OF THE BOYS GOT ARRESTED THAT NIGHT.
I THINK THEY FEELING SORRY FOR WHAT THEY'VE DONE
If you do it again, I'll rat you out to the police.
Mercy!!
HAS SAHARA CONTACTED YOU SINCE?
NOPE.
HE AND HIS DAD SKIPPED OUT DURING THE NIGHT.
WONDER WHERE THEY'VE GONE.
HE'LL BE BACK.

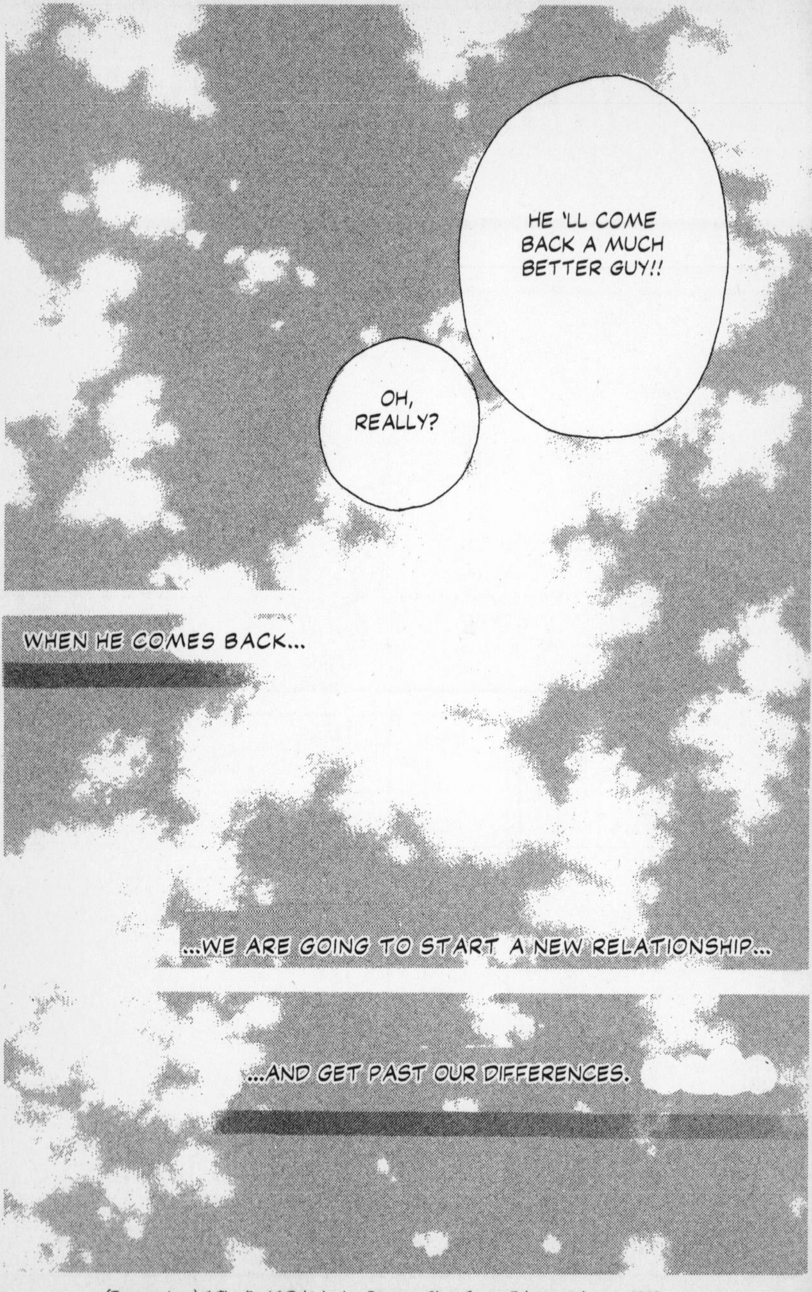
HE 'LL COME BACK A MUCH BETTER GUY!!
OH, REALLY?
WHEN HE COMES BACK...
...WE ARE GOING TO START A NEW RELATIONSHIP...
...AND GET PAST OUR DIFFERENCES.

(Princess Line) * The End * Published in Bessatsu Shojo Comic February 5th issue, 1998

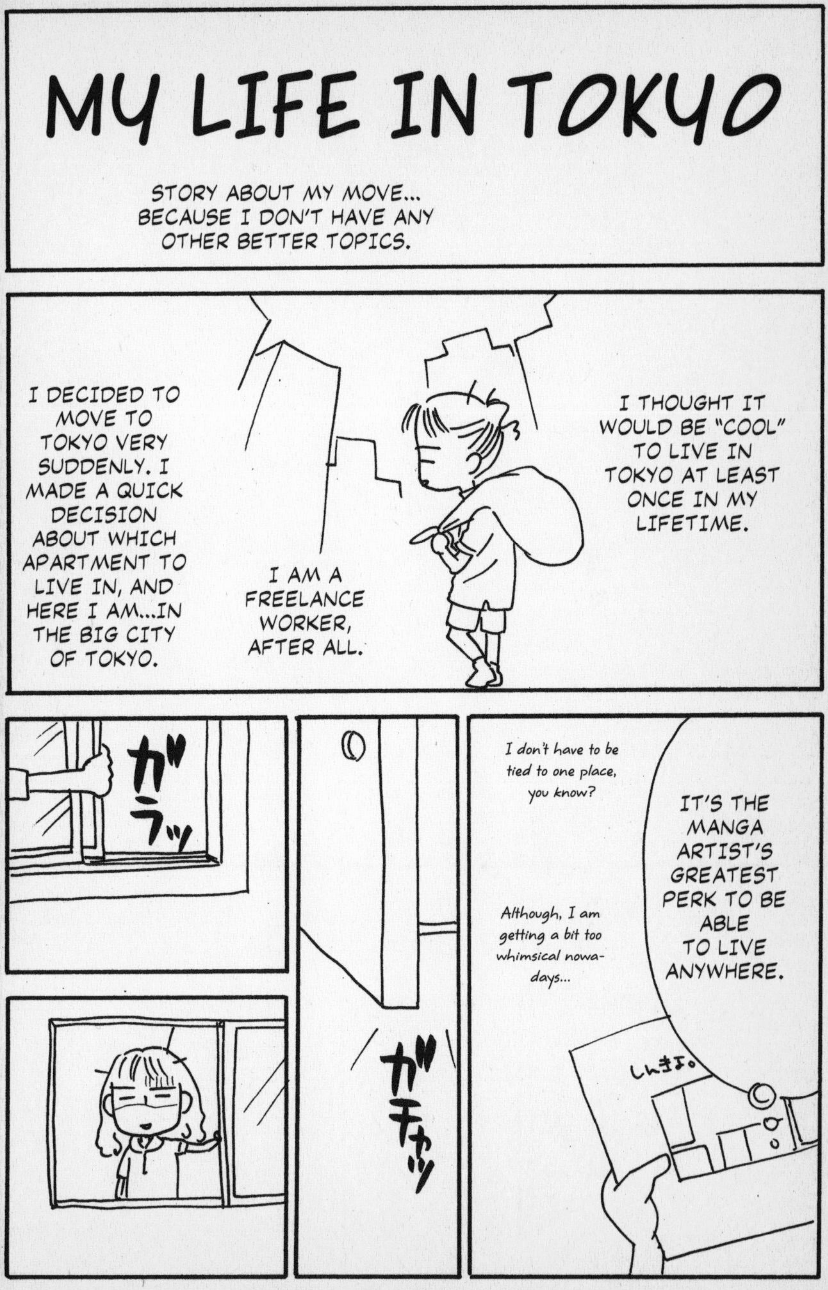
MY LIFE IN TOKYO
STORY ABOUT MY MOVE... BECAUSE I DON'T HAVE ANY OTHER BETTER TOPICS.
I THOUGHT IT WOULD BE "COOL" TO LIVE IN TOKYO AT LEAST ONCE IN MY LIFETIME.
I DECIDED TO MOVE TO TOKYO VERY SUDDENLY. I MADE A QUICK DECISION ABOUT WHICH APARTMENT TO LIVE IN, AND HERE I AM...IN THE BIG CITY OF TOKYO.
I AM A FREELANCE WORKER, AFTER ALL.
IT'S THE MANGA ARTIST'S GREATEST PERK TO BE ABLE TO LIVE ANYWHERE.
I don't have to be tied to one place, you know?
Although, I am getting a bit too whimsical nowa-days...
しんきょ。
ガチャッ
ガラッ

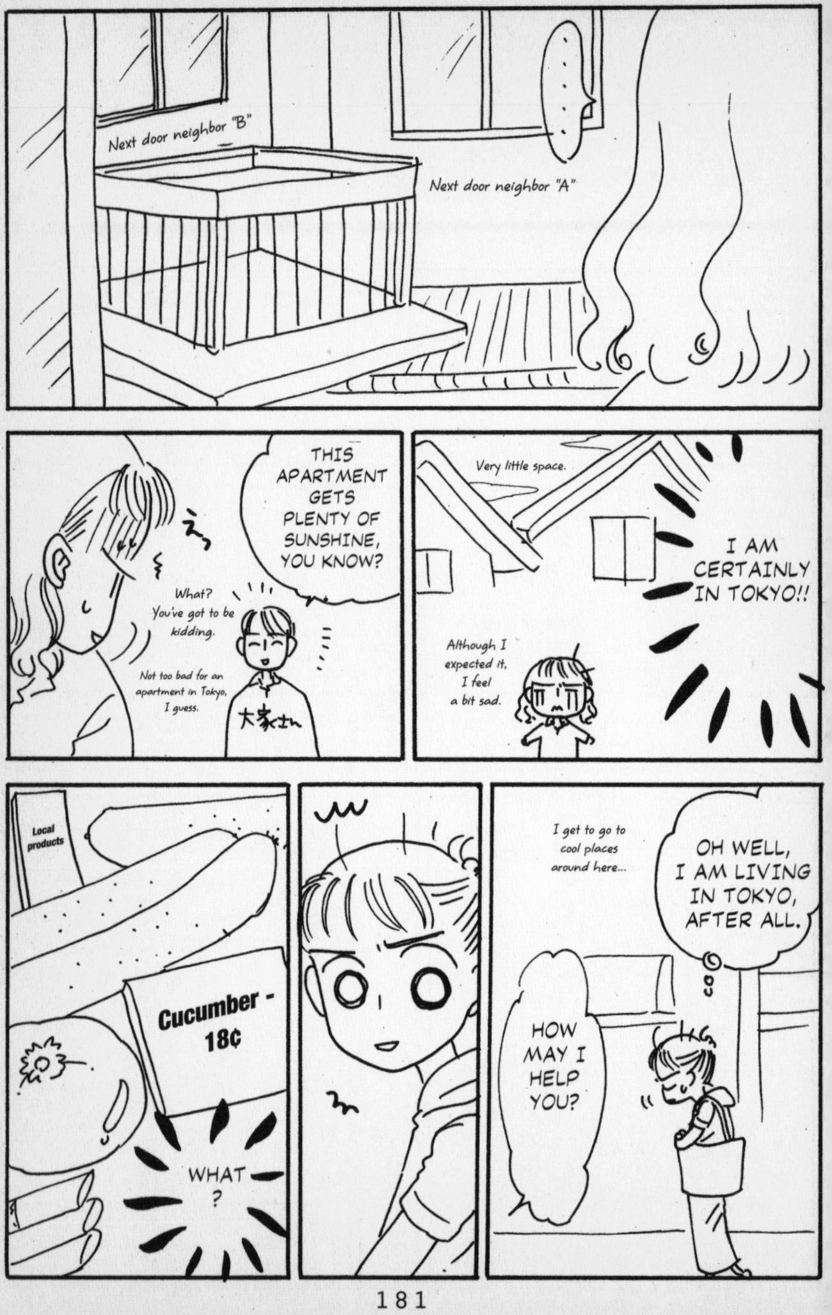
Next door neighbor "A"
Next door neighbor "B"
Very little space.
I AM CERTAINLY IN TOKYO!!
Although I expected it, I feel a bit sad.
THIS APARTMENT GETS PLENTY OF SUNSHINE, YOU KNOW?
What? You've got to be kidding.
Not too bad for an apartment in Tokyo, I guess.
大家さん
OH WELL, I AM LIVING IN TOKYO, AFTER ALL.
I get to go to cool places around here...
HOW MAY I HELP YOU?
Local products
Cucumber - 18¢
WHAT?

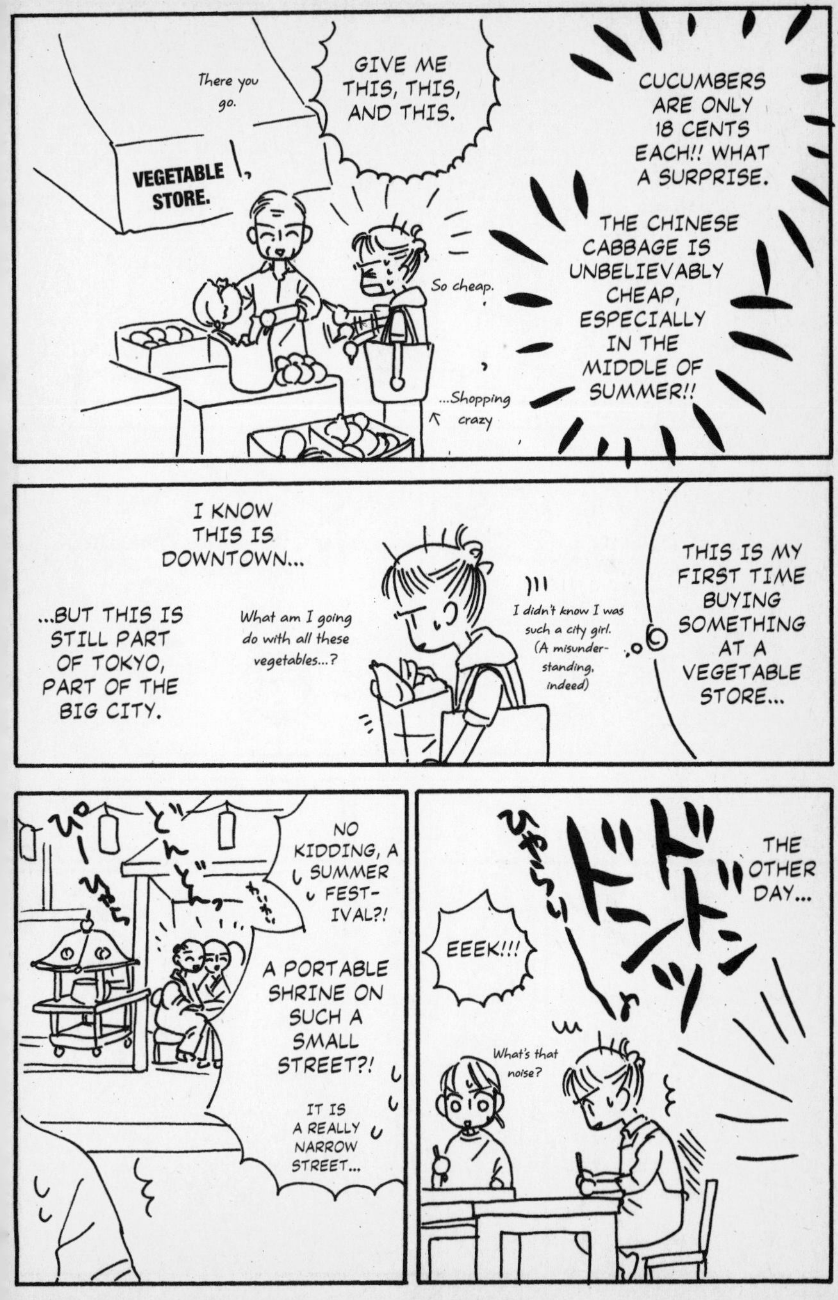
CUCUMBERS ARE ONLY 18 CENTS EACH!! WHAT A SURPRISE.
THE CHINESE CABBAGE IS UNBELIEVABLY CHEAP, ESPECIALLY IN THE MIDDLE OF SUMMER!!
GIVE ME THIS, THIS, AND THIS.
There you go.
VEGETABLE STORE.
So cheap.
...Shopping crazy
THIS IS MY FIRST TIME BUYING SOMETHING AT A VEGETABLE STORE...
I didn't know I was such a city girl. (A misunder-standing, indeed)
I KNOW THIS IS DOWNTOWN...
What am I going do with all these vegetables...?
...BUT THIS IS STILL PART OF TOKYO, PART OF THE BIG CITY.
THE OTHER DAY...
EEEK!!!
What's that noise?
NO KIDDING, A SUMMER FEST-IVAL?!
A PORTABLE SHRINE ON SUCH A SMALL STREET?!
IT IS A REALLY NARROW STREET...

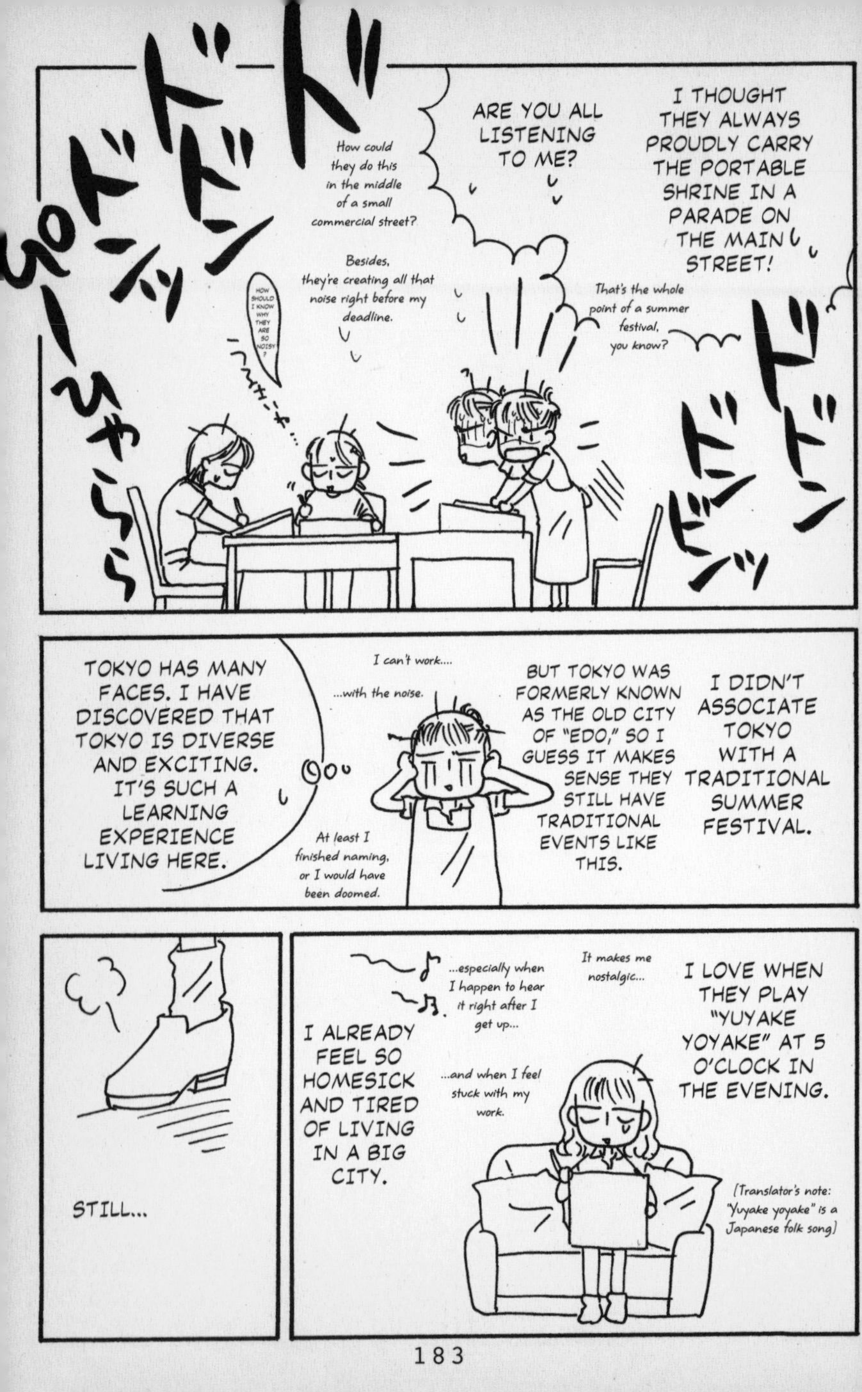
I THOUGHT THEY ALWAYS PROUDLY CARRY THE PORTABLE SHRINE IN A PARADE ON THE MAIN STREET!
That's the whole point of a summer festival, you know?
ARE YOU ALL LISTENING TO ME?
How could they do this in the middle of a small commercial street?
Besides, they're creating all that noise right before my deadline.
HOW SHOULD I KNOW WHY THEY ARE SO NOISY?
I DIDN'T ASSOCIATE TOKYO WITH A TRADITIONAL SUMMER FESTIVAL.
BUT TOKYO WAS FORMERLY KNOWN AS THE OLD CITY OF "EDO," SO I GUESS IT MAKES SENSE THEY STILL HAVE TRADITIONAL EVENTS LIKE THIS.
I can't work....
...with the noise.
At least I finished naming, or I would have been doomed.
TOKYO HAS MANY FACES. I HAVE DISCOVERED THAT TOKYO IS DIVERSE AND EXCITING. IT'S SUCH A LEARNING EXPERIENCE LIVING HERE.
I LOVE WHEN THEY PLAY "YUYAKE YOYAKE" AT 5 O'CLOCK IN THE EVENING.
It makes me nostalgic...
...especially when I happen to hear it right after I get up...
...and when I feel stuck with my work.
I ALREADY FEEL SO HOMESICK AND TIRED OF LIVING IN A BIG CITY.
(Translator's note: "Yuyake yoyake" is a Japanese folk song)
STILL...

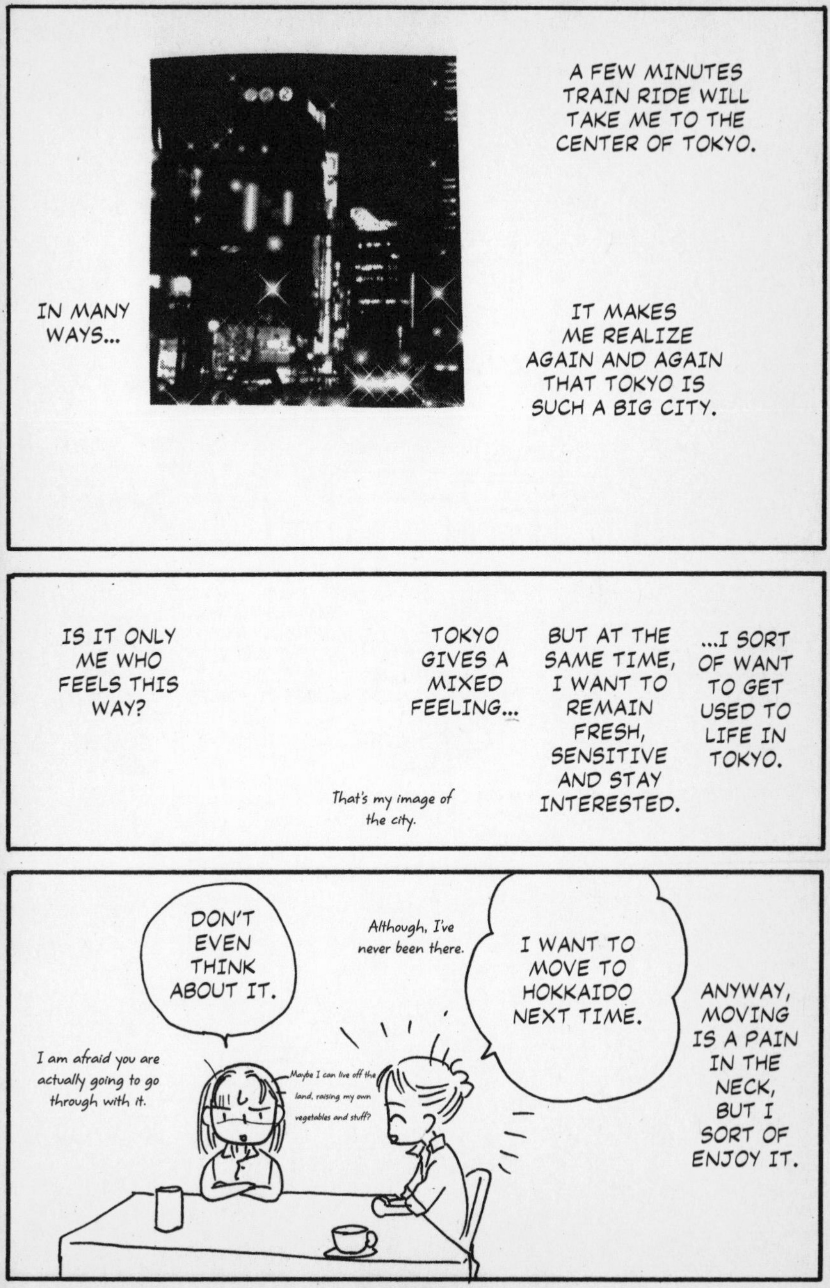
A FEW MINUTES TRAIN RIDE WILL TAKE ME TO THE CENTER OF TOKYO.
IT MAKES ME REALIZE AGAIN AND AGAIN THAT TOKYO IS SUCH A BIG CITY.
IN MANY WAYS...
...I SORT OF WANT TO GET USED TO LIFE IN TOKYO.
BUT AT THE SAME TIME, I WANT TO REMAIN FRESH, SENSITIVE AND STAY INTERESTED.
TOKYO GIVES A MIXED FEELING...
That's my image of the city.
IS IT ONLY ME WHO FEELS THIS WAY?
ANYWAY, MOVING IS A PAIN IN THE NECK, BUT I SORT OF ENJOY IT.
I WANT TO MOVE TO HOKKAIDO NEXT TIME.
Although, I've never been there.
DON'T EVEN THINK ABOUT IT.
Maybe I can live off the land, raising my own vegetables and stuff?
I am afraid you are actually going to go through with it.

The End

In the next volume
of...

Forbidden Dance

After saving the day at the Tokyo performance, Aya is more convinced than ever that she deserves to be a member of COOL. And the fact that she's falling head over ballet slippers for Akira only fuels the fires of her determination. Coincidentally, COOL is perched at a pivotal time... The troupe's anniversary show is fast approaching, but Akira has run off to England to bring back Diana! All is not lost, however, because the ever-diligent Aya has a plan to save the dance company. The question is... will Aya be able to do what it takes to secure COOL's future?

Find out in the dramatic conclusion of...
Forbidden Dance!

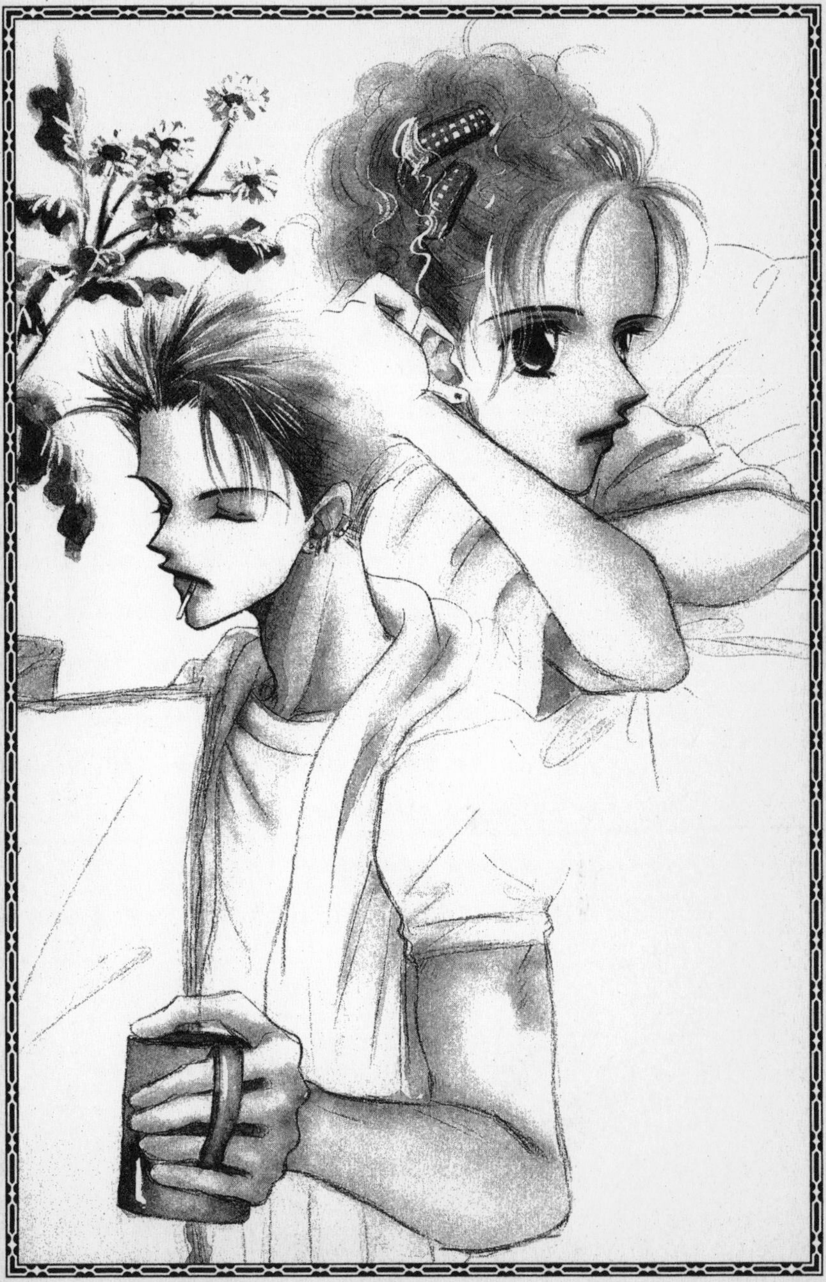

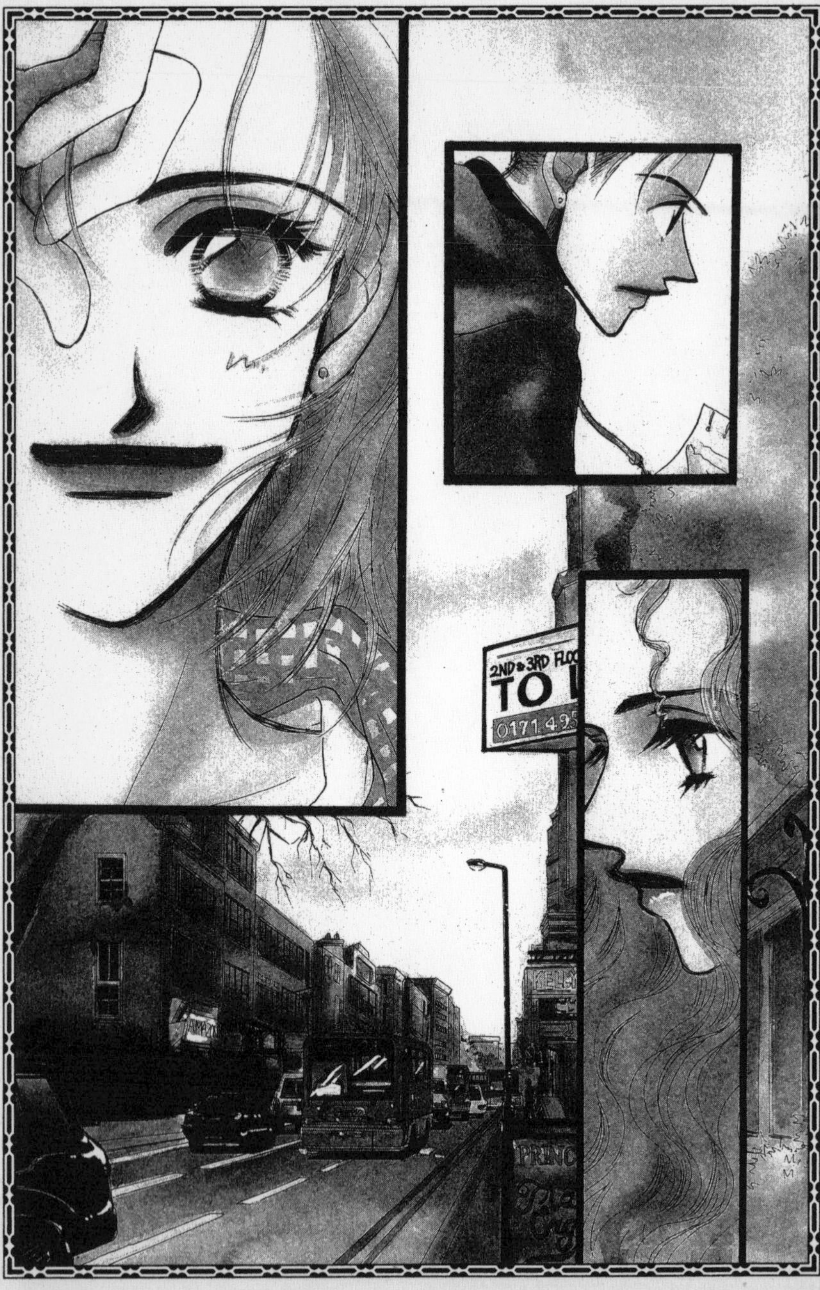
2ND & 3RD FLOO
TO
0171 495

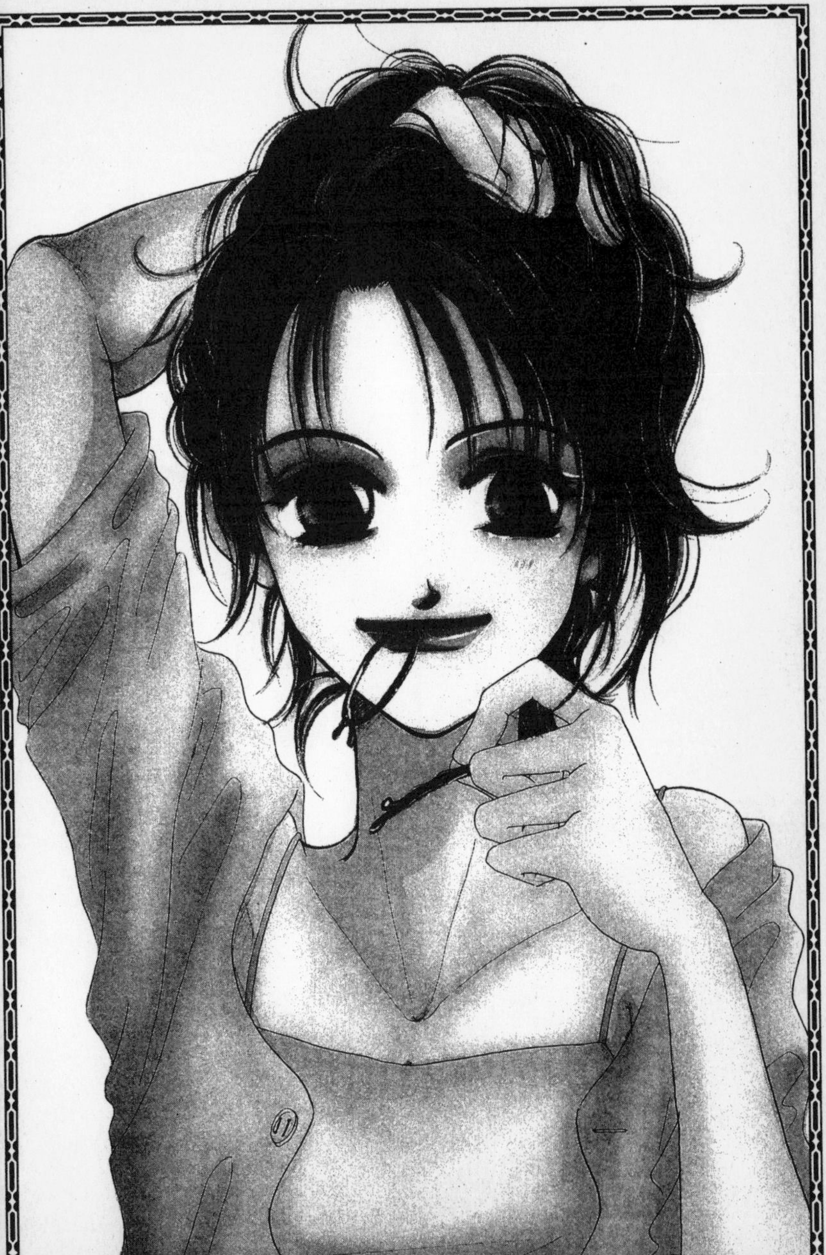

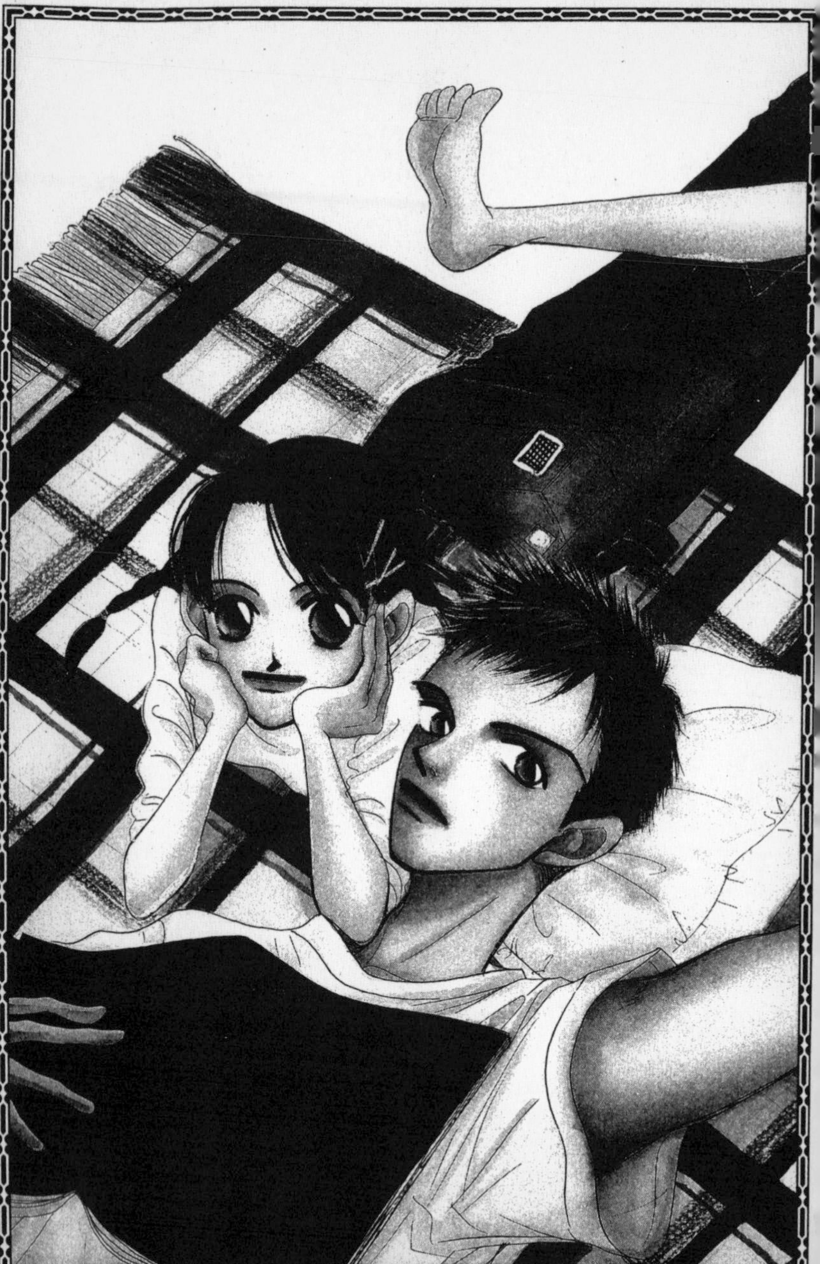

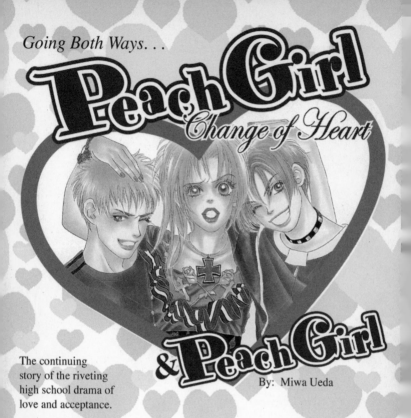

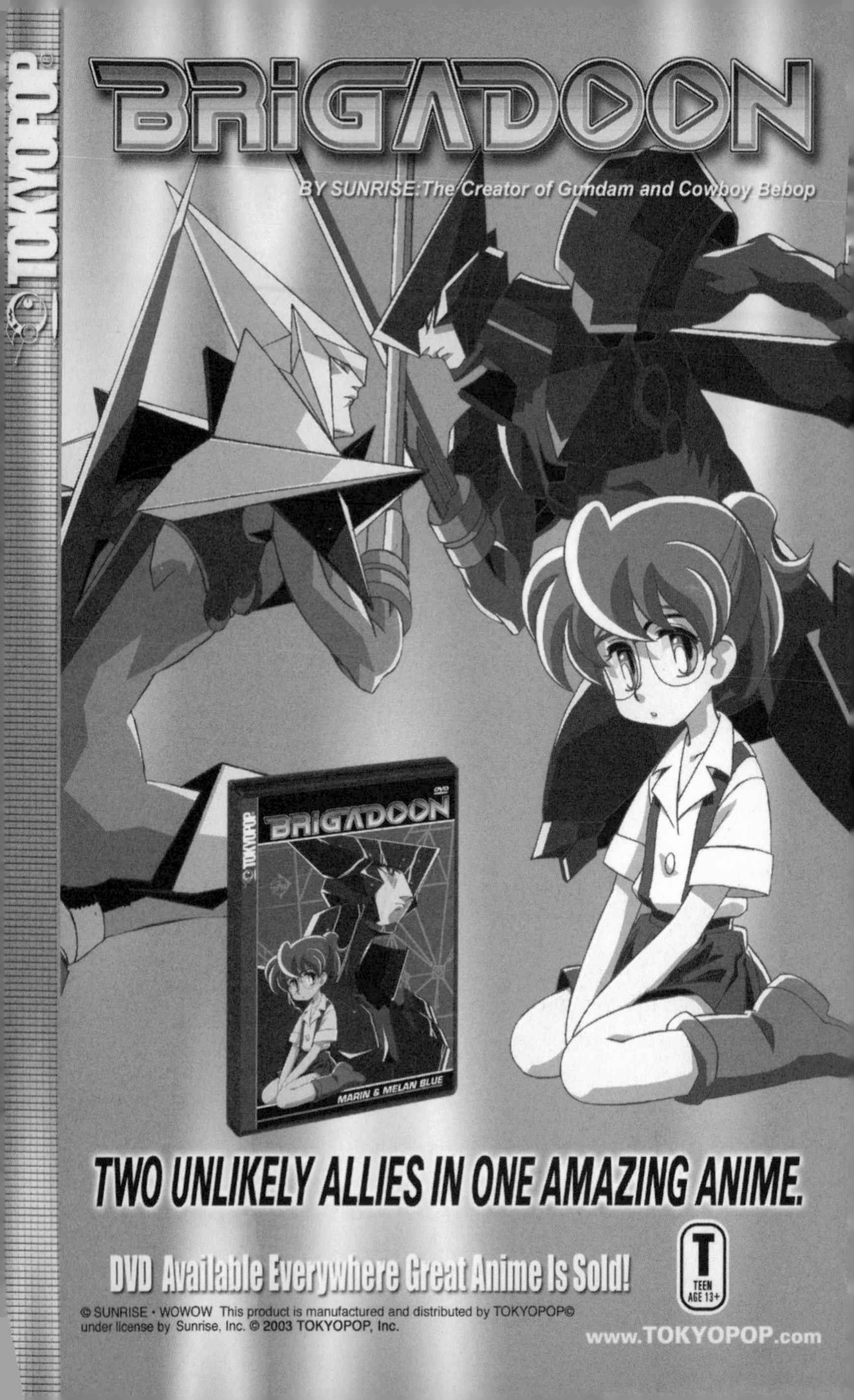
TOKYOPOP
BRIGADOON
BY SUNRISE: The Creator of Gundam and Cowboy Bebop
DVD
BRIGADOON
TOKYOPOP
MARIN & MELAN BLUE
TWO UNLIKELY ALLIES IN ONE AMAZING ANIME.
DVD Available Everywhere Great Anime Is Sold!
T
TEEN
AGE 13+
© SUNRISE • WOWOW This product is manufactured and distributed by TOKYOPOP©
under license by Sunrise, Inc. © 2003 TOKYOPOP, Inc.
www.TOKYOPOP.com

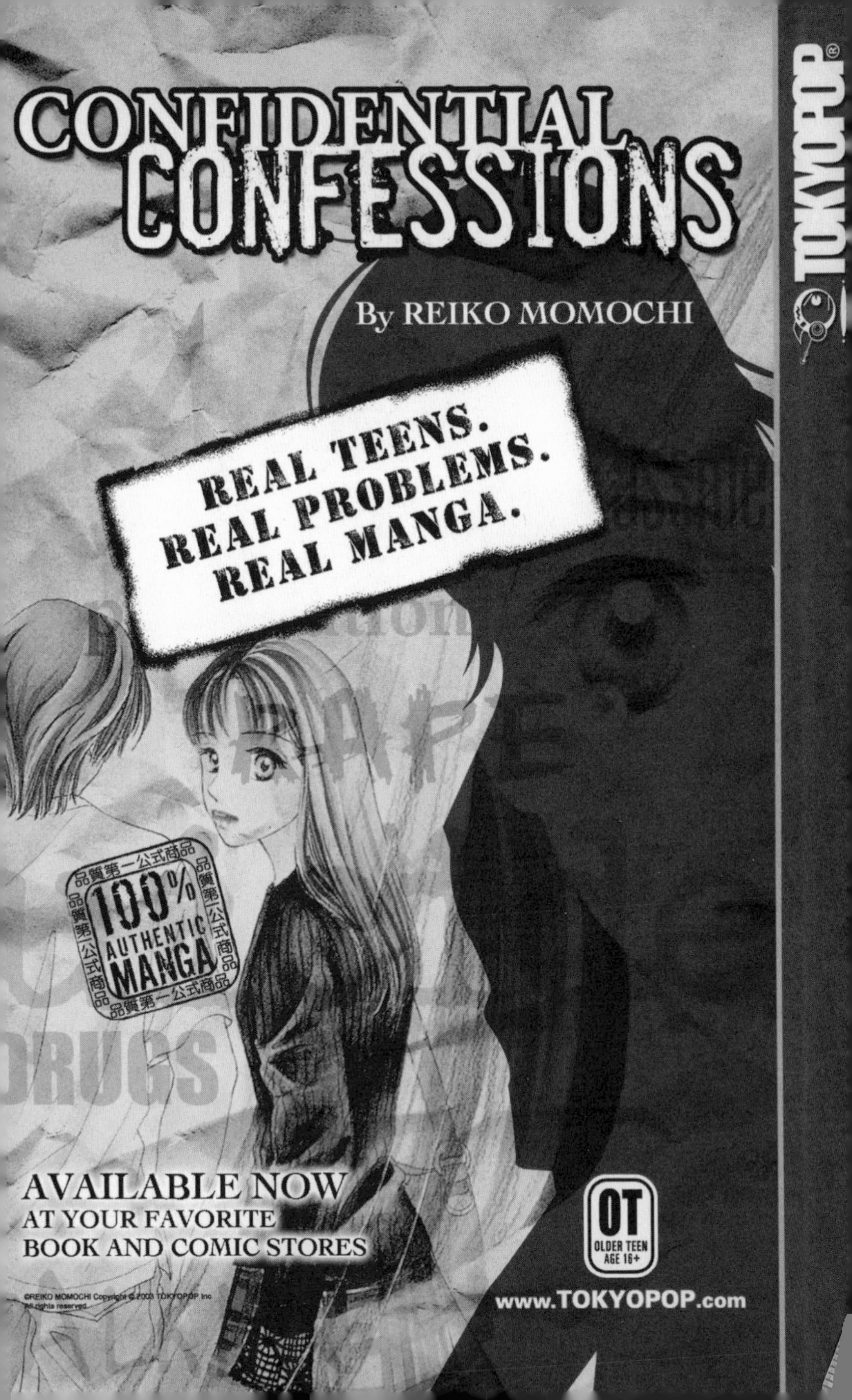
TOKYOPOP®
CONFIDENTIAL CONFESSIONS
By REIKO MOMOCHI
REAL TEENS.
REAL PROBLEMS.
REAL MANGA.
品質第一公式商品
100% AUTHENTIC MANGA
DRUGS
AVAILABLE NOW
AT YOUR FAVORITE
BOOK AND COMIC STORES
OT
OLDER TEEN AGE 16+
©REIKO MOMOCHI Copyright © 2003 TOKYOPOP Inc
All rights reserved.
www.TOKYOPOP.com

TOKYOPOP®

kare kano

his and her circumstances

Story by Masami Tsuda

Life Was A Popularity Contest For Yukino.
Somebody Is About To Steal Her Crown.

Available Now At Your Favorite Book And Comic Stores!

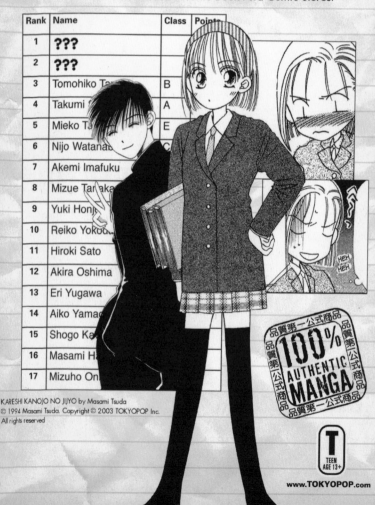

Rank	Name	Class	Points
1	???		
2	???		
3	Tomohiko Ta	B	
4	Takumi S	A	
5	Mieko Ta	E	
6	Nijo Watanab	C	
7	Akemi Imafuku		
8	Mizue Tanaka		
9	Yuki Honjo		
10	Reiko Yokod		
11	Hiroki Sato		
12	Akira Oshima		
13	Eri Yugawa		
14	Aiko Yama		
15	Shogo Ka		
16	Masami Ha		
17	Mizuho On		

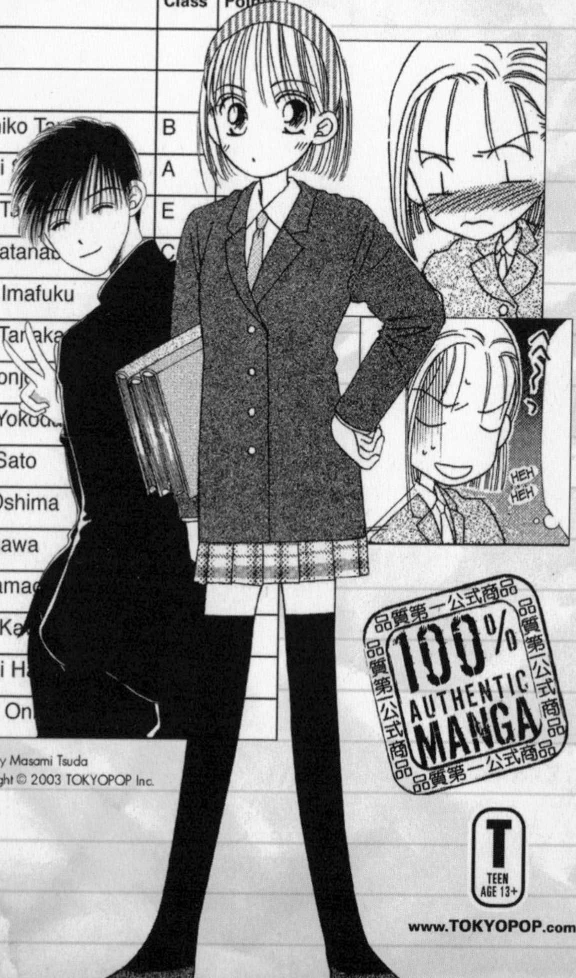
HEH
HEH

100% AUTHENTIC MANGA
品質第一公式商品

T
TEEN
AGE 13+

www.TOKYOPOP.com

STOP!

This is the back of the book.
You wouldn't want to spoil a great ending!

This book is printed "manga-style," in the authentic Japanese right-to-left format. Since none of the artwork has been flipped or altered, readers get to experience the story just as the creator intended. You've been asking for it, so TOKYOPOP® delivered: authentic, hot-off-the-press, and far more fun!

DIRECTIONS

If this is your first time reading manga-style, here's a quick guide to help you understand how it works.

It's easy... just start in the top right panel and follow the numbers. Have fun, and look for more 100% authentic manga from TOKYOPOP®!

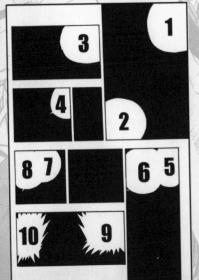

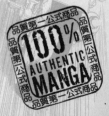

100% AUTHENTIC MANGA